Fake News

Information Policy Series

Edited by Sandra Braman

The Information Policy Series publishes research on and analysis of significant problems in the field of information policy, including decisions and practices that enable or constrain information, communication, and culture irrespective of the legal silos in which they have traditionally been located as well as state-law-society interactions. Defining information policy as all laws, regulations, and decision-making principles that affect any form of information creation, processing, flows, and use, the series includes attention to the formal decisions, decision-making processes, and entities of government; the formal and informal decisions, decision-making processes, and entities of private and public sector agents capable of constitutive effects on the nature of society; and the cultural habits and predispositions of governmentality that support and sustain government and governance. The parametric functions of information policy at the boundaries of social, informational, and technological systems are of global importance because they provide the context for all communications, interactions, and social processes.

Fake News

Understanding Media and Misinformation in the Digital Age

Edited by Melissa Zimdars and Kembrew McLeod

The MIT Press
Cambridge, Massachusetts
London, England

This book was set in Stone Serif and Stone Sans by Westchester Publishing Services. Printed and bound in the United States of America.

Library of Congress Cataloging-in-Publication Data

Names: Zimdars, Melissa, 1985– editor. | McLeod, Kembrew, 1970– editor.
Title: Fake news : understanding media and misinformation in the digital age / edited by Melissa Zimdars, Kembrew McLeod.
Description: Cambridge, Massachusetts : The MIT Press, 2020. | Series: Information policy | Includes bibliographical references and index.
Identifiers: LCCN 2019022931 | ISBN 9780262538367 (paperback)
Subjects: LCSH: Fake news—United States. | Mass media and public opinion—United States. | Disinformation—United States. | Social media—United States. | Media literacy—United States.
Classification: LCC PN4888.F35 F35 2020 | DDC 070.4/3—dc23
LC record available at https://lccn.loc.gov/2019022931

10   9   8   7   6   5   4   3   2   1

Contents

Series Editor's Introduction

Sandra Braman

It has been hard to know where to begin, when it comes to fake news. Not by becoming immersed in it, now a second full-time job for many, a change even among those of us who have been news hounds all of our lives. Not by reading all of the pertinent scholarship and research, a seeming impossibility today given that this is now the largest growth research industry among those who study communication and society, having replaced earlier well-funded topics such as the impact of violence on television and how to diffuse innovations. Not by engaging in never-ending conversations, critiques, and announcements that we will no longer talk about it, the discussions that only—as Mark Andrejevic points out in his chapter in this book—make everything worse.

Where we can begin, now, is with this collection. In *Fake News*, editors Melissa Zimdars and Kembrew McLeod have put together a "who's who" of the authors one would want to read on this subject, and done so with such sophisticated vision that the result is also a map of the field, across disciplines, theories, methods, levels of analysis, and problem frames. Thus the book is an ideal reader for those who are trying to figure out what is happening, why and how it makes a difference, and just what we might do about it. (The "reader" label is structural as well as conceptually curatorial—with an introductory chapter so rich it deserves stand-alone treatment as a course unit and eight additional sections that are all course unit size, the book is a boon for the classroom.)

Fake news, for the purposes of the book, is defined in the introduction as "primarily produced by individuals who are concerned *not* with gathering and reporting information to the world, but rather with generating profit through the social media circulation of false information mimicking the style of contemporary news." Zimdars's introductory chapter makes visible the economic heart of what is so often thought of in solely cultural, now sometimes political, terms. This demonstrates yet again the tedious non-utility of the "battles" between cultural studies and political economy that dominated certain too-closed halls within late twentieth-century academia. More importantly, the point is that these are two among several inextricably intertwined dimensions of the political economic systems involved— but also *only* two; technological change, as is pointed out by several authors in this volume, has also made a difference in what we can do and whether or not what we can do should (or can) be justly and equitably regulated.

The collection has a great deal of conceptual richness to help us think through all these matters. It turns out, for example, that the preferred tactic of the Yes Men, whose work has delighted and inspired so many and is the well-deserved and much appreciated subject of both an oral history and an interview by McLeod in this volume, is what they think of as "identity correction." Andrejevic understands the deliberate production and circulation of fake news as a form of propaganda that shares some features with forms we have known in the past, but also differs from them in ways that are important for research and for policy makers as well as for users who would like to be not only knowledgeable, but also canny, about what they do online. Benjamin Peters points out that the most serious problem with conspiracy theory is shared with all theory—looking further than one can see— but with the important difference that conspiracy theories are by definition unprovable, while it is the point of all assertions of theoretically found fact that they are verifiable. (In the United States, verifiability is among the legal requirements of an assertion that is claimed to be something that should be treated as a fact for legal purposes.)

Across its chapters, *Fake News* tells us a great deal about the techniques that can be used in the production, distribution, and circulation—the use and reuse—of information that presents publicly as "news" and that gets labeled as "fake": manipulating context; enticement (entrapment?) or click-baiting; content aggregation (with its ambiguity reduction functions); cross-medium circulation; and the blurring of genre. Proof by reference to provenance, as Zimdars notes, has become a strategy that no longer is any guarantee of the integrity of provenance or the rigor of information and analytical procedures used. It is impossible to mention all of the book's chapters here, but there are illuminating case studies covering issues as diverse as gun control (Dawn R. Gilpin), abortion (Colin Doty), hate speech (Cherian George), and political campaigns (Benjamin Burroughs). And we learn about the problem of fake news in diverse environments, from platforms (Tarleton Gillespie) to journalism (Claire Wardle) to Twitter (Dan Faltesek).

William Butler Yeats's warnings in the first stanza of "The Second Coming" were written in 1919 and first published in 1920:

> *Turning and turning in the widening gyre*
> *The falcon cannot hear the falconer;*
> *Things fall apart; the centre cannot hold;*
> *Mere anarchy is loosed upon the world,*
> *The blood-dimmed tide is loosed, and everywhere*
> *The ceremony of innocence is drowned;*
> *The best lack all conviction, while the worst*
> *Are full of passionate intensity.*

We know now that there *is* no center, but the general sense of growing anarchy remains the same, clearly innocence can no longer be claimed, and the closing two lines remain unfortunately accurate regarding our times as the long twentieth century continues. That makes the problem all the harder.

The authors in *Fake News* offer ideas, too, about where we might go from here if we all want to continue to be able to live together. The specifics of what those are differ from author to author, focal topic to focal topic, but interestingly enough, the foundations of those answers do not have to do with law and do not have to do with technology—they have to do with learning to trust each other, once again.

Introduction

Melissa Zimdars

Just before the 2016 U.S. presidential election, fake news producers, conspiracy theorists, and alt-right trolls circulated a *Newsweek* cover featuring
Hillary Clinton under the words "Madam President" as "proof" of "the
media" and Democrats conspiring to rig the election.[1] One conspiracy website, D.C. Clothesline, posted the image with the headline "The Fix Is In:
Newsweek Already Has an Issue in Print, Boxed and Ready to Ship, Declaring
Hillary Clinton the Winner."[2] A corresponding "article" linked to another
website found simply through an IP address (http://82.221.129.208), which
is apparently the home of "World Class Investigative Truth" provided by
Jim Stone, a self-identified "deplorable freelance journalist." Stone corroborated the information on his website and linked to a tweet by Milo
Yiannopoulos, an infamous alt-right troll and then a technology editor for
Breitbart, displaying the same photograph captioned, in part, "they are
going to steal it."

Unsurprisingly, this "proof" turned out to be a strategy that news organizations use all the time. *Newsweek* had produced *two* covers, one saying
"President Trump" and the other saying "Madam President," in order to
have the correct cover immediately ready for purchase after the election.
Despite the obvious explanation for the "Madam President" cover, the
decontextualized—and misleadingly selected and captioned—information
became "evidence" of a conspiracy that quickly traveled across a maze of
dubious information sources. This example demonstrates one way that false
information circulates on the web, but more importantly, it also reveals the
need to examine fake news as beyond just a type of misinformation; fake
news is part of much larger political, cultural, and social issues of concern.
Fake news is a symptom of deep-rooted problems as much as it is itself a
problem. Behind the fake news articles capitalizing on the circulation of

this story across social media exists a deeper confluence of issues, including the coordinated politicization and weaponization of information, public distrust of news organizations, and even the failures of technology and information platforms to acknowledge their role in both exacerbating and solving the spread of misinformation.

What Is Fake News?

Fake news has come to mean many things. In communication and media studies it most often referred to satire like *The Onion* or *The Colbert Report*, but now it is also false news exported from Macedonia or created in a living room in Missouri by a guy who just wants to make extra money. The term is used to describe stories created and distributed by propaganda news outlets in Russia attempting to influence global politics. It is used when referring to the hyperpartisan articles on websites like Breitbart that commonly wrap a kernel of truth in a false context in order to rile up their readers. The term *fake news* is used to label conspiracies, junk science presented with clickbait-style headlines, content aggregators circulating misleading gossip, and even national news organizations.

For the purposes of this book, fake news is primarily produced by individuals who are concerned *not* with gathering and reporting information to the world, but rather with generating profit through the social media circulation of false information mimicking the style of contemporary news. Of course, credible news organizations have the potential to distribute false news in the form of "breaking news" errors and inaccuracies that are subsequently corrected or retracted, but spreading false news is not their strategy for profitability. News organizations have a mandate to do journalism, even if it's low-quality journalism, while fake news creators do not. Additionally, the number of false news stories emerging from credible sources tends to be few and far between rather than a constant flow of purposefully crafted sensational, emotionally charged, misleading, or otherwise totally made-up information. Fake news is neither CNN—regardless of its many faults—nor disagreement over particular assessments or interpretations of information; rather, it's unverifiable information rooted in an unreality that hinders our collective abilities to make sense of the world.

Fake news can achieve huge circulation numbers, sometimes earning hundreds of thousands of shares on social media. One of the most shared fake news stories is from the online "newspaper" the *Denver Guardian*, falsely writing, "FBI agent suspected in Hillary email leaks found dead in apartment murder suicide [*sic*]," which earned almost six hundred thousand shares. An article from a fake news website, WTOE 5, alleged, "Pope Francis shocks world, endorses Donald Trump for president," and it engendered almost a million shares by readers both outraged (likely by those on the political left) and excited (likely by those on the political right) by such information. These fake stories achieved similar or higher levels of circulation in comparison to some of the most shared news stories from established organizations like the *Washington Post*, the *New York Times*, and CNN. Of course, hundreds, if not thousands, of other fake news stories are shared only minimally (or not at all), but the same can be said for the wide variations in engagement numbers for actual news stories. Yet some evidence suggests that the top fake news stories circulated between August and November 2016, for example, had more overall social media engagements (shares, likes, and comments) than the top actual news stories circulated during the same period.[3]

However, looking at fake news in isolation downplays the complexity and messiness of our digital age. Fake news is a problem mostly because it exists alongside the massive audience for and influence of unreliable and hyperpartisan websites like Breitbart, which saw 18 million unique visitors per month at its height and whose stories spread across a vast network of propagandistic and fake news websites.[4] These propagandistic websites—as well as corresponding social media accounts and pages—are designed to influence, reinforce, and mobilize people around particular political beliefs while attacking and destabilizing journalism and our faith in certain institutions and figures.[5] When we add satire, native advertising, memes, conspiracy theories, hoaxes, and decontextualized viral videos to this fake news and propaganda mix, it becomes even more challenging for us to make sense of the information we encounter in our daily lives. While we must be intentional in defining and analyzing each of these kinds of misinformation, it's important to consider them interrelated and as constituting a much larger communicative problem in the digital age.

Fake News and the Circuit of Media Study

We need to understand fake news as an emerging type of online misinformation, and as one part of a larger misinformation problem, but we need to do so by making sense of the multiple, overlapping factors that enable, constrain, and shape its production, distribution, and reception. In fact, we need to use an integrated approach to media studies, or what Julie D'Acci refers to as the "circuit of media study," to fully grapple with all of the interconnected aspects of fake news and other forms of online misinformation.[6] This model encourages us to consider the way ideas, discourses, and practices influence, overlap, contradict, and circulate between porous spheres of production (everything from the political economy of fake news to regulation and policy), sociohistorical contexts, reception, and the cultural artifacts or fake news texts themselves. As danah boyd rightly points out, addressing fake news is going to "require a cultural change about how we make sense of information, whom we trust, and how we understand our own role in grappling with information."[7] I would also add that addressing fake news is going to require changes to who produces information, how information is produced, the mechanisms of distribution, and the forces that influence decision-making and specific practices along the way. And considering fake news and other kinds of misinformation through the circuit of media study, through thinking about the mutually constitutive aspects of politics, policy, social media, journalism, and reception, among other things, may offer us the best chance of cultural change, productive policy decisions, technological accountability, and just making sense of our complex and contradictory digital age.

Let's start with thinking about fake news in relation to *news*. Fake news has existed as long as news, and always in a variety of forms, as many of the chapters in this book will explore. Yellow journalism, tabloids, satire, and our long history of magazine and newspaper hoaxes, such as the Great Moon Hoax, reports of a killer hawk terrorizing Chicago, or claims of a seven-headed monster with goat legs in Caledonia, are all inherently connected to news as a historical reality. Newspapers could generate huge profits by printing these fantastic tales, but the eventual professionalization of journalism and increased importance of news prestige and reputation placed greater emphasis on accurately and *objectively* reporting actual events.

However, objectivity itself fosters different types of bias toward maintaining the status quo, or, in other words, toward the interests of business leaders, government officials, and other elites, usually at the expense of everyday citizens.[8] In addition to problems with "objectivity," in order to be profitable in the current media environment, which is characterized by the folding of newspapers, journalist layoffs, ownership concentration, and greater emphases on profit instead of the public good, news organizations have to rely on problematic categories of newsworthiness ("If it bleeds, it leads") and the proliferation of pundits whose only purpose seems to be taking up airtime. Because it's cheaper and easier to do, news organizations focus on short-term stories—horse-race election coverage, the daily twists of the stock market—and not enough deal consistently and seriously with issues that affect people's lives in a way that explores not only what is happening, but also why and what can be done about it. When we also consider the concerted effort to diminish the legitimacy of the press by conservative media makers over the past several decades, it becomes clear why a significant portion of the population distrusts "the media."[9] Of course, distrust varies widely by news outlet and individual, but overall, people trust the press—and increasingly the premise of an objective press—less than they once did.

Although these high levels of news distrust are alarming, they're also understandable. For instance, what does it mean for "news" when dozens of news and entertainment websites report that CNN accidentally aired thirty minutes of pornography in the Boston television market and it's revealed that these stories are entirely based on two hoax tweets? Or when a fake website just a few days old, specifically the *Florida Sun Post*, publishes a made-up story about a millionaire accidentally marrying his granddaughter and it's picked up by AOL News, FoxNews.com, *The Independent*, Complex, and the *New York Post*, among others?[10] Are these indeed examples of the "real" news producing, or at least circulating, fake news, too? These humorous examples are not to suggest that news organizations like *The Independent* should be labeled fake news, but rather to demonstrate both the complexity of the fake news problem and how it's made worse by current journalistic practices. These examples also demonstrate that the line between news and fake news is far blurrier than it should be, and this makes telling the difference between news and fake news far more difficult than it should be.

Although the history and contemporary realities of journalism are particularly important to understanding fake news, we know through the circuit of media study that it's only part of the misinformation problem. To more fully understand the relationship between news and fake news, we need to consider how technologies alter and disrupt news production and distribution practices. Google and Facebook collect about 70 percent of all digital advertising sales in the United States, receiving a vast majority of digital advertising growth year after year.[11] The lack of digital advertising growth for newspapers is a serious problem because traditional advertising revenue also continues to decline.[12] Couple this with the explosion of legitimate and not-so-legitimate online newsrooms and the competition for online advertising dollars and audiences is fierce. Declining advertising revenue and competition for readers mean relying on clickbait-style headlines to try to generate engagement on social media. Financial pressure also means a greater emphasis on entertainment, soft news, and sensationalism that is more likely to be shared on social media. And this means using more native advertising as well as producing more articles based on the information provided by newswires and secondary reporting (too often without checking the information found in the original reporting)[13] because it's cheaper than assigning a reporter to cover a story or investigate an issue. And these practices are likely to further erode public confidence and trust in news.

Not only do changes in the technological landscape affect news and fake news revenue, and thus news and fake news practices, but search engine algorithms and social media play important roles in the production and distribution of all kinds of "news." Shortly after the election of Donald Trump, the number one Google news item for the popular vote was a fake news website, 70news.wordpress.com, erroneously saying that Hillary Clinton lost the popular vote. If you searched Google for information about potential collusion between Russia and Donald Trump in May 2017, the first results that appear are propagandistic, conspiracy-oriented, and unreliable websites like the *Washington Free Beacon*, Infowars, and the Daily Caller, respectively.[14] Google is similarly criticized for the misleading and false, not to mention sexist, racist, nationalist, and hate-filled, queries that auto-fill search boxes and search results that appear first when people look up topics about women, people of color, Judaism, or Islam.[15]

Combine the frequency of specious Google results with millions of Twitter bots synchronously pushing fake news, viral memes on Imgur and Reddit circulating misleading "facts," and Russian agents buying Facebook ads to target specific groups with propaganda, and it's clear that fake news is as much an issue of technology—both how it functions algorithmically and how individuals use it—as it is a matter of journalism.[16] Yet interrogating the context of journalism in relation to technology is also necessary but insufficient for understanding fake news without considering why users of Facebook might knowingly or unknowingly share a fake news article. Paralleling the pressures of immediacy on financially strapped newsrooms is the speed by which we can share information on social media, with some evidence suggesting that many of us share without actually reading what we are sharing.[17] Evidence also suggests that whether we trust a person who shares a news article on social media matters more than the news source in how we assess information, even if the news source is unknown.[18] Furthermore, how do phenomena like filter bubbles or echo chambers—or the "bullshit" emerging from trendy discussions of these things[19]—influence how we individually and collectively understand and engage with fake news? How do we push back against inaccuracies and outright lies when corrections and debunking typically either fail to reach the same audience or fail to gain the same kind of audience reach in comparison to the original information?[20] What should we do when debunking or corrections only serve to reinforce the original misinformation for some readers or watchers?[21] For example, the debunking of #Pizzagate, a conspiracy accusing Hillary Clinton of being at the center of a child sex-trafficking ring run out of a pizza shop, led to a man "self-investigating" the incident and opening fire in the shop.[22] News of the "self-investigation," in another bizarre twist, then inspired a secondary conspiracy circulated by fake news websites: the mainstream media *planted* the Comet Ping Pong pizzeria gunman as a "false flag" in a plot to shut down alternative media sources.[23] Years later and Comet Ping Pong is still defending against these rumors and an attempt to burn the establishment down.[24]

We will neither fully understand fake news and other kinds of misinformation nor make a dent in addressing it, unless we think about it through the circuit of media study, through the reciprocal influences and interactions of our political context, journalism, social media, policy, reception, and fake news as part of a larger misinformation problem. Too often we treat these areas as distinct, which means that we identify media literacy, greater tech company accountability, or changes in contemporary journalism as solutions without considering the intertwined relationships between all of the above. While this project does utilize these categories for organizational purposes, numerous authors think through multiple areas of influence in their analyses. This book is thus an attempt to consider fake news across these areas of inquiry, and from a variety of perspectives and academic disciplines, with the hope of working toward better understanding and changing the underlying issues creating the context for fake news and online misinformation to flourish.

Overview

Many of the chapters in this collection reflect on the hysteria surrounding fake news and other kinds of online misinformation just before and after the 2016 U.S. presidential election. And many of the issues identified during this period remain unchanged or unresolved years later. The aim of this collection goes beyond just analyzing that particular moment in time, although it is an important one. Every day the problem of misinformation seems to get stranger (a fake news website posing as a fact-checking outlet) or more serious (the Taliban's expanding propaganda machine).[25] Thus, this book historicizes and considers various current contexts exacerbating the circulation of misinformation, which will undoubtedly have an impact on the future of our knowledge systems as well as technological, political, regulatory, and cultural changes (or lack thereof).

This collection is organized into eight parts: Politics, Journalism, Law and Policy, Social Media, Reception, History, Media Hoaxes and Satire, and Solutions. Although some chapters could exist in more than one part as many of these issues are interrelated, we placed them in the part in which they are in the most direct conversation. For example, many of the authors in this collection discuss different solutions to fake news as part of their analyses, including the need for technological or regulatory changes to social media platforms, but one part focuses specifically on solutions to online misinformation.

Chapters in this collection primarily come from scholars in the fields of communication, media studies, and journalism, but it also includes the perspectives of scholars of psychology, comparative literature, and computer science, among others. While fake news is a problem that transcends national boundaries, the large number of issues and contexts to consider just within the United States already makes this a huge undertaking. Not every contributor to this collection will agree on what we can or should do about fake news and the underlying problems that create space for the wider circulation of misleading or misinforming information, yet through those very disagreements and contradictions we hope a useful framework emerges for addressing misinformation in many of its iterations and complexities.

Notes

1. James Hamblin, "What Do You Mean by 'The Media?,'" *The Atlantic*, January 24, 2017, https://www.theatlantic.com/technology/archive/2017/01/all-possible-realities-are-playing-out-across-infinite-universes/514130/.

2. Dr. Eowyn, "The Fix Is In: *Newsweek* Already Has an Issue in Print, Boxed and Ready to Ship, Declaring Hillary Clinton the Winner," D.C. Clothesline, November 6, 2016, http://www.dcclothesline.com/2016/11/06/the-fix-is-in-newsweek-already-has-an-issue-in-print-boxed-and-ready-to-ship-declaring-hillary-clinton-the-winner/.

3. Craig Silverman, "This Analysis Shows How Viral Fake Election News Stories Outperformed Real News on Facebook," BuzzFeed News, November 16, 2016, https://www.buzzfeed.com/craigsilverman/viral-fake-election-news-outperformed-real-news-on-facebook.

4. On the number of visitors to Breitbart, see Clare Malone, "Trump Made Breitbart Great Again," FiveThirtyEight, August 18, 2016, https://fivethirtyeight.com/features/trump-made-breitbart-great-again/. On the spread of Breitbart's stories, see Yochai Benkler, Robert Faris, Hal Roberts, and Ethan Zuckerman, "Study: Breitbart-Led Right-Wing Media Ecosystem Altered Broader Media Agenda," *Columbia Journalism Review*, March 3, 2017, https://www.cjr.org/analysis/breitbart-media-trump-harvard-study.php; Kate Starbird, "Examining the Alternative Media Ecosystem through the Production of Alternative Narratives of Mass Shooting Events on Twitter" (paper presented at the International Conference on Web and Social Media, Montreal, May 15, 2017), http://faculty.washington.edu/kstarbi/Alt_Narratives_ICWSM17-CameraReady.pdf.

5. W. Lance Bennett and Steven Livingston, "The Disinformation Order: Disruptive Communication and the Decline of Democratic Institutions," *European Journal of Communication* 33, no. 2 (2018): 122–139.

6. Julie D'Acci, "Cultural Studies, Television Studies, and the Crisis in the Humanities," in *Television after TV: Essays on a Medium of Transition*, ed. Lynn Spigel and Jan Olsson (Durham, NC: Duke University Press, 2004), 418–446.

7. danah boyd, "Did Media Literacy Backfire?," *Points* (blog), Data and Society, January 5, 2017, https://points.datasociety.net/did-media-literacy-backfire-7418c084d88d.

8. See Theodore L. Glasser, "Objectivity and News Bias," in *Philosophical Issues in Journalism*, ed. Elliot D. Cohen (Oxford: Oxford University Press, 1992), 176–185.

9. Pew Research Center, "Beyond Distrust: How Americans View Their Government," November 23, 2015, http://www.people-press.org/2015/11/23/beyond-distrust-how -americans-view-their-government/.

10. Jason Abbruzzese, "Fake-Looking Website Publishes Fake-Looking Story on Man Accidentally Marrying His Granddaughter," Mashable, October 3, 2016, http:// mashable.com/2016/10/03/fake-news-story-man-marries-granddaughter/.

11. Daniel Funke, "What's Behind the Recent Media Bloodbath? The Dominance of Google and Facebook," Poynter, June 14, 2017, http://www.poynter.org/2017 /whats-behind-the-recent-media-bloodbath-the-dominance-of-google-and-facebook /463418/.

12. Pew Research Center, "Newspapers Fact Sheet," June 1, 2017, http://www .journalism.org/fact-sheet/newspapers/.

13. Melissa Zimdars, "Information Infidelity: What Happens When the 'Real' News Is Considered 'Fake' News, Too?," *Flow*, December 16, 2016, http://www.flowjournal .org/2016/12/informational-infidelity/.

14. Roger Sollenberger, "How the Trump-Russia Data Machine Games Google to Fool Americans," *Paste*, June 1, 2017, https://www.pastemagazine.com/articles/2017 /06/how-the-trump-russia-data-machine-games-google-to.html.

15. See Safiya Noble, *Algorithms of Oppression: How Search Engines Reinforce Racism* (New York: New York University Press, 2018).

16. Emilio Ferrara, Onur Varol, Clayton Davis, Filippo Menczer, and Alessandro Flammini, "The Rise of Social Bots," *Communications of the ACM* 59, no. 7 (2016): 96–104; Massimo Calabresi, "Inside Russia's Social Media War on America," *Time*, May 18, 2017, http://time.com/4783932/inside-russia-social-media-war-america/.

17. Maksym Gabielkov, Arthi Ramachandran, Augustin Chaintreau, and Arnaud Legout, "Social Clicks: What and Who Gets Read on Twitter?" (paper presented at ACM SIGMETRICS / IFIP Performance, Antibes Juan-les-Pins, France, June 2016), https://hal.inria.fr/hal-01281190.

18. Media Insight Project (American Press Institute and Associated Press–NORC Center for Public Affairs Research), "'Who Shared It?': How Americans Decide What News to Trust on Social Media," March 2017, http://www.americanpressinstitute.org /publications/reports/survey-research/trust-social-media/.

19. Rasmus Kleis Nielsen, "Social Media and Bullshit," *Social Media + Society* 1, no. 1 (2015): 1–3.

20. On corrections and debunking not reaching the same audience, see Kate Starbird, Jim Maddock, Mania Orand, Peg Achterman, and Robert M. Mason, "Rumors, False Flags, and Digital Vigilantes: Misinformation on Twitter after the 2013 Boston

Marathon Bombing" (paper presented at iConference 2014, Berlin, March 4–7, 2014).

21. James H. Kuklinski, Paul J. Quirk, Jennifer Jerit, David Schwieder, and Robert F. Rich, "Misinformation and the Currency of Democratic Citizenship," *Journal of Politics* 62, no. 3 (2000): 790–816.

22. David A. Graham, "The 'Comet Pizza' Gunman Provides a Glimpse of a Frightening Future," *The Atlantic*, December 5, 2016, https://www.theatlantic.com/politics /archive/2016/12/the-inevitability-of-more-comet-pizza-incidents/509567/.

23. "False Flag Just Staged at Comet Ping Pong Pizza Restaurant to Shut Down Alt Media," Millennium Report, December 4, 2016, http://themillenniumreport.com /2016/12/false-flag-just-staged-at-comet-ping-pong-pizza-restaurant-to-shut-down -alt-media/.

24. Peter Wade, "Someone Started a Fire at Comet Ping Pong, the Infamous Pizzagate Restaurant," *Rolling Stone*, January 26, 2019, https://www.rollingstone.com /politics/politics-news/comet-ping-pong-fire-785020/.

25. Daniel Funke, "This Website Impersonated a Fact-Checking Outlet to Publish Fake News Stories," Poynter, February 15, 2019, https://www.poynter.org/fact-check ing/2019/this-website-impersonated-a-fact-checking-outlet-to-publish-fake-news -stories/; David Stout and Sajjad Tarakzai, "Taliban Confront Fake News and Social Media in Propaganda War," Yahoo! News, February 14, 2019, https://sg.news.yahoo .com/taliban-confront-fake-news-social-media-propaganda-war-044355435.html.

I Politics: Part Introduction

This first part considers the contemporary political context and includes analyses of fake news in relation to propaganda, visuality and objectivity, post-truth, and conspiracy. All of these authors question the role of "truth" as an antidote or counter to misinformation, asking us to move beyond assertions of truth or falsehood to instead understand *why* and *how* (mis) information resonates with people, functions in relation to power, and destabilizes our democracies.

The first chapter of this part by media studies scholar Mark Andrejevic, "The Political Function of Fake News: Disorganized Propaganda in the Era of Automated Media," situates fake news within the history of propaganda. However, unlike top-down state propaganda, fake news operates in a distributed, "disorganized" way that undermines our ability to participate meaningfully in political decision-making. Andrejevic argues that fake news—and the challenges it poses to democratic societies—cannot be addressed just through making technological or regulatory reforms. According to Andrejevic, we also need to build forms of "civic capital" specific to our contemporary media moment that recognize our shared interests and a common good.

The second chapter in this part, "Ways of Seeing…What You Want: Flexible Visuality and Image Politics in the Post-Truth Era," is by Gina Giotta, who is a media historian focusing on visuality and technology. Giotta examines the relationship between news, photography, objectivity, and the production of belief to consider whether and how photography still operates as a warrant of journalistic truth. By reading the popular discourse around contentious news images, Giotta argues that the emergent condition of "visuality" promotes a flexible set of attitudes toward news images. These attitudes, which are politically informed rather than a distinct "ethics of looking," end up enabling the spread of misinformation. Furthermore, Giotta argues that recommendations to address this problem through digital visual literacy or image authentication software not only may be ineffectual, but may also exacerbate the problem.

"A Case against the Post-Truth Era: Revisiting Mouffe's Critique of Consensus-Based Democracy" by media and communication studies scholar Johan Farkas is the third chapter in this part. Farkas examines the way political actors no longer concern themselves with distinctions between fake and real while paradoxically disputing what counts as "true," "real," "false," and "fake" as rhetorical weapons to establish control and attack their opponents. However, rather than trying to assert what is or is not objective political "truth" in our so-called "post-truth" era, Farkas argues that "truth" is not a democratic ideal worth pursuing. Instead, relying on Chantal Mouffe's critique of consensus-based democracies, Farkas argues that agonistic pluralism can help us realize the dangers, not of "fake news" or the blurriness between truth and falsehoods, but of trying to censor and suppress information in order to save democracy—a cure, which represents a bigger potential threat of its own.

Finally, the fourth chapter in this part is by digital culture scholar Whitney Phillips. In "You're Fake News: The Problem with Accusations of Falsehood," Phillips analyzes the #Pizzagate conspiracy in which Hillary Clinton is linked to a satanic child sex ring allegedly run out of the back of a Washington, D.C., pizza shop. Phillips traces the ambivalent spread of the story both by the infamously disruptive website 4chan and by the mainstream journalism outlets that covered it. Phillips argues that focusing on claims of what counts as real and what counts as fake does not bring us any closer to the truth, and limits our discussions to simply asserting that a particular story is false. Thus, Phillips makes the case for a folkloric approach to understanding falsehood, which situates beliefs within existing structures and logics, takes seriously *why* stories resonate with audiences, and reflects on what deeper cultural truths are revealed in the process.

Suggested Reading

Yochai Benkler, Robert Faris, Hal Roberts, and Ethan Zuckerman, "Study: Breitbart-Led Right-Wing Media Ecosystem Altered Broader Media Agenda," *Columbia Journalism Review*, March 3, 2017, https://www.cjr.org/analysis/breitbart-media-trump -harvard-study.php.

W. Lance Bennett and Steven Livingston, "The Disinformation Order: Disruptive Communication and the Decline of Democratic Institutions," *European Journal of Communication* 33, no. 2 (2018): 122–139.

Caroline Jack, "What's Propaganda Got to Do with It?," *Points* (blog), Data and Society, January 5, 2017, https://points.datasociety.net/whats-propaganda-got-to-do -with-it-5b88d78c3282.

Ethan Zuckerman, "Fake News Is a Red Herring," Deutsche Welle, January 1, 2017, https://www.dw.com/en/fake-news-is-a-red-herring/a-37269377.

1 The Political Function of Fake News: Disorganized Propaganda in the Era of Automated Media

Mark Andrejevic

These days, the facts are preceded by their denunciation. We are just as likely to hear about the latest school shooting from a news "flash" as from a shared post about the right-wing trolls denouncing the young victims as "crisis actors" participating in a "false flag operation." The very act of expressing outrage and frustration with those willing to participate in such callous cruelty serves only to amplify their message. Every hard-hitting, deeply reported investigative news report is countered by the savvy skepticism that paints it as a political fabrication woven out of fake photos and invented facts. To compound matters, each story is then redoubled by a counter-narrative that does exactly what it accuses the investigative report of doing. As the philosopher Jacques Ellul puts it, in his study of propaganda, "The propagandist will not accuse the enemy of just any misdeed; he will accuse him of the very intention that he himself has and of trying to commit the very crime that he himself is about to commit."[1] The result is more online noise serving the commercial interests of our social media platforms, but not the informational needs of a democratic society. In the case of the conspiracy theories that sprang up in the wake of the Parkland school shootings in Florida, for example, research revealed that "people outraged by the conspiracy helped to promote it—in some cases far more than the supporters of the story."[2] This outrage was amplified by algorithms that took the frenetic social media response to the conspiracy theories as a sign of user engagement, leading to further automated amplification of the original posts. The algorithms do not measure whether the response is one of febrile support or outraged condemnation: it's all engagement, and that's what the platform privileges.

If, as Ellul wrote in the 1960s, "each medium is particularly suited to a certain type of propaganda," the platform economy lends itself to a profoundly disconcerting type.[3] Although the term *propaganda* has fallen into disfavor in the wake of various sophisticated postwar critiques of "truth" and "objectivity" in all their scare-quoted glory, it tends to make a resurgence during wartime, and the United States has framed itself as being on a wartime footing since the 9/11 attacks.[4] Thus, to describe the rise of "fake news" as an emerging form of propaganda is to highlight the political function of a phenomenon that is typically framed as the result of economic imperatives (the platform economy's privileging of engagement over content) and technological affordances (the "democratization" of access to publication and distribution online).

Even to speak of the "rise" of fake news or to treat it as a form of "emergence" requires a brief engagement with those whose version of historicizing is compelled to remind us that there has always been fake news.[5] Surely this is true, and any number of historical reference points comes to mind, such as yellow journalism or the pamphlet culture of sixteenth- and seventeenth-century Britain. Construed in these terms, fake news is as old as the media, and likely predates speech. However, society and technology march on, and "fake news" takes on new forms in new contexts that have specific consequences for their historical moment. It is just as "ahistorical" to claim that nothing new has happened as it is to imagine that every development is without historical precedent. The goal of this chapter is to explore some of the contemporary characteristics and uses of fake news as a form of propaganda. It argues that, to the extent that fake news can be viewed this way, it corresponds to a significant shift from mass to automated media; it operates in a distributed, "disorganized" fashion; and it corresponds with a broader assault on the forms of sociality and imagined community that undermine what might be described as "civic capital"— the ability to participate meaningfully in political decision-making. The implication of this analysis is that the challenges posed to democratic societies by fake news cannot be addressed through technological or even regulatory reforms. They require strategies for constructing the forms of civic capital adequate to the contemporary media moment. Such a process would, in turn, require the underlying political will to do so, a will that can likely be formed only through a process of societal development that counteracts the logics that have eroded contemporary concepts of the social and the political. Challenging these developments is a disconcertingly tall order.

Fake News and Symbolic Efficiency

Fake news—understood as demonstrably false information that is published and circulated as truth in service of a political or economic agenda—bears a partial resemblance to the forms of top-down propaganda associated with twentieth-century propaganda research.[6] The attempt to forward an agenda based on misleading premises indicates that the purposes are nefarious or objectionable enough to be masked; otherwise the truth would serve. As proposed here, the definition does not cover what might be described as positive propaganda: messaging that uses false information for what might otherwise be construed as a progressive purpose. Much recent work has gone into attempts to provide a more specific definition of fake news, but these tend to abstract away from their context of reception.[7] What makes "fake news" the phenomenon it has become is its reliance on what Slavoj Žižek has described as the demise of symbolic efficiency and thus its nonfalsifiability.[8] For Žižek, symbolic efficiency refers to the mechanisms that make it possible to believe symbolic representations of events that one has not seen with one's own eyes. Barack Obama was born in Hawaii, the horrors of the Holocaust occurred, the earth is round—these are all examples of truths that rely on societal mechanisms of trust and verification. A vertiginous faux freedom results from the suspension of these mechanisms: the truth of everything that one has not witnessed oneself is up for grabs—and even that of what one has seen, given the inability to communicate it to others. One hallmark of fake news—a characteristic attribute of its reception—is that it cannot be disproved, even in principle. This seems to provide it with a marked affinity to truth, with the distinction being the subjective disposition: true news remains, for those who encounter it as such, potentially falsifiable. False news, for those who approach it in the spirit of its circulation, remains, in principle, untouchable. That is, historical verification mechanisms have no purchase on it—not just in real, practical terms, but also in principle. The Gulf of Tonkin incident was false news when circulated—eventually debunked through systems of historical and journalistic research and verification.[9] However, for those who approach it as "fake news," it will always remain true, and the attempts to discredit it merely part of a shady conspiracy.

Another defining attribute of "fake news" is that in its circulation and reception it reproduces its own conditions of possibility. The principle of fake news is not simply that some news is fake and other news is true, but that the grounds for distinguishing the two have shifted from social mechanisms to individual preferences and preconceptions.

The fake news version of propaganda is also differentiated from its twentieth-century predecessors by its relationship to the notion of a dominant narrative. Mass media propaganda was predicated on a logic of media scarcity and thus on the principle of message "organization." As public relations pioneer Edward Bernays puts it in his 1928 book on propaganda, "The instruments by which public opinion is organized and focused may be misused. But such organization and focusing are necessary to orderly life."[10] Similarly, for Ellul, "an organization is required that controls the mass media, is capable of using them correctly, of calculating the effect of one or another slogan."[11] Such models of propaganda operate in the register of scientific management of public opinion via centralized mass media. They assume the ability to dominate a media narrative via control over the message—an assumption that reflects the barriers of entry to mass media messaging characteristic of the era. Challenging propaganda, in such a context, takes the form of speaking truth to power, that is, challenging and subverting the dominant narrative organized by the institutional powers that be. Truth, as media representations from *All the President's Men* to *The Paper* suggest, can be the Achilles' heel of power in the mass media model, and the investigative reporter plays the role of Hector.

The rise of the internet and the shift to automated media, however, provide those in power with new challenges and new propaganda strategies. An environment of information overload makes it harder to secure a dominant narrative because barriers of entry to media production and distribution are lowered. It is no longer enough to be able to capture and shape the narratives that appear on the evening news or in the morning paper. These can be countered and in some cases eclipsed by a torrent of online information. One response is to replace the principle of organization described by Ellul with that of *disorganized* messaging: the goal is no longer to sustain a dominant narrative, but to prevent any sustainable counter-narrative to emerge. When President Donald Trump's administration repeats palpably false stories—about the size of the inauguration crowd, for example—the goal is not to replace one narrative with another, but to sow doubt that renders all narratives suspect.

In what now looks like a presentiment of the U.S. context, military consultants at the RAND Corporation wrote a report on disorganized propaganda that ostensibly focuses on Russia, dubbing this form of propaganda "the firehose of falsehood."[12] The report describes this allegedly novel approach as one that takes advantage of a proliferating and often unaccountable multichannel environment. Firehose propaganda relies on "high numbers of channels and messages and a shameless willingness to disseminate partial truths or outright fictions."[13] The goal is not to provide a clear, dominant narrative, but to sow mistrust of the media themselves: "'[It] entertains, confuses and overwhelms the audience.'…It is also rapid, continuous, and repetitive, and it lacks commitment to consistency."[14] The report notes that such strategies "run directly counter to the conventional wisdom on effective influence and communication," suggesting that the combination of political goals and media tools reconfigures the workings of propaganda.[15] Such methods clearly rely not just on ease of access and distribution, but also on contemporary commercial platform logics.

Mirroring the online economy, disorganized propaganda off-loads much of the work of content production onto the populace. It also relies on circuits of individual and automated sharing to amplify messages. As has been repeatedly demonstrated, these systems (both human and automated) tend to prioritize the most polarizing and extreme forms of online content.[16] In the digital information environment, every account can be undermined and contested, every representation deconstructed, every proof counterfeited, every theory transformed into a conspiracy and vice versa. When even the most extreme perspectives can readily find themselves reinforced by a range of media sources and resources (as well as a core of like-minded supporters, who might previously have been difficult to find), it is easier to feel that one has not only the right but also the obligation to choose one's own facts. If in an "echo chamber" one's prejudices are confirmed through the repeated confirmation and reiteration of one's preconceptions, in an environment of media surfeit one is cast adrift on a sea of narratives and counter-narratives, equipped only with the polestar of preexisting preconceptions and prejudices.

The Demolition of Civic Dispositions

Although Ellul's formulation of the relationship between a particular medium and its characteristic form of propaganda is a compelling one, technological changes, on their own, cannot explain the shift from organized to disorganized propaganda. Broader damage to the social fabric plays a crucial role in the demise of symbolic efficiency and the savvy skepticism with which it is associated. What drives disorganized capitalism is not unwitting gullibility—the willingness to believe the lies of power—but rather a hypertrophied, generalized critique of representation. Bruno Latour, for example, laments the fate of a knee-jerk critical stance that no longer realizes power has shifted its coordinates so that the debunking of accepted truths can be just as retrograde as their unquestioning acceptance.[17] He describes, for example, the ways his own critique of "closure" in scientific investigations can be embraced by climate change deniers to claim that the science on global warming is not yet settled.

Generalized critique is further facilitated by the rapid switch from information scarcity to glut: it has become readily apparent that the mediated representations we received were always only part of the picture and that getting to the bottom of things is a much more difficult task than once imagined, not least because the bottom recedes infinitely before us. Theoretical and technological shifts provide important pieces of the fake news puzzle, but they need to be supplemented with a consideration of the socioeconomic transformations of what Wendy Brown calls "statist neoliberalism."[18] This political and social regime is predicated on the suppression of the social bonds, dependencies, and trust that foster a civic disposition and enable symbolic efficiency. As Richard Pratte puts it, "Civic virtue is not a matter of mere behavior; it is a matter of forming a civic disposition, a willingness to act, in behalf of the public good while being attentive to and considerate of the feelings, needs, and attitudes of others."[19] As our platforms invite us into solipsistic media cocoons where we communicate with others at our convenience and on our own customized terms, the very social structures come to reinforce a version of isolated individualism. Brown describes the regulatory approach of the Trump administration as one that "literally takes apart social bonds and social welfare—not simply by promoting a libertarian notion of freedom and dismantling the welfare state, but also by reducing legitimate political claims only to those advanced by and for families and individuals, not social groups generated by social powers."[20] The systematic nonrecognition of the claims of others has become a defining feature of the administration's policies, from the detention of immigrant children to the demolition of environmental protection and government health insurance programs.

The combined political, social, technological, and cultural environ-ment exhibits a shared pattern: collective goods like vaccination and public health care come under attack even as we find ourselves increasingly iso-lated in our consumption and communication practices. The dismantling of shared media experiences affects not just news but also entertainment: college students watch Netflix shows on their own, plugged into their per-sonal earphones only feet away from each other. Cell phone operating sys-tems devise automated text messaging that replaces our interactions with others. Even the most basic forms of consumption become desocialized as we order online and pick packages up on our doorstep without having to interact with another human during the entire process. Tech companies develop machines to take care of children and apps to teach them. In keep-ing with this logic, the economic success of the commercial tech industry devastates the local communities in which the companies are based. Face-book assaults civic dispositions both online and off.

From the mundane rhythms of everyday life to the overarching frame-works that shape our life chances, the suppression of underlying social bonds is the order of the day. The irreducible element of sociality that makes pos-sible the fantasy of the autonomous subject is off-loaded onto social plat-forms and misrecognized in the form of commercial relations. This makes it easier to imagine that our thoughts and beliefs spring solely from within ourselves and act as the unique determinant of our preferences and precon-ceptions. The role of community, sociality, and collectivity is systematically suppressed in ways that facilitate the forms of social fragmentation that make disorganized propaganda possible. Until this suppression is addressed and countered, no program of regulatory or technological tweaks will have much of an effect on the challenges posed by the rise of "fake news."

Is It Propaganda?

It seems somewhat paradoxical to call "fake news" a form of propaganda, given that the term generally implies some form of belief on the part of those who are subject to it. Indeed, one of the criteria that Ellul uses to eval-uate the effectiveness of propaganda is the extent to which it is believed. For Bernays, the public mind is "made up for it by the group leaders in whom it believes and by those persons who understand the manipulation

of public opinion."[21] The authors of the RAND report on falsehood as propaganda use Russian president Vladimir Putin as an example of an inconsistent and constantly changing source of fake news, although Trump would
also fit the bill, given his facility with falsehood. According to the report,
a reliance on inconsistent, contradictory, and shifting news sources and
stories "flies in the face of the conventional wisdom on influence and persuasion. If sources are not consistent, how can they be credible? If they are
not credible, how can they be influential?"[22] To say that false news operates as propaganda, however, is not to suggest that it is necessarily believed;
rather, it is to consider how it preserves and fortifies power relations. The
end goal of fake news campaigns is to disable the role played by news and
information in challenging either individual beliefs or existing power relations, thereby allowing those in power to pursue their agendas unharassed.
As propaganda, "fake news" serves a fundamentally conservative purpose,
which helps explain the fact that extreme right-leaning content is more
prevalent and profitable.[23] It does not agitate for changes in existing power
relations, but works to preempt change. In this respect, the propaganda role
played by fake news takes place at one remove from content: the goal is to
prevent a Pentagon Papers or Watergate scenario, that is, the possibility that
a coherent critique of power might emerge. "Fake news" doesn't need to
be believed to work; rather, it needs to foster the spread of disbelief in the
form of a generalized savviness that portrays all belief (at least in the realm
of politics) as the province of the dupe. The mobilization of fake news as a
weapon that slays belief and relegates conviction to the realm of preexisting prejudices helps explain the subject position of the Trump-era political
Right: that of the "troll" who uses irony as a weapon.[24] Even the most vocif-
erous members of the extreme Right adopt the attitude that it might all be
staged with an eye to trolling the "normies." Belief is the province of the
dupe; language has become purely *operational*: what matters is not the content of what it says, but what it can get done. Countering fake news with
more fake news is simply a gesture of capitulation and defeat. In the face
of this widespread strategy of demobilization, what is called for is a recon-
struction of conditions for recognition of shared interests and a common
good. This cannot be achieved on Facebook, but requires the development
of forms of community and mutual recognition that are systematically
thwarted by our commercial online economy and the neoliberal logics in
which it is embedded.

Notes

1. Jacques Ellul, *Propaganda* (New York: Knopf, 1966), 58.

2. Molly McKew, "How Liberals Amped Up a Parkland Shooting Conspiracy Theory," *Wired*, February 27, 2018, https://www.wired.com/story/how-liberals-amped-up-a -parkland-shooting-conspiracy-theory/.

3. Ellul, *Propaganda*, 10.

4. See Nancy Snow and Philip M. Taylor, "The Revival of the Propaganda State: US Propaganda at Home and Abroad since 9/11," *International Communication Gazette* 68, nos. 5–6 (2006): 389–407.

5. Stephen Marche, "How We Solved Fake News the First Time," *New Yorker*, April 23, 2018, https://www.newyorker.com/culture/cultural-comment/how-we-solved-fake-news -the-first-time.

6. See Harold D. Lasswell, *Propaganda Technique in the World War* (New York: Knopf, 1927); Ellul, *Propaganda*; Edward Bernays, *Propaganda* (1928; New York: Ig Publishing, 2005).

7. See Robyn Caplan, Lauren Hanson, and Joan Donovan, *Dead Reckoning: Navigating Content Moderation after "Fake News"* (New York: Data and Society Research Institute, 2018).

8. Slavoj Žižek, *The Ticklish Subject* (London: Verso, 1999).

9. For more information about the Gulf of Tonkin incident, see Richard Kreitner, "Gross Cruelty and Fraud in the Gulf of Tonkin: A Brief History," *The Nation*, July 31, 2014, https://www.thenation.com/article/gross-cruelty-and-fraud-gufl-tonkin-brief-history/.

10. Bernays, *Propaganda*, 39.

11. Ellul, *Propaganda*, 20.

12. Christopher Paul and Miriam Matthews, *The Russian "Firehose of Falsehood" Propaganda Model* (Santa Monica, CA: RAND Corporation, 2016).

13. Ibid., 1.

14. Giorgio Bertolin, "Conceptualizing Russian Information Operations: Info-War and Infiltration in the Context of Hybrid Warfare," *IO Sphere*, Summer (2015): 10, quoted in Christopher Paul and Miriam Matthews, *The Russian "Firehose of Falsehood" Propaganda Model* (Santa Monica, CA: RAND Corporation, 2016).

15. Ibid.

16. Paul Lewis, "'Fiction Is Outperforming Reality': How YouTube's Algorithm Distorts Truth," *The Guardian*, February 2, 2018, https://www.theguardian.com /technology/2018/feb/02/how-youtubes-algorithm-distorts-truth.

17. Bruno Latour, "Why Has Critique Run out of Steam? From Matters of Fact to Matters of Concern," *Critical Inquiry* 30, no. 2 (2004): 225–248.

18. Wendy Brown, *Undoing the Demos: Neoliberalism's Stealth Revolution* (Cambridge, MA: MIT Press, 2015).

19. Richard Pratte, "Civic Education in a Democracy," *Theory into Practice* 27, no. 4 (1988): 308.

20. Wendy Brown, "Where the Fires Are: Wendy Brown Talks to Jo Littler," *Soundings: A Journal of Politics and Culture*, no. 68 (2018): 14.

21. Bernays, *Propaganda*, 109.

22. Paul and Matthews, *Russian "Firehose of Falsehood,"* 8.

23. Andrew Higgins, Mike McIntire, and Gabriel J.x. Dance, "Inside a Fake News Sausage Factory: 'This Is All about Income,'" *New York Times*, November 25, 2016, https://www.nytimes.com/2016/11/25/world/europe/fake-news-donald-trump-hillary-clinton-georgia.html; Craig Silverman and Lawrence Alexander, "How Teens in the Balkans Are Duping Trump Supporters with Fake News," BuzzFeed News, November 3, 2016, https://www.buzzfeed.com/craigsilverman/how-macedonia-became-a-global-hub-for-pro-trump-misinfo; Alex Hern, "Fake News Sharing in US Is a Rightwing Thing, Says Study," *The Guardian*, February 6, 2018, https://www.theguardian.com/technology/2018/feb/06/sharing-fake-news-us-rightwing-study-trump-university-of-oxford.

24. Jason Wilson, "Hiding in Plain Sight: How the 'Alt-Right' Is Weaponizing Irony to Spread Fascism," *The Guardian*, May 23, 2017, https://www.theguardian.com/technology/2017/may/23/alt-right-online-humor-as-a-weapon-facism.

2 Ways of Seeing … What You Want: Flexible Visuality and Image Politics in the Post-Truth Era

Gina Giotta

A widely reported 2017 research study confirmed what most have suspected for a long time: people are terrible at identifying photo manipulations.[1] The study, however, was remarkable less for what it revealed about the fallibility of the human eye than for what it unintentionally illustrated about the flexibility of visuality. Instead of producing original photographic stimuli for the experiment, researchers sourced their "undoctored" image set from Google—a vast and mysteriously juried index of some 30 trillion web pages from around the globe. Their confidence in the unretouched quality of images discovered online in a study concerned with our capacity to be duped by Photoshop ironically demonstrates the extent to which a naive faith in photographic truth can exist comfortably alongside a persistent skepticism of it.

Although this dialectic of indiscriminate faith and skepticism has lingered in the background of photographic culture since the medium's inception in the mid-nineteenth century, it has become an especially prominent feature of political visual discourse. As this chapter argues, the new landscape of digitally networked news—marked as it is by speed, abundance, and radical decontextualization—both demands and makes possible more supple viewing habits vis-à-vis the public image. After sketching photography's fraught relationship to truth and objectivity, the chapter analyzes several contentious images in the Donald Trump era to illustrate the emerging condition of flexible visuality and theorize its growth within the context of digitally networked politics. It concludes by arguing that righteous calls for enhanced visual literacy and digital forensic software are largely impotent in the fight against "demand-side propaganda,"[2] and may well reproduce the very discursive conditions that engendered this crisis of the image in the first place.

Photographic Realism and Skepticism

Contrary to the suspicion that permeates images today, photography enjoyed a uniquely privileged and comparatively untroubled relationship to truth throughout the nineteenth and early twentieth centuries. Not long after the debut of the daguerreotype in 1839, Edgar Allan Poe enthusiastically described the incipient medium as "the most important, and perhaps the most extraordinary, triumph of modern science" by virtue of its ability to disclose "a more absolute truth."[3] Oliver Wendell Holmes, likewise, hailed photography as a wonder of human progress and technical ingenuity, famously characterizing the camera as a "mirror with a memory" for its enchanting fidelity to nature.[4] Free from the inescapable sin of subjectivity and lacking the type of personal ambition that corrupts human authors,[5] the camera came to represent the perfectly disinterested observer of an ascendant positivism.

Where men of letters saw in the camera a wondrous instrument of science, many journalists saw a collaborator. The commercial penny press, which emerged in the 1830s as an unbiased alternative to the politically subsidized partisan press, seized upon the new medium's special epistemic authority to strengthen its vaunted claims to neutrality. Unlike woodcuts and metal engravings, which had served to merely illustrate news stories and make the penny papers accessible to a broader audience, photographs performed the more significant task of corroborating—and occasionally altogether replacing—a reporter's account. Because they appeared to trade in "unalloyed facts peeled from the surface of the real world,"[6] photographs helped reinforce the remarkably resilient alibi that news could be selected, framed, and positioned on a page without prejudice. By the end of the late nineteenth century, objectivity had become the press's primary product, and photographic realism a primary means by which it was manufactured.[7]

The appearance of digital imaging devices in the late 1980s challenged the prevailing belief in photography as an innocent, stable record of reality. As a radical transformation of the materiality of the image, digital photography initiated what some observers described as a historic "rupture," a pressing "crisis," and the dawn of a new "post-photographic" era.[8] Unlike its mechanical forerunner, which *transcribed* information from the physical world onto a light-sensitive surface, the digital camera *converted* information into discrete electrical charges configured as either 0 or 1, thereby attenuating the direct connection between the object and its sign.[9] Without a physical inscription to fasten it to its referent, the digital photograph became unable to certify that it had been there, so to speak, and susceptible to "practically infinite manipulability."[10] And far from retroactively fortifying the truth claims of mechanically reproduced photographs, which could still boast a causal connection to their referent, digital photographs cast a pall over *all* images. Since all images, regardless of their technical provenance, could be digitized, all images had to be regarded with suspicion in the digital age.[11]

Further compounding this accelerating loss of confidence in photography were ongoing—and highly public—revelations of surreptitious image manipulation by professionals throughout the news industry. In 1982, *National Geographic* was roundly mocked for repositioning two pyramids in a photograph of Giza so that they would both fit neatly on its February cover, while *Time* had to answer in 1993 to allegations that it had published a fully staged photo feature of homeless child prostitutes in Russia.[12] Additionally, Reuters news agency was publicly disgraced in 2006 by a small-time political blog that detailed how a photograph published on the agency's website had been crudely manipulated to exaggerate the intensity of an Israeli airstrike during the Lebanon War.[13] One day later, another small blog revealed that a second Reuters image by the same photographer had been doctored and miscaptioned to similar effect. After purging all 920 of the disgraced photographer's images from its website and expressing confidence in the veracity of the rest of its news products, Reuters praised the growing weblog community for making the media "much more accountable and more transparent."[14]

Revelations of staging, postproduction retouching and compositing, and image repurposing emerged so routinely in the first decade of the twenty-first century that such reports eventually ceased being news altogether. Instead, the increasingly mundane announcements of photo fraud largely came to be regarded as part of the cost of producing news with a skeleton staff in a relentlessly competitive twenty-four-hour news cycle. Editors blamed Photoshop for making photo manipulation fast, easy, and undetectable, while photographers cited shrinking deadlines and new competition from cheaper alternatives like cell phone–equipped "citizen journalists" and commercial stock photo archives.[15] Few were willing to acknowledge publicly that very little had actually changed within the industry, as newspapers and news magazines had been retouching and staging reality since the invention of the halftone process in the late nineteenth century.

What had changed were the broader sociotechnical conditions within which news images circulated. The new internet-enabled culture of inspection and comparison, in concert with new opportunities to build and access interpretive communities concerned with photographic authenticity, gave lie to sloppy and sensational practices that have funded the commercial news industry for more than a century. The news image, it turned out, was as protean as all images, and the news industry as trustworthy as the partisan press it nobly replaced under the pretext of objectivity.

The Condition of Flexible Visuality

A product of critical theory's "visual turn" in the 1990s, "visuality" refers to the way that we encounter, look at, and interpret images based on the social, cultural, technological, and economic conditions of their viewing. Unlike vision, which is a purely biological process involving the eyes and processing centers in the brain, visuality is a cultural practice with a history marked by different habits or ways of seeing, as well as different types of spectators.[16] The extent to which we have accepted photography as a reliable index of "reality"—and, by extension, how we approach and read individual photographs—has been anything but stable. Epistemological ruptures, changes in the apparatus of production, and troubling disclosures about image tinkering by professional journalists fostered new attitudes toward the image and the truth it allegedly contained. While early spectators of photographs are routinely portrayed as naive and their contemporary analogues as skeptical or savvy, a more accurate description of the present-day image consumer is "flexible."

"Flexible" spectators are characterized not by naïveté or skepticism, but by the relative ease with which they slide between these opposed viewing positions. Their "way of looking" is not deeply invested in the realism that pervaded early attitudes toward the photograph or the cynicism that emerged out of the various "crises" of the image, but neither is it hostile to these viewing practices. Rather, they adopt and occupy these positions strategically at will. Such spectators assume a realist style of looking when confronted with images that authenticate their preexisting experiences and ideas, and a skeptical mode vis-à-vis those images that threaten to destabilize or invalidate their views. This variability has become a privilege licensed by the unresolved discursive battles over photography's evidentiary status, but it has equally become a necessity engendered by the new online context of reception, where the sheer volume of images, the breakneck speed and promiscuity of their circulation, and the often unverifiable nature of their origin demand a certain suppleness of viewing.

While flexible visuality has typified spectators' encounters with their own photographic likenesses since the birth of photography,[17] it has only recently come to suffuse encounters with steadfastly nonaesthetic genres like the photo document. A paradigmatic case of this new flexible attitude toward the documentary image erupted on November 12, 2016, when two photographs of a protester holding a sign reading "Rape Melania" at an anti-Trump demonstration outside Trump International Hotel in Washington, D.C., began spreading quickly across Twitter and other social media platforms. Originally propagated from an otherwise unremarkable Twitter account (@thereal_beck), the photographs immediately attracted a flurry of likes, retweets, and replies that pushed "Rape Melania" into the platform's trending topics sidebar within a matter of hours.

Believers and skeptics alike were swift to weigh in on the images. Those in the former camp took the photographs as damning evidence of the hypocrisy of "the Left," which appeared to be advocating the very hatred and violence it claimed to condemn in Donald Trump and his "deplorable" base. "Oh they're just so tolerant ... #MakeAmericaGreatAgain," offered one such Twitter rebuke, while another declared smugly, "Rape Melania is trending. You know, because liberals love women and immigrants so much."[18] Meanwhile, skeptics moved to discount and discredit the images as a desperate bid by Trump operatives to smear the opposition. Although some merely dismissed the images out of hand as "obviously photoshopped," others adopted a more forensic gaze, noting lighting and angle inconsistencies that defied the laws of physics.[19] The more industrious among them built complex animated image overlays to illustrate the striking discrepancies between what they contended were two poorly doctored images.[20] Still others digitally replaced the reprehensible message with "Fake Sign" or "Beck Photoshops" as a testament to how easy it is to tinker with photographic "evidence."[21]

The question of truth became even murkier when news media entered the fray with eyewitness reports that undermined the hasty judgments of both sides. According to a handful of protesters interviewed in the aftermath

of the controversy, the sign did, in fact, appear at the event, but under suspicious circumstances that found the owner holding it backward and retreat-
ing quickly once confronted by others about its incendiary message.[22]
Such reports were corroborated two months later when another news outlet
published screenshots of text messages obtained from a Trump supporter
involved in staging the event for the camera. When contacted by the reporter
for comment on the screenshots implicating him in the stunt to discredit
peaceful protesters, right-wing propagandist and cable channel One America News (OAN) correspondent Jack Posobiec denied being involved in the
affair and dismissed the text message images as likely fakes[23]—an assessment unreflectively echoed in several reader comments on the story.

Both Posobiec and the commenters who were quick to accept or dismiss
the images offer instructive examples of flexible visuality and the danger
it represents to the lofty goal of reasoned public discourse and deliberation. Although Posobiec's perfunctory acceptance of the disturbing protest
images in tweets that he later deleted, and equally perfunctory dismissal
of the incriminating screenshots in the news story linking him to the disinformation campaign, appears motivated by personal ambition and self-
preservation, his pragmatically capricious attitude toward images is widely
reflected in the attitudes of average spectators with much less invested in
either individual photographs or the flexibility that increasingly attends
their reception. For Posobiec, as for all flexible viewers, images have largely
become hollowed-out signs refashioned into screens for the projection of
existing perceptions. Within this emergent scopic regime, images persuade
only insofar as they ratify what a spectator already knows to be true. In the
absence of such correspondence, images become evidence of a different
sort. They serve to testify to the unreliability of photographs and those
who produce and distribute them. Contrary to the predictions of scholars
reckoning with digital photography in the late 1990s and early 2000s, the
new apparatus of production did not cast a pall over all images. Rather, it
just made it easier to discount those that challenge our entrenched beliefs
about the world. Faith in certain images is stronger than ever. Faith in the
image, as such, is flexible.

While propagandists like Posobiec did not invent these new spectators,
propagandists have exploited them with great success in the political arena.
In addition to using them to mask their practiced rejection and acceptance
of politically significant photographs, propagandists have also effectively

leveraged them to foster divisiveness, distrust, and confusion. Understanding all too well that the low-effort flexible viewers stand ready to merely project their beliefs onto images rather than "read" them to gain a larger understanding of the world, disinformation peddlers frequently steal and recontextualize photographs from other sources to lend credence to manufactured news stories. In the so-called #Pizzagate disinformation scandal that Posobiec signal boosted on his social media accounts, personal family photographs of minors were unwittingly scraped from disparate Facebook and Instagram user profiles to corroborate a bogus story alleging that high-ranking members of the Democratic Party were operating an elaborate child sex ring from the basement of a popular Washington, D.C., restaurant.[24] The repurposed images helped cultivate an air of legitimacy around a fever dream about the moral turpitude of Democrats at a moment when that of Republicans was being laid bare by prominent "alt-right" figures like Milo Yiannopoulos and Richard Spencer.

While #Pizzagate was remarkable for the level of hysteria and physical violence it inspired, its reliance on recontextualized images to support pure political fiction was not. For example, a vernacular portrait of a young blond woman who appears bloodied and bruised underneath a caption warning, "Here's what happened to a female Trump supporter when she met 'peaceful' and 'tolerant' liberals," catalyzed more than thirty thousand shares on Facebook before it was revealed that the woman featured in the image was an actor preparing for a scene in a television horror series.[25] Only one day earlier, a different viral image of a battered woman allegedly assaulted by protesters at a Trump rally was similarly debunked as a still from a Mexican telenovela.[26]

Widely published professional news images, too, are not immune to the bold recycling efforts of the disinformation industry. No less than one month after the publication of an aerial image of protests in South Korea, a host of recognized fake news sites like the Geller Report repurposed the popular-but-generic image to illustrate a story about a purported "massive movement to overthrow George Soros" in Macedonia.[27] As the industry's quick cannibalization of the image suggests, there was little fear among propagandists that flexible viewers would venture into one of the many spaces where the image had been legitimately used or expend much effort interrogating its frictionless "truths." And even if they had, the costs—both economic and legal—associated with the purloined image are negligible, particularly as compared to those of the staged image. At worst, such appropriations invite a Digital Millennium Copyright Act (DMCA) takedown notice for copyright violation. At best, they sow the seeds of suspicion that nourish the industry, its adjacent political actors, and the flexible visuality evolving to help negotiate photographs in the digital age.

In addition to choreographing reality for the camera and pirating images from other sources to lend credibility to otherwise groundless stories, the industry and its benefactors have also leveraged flexible visuality to vigorously discount photographic evidence that conflicts with their political narratives. Among the clearest examples of this tactic was the Trump administration's response to an aerial photograph taken by Reuters of the president-elect's poorly attended 2017 inauguration. After the public rejected the administration's facile efforts to discredit the image based on its provenance in the "dishonest media," Trump and his surrogates shifted their campaign of doubt from source to text and context.

White House press secretary Sean Spicer initiated efforts to scramble interpretations of the damning image by enumerating platform crowd capacity numbers, D.C. Metro ridership figures on the day of the event, and the recent vintage of white ground coverings missing from an analogous photograph of Barack Obama's 2013 inauguration. Meanwhile, anonymous online commenters began a more pointed forensic investigation of the photograph, claiming that image enlargement revealed a discrepancy between the time shown on the face of the Smithsonian tower clock and the purported time of the photograph's production—an observation that editors at *The Atlantic* determined was true, but only because the clock had been broken for some time.[28]

After an exhausting week of performed suspicion about the image in question and photographic truth, more generally, Trump and his team used national television to pivot from abiding disbelief in one inauguration photograph to wide-eyed confidence in another. Speaking to news anchor David Muir in the West Wing before an alternate inauguration photograph captured from a lower angle and cropped so that the crowd appears to spill beyond the frame, Trump bloviates, "One thing this [photo] shows is how far over [the crowds] go here. Look. Look how far this is. This goes all the way down here. All the way down. Nobody sees that. You don't see that in the pictures."[29]

Trump's strenuous rejection of the Reuters photograph and subsequent promotion of an alternate image of the event depends on spectators whose confidence lies less in photography than in their own beliefs and instincts, which serve as the basis for their acceptance or rejection of a given image. Thus, what looks like faith in the veracity of an image is really appreciation for the way it flatters what Walter Lipmann calls "the pictures in our heads."[30] Within such a scopic regime, photographs lose their evidentiary and rhetorical value, and are, instead, reduced to mere extensions of our existing ideas and impressions of the world, including and especially the idea that photographic truth is malleable. Emptied of their capacity to inspire doubt (and thus inquiry) about anything other than the medium itself, images primarily become comforting objects of affirmation, ratifying experience and confirming what we already know to be true, even, paradoxically, as the very notion of truth crumbles around us.

As the example of Twitter users' gut-level dismissals of the "Rape Melania" photographs (e.g., "obviously photoshopped") illustrate, a flexible relationship to images is not unique to Trump supporters. Nor is it specific to our encounters with expressly political imagery, as the case of the researchers who looked to Google for their unmanipulated photographic stimuli demonstrates. Moreover, this style of spectatorship is not entirely new, as it has epitomized our reading of personal portraits for well over a century, and increasingly came to figure in our reading of other photo documents when cracks in the foundation of photographic fidelity became more noticeable throughout the second half of the twentieth century. Significantly, though, this tendency to shift between unreflective faith and skepticism based on whether an image aligns with our prior knowledge has become more pronounced with the rise of digitally networked visual culture.

Awash in ever more images that flicker in and out of public consciousness with unprecedented speed, spectators have had to adopt modes of looking that economize the time and energy they dedicate to any one image. This retreat from our responsibility to the image and reading process has been justified by the declining value of images within contemporary conditions of surplus. That is, because the image has been cheapened by the democratization of its production and distribution, it no longer commands the deep attention it once did. Scrutiny once directed at a handful of images in the daily newspaper is now distributed across multiple online platforms actively pushing all manner of images into our field of vision for consideration. Under such conditions of viewing, flexible visuality becomes a matter of not just convenience but necessity. Likewise, as images become progressively unmoored from the traditional enunciative structures that have helped to both authenticate and organize their meaning for the spectator, flexibility emerges as a strategy for undertaking the work that trusted newspapers, magazines, and television news programs once did.

While a deeper history of contemporary visuality reveals that the disinformation industry did not invent these new conditions of viewing or the visuality they demand, it is clear that propagandists have leveraged our emerging relationship to images for financial gain and political benefit. In addition to crowding the already thick flow of visual material with inflammatory images designed to communicate efficiently, such figures have also worked tirelessly to delegitimize traditional news institutions by cultivating an ecology of doubt around them. The goal of the tiresome fake news rejoinder lobbed at the press, as Trump revealed to journalist Lesley Stahl off the record in 2016, is not to ensure that the facts get reported correctly, but rather to make sure that when they do, no one believes them.[31]

The False Hope of Digital Image Literacy and Forensic Technology

The growing concern over staged, doctored, recontextualized, and disingenuously dismissed photographs has given rise to a robust body of popular and scholarly work on ways to avoid being duped by images and political actors who manipulate them. The recommendations in this literature typically boil down to either digital visual literacy or image authentication software. Although seemingly noble antidotes to the scourge of visual disinformation, neither is capable of ameliorating the problem, and might, in fact, exacerbate it.

Historically, visual literacy has referred to the development of interpretive faculties that help an observer recognize how images coordinate meaning and thus come to persuade audiences. Literacy of this sort equips an observer to "read," for example, the celebratory images of George W. Bush's 2003 "Mission Accomplished" speech as an effort to manufacture approval for a deeply unpopular president and war. Calls for such training in primary and secondary schools emerged in the second half of the twentieth century under the more general banner of "media literacy," and were primarily motivated by anxiety over the corrosive effects of ubiquitous commercial media messaging on young people.[32]

The *digital* visual literacy promoted in much of the contemporary work on fake news represents a literacy of a very different kind. It is not a critical literacy concerned with the rhetorical or ideological dimensions of images, but a forensic literacy centered on their computational or operational logics. It is the study of image signals rather than signs. Exercising this counterstrike against deceptive images entails using Google's image search tool or the website TinEye to track down the source of an image, Amnesty International's YouTube DataViewer to verify a video's upload time, and Google Maps to confirm locations in photographs. It might also include reviewing image metadata to determine details like the type of camera used, and scrutinizing pixel uniformity and shadow and lighting consistency in the image to rule out postproduction tinkering.[33]

Frequently described as simple but powerful techniques to spare netizens from the embarrassment of inadvertently sharing fake images online, digital visual literacy amounts to a dizzying, software-enabled game of online Clue. The viewer is called upon to expend great time and effort cataloging supplementary details and extravisual evidence in a manner reminiscent of Giovanni Morelli's method for exposing fine art forgeries,[34] all before the more significant task of interpretation and understanding can even begin.

In addition to the problem of supplanting reasoned deliberation with mechanistic verification, such "tricks" turn out to be mostly worthless in practice. As social media platforms like Facebook and Instagram integrate more of the web into walled gardens that prevent search engines like Google from indexing their contents, reverse image searches become increasingly impotent in the war on fake images. The call to investigate image metadata, too, is largely ineffectual since only about a quarter of images on the web contain any such information.[35] In legitimate efforts to reduce server costs and optimize websites for faster loading, as well as illegitimate efforts to erase the traces of disinformation campaigns, metadata is often the first casualty. Likewise, as the experimental research study referenced at the beginning of this chapter found, identifying photo manipulations is incredibly difficult for the average person.[36] Even the World Press Photo competition does not trust its expert judges with such detective work anymore. Instead, it utilizes Photoshop and two independent forensic analysts to evaluate the files.[37] As this practice makes clear, image authentication is a job for machines and people trained to think like them.

The second recommendation that frequently appears in work concerned with the epidemic of photo manipulation offers to relieve humans of the onerous—if not impossible—task of evaluating the integrity of an image by altogether off-loading that work onto machines. In this market-based approach to the problem, we find a variety of start-up companies scrambling to develop software to automate many of the techniques central to digital visual literacy. Some programs promise to verify images by digitally "notarizing" them at the point of capture and transmitting these digital signatures to distributed public ledgers like Bitcoin for future retrieval, while others pledge to authenticate "un-notarized" images by examining their content and packaging to assign them an originality score.[38] Despite how elegant such solutions sound, even software developers are skeptical about their viability. As a computer scientist working on an image detection tool sponsored by the Defense Advanced Research Projects Agency (DARPA) mused, "My hope is that when you run a photo through *20 or so different forensic techniques*, and every single one, from the packaging to the shadows to the colour to the noise is completely consistent, it is more likely that the photo is real."[39] Even computers, it turns out, are not particularly up to the task of protecting the world from propagandists.

In both digital visual literacy and image authenticity detection software we find little more than rhetorical panaceas and a troubling promise to recuperate the myth of photographic objectivity, in which the seeds of our contemporary crisis of images lie. Had we had the foresight in 1839 to describe the daguerreotype as simply "more real" than a painting and not, for example, a "mirror with memory," we would not have set photography up to become the source of weaponized doubt that it is today. The sooner we stop trying to shape the medium into a vehicle of absolute truth, the sooner it will lose its capacity to propagate fiction.

Notes

1. Sophie Nightingale, Kimberley Wade, and Derrick Watson, "Can People Identify Original and Manipulated Photos of Real-World Scenes?," *Cognitive Research: Principles and Implications* 2, no. 30 (2017): https://doi.org/10.1186/s41235-017-0067-2.

2. Lawrence Grossberg, "Tilting at Windmills: A Cynical Assemblage of the Crises of Knowledge," *Cultural Studies* 32, no. 2 (2018): 149–193.

3. Edgar Allan Poe, "The Daguerreotype," *Alexander's Weekly Messenger*, June 15, 1840, http://www.daguerreotypearchive.org/texts/P8400008_POE_ALEX-WEEKLY_1840-01 -15.pdf.

4. Oliver Wendell Holmes, "The Stereoscope and the Stereograph," *Atlantic Monthly*, June 1859, https://www.theatlantic.com/magazine/archive/1859/06/the-stereoscope -and-the-stereograph/303361/.

5. André Bazin, "The Ontology of the Photographic Image," trans. Hugh Gray, *Film Quarterly* 13, no. 4 (1960): 4–9.

6. Andy Grundberg, "Ask It No Questions: The Camera Can Lie," *New York Times*, August 12, 1990, https://www.nytimes.com/1990/08/12/arts/photography-view-ask -it-no-questions-the-camera-can-lie.html.

7. Dan Schiller, "Realism, Photography and Journalistic Objectivity in 19th Century America," *Studies in the Anthropology of Visual Communication* 4, no. 2 (1977): 86–98.

8. For example, see Lev Manovich, *The Language of New Media* (Cambridge, MA: MIT Press, 2002); William J. Mitchell, *The Reconfigured Eye: Visual Truth in the Post-Photographic Era* (Cambridge, MA: MIT Press, 1992); Fred Ritchin, *After Photography* (New York: W. W. Norton, 2009).

9. David Rodowick, *The Virtual Life of Film* (Cambridge, MA: Harvard University Press, 2007).

10. Philip Rosen, *Change Mummified: Cinema, Historicity, Theory* (Minneapolis: University of Minnesota Press, 2001), 322.

11. Ibid.

12. Susan Goldberg, "How We Spot Altered Pictures," *National Geographic*, July 2016, https://www.nationalgeographic.com/magazine/2016/07/editors-note-images-and -ethics/; Fred Hiatt, "Boy Prostitute Photos Staged," *Washington Post*, September 11, 1993, https://www.washingtonpost.com/archive/lifestyle/1993/09/11/boy-prostitute -photos-staged/ae989182-0200-41b0-a8ea -9be6be60bd50/?utm_term=.67da3e89aa19.

13. Maria Aspan, "Ease of Alteration Creates Woes for Picture Editors," *New York Times*, August 14, 2006, https://www.nytimes.com/2006/08/14/technology/14photo shop.html.

14. "Reuters Drops Beirut Photographer," BBC News, August 8, 2006, http://news .bbc.co.uk/2/hi/5254838.stm.

15. Michael Agresta, "The Image in the 21st Century: How Digital Photo Archives Have Changed the Way the World Looks," *Slate*, December 16, 2014, http://www .slate.com/articles/life/design/2014/12/images_on_the_internet_how_digital_photo _archives_have_changed_the_way_the.html.; Marco Solaroli, "Toward a New Visual

Culture of the News: Professional Photojournalism, Digital Post-Production, and the Symbolic Struggle for Distinction," *Digital Journalism* 3, no. 4 (2015): 513–532.

16. Hal Foster, "Preface to *Vision and Visuality*," in *Visual Culture: Critical Concepts in Media and Cultural Studies*, ed. Joanne Morra and Marquard Smith (New York: Routledge, 1988), 116–119.

17. Gina Giotta, "Disappeared: Erasure in the Age of Mechanical Writing" (Ph.D. diss., University of Iowa, 2011).

18. Quoted in Callum Borchers, "'Rape Melania' Sign at Anti-Trump Protest Draws Strong Rebuke, Sparking Twitter Trend," *Washington Post*, November 13, 2016, https://www.washingtonpost.com/news/post-politics/wp/2016/11/13/protesters -rape-melania-sign-draws-strong-rebuke-sparking-twitter-trend/.

19. James Miller (@Millermena), "'Rape Melania' was fake. I knew it but didn't have time to prove it. Malcolm Gladwell was right, trust my gut," Twitter, November 16, 2016, https://twitter.com/Millermena/status/798865781194944512; Anya (@any-abike), "That 'rape Melania' sign is fake btw. Same sign facing straight to camera but shots taken from very different angles," Twitter, November 13, 2016, https://twitter .com/anyabike/status/797838984156250114.

20. Melanie Ehrenkranz, "Was That 'Rape Melania' Sign Fake or Photoshopped?," Mic, November 14, 2016, https://mic.com/articles/159392/was-that-rape-melania -sign-fake-or-photoshopped-extremely-unlikely-expert-says#.bLptzarzd.

21. Absentee Voter (@absentee_voter), "@thereal_beck #photoshopped #photoshops Rape Melania #protest signs. Rape is not a joke, nor a tool with which to attack your opponents," Twitter, November 14, 2016, https://twitter.com/absentee_voter/status /798294944196788224.

22. Callum Borchers, "How One Deplorable Sign at an Anti-Trump Protest Fore-shadows the Fight over Fake News," *Washington Post*, November 26, 2016, https:// www.washingtonpost.com/news/the-fix/wp/2016/11/15/how-one-deplorable-sign -at-an-anti-trump-protest-foreshadows-the-fight-over-fake-news/.

23. Joseph Bernstein, "Inside the Alt-Right's Campaign to Smear the Trump Pro-testers as Anarchists," BuzzFeed News, January 11, 2017, https://www.buzzfeed.com /josephbernstein/inside-the-alt-rights-campaign-to-smear-trump-protesters-as?utm _term=.kvpAgNko2#.fnR6A479w.

24. Laura Hayes, "The Consequences of 'Pizza Gate' Are Real at Comet Ping Pong," *Washington City Paper*, November 15, 2016, https://www.washingtoncitypaper.com /news/article/20842321/the-consequences-of-pizza-gate-are-real-at-comet-ping -pong.

25. Nick Logan, "Bloodied 'Trump Supporter' in Hoax Photo Is 'Ash vs Evil Dead' Actress Samara Weaving," Global News, June 8, 2016, https://globalnews.ca/news

/2750098/bloodied-trump-supporter-in-hoax-photo-is-ash-vs-evil-dead-actress
-samara-weaving/.

26. Brian Feldman, "Look at the Horrific Injuries 'Tolerant' Liberals Gave This
Meme Just for Supporting Trump," *New York*, June 7, 2016, http://nymag.com
/selectall/2016/06/intolerant-liberals-lash-out-at-trump-supporters-in-very-real-and
-true-tweets.html#comments.

27. Pamela Geller, "Stop Operation Soros (SOS): Massive Movement to Overthrow
George Soros Explodes in Macedonia," Geller Report, January 22, 2017, https://
gellerreport.com/2017/01/stop-operation-soros-sos.html/.

28. Alan Taylor, "'All of This Space Was Full': A Photographic Fact Check," *The
Atlantic*, January 24, 2017, https://www.theatlantic.com/photo/2017/01/all-of-this
-space-was-full-a-photographic-fact-check/514253/.

29. Donald Trump, "President Donald Trump: The White House Interview by David
Muir," *ABC News Specials*, January 25, 2017, http://abc.go.com/shows/abc-news-specials
/episode-guide/2017-01/25-President-Donald-Trump-The-White-House-Interview.

30. Walter Lippmann, *Public Opinion* (New York: Harcourt, Brace, 1922).

31. Eli Rosenberg, "Lesley Stahl: Trump Admitted He Attacks Journalists to Shield
Himself from Negative Coverage," *Washington Post*, May 22, 2018, https://www
.washingtonpost.com/news/the-fix/wp/2018/05/22/trump-admitted-he-attacks
-press-to-shield-himself-from-negative-coverage-60-minutes-reporter-says/.

32. Kathleen Tyner, *Literacy in a Digital World: Teaching and Learning in the Age of
Information* (Mahwah, NJ: Lawrence Erlbaum, 1998).

33. Isaac Kaplan, "We're in the Age of Fake Photos and Videos—Here's How to Spot
Them," *Artsy*, September 25, 2017, https://www.artsy.net/article/artsy-editorial-age
-fake-photos-videos-spot; Annette Lamb, "Fact or Fake? Curriculum Challenges for
School Librarians," *Teacher Librarian* 45, no. 1 (2017) 56–60; David Nield, "How
to Spot Fake Photos on the Web," Gizmodo, October 13, 2017, https://fieldguide
.gizmodo.com/how-to-spot-fake-photos-on-the-web-1819434333.

34. Carlo Ginzberg, "Clues: Morelli, Freud, and Sherlock Holmes," in *The Sign of
Three: Dupin, Holmes, Peirce*, ed. Umberto Eco and Thomas A. Sebeok (Bloomington:
Indiana University Press, 1988), 81–118.

35. Emad Isa Saleh, "Image Embedded Metadata in Cultural Heritage Digital Collections on the Web: An Analytical Study," *Library Hi Tech* 36, no. 2 (2018): 339–357.

36. Nightingale, Wade, and Watson, "Can People Identify."

37. Ye Ming and Oliver Laurent, "World Press Photo Disqualifies 20% of Its Contest
Finalists," *Time*, February 12, 2015, http://time.com/3706626/world-press-photo
-processing-manipulation-disqualified/.

38. Daven Mathies, "How a Blockchain-Based Digital Photo Notary Is Fighting Fraud and Fake News," Digital Trends, January 25, 2018, https://www.digitaltrends.com/photography/truepic-blochain-image-verification/; Tiffanie Wen, "The Hidden Signs That Can Reveal a Fake Photo," BBC, June 30, 2017, http://www.bbc.com/future/story/20170629-the-hidden-signs-that-can-reveal-if-a-photo-is-fake.

39. Quoted in Wen, "Hidden Signs" (emphasis added).

3 A Case against the Post-Truth Era: Revisiting Mouffe's Critique of Consensus-Based Democracy

Johan Farkas

The rapid rise of *fake news* as a ubiquitous term in global politics has caused widespread debate in democratic societies concerning the distinction between true and false. A number of scholars and journalists have argued that we might be entering a *post-truth* or *post-factual* era.[1] Post-truth was even named *word of the year* in 2016 by Oxford Dictionaries, defining the concept as "circumstances in which objective facts are less influential in shaping public opinion than appeals to emotion and personal belief." Based on this societal diagnosis, analysts have concluded that facts are moving to the background of contemporary politics. Politicians no longer concern themselves with the distinction between fake and real, making democracy shift from a rational to an emotional political system.[2]

If we consider this characterization of the post-truth era, one aspect of contemporary politics appears paradoxical: rather than neglecting facts, it seems that democracy is increasingly saturated with disputes over what counts as "true," "real," "false," and "fake." Political actors routinely label their opponents as frauds, while claiming to be the bearers of truth themselves. As U.S. president Donald Trump exemplifies, terms such as *fake news* have become a means of bolstering authority and attacking perceived enemies. It has become a way of obtaining and enforcing dominance in the political landscape. Facts are not simply dismissed. As part of a much more complex development, the very meaning or interpretation of the term *facts* seems to have become the epicenter of political struggles. If this is the case, we might consider whether the notions of the "post-truth" or "post-factual" era truly encapsulate the current state of democratic politics.

This chapter argues that there is more to the story than what is often told: that facts are not becoming obsolete, but rather are becoming highly politicized. The term *fake news* has become a rhetorical weapon, increasingly mobilized by political actors to attack their opponents. As a consequence, the notion of "fake" shifts from a question of information validity to a question of political control: Who gets to draw the line between "fake" and "real"? And who gets to establish himself or herself as an authority and dismiss others as "fakes"? Opposing political actors propose incompatible answers to these questions.[3] The ubiquity of terms such as *fake news* thus becomes detached from the actual amount of false information in circulation. *Fake* becomes a placeholder for power and dominance—a means of delegitimizing conflicting ideas. This has fundamental implications for the way we can assess the current state of democratic politics. More importantly, it changes the way we can prescribe a viable future trajectory for democracy as a political system. To understand why this is the case, we need to delve into democracy's innermost logics of operation.

Agonistic Pluralism and the Critique of Consensus-Based Democracy

Chantal Mouffe's theory of agonistic pluralism builds on the fundamental premise that democracy—as a political system—should not strive toward consensus based on rational discussion. This is due to the fact that "any social objectivity is ultimately political,"[4] meaning that any seemingly "neutral" or "objective" solution to any social issue will always materialize as the result of power relations. All human norms, policies, and mechanisms of control derive from political struggles between conflicting discourses. No procedure, decision, or consensus can arise from pure rational thought, as all "agreements in opinions" must first rely on "agreement in forms of life."[5] There is no truly neutral, rational, or objective outcome, as neutrality cannot exist independent of human consciousness. Indeed, the very notion of neutrality is fully contingent upon human existence—an argument Mouffe derives from Ludwig Wittgenstein.[6] What might appear as politically objective at any given moment in time will thus always rest on the exclusion of opposing ideas and worldviews. And what might appear as unanimous agreement will always be a manifestation of one discourse dominating over others (i.e., *hegemony*). Following this line of argument, Mouffe contends that politicians, scholars, and citizens must all "give up the dream of a rational consensus, which entails the fantasy that we could escape from our human form of life."[7]

To Mouffe, consensus-based democratic ideals rely on a fundamental misconception about democracy's justification of existence. Their principal error lies in a failure to acknowledge "the impossibility of finding rational, impartial solutions to political issues but also the integrative role that conflict plays in modern democracy."[8] Democratic institutions, Mouffe argues, should acknowledge and accommodate the contingency of political decision-making and sustain the inherent struggles that shape democratic societies.[9] As in all political systems, democracies contain a multitude of conflicting voices, all constructing their collective identities around divergent agendas and perceived enemies. The core value of a democracy lies in its ability to give voice to these opposing groups and mitigate between them. What distinguishes democratic politics, then, from, say, a dictatorship is *not* the degree of consensus it can produce, but rather the degree of accepted disagreement it can contain. To rephrase this slightly: democracy's strength lies in its ability to accommodate crosscutting goals and conflicting worldviews, refusing to suppress opposition "by imposing an authoritarian order."[10]

Instead of idealizing objectivity and consensus, Mouffe asserts that democracy's key goal should be to foster accepted disagreement between conflicting groups. Democratic institutions should serve to soften hostilities between perceived enemies, ideally making them see each other as "somebody whose ideas we combat but whose right to defend those ideas we do not put into question."[11] She conceptualizes this as a transformation from *antagonistic enemies* into *agonistic adversaries*. To Mouffe, consensus-based ideals fail to recognize the significance of this transformational process. This represents not only a flaw, she argues, but also a potential threat to the very foundation of democracy as a political system. By putting objectivity, rationality, and agreement at the center of democracy, consensus-based ideals reinforce what Mouffe defines as a "post-political *Zeitgeist*."[12] From within this worldview, conflicting groups and ideas are seen as an obstacle for democratic decision-making rather than as its constitutive core. By idealizing consensus over compromise, objectivity over opposition, the post-political zeitgeist neglects how *all* societal outcomes derive from power relations. This potentially undermines democracy's functioning, as hegemonic discourses become presented as stable and unchallengeable "truths" instead of contingent results of political struggles. Agonistic conflict is relegated to the margins of society, perceived as a disturbing element instead of democracy's cornerstone.

According to Mouffe, democratic institutions should mitigate between groups and make visible how each and every "objective" outcome is always *as* political as the conflicting ideas they suppress. Accordingly, institutions should *not* claim to operate based on any kind of "true" or "objective" mode of organization. Political disagreement should be brought to the forefront of democratic institutions—not as destructive conflicts, but as constructive disagreement between agonistic adversaries: a democratic system based on agonistic pluralism.

The Impossibility of a "Truth Era"

From the perspective of agonistic pluralism, ideals of finding one true solution to any societal issue are inherently problematic, as they fail to acknowledge how political solutions arise as the result of discursive constellations. Instead of offering truly objective approaches to politics, they obscure the political core of all decision-making, neglecting how everything that is "accepted as the 'natural' order...is never the manifestation of a deeper objectivity."[13] Truly objective or rational politics is an oxymoron.

Drawing on this theoretical foundation, let us return to the idea of a "post-truth era" and its potential remedy, the "truth era." As stated in the introduction to this chapter, numerous scholars and journalists have argued that we might be entering a "post-truth era," a dysfunctional state of democracy where political decision-making relies "on assertions that 'feel true,' but have no basis in fact."[14] According to this position, the power of facts is waning, as politicians increasingly rely on emotional engagement rather than rational argumentation.[15] Social media environments are said to play a key role in this development, as they enable politicians and disseminators of "fake news" to communicate directly to potential voters without interference from fact-checking journalists.[16] The technological architecture of these online platforms amplifies these processes, as citizens become "inhabitants of internet-created bubbles, where algorithms feed their prejudices and misconceptions with cosseting confirmations of whatever they have selected for their...truth."[17] People become not only misinformed, but also completely indifferent to the truth. The result is a state of "post-truth" politics torn by hyperpartisan divides: "When lies make the political system dysfunctional, its poor results can feed the alienation and lack of trust in institutions that make the post-truth play possible in the first place. To counter this, mainstream politicians need to find a language of rebuttal (being called 'pro-truth' might be a start)."[18]

As numerous scholars and media professionals have argued, the key goal of contemporary democracy is to reposition facts at the center of political decision-making in order to solve the post-truth crisis. By doing so, hyperpartisan divides will dissolve and politics can once again return to a constructive state of operation. Political actors should thus actively seek to counterweigh the post-truth era by establishing themselves as "pro-truth." If successful, these efforts will not only bring facts to the forefront, but also unify a divided and antagonistic society. Ideally, we could imagine that these efforts could mark the beginning of a "truth era" in which fake news and hyperpartisanship is replaced by fact-based politics. This might sound ideal on the surface, but is this truly the best prescription for contemporary democracy? If we accept the argument that being "pro-truth" could potentially solve the post-truth crisis, we are quickly faced with a paradoxical question: Who gets to decide who are the "pro-truth" politicians and who are the "fake" ones? Asking oppositional political actors undoubtedly leads to conflicting answers.

In early January 2017, the newly elected president, Donald Trump, defended himself and his allies against accusations of spreading fake news. On Twitter, his favorite platform of choice, he wrote: "FAKE NEWS—A TOTAL POLITICAL WITCH HUNT!"[19] Trump saw himself and his trusted media channels, such as the national-conservative Breitbart News, as victims. Yet, soon after, Trump switched the roles in this so-called witch hunt, systematically attacking media outlets, including CNN, BuzzFeed, and the *New York Times*, as the "fake news media."[20] "Fake news" thus became a potent political weapon in a struggle between himself and his perceived enemies. This struggle reached a peak when Trump proclaimed that he himself had come up with the very term *fake* to capture the wrongdoings of the "mainstream media."[21] If we hypothetically asked Trump if he was "pro-truth" or "fake," there could be little doubt that he would reply that he is profoundly "pro-truth," while his perceived opponents are "fakes." If we ask these very same opponents, the answer would likely be the opposite. But who is right, then?

It could be argued that we should simply fact-check each political actor and figure out who is "pro-truth" and who is "fake." In the case where Trump claimed to have invented the term *fake*, the answer is obviously that Trump is spreading misinformation. Yet, as Mouffe reminds us, political decision-making is much more complicated than simply questions of "true" and "false." In relation to political outcomes, nothing is ever truly "objective" or "rational," as all decisions arise from different actors asserting dominance over one another. Finding the most "true" political outcome is an impossible task. Recently, Stephen Coleman, professor of political communication at the University of Leeds, echoed this position, arguing that proponents of a "truth"-based democracy should "come to terms with the inevitability that political conflicts have no single, 'correct' conclusion, but can only ever be contested and resolved as battles of competing interests."[22] The proposed solution of supporting "pro-truth" politicians and delegitimizing "fake" ones seems to miss this point. In order for there to be widespread consensus on who is "pro-truth" and "fake," some politicians would have to assert themselves as such by hegemonizing the social, obtaining total dominance. This would most likely *not* be positive for democracy as a political system.

In the characterization of the "post-truth era," one argument put forth is that "facts...seem to be losing their ability to support consensus."[23] Yet, as Mouffe underlines, consensus always requires the suppression of opposing voices, potentially undermining the very foundation of democracy. A consensus-based "truth society," in other words, could quickly resemble an authoritarian regime more than a free democratic state characterized by agonistic pluralism. Consider China or Russia, for example: in these countries, speaking against the "truths" of the government can lead to imprisonment or even death. Within these political systems, this ensures that there is little (visible) opposition to the political consensus and very little (visible) political conflict. Yet this consensus does not result from a well-functioning democracy. Following Mouffe, it results from the opposite—a lack of agonistic pluralism. With this in mind, a "truth society" becomes a democratic ideal hardly worth pursuing. Additionally, it raises the question of whether the "post-truth era" truly encapsulates the current state of democracy in the first place.

Conclusion

Based on the presented critique of the "post-truth" and "truth" eras, it might seem that we are left with political meaninglessness: all solutions are equally good, as there is no "objective" political outcome, making politics futile. Building on Mouffe, however, I will argue that the opposite is the case. Faced with similar criticism, Mouffe contends: "I have no doubt that the liberals who think that rational agreement can be reached in politics…will accuse my conception of the political of being 'nihilistic.'…I hope to demonstrate that acknowledging the ineradicability of the conflictual dimension in social life, far from undermining the democratic project, is the necessary condition for grasping the challenge to which democratic politics is confronted."[24]

The fact that there is no political "objectivity" does not make the world meaningless. On the contrary, it highlights the fundamental importance of political decision-making for the human condition. Democratic politics should not reflect any "objective truths" in the world, but instead reflect the wide array of perspectives of the very same people who are affected by political outcomes. This underlines the merits of democracy as a political system, including agonistic pluralism, as it enables citizens to influence the contingent discourses that shape the social world. In contrast, citizens within authoritarian regimes remain subjected to supposedly "objective" or "true" decisions of their leaders. Based on these conclusions, I argue that if there is a crisis of contemporary democracy, the crisis cannot be described in terms of a "post-truth era," as this implies a democratic ideal not worth pursuing. This does *not*, however, infer that new forms of misinformation, deception, and disguised propaganda—what we might call "fake news"— are harmless to democracy. In fact, most of my own research explores manifestations and implications of such phenomena.[25] Rather, Mouffe's theory of agonistic pluralism can help us realize the dangers, not of fake news, but of trying to censor and suppress it in order to save democracy—a cure, which represents a bigger potential threat of its own. Beyond the scope of this chapter, then, lies what can best capture the present state of democracy. But looking for objective political truths is at least not the right place to start.

Notes

1. William Davies, "The Age of Post-Truth Politics," *New York Times*, August 24, 2016, https://www.nytimes.com/2016/08/24/opinion/campaign-stops/the-age-of-post -truth-politics.html; Jonathan Freedland, "Post-Truth Politicians Such as Donald

Trump and Boris Johnson Are No Joke," *The Guardian*, May 15, 2016, https://www
.theguardian.com/commentisfree/2016/may/13/boris-johnson-donald-trump-post
-truth-politician; Fabio Giglietto, Laura Iannelli, Luca Rossi, and Augusto Valeriani,
"Fakes, News and the Election: A New Taxonomy for the Study of Misleading Information within the Hybrid Media System," *Convegno AssoComPol*, December (2016):
1–41; Kathleen Higgins, "Post-Truth: A Guide for the Perplexed," *Nature* 540 (2016):
9, http://doi.org/10.1038/540009a; Brian McNair, "After Objectivity? Schudson's
Sociology of Journalism in the Era of Post-Factuality," *Journalism Studies* 18, no. 10
(2017): 1–16, http://doi.org/10.1080/1461670X.2017.1347893; Matthew Norman,
"Whoever Wins the US Presidential Election, We've Entered a Post-Truth World—
There's No Going Back Now," *The Independent*, November 8, 2016, http://www
.independent.co.uk/voices/us-election-2016-donald-trump-hillary-clinton-who
-wins-post-truth-world-no-going-back-a7404826.html.

2. "Post-Truth Politics: Art of the Lie," *The Economist*, September 10, 2016, https://
www.economist.com/leaders/2016/09/10/art-of-the-lie; Luciano Floridi, "Fake News
and a 400-Year-Old Problem: We Need to Resolve the 'Post-Truth' Crisis," *The Guardian*, November 29, 2016, https://www.theguardian.com/technology/2016/nov/29
/fake-news-echo-chamber-ethics-infosphere-internet-digital.

3. Johan Farkas and Jannick Schou, "Fake News as a Floating Signifier: Hegemony,
Antagonism and the Politics of Falsehood," *Javnost—The Public* 25, no. 3 (2018):
298–314.

4. Chantal Mouffe, "Deliberative Democracy or Agonistic Pluralism," Political Science Series 72 (Vienna: Institute for Advanced Studies, 2000), https://www.ihs.ac.at
/publications/pol/pw_72.pdf.

5. Ibid., 11.

6. Ludwig Wittgenstein, *Philosophical Investigations* (Oxford: Basil Blackwell, 1953).

7. Mouffe, "Deliberative Democracy," 12.

8. Chantal Mouffe, *On the Political* (London: Routledge, 2005), 30–31.

9. Ibid.; Mouffe, "Deliberative Democracy."

10. Mouffe, *On the Political*, 30.

11. Mouffe, "Deliberative Democracy," 15.

12. Mouffe, *On the Political*, 8 (original emphasis).

13. Chantal Mouffe, "Democratic Politics and Conflict: An Agonistic Approach,"
Política Común 9 (2016), http://dx.doi.org/10.3998/pc.12322227.0009.011.

14. "Post-Truth Politics: Art of the Lie."

15. Davies, "Age of Post-Truth Politics"; Floridi, "Fake News."

16. Alison Flood, "'Post-Truth' Named Word of the Year by Oxford Dictionaries," *The Guardian*, November 15, 2016, https://www.theguardian.com/books/2016/nov /15/post-truth-named-word-of-the-year-by-oxford-dictionaries; Freedland, "Post-Truth Politicians."

17. Norman, "Whoever Wins the US Presidential Election."

18. "Post-Truth Politics: Art of the Lie."

19. Donald Trump (@realDonaldTrump), "FAKE NEWS—A TOTAL POLITICAL WITCH HUNT!," Twitter, January 20, 2017, https://twitter.com/realdonaldtrump /status/818990655418617856?lang=en.

20. Donald Trump (@realDonaldTrump), "@CNN is in a total meltdown with their FAKE NEWS because their ratings are tanking since election and their credibility will soon be gone!," Twitter, January 12, 2017, https://twitter.com/realdonaldtrump /status/819550083742109696?lang=en; Donald Trump, "'BuzzFeed Runs Unverifiable Trump-Russia Claims' #FakeNews," Twitter, January 20, 2017, https://twitter .com/realDonaldTrump/status/819000924207251456; Donald Trump, "Somebody with aptitude and conviction should buy the FAKE NEWS and failing @nytimes and either run it correctly or let it fold with dignity!," Twitter, January 29, 2017, https:// twitter.com/realDonaldTrump/status/825690087857995776?ref_src=twsrc%5Etfw &ref_url=http%3A%2F%2Fthehill.com%2Fhomenews%2Fadministration%2F3167 23-trump-blasts-fake-news-and-failing-new-york-times.

21. Michael Schaub, "Trump's Claim to Have Come Up with the Term 'Fake News' Is Fake News, Merriam-Webster Dictionary Says," *Los Angeles Times*, October 9, 2017, http://www.latimes.com/books/jacketcopy/la-et-jc-fake-news-20171009-story.html.

22. Stephen Coleman, *Can the Internet Strengthen Democracy?* (Cambridge, UK: Polity Press, 2017), 76–77.

23. Davies, "Age of Post-Truth Politics."

24. Mouffe, *On the Political*, 3–4.

25. Johan Farkas, Jannick Schou, and Christina Neumayer, "Platformed Antagonism: Racist Discourses on Fake Muslim Facebook Pages," *Critical Discourse Studies* 15, no. 5 (2018): 463–480, https://doi.org/10.1080/17405904.2018.1450276; Johan Farkas and Marco T. Bastos, "IRA Propaganda on Twitter: Stoking Antagonism and Tweeting Local News," in *Proceedings of the 9th International Conference on Social Media and Society* (New York: ACM, 2018), 281–285, https://doi.org/10.1145/3217804.3217929.

4 You're Fake News: The Problem with Accusations of Falsehood

Whitney Phillips

In an era plagued by alternative facts, adjustable data, and social media sleight of hand, falsehood—or at least the threat of falsehood, whether born of maliciousness, ignorance, or greed—permeates the political landscape. It is therefore critical to hone best practices for identifying, assessing, and countering falsity. Not all approaches to true versus false are equally effective, however. Focusing on the "fake news" frame, this chapter will argue that external claims of what counts as real and what counts as fake—regardless of whether a person uses the term *fake news* specifically—doesn't bring us any closer to the truth. In fact, *etic* claims of veracity, which impose external standards onto the indigenous values and assumptions of a particular group, often limit discussions to the basic assertion *that* a particular story is false, rather than encouraging reflection on *why* the story resonates with audiences, how the story spreads, and what deeper cultural truths are revealed in the process.

The chapter will advocate instead for a folkloric approach to falsehood, one that situates belief within existing structures and logics, and actively embraces *emic* analyses, which take seriously—and explore the organic functionality of—the values and behaviors of participants. As an anchoring case study, the chapter will explore the satanic, pedophilic, sometimes ironic, sometimes sincere conspiracy theory known as #Pizzagate, which mushroomed into a very real news story, with very real political, professional, and interpersonal implications for those targeted, despite its utter fictitiousness.

This analysis of #Pizzagate and other cases discussed throughout the chapter will not, to be clear, apologize for slippery relativistic thinking, the notion that if something is believed to be true, that's close enough. "Close enough" neither is close to the truth nor provides nearly enough of it. However, without fully understanding the broader historical, cultural, and interpersonal context of belief, and, more basically, why a particular false claim is true to the person who believes it, one is much less likely to know where to even begin pushing back—a point of particular importance when the issues in question pose a direct threat to life, liberty, and even democracy itself.

Heard Any Fake News Lately?

First up is the handful of problems ushered in by the "fake news" frame, which, as the term would suggest, hinges on objective assessment of veracity. At least that's the idea; after reaching critical mass as a concept, the term has become hopelessly muddled through imprecise use. In addition to describing purposefully deceptive clickbait published by bogus websites and then spread via social media (the original sense of the term), the "fake news" label has been adopted to describe a variety of gossipy claims and conspiracy theories that may or may not be sincerely believed by those sharing. "Fake news" has also proved to be a handy way of undermining one's critics. The *"you're* fake news" schoolyard insult sense of the term has been employed most conspicuously by U.S. president Donald Trump, a habit that can only be described as ironic, given Trump's, let's say, shaky relationship with the truth, and enthusiastic amplification of a variety of verifiably false assertions over the years.[1] Ironic or not, Trump has taken to calling all unfriendly news organizations fake news, with particular rancor aimed at CNN; in May 2017, he denounced the cable organization for being (double? triple?) fake news for not running an advertisement that accused CNN of being fake news.[2] He also spent a great deal of time during his first one hundred days in office deriding the increasingly demonstrable claims of collusion between his presidential campaign and Russia as, you guessed it, "FAKE NEWS" (Trump's Caps Lock).[3]

One problem with this approach—particularly when someone uses the term *fake news*, but also when a story is dismissed out of hand as false—is that such frames tend to trivialize the impact of these stories, as if their falsity somehow mitigates their impact. In "classic" cases of fake news, for example, stories claiming that Pope Francis endorsed Trump for president or that Hillary Clinton sold weapons to the Islamic State in Iraq and Syria (ISIS), both false narratives—narratives that, as Craig Silverman illustrates, frequently outperformed legitimate news stories in terms of Facebook engagement and spread[4]—can still have a very real impact on individual behavior, from decisions about whom to follow and whom to ignore on social media to whom one chooses to vote for on Election Day. Similarly, erroneous conspiracy theories can have just as much impact as provable claims, as evidenced by the very false yet widespread assertion that Hillary Clinton was running a satanic child sex ring out of the back of Comet Ping Pong, a Washington, D.C., pizza parlor—a conspiracy theory known broadly as "#Pizzagate." Clinton was, of course, doing no such thing. That said, #Pizzagate was all too real for the owners of Comet Ping Pong, whose lives were upended by the sudden frenzy of attention from true believers, cynical pot-stirrers, and mainstream journalists alike. One proponent even traveled all the way from North Carolina to D.C. to conduct his own investigation—and ended up opening fire on the restaurant.

In addition to collectively sustained conspiracy theories, false accusations made by individuals can have a similarly serious impact. Donald Trump's utterly unfounded March 2017 accusation that then president Barack Obama had ordered a parting-gift wiretap of Trump provides one example. Though these claims were ultimately traced to a Breitbart News write-up of a far-right radio host's unfounded suspicions, Trump's assertion led the news cycle for weeks on end, triggered a formal probe within the U.S. intelligence community, and even resulted in the recusal of California representative Devin Nunes, ranking Republican on the House Intelligence Committee's investigation of Russian meddling in the 2016 election, for attempting (and failing) to validate Trump's wiretapping claims. Even the fakest, most absurd news, in other words, is in a very basic sense *real*—at least in terms of the havoc it can wreak.

Perhaps the greatest drawback of the "fake news" frame, however (again, regardless of whether that term is explicitly used), is that it tends to direct focus to the veracity of the text itself, not on the social processes that facilitate the text's spread, or how particular stories align with the interests and biases of those sharing. It is geared toward surface phenomena, in other words, not to underlying currents. Illustrating this point—as well as what is missed when the primary focus is truth versus falsehood—is Edgar Welch, the #Pizzagate crusader who opened fire on Comet Ping Pong. As noted in an interview with Adam Goldman of the *New York Times*, Welch didn't just reject the "fake news" frame (in this case, he was referring to the plethora of unsubstantiated rumors circulating in parts of Reddit and 4chan), he out-right inverted it.[5] Echoing many far-right conspiracy "truthers" suspicious of corporate media, he asserted that mainstream journalists were biased to the point of fakery;[6] for him, these journalists' proclamations of "fake news" pointed to the veracity of the story they were refuting.

The glaring disconnect between Welch and those who scoffed at #Pizza-gate highlights the limitations of etic truth claims—most succinctly cap-tured by the paradox that one person's marker of truth is another person's marker of falsehood. There are, of course, such things as actual things, and it is critical to keep track of which is which. That said, people are often memetically, and not strictly empirically, situated, a fact that complicates how best to respond to subjective experiences of truth. Ryan M. Milner and I highlight the power—and potential destructiveness—of subjectivist, memetic thinking in our discussion of the most successful memes of the 2016 U.S. presidential election.[7] These memes were not traditional internet memes, with specific resonant images superimposed with text. Sorry, Pepe the Frog; sorry, Ken Bone. Rather, the most successful election memes—the memes that spread the farthest with the most people across the broadest variety of media—aligned with ideas much older than the internet, from harmful racial stereotypes to restrictive gender norms to sweeping nativist sentiment. Cries of "Lock her up," "Build the wall," and "Drain the swamp" are all memes in this sense, with objective truth having very little to do with their subjective emotional resonance. In fact, the resonance of these memes was often entirely unmoored from the objective truth of the claims being made.

It is easy to decry memetic thinking in these cases, particularly when the message so explicitly denigrates an entire racial or religious group. But memetic thinking can be much more subtle, both in terms of the messages communicated and the implications of these messages. We—all of us, at some point in our lives, to varying degrees—believe things because they align with our existing worldviews, or because we were told these things by people we trust, or because we desperately want to believe them, *not* because we have independently verified these things using anything even vaguely resembling an analytic methodology. This point is supported by Sandra Harding's articulation of feminist standpoint theory, which fore-grounds the extent to which political standpoint—literally and figuratively, where one is standing in relation to power, due to race, gender, or class, for example—directly influences what one sees, and therefore what one knows, or thinks one knows, about the world.[8] The mere assertion that a false belief is false downplays the degree to which the belief hinges on memetic resonance, and the degree to which memetic resonance hinges on political standpoint. This, in turn, renders untenable any nuanced understanding of *why* something is believed, and *how* this belief coheres within a broader value system.

It's not just that "fake news" frames obscure the why and how of belief. Etic assertions of falsity posit a worldview and set of assumptions that may not even be *perceivable* to believers, further convincing these believers that their detractors are the crazy ones. For Welch, for example, it was logically impossible—from his standpoint, anyway—that mainstream reports debunking the #Pizzagate story could possibly have been true. Journalists always lie, the logic went. So if they're saying this didn't happen, it definitely did. Welch's case also illustrates Stephan Lewandowsky, Ullrich K. H. Ecker, and others' findings that attempts to correct misinformation may ultimately serve to reinforce false beliefs, as entrenched repetition inadvertently reinforces one's subjective understanding of a particular argument, its (presumed) evidence, and even its broader political stakes.[9]

For both these reasons, etic attempts to set the record straight risk strengthening precisely the emic monster that's been placed under quarantine. The possibility of fact-checks backfiring is rendered even more fraught when considering the difficulty imposed by Poe's law, an internet axiom that was formulated by Nathan Poe in the middle of the first decade of the twenty-first century and stipulates that sincerity and satire are often impossible to parse online. In the case of #Pizzagate, it wasn't clear as the conspiracy unfolded how many of the people sharing the story and posting theories to various online forums genuinely believed the story was true, and how many were engaged in trollish pro-Trump "shitposting"—*shitposting* being a term adopted by trolls / white nationalists / white nationalist trolls / who know to describe their efforts to seed as much Trump-flavored chaos as possible, with the ultimate goal of bolstering Trump, who they describe perhaps ironically, perhaps sincerely, perhaps as some unholy combination of both, as their "God Emperor."

The range of (often unverifiable) participant motivations in the #Pizzagate case raised a number of questions about the relative benefits and drawbacks of pushing back against the story. Explainers and other articles debunking the conspiracy were appropriate for those already aligned with the reporters' basic worldview. For truthers like Welch, however, who inverted every factual claim made by journalists on the grounds that journalists lie, these articles inadvertently reinforced the veracity of the story being debunked. For those who weren't true believers, but rather were just trying to bolster Trump, these articles had an even more insidious impact. Most basically, they incentivized further trollish engagement with and amplification of the story, because these pot-stirring behaviors worked; they spurred journalists to jump into the conspiracy-theorizing fray. This simultaneously incentivized the filing of additional articles (even articles of the "look at what these trolls on 4hcan are doing" ilk) and provided additional proof, or what looked like proof, for people like Welch. The objectively correct claim that nobody, and certainly not Hillary Clinton, was running a satanic child sex ring out of the back of a Washington, D.C., pizza shop completely sidestepped this complex intertwine of belief, standpoint, and play. It certainly couldn't begin to try and untangle it.

The Lore (and Lure) of the Folk

But if not "fake news," or some other etic framing of the truth, then what? Although less catchy, and a decidedly less fun insult, a folkloric framework—one that could be described as "folkloric news," or even the clipped "folk news," though the specific terminology is less important than the underlying theoretical approach—provides one possibility. Again, this is not to court relativism, or to minimize the value of true claims, or to give liars a free pass. This should go without saying, but warrants explicit spelling out in a climate so suffused by prevarication, outright deception, and questions of motive.

What a folkloric framing does do is foreground the resonance of a particular narrative or claim, and the realness of this resonance, within and across existing folk groups. This resonance might be born of sincere belief, sincere satire, or sincere shit-stirring; participants might be truthers or trolls. Regardless of motives, one basic insight always holds when considering participant behavior: something about whatever narrative or claim connects with those participating. This point of connection might accurately reflect the world, that is, *be true*. It might not. In either case, and in contrast to etic analyses, an emic folkloric frame doesn't hinge on the veracity of a given claim. It hinges on the resonance of a claim, and the ways this resonance aligns with participants' individual and collective standpoint. From there, one can ask why this alignment matters, and how best to respond given the context, community, and stakes. The point of a folkloric framing isn't to minimize truth, in other words. It's to extract more meaningful kinds of truth.

The most basic entry point into these deeper truths is the fact that folklore is, to quote the American folklorist Alan Dundes, "always a reflection of the age in which it flourishes."[10] What gets reflected isn't restricted just to the behaviors themselves, but rather is all the hybrid, overlapping forces—institutional and populist, corporate and grassroots, and emergent and established—that constitute the jumble of affect, tradition, and communication we refer to collectively as culture. To talk about folkloric expression of any kind, objectively true or objectively false, is to talk about this broader cultural context, encouraging a much more nuanced approach to unfolding narratives.

In the case of #Pizzagate, satanic sex ring claims against Hillary Clinton (and her campaign chair, John Podesta, her alleged coconspirator) spread, first and most basically, because they resonated. To reiterate, this resonance could have been born of trutherism or trollishness or anything in between. In any case, for any reason, these ideas connected with participants, prompting them to share, comment on, and generally play with the story. One recurring point of this engagement—again, whether framed winkingly or earnestly—was the presumption of Clinton's corruption, evidenced by the "Lock her up!" meme, stemming from Clinton's use of a private server to send State Department e-mails, that echoed throughout the election cycle. The sexist undercurrent of this meme cannot be overstated; as a number of journalists and cultural critics have highlighted, reaction to Clinton's candidacy was suffused with misogyny, making the chant "Lock her up" an implicit referendum not just on Clinton, not just on her gender, but on female empowerment more broadly.[11]

For truthers and trolls alike, #Pizzagate thus provided a perfect memetic vessel for the idea that Clinton wasn't just up to no good, she was up to the worst kinds of crimes imaginable, a feminist Satan unto herself. The meme of Clinton *as* ultimate evil *doing* ultimate evil, and getting away with it to boot, also tapped into much older memes about the (presumed) threat of Satanism and satanic ritual, which underscored a deluge of conspiracy theorizing in the 1980s and 1990s across media, now broadly referred to as the satanic panic.[12] Although a relatively recent phenomenon, the satanic panic was itself drawing from centuries of occultist conspiracies, as Kembrew McLeod adeptly chronicles.[13] Resonant memes layered over resonant memes layered over resonant memes, in this case with Satan all the way down.

The spread of the #Pizzagate conspiracy theory didn't just hinge on the resonance of mutually reinforcing memes, however. It also spread thanks to a broad range of institutional gatekeepers, including the journalists who covered the story, the social media platforms that hosted links to the story, the algorithms used by these platforms that influence what on-site content is seen by whom, and the search engines that allowed people to easily find information about the story. Average citizens—beyond those actively bolstering the conspiracy—were also part of this jumble, as their collective engagement, outcry, and commentary on social media looped back into the overall cycle of amplification, spurring further coverage and further fodder for those actively peddling the narrative.

Etic accounts of #Pizzagate miss these deeper strata of cultural connectedness, getting stuck, instead, at the moment untruth is declared. But there is so much more to say and understand than the fact that #Pizzagate—that anything—is false. In some ways, that's just the beginning of the conversation. Another caveat: this does not mean that one must *sympathize* with whatever resulting explanation, or maintain complicity in the face of violence, ignorance, and bigotry. It's not OK, for example, that the owners of Comet Ping Pong had their lives upended because there is a nuanced folkloric explanation for why the story resonated. It's not OK that Hillary Clinton's campaign was torpedoed, at least in part, because people simply couldn't stomach the idea of a female president.

That said, without considering how a particular belief coheres within a particular paradigm, censorious fact-checking risks being heard only by already sympathetic ears, thus becoming its own kind of fake news to those who disagree. Lewandowsky, Ecker, and colleagues' findings affirm this point, noting that misinformation is best corrected not merely by saying facts at someone, but by filling coherency gaps left in the wake of a retraction.[14] And that's precisely what a folkloric approach has the power to do: rather than approaching narratives as true/false binaries, it allows observers to peer beyond the memes and identify—and, when necessary, to exactingly challenge—deeper cultural logics. It lets a different story be told, in other words, one that will help maintain our collective grip on what's really real, and why that really matters.

Notes

1. Kali Holloway, "14 Fake News Stories Created or Publicized by Donald Trump," AlterNet, January 17, 2017, http://www.alternet.org/media/14-fake-news-stories-crea ted-or-publicized-donald-trump.

2. Will Oremus, "Trump Calls CNN 'Fake News' for Refusing to Run Ad Calling CNN 'Fake News,'" *Slate*, May 2, 2017, https://slate.com/news-and-politics/2017/05 /trump-calls-cnn-fake-news-for-refusing-to-run-ad-calling-cnn-fake-news.html.

3. Louis Nelson, "Trump: Everyone Knows Russia Allegations Are 'Fake News,'" *Politico*, March 20, 2017, http://www.politico.com/story/2017/03/trump-tweets-russia-ties -236243.

4. Craig Silverman, "This Analysis Shows How Viral Fake Election News Stories Out-performed Real News on Facebook," BuzzFeed News, November 16, 2016, https:// www.buzzfeed.com/craigsilverman/viral-fake-election-news-outperformed-real -news-on-facebook.

5. Adam Goldman, "The Comet Ping Pong Gunman Answers Our Reporter's Ques-tions," *New York Times*, December 7, 2016, https://www.nytimes.com/2016/12/07 /us/edgar-welch-comet-pizza-fake-news.html.

6. Jeremy W. Peters, "Wielding Claims of 'Fake News,' Conservatives Take Aim at Mainstream Media," *New York Times*, December 25, 2016, https://www.nytimes.com /2016/12/25/us/politics/fake-news-claims-conservatives-mainstream-media-.html.

7. Ryan M. Milner and Whitney Phillips, "Dark Magic: The Memes That Made Donald Trump's Victory," US Election Analysis 2016 (Centre for the Study of Jour-nalism, Culture, and Community, Bournemouth University), November 15, 2016, http://www.electionanalysis2016.us/us-election-analysis-2016/section-6-internet /dark-magic-the-memes-that-made-donald-trumps-victory/.

8. Sandra Harding, "Rethinking Standpoint Epistemology: What Is 'Strong Objectiv-ity'?," in *Feminist Epistemologies*, ed. Linda Alcoff and Elizabeth Potter (New York: Routledge, 1993), 49-82.

9. Stephan Lewandowsky, Ullrich K. H. Ecker, Colleen M. Seifert, Norbert Schwarz, and John Cook, "Misinformation and Its Correction: Continued Influence and Suc-cessful Debiasing," *Psychological Science in the Public Interest* 13, no. 3 (2012): 106–131.

10. Alan Dundes, *Cracking Jokes: Studies of Sick Humor Cycles and Stereotypes* (Berke-ley, CA: Ten Speed Press, 1987), 12.

11. Peter Beinart, "Fear of a Female President," *The Atlantic*, October 2016, https://www.theatlantic.com/magazine/archive/2016/10/fear-of-a-female-president/497564/; Emma Gray, "Can We Finally Admit It Was Always about Sexism, Never Emails?," *Huffington Post*, March 7, 2017, http://www.huffingtonpost.com/entry/hillary-clinton-mike-pence-emails_us_58bde0cce4b033be1467d150.

12. Richard Beck, "A Moral Panic for the Age of Trump," *Slate*, December 6, 2016, http://www.slate.com/articles/news_and_politics/politics/2016/12/the_comet_ping_pong_pizzagate_scandal_is_a_child_sex_ring_myth_for_the_age.html.

13. Kembrew McLeod, *Pranksters: Making Mischief in the Modern World* (New York: New York University Press, 2014).

14. Lewandowsky et al., "Misinformation and Its Correction," 116.

II Journalism: Part Introduction

Understanding news is particularly important for understanding fake news. In fact, the first two chapters in this part consider how news organizations may have created an information environment conducive to the spread of fake news through the use of clickbait, breaking news errors, and native advertising. These kinds of practices, while perhaps necessary in a period of diminishing advertising revenue, may exacerbate their delegitimization with some publics. The second two chapters in this part look at how our trust in news is *purposefully* destabilized by different groups, specifically the National Rifle Association (NRA) and antiabortion activists posing as an alternative news source. Both these internal and external factors destabilizing journalism ultimately enable various kinds of misinformation to instead fill our informational needs.

In the first chapter of this part, "Journalism and the New Information Ecosystem: Responsibilities and Challenges," Claire Wardle, who is a cofounder and the director of First Draft News, defines and maps different types of problematic content circulating online. This necessary endeavor looks at how the phrase *fake news* is used to describe entirely fabricated content masquerading as news to turn a profit while it is simultaneously weaponized to call out journalists for political or ideological reasons. Furthermore, Wardle argues that the term fails to capture the complexity of our polluted information ecosystem, including how news organizations use clickbait headlines or circulate rumors during breaking news events. In addition to identifying seven different types of problematic online information, Wardle asks: What are the responsibilities of journalists to help audiences navigate this misleading or false information? Additionally, how can journalists debunk misleading or false information without amplifying it?

The second chapter in this part, "Native Advertising as Counterfeit News," is by communication scholars Theodore L. Glasser, Sheng Zou, and Anita Varma. They argue that conceptions of fake news need to make room for another pernicious form of counterfeit journalism: native advertising. Native advertising is a web-based form of "stealth marketing" that succeeds as it deceives by blending undetected into online news content. Native advertising, at least when it is successful, is understood by readers to be journalism instead of advertising, much like fake news may be confused with actual news. According to Glasser, Zou, and Varma, this lack of clarity about where news ends and advertising begins sows confusion about the distinctions between journalism and commercialism and breeds distrust among news consumers.

Dawn R. Gilpin, who researches the interplay between media, organizations, and public policy, contributes the third chapter in this part, "The Second Amendment vs. the First: The NRA's Constitutional Bias Perspective on Fake News." Gilpin explores the NRA's shift in focus from improving members' shooting skills and firearm safety to becoming both the largest political lobby in the United States and a social movement. As part of its recruitment and retention strategy, the NRA has created a vast media empire that takes full advantage of social media to foster member identification, with dozens of accounts ranging from Facebook to Twitter, Instagram to Pinterest, and numerous YouTube channels. These accounts are directed at different publics, but most share a common narrative cultivated through propagandistic curation of news, opinions, images, and fake news. Gilpin argues that the NRA uses the term *fake news* as a way to compete with mainstream news organizations and discredit their reporting generally and their reporting about guns specifically.

The final chapter of this part is from information studies scholar Colin Doty, "Media Credibility before 'Fake News': Interpreting an Antiabortion Activist Undercover Video." The heavily edited video central to Doty's case study was produced by the Center for Medical Progress, a front organization for antiabortion activists, which covertly recorded conversations with officials at Planned Parenthood discussing the donation of postabortion tissue for use in research. By analyzing the public debate over the first in a series of videos, represented through online comments on news articles from ideologically diverse websites, Doty argues that we can observe the antecedents of fake news. Doty also shows how news commenters debated the credibility of the video and articles about the video, while leveling accusations of bias, deception, and manipulation in ways that challenge the credibility and legitimacy of mainstream news organizations.

Suggested Reading

Pablo Boczkowski and Zizi Papacharissi, eds., *Trump and the Media* (Cambridge, MA: MIT Press, 2018).

Whitney Phillips, "The Oxygen of Amplification: Better Practices for Reporting on Extremists, Antagonists, and Manipulators Online," Data and Society, May 22, 2018, https://datasociety.net/output/oxygen-of-amplification/.

Silvio Waisbord, "Truth Is What Happens to News: On Journalism, Fake News, and Post-Truth," *Journalism* 19, no. 13 (2018): 1866–1878.

5 Journalism and the New Information Ecosystem: Responsibilities and Challenges

Claire Wardle

The term *fake news* has become a mechanism for undermining individual journalists and the professional media as a whole. As a result, the term is now almost entirely meaningless: when audiences are asked about the term, they believe it describes poor reporting by the "mainstream media."[1] The term is also grossly inadequate at capturing the variety of information pollution choking public discourse. Misleading content can take many forms: satire; clickbait; inaccurate captions, visuals, or statistics; genuine content shared out of context; manipulated quotes and imagery; and outright fabricated stories. Almost none of this detail is captured by the term *fake news*. For these two reasons, I argue that the term *fake news* should be avoided where possible.

Much of the discourse about information pollution conflates two notions: misinformation and disinformation. In our report *Information Disorder*, Hossein Derakhshan and I argue that it's important to distinguish true and false messages, as well as messages that are and are not created, produced, or distributed with intent.[2] We defined *misinformation* as false information shared by someone who believes it to be true. *Disinformation*, by contrast, is false information shared with knowledge of its falsity and thus intention to deceive or otherwise do harm. It is a deliberate, intentional lie. We also defined a third category, *malinformation*, which is information based in reality that is shared to do harm to a person, organization, or country. This term can refer to instances where private information is made public (e.g., revenge porn) or genuine imagery is reshared in the wrong context. Finally, we chose *information disorder* as an umbrella term encompassing all forms of disinformation, misinformation, and malinformation.

TYPES OF INFORMATION DISORDER

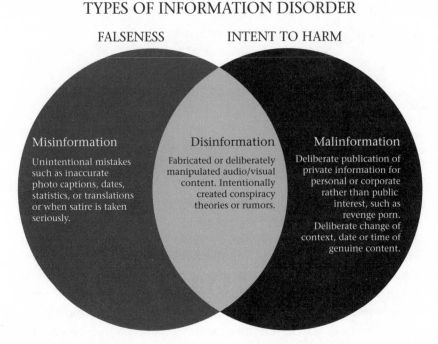

Figure 5.1
Three types of information disorder.

As I noted above, there are many aspects to this issue, and many of the debates are not grasping its complexity. If we want to think about remedies to the various kinds of information disorder polluting our social media streams, we need to start thinking about the problem with more care. We also need to give more thought to the people who are creating this content. What is motivating them? What types of content are they producing, and how are they being received by audiences? And when audiences reshare their posts, what's motivating *them*? In the first place, however, we still don't have enough empirical evidence about the scale of the different varieties of information disorder and the impact it has on audiences.

This chapter examines seven different categories of information disorder, underlining the complexity of this ecosystem. They are used as a foundation for discussing the responsibilities of journalists in helping audiences navigate information that is circulating online, in this new information environment. If journalists debunk rumors or misleading content too early, they can give unnecessary oxygen to something that may have died out on its own accord. If a rumor is left unchecked, it can take hold and can be very hard to effectively debunk. What are the new professional guidelines for reporting on disinformation?

The Seven Categories of Information Disorder

1. Satire and Parody
Including satire in a typology about information disorder is uncomfortable. Satire and parody should be considered forms of art. However, in a world where people increasingly receive information via their social media feeds and all types of information appear identical, some fail to realize that content is satirical.

Did Planned Parenthood Defend Bill Cosby?

Reports that the nonprofit organization defended the comedian after his felony sexual assault conviction stemmed from a Christian-themed satire site.

Figure 5.2
A story by the debunking organization Snopes, about a story in the Babylon Bee, a Christian satirical site.

Figure 5.3
A screenshot from the Political Insider using a classic clickbait headline.

2. False Connection

When headlines, visuals, or captions don't support the content, we call this an example of false connection. Unfortunately, the most common example of this type of content is clickbait headlines. Competing for eyeballs, editors increasingly have to write headlines to attract clicks, and may not remain faithful to the content of the article.

3. Misleading Content

This type of content is the use of information in a misleading manner to frame an issue or individual in a particular way, such as by cherry-picking images, quotes, or statistics.

4. False Context

Information doesn't have to be wrong to be misleading. This is one of the reasons why the term *fake news* is so unhelpful. For example, during breaking news situations, we often see old imagery from similar, past events recirculate.

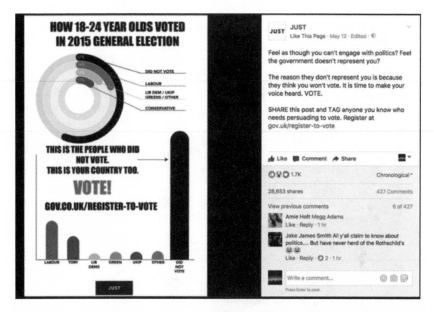

Figure 5.4
An infographic that circulated widely during the U.K. general election in May 2018. The diagram is misleading, as the black "did not vote" bar does not use the same scale as the rest of the graph.

5. Impostor Content

One increasingly common issue is when journalists have their bylines used alongside articles they did not write or organizations' logos are attached to videos or images they did not create. For example, in the run-up to the Kenyan election in August 2017, BBC Africa found a video it had not created that was using a BBC logo and tagline. It was circulating on WhatsApp. In response, BBC Africa made a video warning people not to be fooled by the impostor report and shared it on social media.

6. Manipulated Content

Manipulated content is genuine content that is manipulated to deceive. In the example below, two genuine images have been stitched together. The first is a photograph of people waiting in line to vote. It was captured in March 2016 in Arizona, during the primary election. The second photograph is a stock image of an arrest by a U.S. Immigration and Customs Enforcement officer; one can it find online by simply searching "ICE arrest." This

Na-Son Nguyen   ⚙ +⚑ Follow
@nasonnguyen

This is my photo about two Vietnamese
Hmong ethnic children taken in 2007 in Ha
Giang province, it's not about Nepal

RETWEETS   FAVORITES
3,097   1,692

Figure 5.5
This tweet was put out after a Twitter account, @HistoricalPics, shared the photo and
claimed that it was taken in Nepal shortly after the earthquake.

Figure 5.6
A video put out by BBC Africa on its Twitter account to explain that a fake video was circulating that purported to be a broadcast from BBC Africa.

composite image was shared in the weeks leading up to the November 2016 presidential election.

7. Fabricated Content

This type of content can be text-based, such as the article suggesting that the Pope had endorsed Donald Trump, published by a completely fabricated "news" site. It can also be visual, as in the case of a graphic that incorrectly suggested that people could vote for Hillary Clinton via short message service, or SMS. These graphics targeted minority communities on social networks in the lead-up to the U.S. presidential election.

Figure 5.7
A photo that circulated in the lead-up to the 2016 U.S. presidential election. The photo is made up of two images stitched together.

Figure 5.8
An image that circulated on Twitter and Facebook in the lead-up to the 2016 U.S. presidential election.

In our report, Derakhshan and I also argue that, in addition to understanding these different categories of information disorder, we must separately examine the "elements" of information disorder: the agent, messages, and interpreters. In the matrix below, we pose questions that need to be answered for each element. As we explain, the "agent" who *creates* a fabricated message might be different from the agent who *produces* that message—who might still be different from the "agent" who *distributes* the message. Similarly, we need a thorough understanding of who these agents are and what motivates them. We must also understand the different types of messages being distributed by agents, so that we can estimate the scale of—and address—each. (The debate to date has been overwhelmingly focused on fabricated text news sites, although visual content is just as widespread and much harder to identify and debunk.)

Finally, we also emphasize the need to consider the three different "phases" of information disorder: creation, production, and distribution. In particular, it's important to consider the phases of information disorder alongside the elements, because the agent that creates the content is often fundamentally different from the agent who produces it.

For example, the motivations of the mastermind who "creates" a state-sponsored disinformation campaign are very different from those of the low-paid "trolls" tasked with turning the campaign's themes into specific

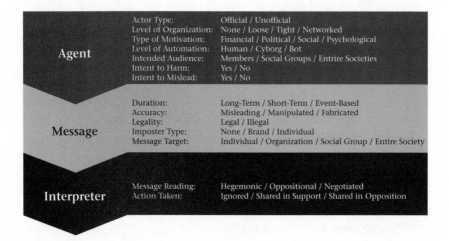

Figure 5.9
The three elements of information disorder.

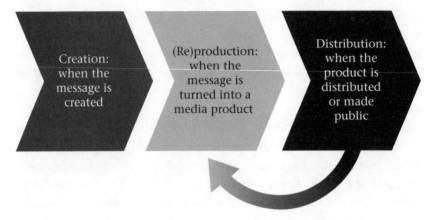

Figure 5.10
The three phases of information disorder.

posts. And once a message has been distributed, it can be reproduced and redistributed endlessly—by many different agents, all with different motivations. Only by dissecting information disorder in this manner can we begin to understand its many nuances.

Discussion

The bedrock of professional journalism is accurate reporting. As such, journalists have not previously had to think about ways to responsibly report what wasn't true. When rumors or hoaxes passed across their desks, the newsroom was warned to be on its guard, but rarely would any reporting take place. As gatekeepers to the information that people consumed, there was no responsibility to discuss false information with audiences. The arrival of the widespread adoption of social media late in the first decade of the twenty-first century changed conversations inside the newsroom.

The Iranian revolution in June 2009 is often cited as the news event that convinced journalists of the value of Twitter. I would argue that the Arab Spring was the moment when questions of how to report false information became much more widespread. Andy Carvin, who was working at NPR at the time, developed a following on Twitter by sharing information and asking his community to help him verify imagery.[3]

At the time, I was working with BBC News, designing a training course to help journalists find and verify sources and "content" on the social web. Carvin's tweets were being discussed at length among those interested in this new form of news gathering. Should a public broadcaster share information that hadn't been 100 percent verified? Would that confuse the audience? A concern shared by many journalists was that if the BBC began "debunking" rumors and false information, would that mean they would have to do that for all information that was false? If the audience got used to the service, would the absence of a "false" stamp suggest that it was automatically true. There was a great deal of heated debate, and the decision was taken that the BBC should not report—on either official channels or social media accounts—any information unless it had been fully verified. And while the newsroom's user-generated hub played a crucial role in helping the organization discern what was true and false, it was not a public debunking service.

If the Arab Spring was the story that thrust these questions into journalists' collective consciousness, Hurricane Sandy, the storm that hit the United States' eastern coast in October 2012, was the story where newsrooms began to actively help audiences differentiate fact from fiction. Alexis Madrigal in *The Atlantic* published a stream of images with yellow "true" or "false" stickers, and journalists worked overtime on Twitter to verify tweets, such as those of the flooded New York Stock Exchange from @ComfortablySmug, manipulated images of the Statue of Liberty shrouded in storm clouds, or old, recirculated imagery from Arlington Cemetery.[4]

The Boston Marathon bombing in 2013 provided another turning point. Active, amateur sleuths on Reddit worked to identify the two young men whose images had been shared by the Boston Police Department. Incorrect names were shared widely, and the dangers of crowdsourcing from social media became clear.[5] When CNN made a couple of serious on-air errors, it renewed concern about the role of mainstream media in helping audiences parse their increasingly chaotic information streams, particularly during breaking news events.[6]

These conversations seem quaint in the context of the current reality of the information ecosystem. Early discussions about whether professional journalists should play a role in helping audiences navigate hoaxes online took place when the only real concern was mistakes happening in the heat of a breaking news situation—old photos and false casualty figures. We hadn't yet recognized the potential of sophisticated, social media–focused campaigns to manipulate.

We now have agents of *dis*information—people deliberately creating and disseminating false information to cause harm and targeting technology companies' trending topics or search algorithms.[7] These techniques are designed to deceive, and their ultimate goal is to get journalists to publish their work—even if it's just to report on the campaign, and not its claim. For agents of disinformation, this coverage is as valuable, because they see it as amplifying their message.

As Alice Marwick and Rebecca Lewis noted in their 2017 report *Media Manipulation and Disinformation Online*, "For manipulators, it doesn't matter if the media is reporting on a story in order to debunk or dismiss it; the important thing is getting it covered in the first place."[8] BuzzFeed's Ryan Broderick confirmed these concerns when, on the eve of the French presidential vote, he tweeted that 4channers were celebrating sober news stories about #MacronLeaks as a "form of engagement."[9]

In actuality, we know little about how reporting on disinformation campaigns and tactics influences audiences. Experiments suggest that conspiracy-like stories can inspire feelings of powerlessness and lead people to report lower likelihoods to engage politically.[10] With trust in institutions in decline, reporting that highlights these campaigns of manufactured amplification could run the risk of further weakening trust in institutions. Again, we need further research into these issues.

Figure 5.11
A tweet by Ryan Broderick highlighting how "debunks are a form of engagement."

Scott Shane, in an article in the *New York Times*, points out the new challenges posed when foreign governments are involved in leaking information.[11] He states:

> The old rules say that if news organizations obtain material they deem both authentic and newsworthy, they should run it. But those conventions may set reporters up for spy agencies to manipulate what and when they publish, with an added danger: An archive of genuine material may be seeded with slick forgeries.

He is right to draw attention to the need for additional protocols for reporting on this form of information. However, the same challenges exist for reporting on any form of disinformation. When getting a falsehood debunked is the ultimate goal of the person pushing the false information, how should journalists respond? Choosing not to report on something makes many journalists feel uncomfortable, as it challenges their professional ethics. Journalists are taught from their first day at journalism school or in the newsroom that transparency is the central tenet of the profession. But this belief is now being used as a powerful weapon against the news industry itself. What does responsible coverage look like here?

As danah boyd argues, newsrooms know how to report on the powerful. Attempts by the Pentagon to suppress reporting results in long meetings, including with all senior editors, to assess the potential fallout in terms of national security. Similarly, when presented with public relations stunts by corporations, newsrooms know how to act responsibly. In this new information environment, when reporting on niche communities and their conspiracy theories can provide much-needed oxygen and legitimacy, where are the ethics policies that deal with this type of reporting?

At First Draft, when we work on debunking projects, we regularly talk about the journalists' need to understand the tipping point—the point at which debunking a rumor becomes necessary and advantageous.[12] If you debunk a rumor too early, you provide unnecessary oxygen and risk playing a role in spreading it further. If you wait too long to debunk, the rumor becomes extremely difficult to dislodge.

Identifying this tipping point is a complex task, partly because there is no one tipping point. In different countries, where popular platforms and population sizes vary, news industries have to work collaboratively to discuss when and how to publish. News industries are vulnerable exactly because of their competitive nature. If one news organization reports, it puts pressure on others to do the same—a particularly dangerous fact, as not all newsrooms undertake their own verification checks, seeing another newsroom's reporting as enough of an insurance policy. This is another reason why disinformation agents are so keen to use the news industry as a source of amplification. If you get one, you can get them all.

Another challenge we face is the limited amount of academic literature on effective debunks. John Cook and Stephan Lewandowsky's *The Debunking Handbook* underlines the need for falsehoods to be dealt with thoughtfully. Repeating falsehoods in headlines, for example, can improve someone's memory of the false information.[13] As little as we know about how to write effective text-based debunks, we know far less about how to effectively debunk false or fabricated imagery. A professional norm of stamping false imagery with a red "false" or "fake" label on an image has developed, but we do not know the impact this has on the way people process the image.

The news industry is wholly unprepared for the contemporary information ecosystem. Journalists and platforms are being targeted. We need new ethics guidelines and new training courses. We also need more research to understand the scale and complexity of the challenges before us, as well as the best remedies for them. Silencing coverage is not the answer, but we need to understand the most effective ways of reframing the narrative to minimize unintended consequences.

Notes

1. Rasmus Kleis Nielsen and Lucas Graves, *"News You Don't Believe": Audience Perspectives on Fake News* (Oxford, UK: Reuters Institute for the Study of Journalism, 2017), https://reutersinstitute.politics.ox.ac.uk/sites/default/files/2017-10/Nielsen%26Graves_factsheet_1710v3_FINAL_download.pdf.

2. Claire Wardle and Hossein Derakhshan, *Information Disorder: Toward an Interdisciplinary Framework for Research and Policy Making* (Strasbourg: Council of Europe, 2017), https://firstdraftnews.org/wp-content/uploads/2017/11/PREMS-162317-GBR -2018-Report-de%CC%81sinformation-1.pdf?x11466.

3. Andy Carvin, *Distant Witness: Social Media, the Arab Spring, and a Journalism Revolution* (New York: CUNY Journalism Press, 2013).

4. Alexis Madrigal, "Sorting the Real Sandy Photos from the Fakes," *The Atlantic*, October 29, 2012, https://www.theatlantic.com/technology/archive/2012/10 /sorting-the-real-sandy-photos-from-the-fakes/264243; Jack Stuef, "The Man behind @ComfortablySmug, Hurricane Sandy's Worst Twitter Villain," BuzzFeed, October

30, 2012, https://www.buzzfeed.com/jackstuef/the-man-behind-comfortablysmug -hurricane-sandys; Meredith Bennett-Smith, "Fake Hurricane Sandy Photos Spread on Internet as Storm Barrels toward Northeast," *Huffington Post*, October 30, 2012, https://www.huffingtonpost.com/2012/10/29/fake-hurricane-sandy-photos -internet-northeast_n_2041283.html; Sam Laird, "Incredible Viral Soldier Pic Debunked by Military," Mashable, October 29, 2012, https://mashable.com/2012 /10/29/viral-soldier-pic-debunked/.

5. Chris Wade, "The Reddit Reckoning," *Slate*, April 15, 2014, http://www.slate.com /articles/technology/technology/2014/04/reddit_and_the_boston_marathon_bomb ings_how_the_site_reckoned_with_its_own.html.

6. David Carr, "The Pressure to Be the TV News Leader Tarnishes a Big Brand," *New York Times*, April 21, 2013, https://www.nytimes.com/2013/04/22/business/media /in-boston-cnn-stumbles-in-rush-to-break-news.html.

7. Melanie Ehrenkranz, "Google's Top Stories Promoted Misinformation about the Las Vegas Shooting from 4chan," Gizmodo, October 10, 2017, https://gizmodo.com /googles-top-stories-promoted-misinformation-about-the-l-1819053288.

8. Alice Marwick and Rebecca Lewis, *Media Manipulation and Disinformation Online* (New York: Data and Society Research Institute, 2017), 39, https://datasociety.net /pubs/oh/DataAndSociety_MediaManipulationAndDisinformationOnline.pdf.

9. Ryan Broderick (@broderick), Twitter thread about the #MacronLeaks response on 4chan, May 5, 2017, https://twitter.com/broderick/status/860423715842121728 ?lang=en.

10. Daniel Jolley and Karen M. Douglas, "The Social Consequences of Conspiracism: Exposure to Conspiracy Theories Decreases Intentions to Engage in Politics and to Reduce One's Carbon Footprint," *British Journal of Psychology* 105, no. 1 (2014): 35–56, https://doi.org/10.1111/bjop.12018.

11. Scott Shane, "When Spies Hack Journalism," *New York Times*, May 12, 2018, https://www.nytimes.com/2018/05/12/sunday-review/when-spies-hack-journalism .html.

12. Claire Wardle, "10 Questions to Ask before Covering Misinformation," First Draft, September 29, 2017, https://firstdraftnews.org/10-questions-newsrooms/

13. John Cook and Stephan Lewandowsky, *The Debunking Handbook* (St. Lucia, Australia: University of Queensland, 2011).

6 Native Advertising as Counterfeit News

Theodore L. Glasser, Sheng Zou, and Anita Varma

Native advertising and fake news are two sides of the same coin. Both involve phony journalism and both involve the production of counterfeit news. Like fake news, native advertising succeeds as it deceives; both masquerade as content judged by journalists to be acceptable and appropriate. A form of covert marketing as pernicious as the fabricated facts of fake news, native advertising tries to fool the public not by pretending to be true, but by pretending to be authentic.[1]

Unlike fake news, however, which finds no sanctuary among reputable journalists, native advertising enjoys a quiet acquiescence in many newsrooms. Indeed, some of the oldest and most prestigious news organizations in the United States and elsewhere—the *New York Times*, the *Washington Post*, and the *Guardian*, among many others—not only accommodate native advertising, but produce it as well. For example, the *New York Times'* T Brand Studio, the newspaper's "brand marketing unit" with a "global network" of offices in New York, London, Paris, and Hong Kong, uses the newspaper's "proven recipe for storytelling" to create and distribute "stories that influence the influential."[2] This, of course, raises the question: What does the newsroom create and distribute if not stories that influence the influential? Tellingly, the pitch to advertisers bears a striking resemblance to a pitch to the Pulitzer board: here's a story that makes a difference.

That both types of content—material produced by its newsroom and material produced by its marketing unit—meet the *Times'* exacting standards of quality, particularly its standards of style, and thus deserve the *Times'* imprimatur obscures the fact that marketing material eludes the judgment of journalists, judgments that account for not only the quality of content but its *value* as well. Native advertising invites us to forget that advertising advances the commercial interests of the advertiser and only coincidentally the interests of the public.

Understood as content of purposely unclear provenance, native advertising benefits from a deliberate lack of clarity about where journalism ends and commercialism begins; it exploits the problematic distinction between "journalism" and what the *New York Times* calls "a journalistic approach" to crafting stories; it flourishes amid the "blurred content boundaries" that bedevil online journalism. In short, native advertising stakes a place for itself as vanishing lines and crumbling walls leave journalists without the markers that for nearly two centuries defined, metaphorically, the ethics and ethos of Western journalism.[3]

Advocates of native advertising position themselves as entrepreneurs who view native advertising as an innovative—and lucrative—alternative to banner ads, pop-up ads, autoplay videos, and other obtrusive, disruptive, and altogether annoying (and not very profitable) forms of web-based marketing. They regard the lines and walls that separate advertising from other content as arbitrary, antiquated, and antithetical to native advertising's basic premise: sites with integrated content of high quality trump sites with segregated content of mixed quality. Critics, however, contend that whatever the quality of its content, native advertising depends on deception, an egregious breach of ethics. They point out, as journalists do in their coverage of other distressed industries, that the vagaries of the marketplace do not justify dishonesty; economics does not trump ethics. While proponents of native advertising believe that explicit and conspicuous disclosures, as required by the Federal Trade Commission (FTC), remedy any legal or ethical concerns, opponents believe that disclosures do not undo deceit; they merely acknowledge it. Mark Coddington usefully sums up native advertising's "core tension" as the "inherent conflict" between "blurring the boundary between news and advertising" and at the same time "creating more compelling advertising that's honestly labeled."[4]

The conflict reveals itself in what Coddington calls the "rhetoric of survival," illustrated by a News Corp executive who views critics of native advertising as scolds who "would rather hide behind ossified church and state walls with absolute positions than find flexible ways to protect both journalism and the business of journalism."[5] The rhetoric of survival preys on the fear that journalism cannot succeed unless it succeeds as a business; a well-worn fiction contradicted by the scores of new and successful news sites unaffected by the exigencies of market forces. It also invites journalists to embrace, in the name of success, the prospects for an unprecedented role for advertising: "Instead of editorial content being used to attract audiences who are then exposed to advertising, advertising itself begins to attract audiences."[6] Advertising would continue to subsidize news and other editorial content, as it has since the 1830s, but now, "wearing the uniform of journalism, mimicking the storytelling aesthetics of its host site," it would not be easily distinguishable from the content adjacent to it.[7] Put in starker terms, protecting both journalism and the business of journalism now comes with the expectation that journalists will accept the idea of a seamless news site that mingles their content with stylistically identical content produced by advertisers.

Notwithstanding its prehistory in the form of advertorials in newspapers and infomercials on radio and television, native advertising's near ubiquity,[8] particularly online, signals a new and different understanding of journalism's interest in advertising, namely, a willingness to work with advertisers as partners, not simply clients. We expand on this with a brief account of journalism's deliberate abuse of disclosures, which we take as evidence of a lack of commitment to reveal native advertising as advertising—and a missed opportunity for an important media literacy lesson: with rare exceptions, advertising has no public purpose analogous to journalism's public purpose. We conclude with an even briefer discussion of how we might quarantine native advertising in ways that wouldn't readily apply to other forms of counterfeit news.

Native Advertising and the Disclosure Debacle

News executives defend practices of native advertising on the grounds that disclosure mitigates deception, and the FTC condones native advertising as long as it is clearly labeled.[9] However, the FTC does not mandate that advertisers use the word *advertising* in those labels. From a marketing perspective, native advertising loses its value if it loses its *stealth* status through explicit disclosure,[10] which is why news outlets publishing native advertising prefer euphemistic terms such as *sponsored*, *promoted*, and *paid post*. Yet, as discussed below, this latitude in nomenclature for labels results not only in deceiving consumers, but also in breeding consumer distrust of news outlets.

The use of euphemistic terms to refer to native ads has become a common practice. A review of native advisements for sixty-three publishers reveals that the most commonly used terms are *sponsored, presented by, sponsor story,* and *sponsored story*.[11] The argument could be made that *sponsored* and *advertising* are synonymous, but there is little evidence to support such a defense. For example, in an eye-tracking survey in which advertisements with different labels appeared on a website, native ads labeled "advertisement" were viewed less often by participants (23 percent) compared to other labels, which respondents saw more frequently, such as "brought to you by" (24 percent), "promoted by" (26 percent), "sponsored by" (29 percent), and "presented by" (39 percent).[12] This is likely because people tend to avoid advertising, and these other labels are less likely to be understood as advertising. The integrative format of native advertising is less likely to trigger consumer awareness of the persuasive intent of native advertising.[13]

In fact, in an online experiment, only 17 percent of 443 participants correctly identified material labeled "sponsored content" as native advertising.[14] Even a disclosure label is insufficient for signaling to the audience the commercial nature of the advertising material.[15] In a separate experiment, 598 respondents were shown a simulated blog page with three articles, one of which was a native advertisement labeled as "sponsored report." Even with the disclosure label, 27 percent of the respondents thought a journalist or reporter wrote the native ad. Terms such as *sponsored* are too ambiguous to serve as disclosure, for they do not necessarily mean "advertising" but apply to other funding situations, as in the case of sponsors for public programming. Thus, it is evident that consumers are not thoroughly informed through existing disclosure practices.

Furthermore, when readers do recognize articles as native advertising, it leads to unfavorable perceptions of article quality and unfavorable attitudes toward sponsors.[16] And if the advertisement disguised as news comes from a trusted journalistic outlet, individual attitudes toward the news outlet become more negative overall.[17] This suggests that, far from viewing native advertising as an innocuous storytelling format, readers who recognize native advertising as such view it as grounds for being skeptical or distrustful of the news outlet's coverage.[18] Native advertising is thus a lose-lose-lose situation: ineffective disclosure deceives readers into believing that content is journalistic when it is not, effective disclosure obliterates native advertising's unique value proposition (unobtrusiveness) for brands, and reader awareness of native advertising destabilizes the perceived legitimacy and trustworthiness of news outlets.

Counterfeit News and the Future of Journalism

Native advertising and fake news take different paths to the same place: the land of counterfeit news. Fake news gets there by virtue of its lack of veracity. Native advertising gets there by virtue of its lack of authenticity. Their different paths, as well as their different pathologies, explain the vastly different responses to them. No one celebrates fake news as a worthwhile endeavor; with two possible exceptions—as satire and as a weapon used to confuse an enemy of the state—no one sees a legitimate public purpose for it. In contrast, native advertising, while controversial, garners considerable praise from owners and managers of news sites, who are understandably eager to accommodate a new revenue stream that might head off the trend toward fewer and smaller newsrooms, and from advertisers, who are understandably delighted with the prospect of taking an unassuming "journalistic approach" to getting their story out.

If we can't legally eliminate counterfeit news—at least not in the United States—we can regulate some of it. As a matter of U.S. law, more can be done to protect us from advertising that is deceptive than from news that is false. Commercial speech (like native advertising) receives less constitutional protection than noncommercial speech (like fake news), which makes room for the FTC and other administrative agencies to promulgate rules and regulations designed to protect the public from commercial content that pretends to be something else. To be sure, the FTC has the authority to demand, though not the resources to monitor, the use of what it calls "clear and conspicuous" disclosure, a requirement designed to quarantine advertising in ways that make clear that an ad is an ad.[19]

Arguably illegal and decidedly unethical, the disingenuous use of disclosures, where news sites make it a point to identify an advertisement as an advertisement without using the word *advertisement* underscores the intractable conflict between candor and deception, between journalism and the business of journalism. As a matter of ethics, news sites populated with native advertising owe the public more than disclosures of marginal efficacy. If we accept the proposition that deception, like lying, is presumptively wrong, then the burden is on the deceiver to justify the deception.[20]

And the justification must move beyond the rationalizations associated with the rhetoric of survival, where journalists and others are bullied into accepting an otherwise unacceptable arrangement on the grounds that their jobs, their profession, hang in the balance. In our deep dive into the literature on native advertising—books, articles, papers, magazines (popular and trade), websites—we found nothing close to what publishers of native advertising owe the public: a morally rigorous defense of publishing material that intentionally appears to be what they know it's not.

Notes

1. This chapter is based on an earlier article: Theodore L. Glasser, Anita Varma, and Sheng Zou, "Native Advertising and the Cultivation of Counterfeit News," *Journalism* 20, no. 1 (2019): 150–153.

2. "About Us," T Brand Studio, accessed June 17, 2019, http://www.tbrandstudio .com/about-us/.

3 "Marketing," The New York Times Company, accessed June 17, 2019, https://www .nytco.com/careers/marketing/; Matt Carlson, "When News Sites Go Native: Redefining the Advertising-Editorial Divide in Response to Native Advertising," *Journalism* 16, no. 7 (2015): 862.

4. Mark Coddington, "The Wall Becomes a Curtain: Revisiting Journalism's News-Business Boundary," in *Boundaries of Journalism: Professionalism, Practices and Participation*, ed. Matt Carlson and Seth C. Lewis (New York: Routledge, 2015), 76–77.

5. Ibid.

6. Carlson, "When News Sites Go Native," 861.

7. David Carr, "Storytelling Ads May Be Journalism's New Peril," *New York Times*, September 15, 2013, https://www.nytimes.com/2013/09/16/business/media/storytelling -ads-may-be-journalisms-new-peril.html.

8. Now a global phenomenon, native advertising has its own international trade association, Native Advertising Institute, based in Copenhagen.

9. Federal Trade Commission, *.com Disclosures: How to Make Effective Disclosures in Digital Advertising* (Washington, DC: Federal Trade Commission, 2013), https:// www.ftc.gov/sites/default/files/attachments/press-releases/ftc-staff-revises-online -advertising-disclosure-guidelines/130312dotcomdisclosures.pdf; Federal Trade Commission, "Native Advertising: A Guide for Businesses," December 2015, https://www .ftc.gov/tips-advice/business-center/guidance/native-advertising-guide-business.

10. Ellen Goodman, "Stealth Marketing and Editorial Integrity," *Texas Law Review* 85 (2006): 83–152.

11. Lucia Moses, "The Publishers That May Need to Change Their Native Ads under New FTC Rules," *Digiday*, December 24, 2015, https://digiday.com/media/publishers -may-need-change-native-ads-new-ftc-rules/.

12. Lucia Moses, "How Native Advertising Labeling Confuses People, in 5 Charts," *Digiday*, May 4, 2015, https://digiday.com/media/5-charts-show-problem-native-ad -disclosure/.

13. Sunny J. Kim and Jeffrey T. Hancock, "How Advertorials Deactivate Advertising Schema: MTurk-Based Experiments to Examine Persuasion Tactics and Outcomes in Health Advertisements," *Communication Research* 44, no. 7 (2016): 1019–1045; Miceal Dahlén, and Mats Edenius, "When Is Advertising Advertising? Comparing Responses to Non-traditional and Traditional Advertising Media," *Journal of Current Issues and Research in Advertising* 29, no. 1 (2007): 33–42, https://doi.org/10.1080 /10641734.2007.10505206.

14. Michelle A. Amazeen and Bartosz W. Wojdynski, "The Effects of Disclosure Format on Native Advertising Recognition and Audience Perceptions of Legacy and Online News Publishers," *Journalism*, February 7, 2018, https://doi.org/10.1177 /1464884918754829.

15. Chris J. Hoofnagle and Eduard Meleshinsky, "Native Advertising and Endorsement: Schema, Source-Based Misleadingness, and Omission of Material Facts," *Technology Science*, December 15, 2015, http://techscience.org/a/2015121503/.

16. Bartosz W. Wojdynski, "The Deceptiveness of Sponsored News Articles: How Readers Recognize and Perceive Native Advertising," *American Behavioral Scientist* 60, no. 12 (2016): 1475–1491.

17. Michelle A. Amazeen and Ashley R. Muddiman, "Saving Media or Trading on Trust? The Effect of Native Advertising on Audience Perceptions of Legacy and Online News Publishers," *Digital Journalism* 6, no. 2 (2018): 176–195, https://doi.org /10.1080/21670811.2017.1293488; Amazeen and Wojdynski, "Effects of Disclosure."

18. Goodman, "Stealth Marketing and Editorial Integrity."

19. "Full Disclosure," Federal Trade Commission, September 23, 2014, https: www .ftc.gov/news-events/blogs/business-blog/2014/09/full-disclosure.

20. Sissela Bok, *Lying: Moral Choice in Public and Private Life* (New York: Random House, 1978).

7 The Second Amendment vs. the First: The NRA's Constitutional Bias Perspective on Fake News

Dawn R. Gilpin

As this volume attests, the seemingly ubiquitous term *fake news* has been widely adopted to attack mainstream news organizations. Media scholars have scrambled to develop definitions and taxonomies to describe the range of practices that may be classified under its umbrella, from propaganda to hoaxes, from satire to fabricated stories.[1] This chapter takes a slightly different approach. In it I argue that, for at least some actors within the right-wing media context, fake news refers to not solely what a media organization or journalist *does*, but what they *are*. In other words, beyond referring to a set of practices, "fake news" is an ontological label. Understanding the framework of beliefs that guide this line of thinking can help shift the focus of scholarly attention from taxonomies of media output to a richer vein of theoretical development.

Through qualitative analysis of National Rifle Association (NRA) media artifacts gathered over the course of several months, I first identify a set of axioms that clarify how the NRA perceives the mainstream media, followed by practices stemming from those axioms. Like many right-wing media outlets, the NRA assumes a priori ideological bias against gun owners and conservatives and the inherent dishonesty of media organizations. In addition, it perceives journalists as selfishly favoring the First Amendment over the Second, which it frames as a disrespectful, à la carte approach to the Constitution. Together, these constitute the framework of beliefs that undergirds its cries of "fake news." This belief system also serves as the foundation upon which NRA media actors construct their own identity and situate themselves within the broader media landscape as more fairly upholding all rights and serving the Truth.

The Mediatization of the NRA

The NRA is the largest gun rights organization in the United States, claiming approximately 5 million members.[2] Founded in 1871, it for decades distributed publications for members and gun enthusiasts, such as the hobby and hunting magazine *American Rifleman* (launched in 1923) and the more politically focused *America's 1st Freedom* (first issued in 2000).

In 2004, the NRA announced its plan to formally establish its own news organization, with an online talk show, radio station, and televised programming. *The Quill* reported in 2004 that the organization intended to establish a major media conglomerate in an effort "to bring back the First Amendment."[3] Fox News noted that this goal arose from financial and political motivations, as the NRA aimed to "operate free of political spending limits" and take advantage of so-called soft money to fund its issue messaging and support of sympathetic candidates.[4] According to Executive Vice President Wayne LaPierre, the goal was to develop into a "'legitimate packager of news' like newspapers and TV networks."[5]

These programs were originally hosted on YouTube and publicized through various social media accounts and subsites. In 2016, NRATV was spun off into its own platform, and it currently offers programs via SiriusXM, Apple TV, Roku, and other distribution systems, as well as the NRATV .com website. The NRA also publishes online news through its lobbying arm, the Institute for Legislative Action (ILA), and electronic editions of its print magazines.

The NRA mediasphere represents a form of alternative media, established in opposition to legacy outlets and to serve constituencies who may in turn feel alienated from mainstream media.[6] One iteration of the NRATV.com website highlighted this antagonism with the tagline "At NRATV, We're Not Members of the Media. We're Members of the NRA. And Our Ultimate Weapon Is Truth."[7] It is not surprising, then, that NRA commentators and writers have embraced the mantra of "fake news" to discredit their adversaries and competitors. However, as Tony Harcup notes, the realities of alternative and mainstream media are more complex than a simple opposition might suggest.[8] It therefore seems warranted to examine in greater depth how the NRA views the mainstream media and how it characterizes itself as a media entity.

Analyzing the NRA and "Fake News"

To investigate these questions, I examined articles and video segments from all NRA media subsites posted to the NRA.org front page between June 2017 and March 2018. The front page changes most weekdays, with a rotating scroll of links to various NRATV segments and articles on subsites such as the ILA's. Since the organization curates this set of daily links, they would seem to represent its core values and identity.

My first step was to cull, from the 720 total media artifacts gathered during this period, those that specifically leveled criticisms at mainstream media. Rather than limiting myself to those containing the specific phrase "fake news," I included all articles and video segments that dedicated meaningful time or space to criticizing media for lying, misleading, or engaging in unsound journalistic practices. The result of this culling process was a set of one hundred media items: five articles from the site of the ILA, the NRA's lobbying arm; three from the online edition of *America's 1st Freedom*; and the remaining ninety-two from various NRATV programs.

In immersing myself in these texts, I adopted Karen Barad's methodology of diffraction.[9] Diffraction posits the inherent materiality of communication, ascribing to it the physical qualities of waveforms. Specifically, it refers to "the way waves combine when they overlap and the apparent bending and spreading of waves that occurs when waves encounter an obstruction."[10] Given that the NRA occupies multiple roles (media producer, special interest organization, leader of a social movement), its enunciations may be conceptualized as waves issued at multiple frequencies, which may diffract in different ways depending on object and context.

This approach makes it possible to tease out epistemological and ontological principles by examining the ways communicative processes and agents interact. One advantage of envisioning communication as a waveform, rather than, for instance, a series of binary oppositions, is that it permits us to notice continuities as well as contrasts. NRA media emerge from the same mediatized environment as the journalistic enterprises they decry and share many of the same formal characteristics, placing their works alongside other alternative media sources, such as online news or talk radio.

Fake News: Identity and Practice

It quickly emerged that the NRA approached "fake news" not merely as an output or practice, but as an a priori identity descriptor distinct from any specific action. For example, in a segment titled "The Fake News Fight," commentator Bill Whittle states, "'Fake news' is being applied to the mainstream media, and in particular it's being applied to CNN, and there's a perfectly good reason for that."[11] In "Dousing Fake News Wildfires," Grant Stinchfield draws a distinction between the noun and the adjective forms when he vows, "I promise you I will not let fake news and the fake news media get away with their nonsense any longer."[12] In another segment, Stinchfield drives home the point with multiple variations on the theme, including "the lying fake news media" and "the fake news socialist media."[13] These are just a few examples of how the NRA repeatedly labels the news media as "fake" without alleging specific instances of fabrication.

Axioms about Journalism and Mainstream Media

The NRA engages with mainstream media on three levels: as an interest group promoting gun ownership and Second Amendment advocacy; in its role as part of a right-wing social movement;[14] and as a competitor within the media attention economy. These three levels are not separate and distinct, but present numerous points of overlap and blurred boundaries. The diffractive analysis of NRA media critiques lodged against "fake news" and related topics similarly produced three overlapping axioms, ontological characterizations of the mainstream or "legacy" media. These act as catalysts for what the NRA derides as negligent or inept journalistic practices, especially insofar as they are seen to influence coverage of issues surrounding firearms and Second Amendment policy. Finally, they influence the relational self-perceptions and positioning of the NRA as a competing media organization. Collectively, these offer a nuanced portrait of how the NRA characterizes media in general, and what constitutes "fake news" according to this belief system.

Axiom 1: Mainstream media are ideologically biased   Nicole Hemmer notes that one consistent thread linking conservative media activists is the conviction that all institutions are inherently ideological.[15] According to the NRA, mainstream media are liberal-leftist, tools of the Democratic

Party. For instance, in the segment "Trump's Fake News Awards," spokesperson Dana Loesch claims a crisis of media credibility because "no one has faith in an institution that exists to prop up one particular ideology in the United States."[16] In another segment, conservative political analyst Gayle Trotter ascribes the problem to a dearth of conservatives working in the industry.[17] Overall, Stinchfield asserts, "that anyone would pretend that these media entities are unbiased is a joke. It's an absolute joke."[18]

NRA media focus on two general categories of bias: against guns and gun owners and, more broadly, against conservatives, Christians, and President Donald Trump and his supporters. Stinchfield harshly criticizes CNN, saying the cable network "has continued its trend of not only being devious and deceitful, but making up stories specifically in an effort to slam gun owners, slam the NRA, slam all of you, slam our president. They are the chief purveyors of fake news."[19] Loesch focuses instead on the *New York Times*, condemning the newspaper for unfairness: "You always blame the gun when publishing stories on the Chicago crime rate."[20] A guest explaining why he organized a protest march at CNN headquarters in Atlanta outlined his complaint in terms of prejudice: "They don't want to admit the problems that exist in other ethnicities, national origins and religions. They will be the first to run to the scene to report about Christians or gun owners or white people, and they will do nonstop wall-to-wall coverage."[21]

Axiom 2: Mainstream media are dishonest NRA commentators ascribe their lack of trust in mainstream news outlets not just to their assumed partiality, but also to active dishonesty on the part of journalists. LaPierre stated bluntly, "Your claim to the truth is as legitimate as a thief's."[22]

Media dishonesty is frequently described in violent terms. Commentator Dan Bongino, in announcing the imminent launch of his new show *We Stand*, warns, "Today, that very Truth upon which our nation was built, which holds our country together, is under threat. Tainted every time we turn on our televisions. Vandalized in the pages of newspapers."[23] News media, and ideological opponents of the NRA, are all charged with violent acts against Truth itself.

One specific form of dishonesty is hypocrisy, which takes place when people or organizations "implicitly or explicitly endorse principles that their behavior contradicts."[24] Accusations of media hypocrisy are plentiful, including a segment with that very title. During that segment, which focuses on reactions to Trump's reference to "shithole countries," Stinchfield complains, "The president is now being demonized for telling the truth. No one knows what that's like more than the NRA, an organization demonized for decades by the devious fake news media simply for what? Telling the truth.... We must push back and call out the hypocrisy of these so-called reporters."[25]

Axiom 3: The mainstream media disregard the Constitution   A final thread that emerges from the analysis is the belief that mainstream media organizations and journalists do not respect the United States Constitution, or do so only selectively. Trotter, as a guest on *Stinchfield*, argues, "People on the left want to take some of the black and white lettering of the Constitution and airbrush it out. At the same time, they're adding all these additional rights that are not actually in the text of the Constitution."[26] Host Bongino frequently refers to "big-R Rights," which he says are "rights granted by God and not the state."[27] These rights include the First and Second Amendments, both of which he claims are at risk. As a guest on *Stinchfield*, he goes into detail about the ways in which the media, in his view, show disrespect for these rights, claiming that the "fake news media" are "taking a machete to the First Amendment." "They've abused it" and "used their airwaves and newspapers not to hold power to account but to spread lies, leaks and deceit; to smear NRA members; to attack gun owners; to belittle all those they disagree with." Ultimately, he maintains, "the fake news media hates the NRA and its members."[28]

A provocative spot by commentator Colion Noir pretends to call for limitations on the press to prevent it from glorifying mass shooters and encouraging copycats, to highlight what he claims is the unmistakable absurdity of seeking to limit any constitutional amendment.[29] In a follow-up segment, Noir argues that the backlash to the spot highlights the failings of a self-serving media industry that cares only about the First Amendment, "because it directly correlates to them," but doesn't believe the Second Amendment warrants the same respect.[30]

It follows that these axioms are not separate and distinct: bias, dishonesty, and disregard for the Constitution overlap to produce what the NRA perceives as tendentious coverage of Second Amendment issues. The NRA does so primarily through three categories of practices, briefly outlined below.

"Fake News" Journalistic Practices

The first practice responsible for what the NRA calls out as "fake news" involves *biased gatekeeping*. The organization claims that mainstream media ignore data and cherry-pick facts to push an antigun narrative, avoiding positive news about guns or gun ownership. Writing for *America's 1st Freedom*, conservative pundit Stacy Washington claims that mainstream media underreport cases of women who successfully use firearms for self-defense: "They don't fit their 'guns are bad' narrative."[31]

The second practice, the NRA argues, is that liberal journalists are ignorant about guns and too lazy to learn the facts necessary for fair and accurate coverage. This results in *sloppy reporting*. Dan Gainor of the Media Research Center blames this failing on bias and ignorance, claiming, "The problem is so many journalists are not just anti-gun, but they've never touched, handled, shot a gun, carried a gun. The whole world of gun use and ownership is foreign to them, and so they get a lot of things wrong. A ton of things wrong."[32]

Finally, the third practice is that when these news sources do report about guns, they employ *distorted framing* to unfairly influence audiences. One article complains of misleading reporting on New York gun legislation, claiming that it fits into a long-standing pattern of coverage:

> In the same way that anti-gun advocates consistently seek to disguise restrictive gun control measures under the veneer of "common sense," "gun safety," or "gun law reform," they aim to influence public opinion towards "strengthening" gun laws by dismissing opposition to such laws by ordinary, informed Americans as the "mindless" nattering of a handful of extremists.[33]

LaPierre addresses the media accusingly, saying, "All you had to do was just get the facts right about our guns and our freedom, but you never even pretended to listen."[34]

Conclusion

In critiquing the mainstream media, NRA commentators both implicitly and explicitly traced the contours of the organization's own media presence, which might be described as the product of diffraction. The NRA, as a media entity, "bumps up against" traditional media organizations in ways that influence how it expresses its own identity.

Based on statements by its media commentators, the NRA conceives of "fake news" as both a practice and a state of being, a sort of preexisting condition that persists independent of any tangible action. As a practice, "fake news" exists along a continuum of commission to omission: it may be invented, inaccurate, misleading, unfavorable, or incomplete, or it may exist as negative space surrounding events the NRA deems newsworthy (such as positive stories about guns and gun owners). While the motivations ascribed to fake news production anywhere on the spectrum may be generalized as "bias," a more textured interpretation emerges from close analysis: mainstream media are seen as inherently ideological, dishonest, and without regard for the Constitution.

According to Scott Melzer, the NRA primarily uses fear and culture war tensions to drive its public messaging.[35] This perspective is in keeping with the organization's framing of fake news, which claims that mainstream "legacy" media exploit and abuse the public trust in order to push a liberal ideological agenda. According to this view, these organizations are failing to uphold their role in our democracy.

For the NRA, "fake news" thus describes both the product and the essence of mainstream news outlets. Ultimately, much "fake news" is seen as originating from favoritism among journalists toward the First Amendment and against (or, at best, indifferent to) the Second. According to the NRA's formulation, the Second and First Amendments are intertwined such that only by staunchly defending a maximalist interpretation of the former is it possible to protect the latter.

What mostly sets the NRA's accusations of "fake news" apart from other right-wing media sources is this claim of constitutional bias. By adopting this lens, NRA commentators can position themselves as the leading defenders of all rights and claim the moral high ground over their competitors. The NRA emerges as a champion not only of the Second Amendment, and the First, but also of the Truth itself, against mainstream media "purveyors of propaganda" working to undermine the United States Constitution and the interests of its citizens.[36]

Notes

1. See David M. J. Lazer, Matthew A. Baum, Yochai Benkler, Adam J. Berinsky, Kelly M. Greenhill, Filippo Menczer, Miriam J. Metzger, Brendan Nyhan, Gordon

Pennycook, David Rothschild, Michael Schudson, Steven A. Sloman, Cass R. Sunstein, Emily A. Thorson, Duncan J. Watts, and Jonathan L. Zittrain, "The Science of Fake News," Policy Forum, *Science* 359, no. 6380 (2018): 1094–1096.

2. "A Brief History of the NRA," NRA, accessed June 17, 2019, https://home.nra.org/about-the-nra/.

3. "NRA Moves into the Media Business," *The Quill* 92, no. 5 (2004): 7.

4. Associated Press, "NRA to Launch News Company," Fox News, April 16, 2004, http://www.foxnews.com/story/2004/04/16/nra-to-launch-news-company.html.

5. Ibid.

6. Tony Harcup, "'I'm Doing This to Change the World': Journalism in Alternative and Mainstream Media," *Journalism Studies* 6, no. 3 (2006): 361–374. https://doi.org/10.1080/14616700500132016.

7. NRATV, accessed February 22, 2018, http://graphics.nra.org/special_announcements/2018-02-nratv.html.

8. Harcup, "'I'm Doing This to Change the World.'"

9. Karen Barad, *Meeting the Universe Halfway: Quantum Physics and the Entanglement of Matter and Meaning* (Durham, NC: Duke University Press, 2007).

10. Ibid., 74.

11. *Bill Whittle's Hot Mic*, "The Fake News Fight," NRATV, July 20, 2017, https://www.nratv.com/series/bill-whittles-hot-mic/episode/bill-whittles-hot-mic-season-1-episode-23.

12. *Stinchfield*, "Dousing Fake News Wildfires," NRATV, January 8, 2018, https://www.nratv.com/series/stinchfield/video/stinchfield-gayle-trotter-putting-out-fake-news-wildfires/episode/stinchfield-season-2-episode-5.

13. *Stinchfield*, "Sledgehammer of Truth," NRATV, February 14, 2018, https://www.nratv.com/videos/stinchfield-dan-bongino-sledgehammer-of-truth.

14. Scott Melzer, *Gun Crusaders: The NRA's Culture War* (New York: New York University Press, 2009).

15. Nicole Hemmer, *Messengers of the Right: Conservative Media and the Transformation of American Politics* (Philadelphia: University of Pennsylvania Press, 2016).

16. *Stinchfield*, "Trump's Fake News Awards," NRATV, January 19, 2018, https://www.nratv.com/series/stinchfield/video/stinchfield-dana-loesch-president-trumps-fake-news-awards/episode/stinchfield-season-2-episode-13.

17. *Stinchfield*, "Dousing Fake News Wildfires."

18. *Stinchfield*, "Calling out Fake News," NRATV, October 27, 2017, https://www .nratv.com/series/stinchfield/video/stinchfield-dana-loesch-calling-out-fake-news -and-journalists/episode/stinchfield-season-1-episode-208.

19. Ibid.

20. *Commentators*, "Taking on the Times," NRATV, accessed August 4, 2017, https:// www.nratv.com/series/commentators/episode/commentators-season-7-episode-1 -taking-on-the-times.

21. Brian Crabtree, *Bill Whittle's Hot Mic*, "The Fake News Fight."

22. *Freedom's Safest Place*, "Why the Media Is Failing," NRATV, accessed September 7, 2017, https://www.nratv.com/series/freedoms-safest-place/episode/freedoms-safest -place-season-2-episode-1-why-the-media-is-failing.

23. "Bongino: New Show Starts Monday," NRATV, February 26, 2018, https://www .nratv.com/home/video/dan-bonginos-new-show-we-stand-comes-to-nratv-next -monday.

24. Mark Alicke, Ellen Gordon, and David Rose, "Hypocrisy: What Counts?," *Philo-sophical Psychology* 26, no. 5 (2013): 674.

25. *Stinchfield*, "Media Hypocrisy," NRATV, January 15, 2018, https://www.nratv .com/series/stinchfield/video/stinchfield-dana-loesch-medias-hypocrisy-cannot-be -ignored/episode/stinchfield-season-2-episode-10. On Trump's statement, see Josh Dawsey, "Trump Derides Protections for Immigrants from 'Shithole' Countries," *Washington Post*, January 12, 2018, https://www.washingtonpost.com/politics/trump -attacks-protections-for-immigrants-from-shithole-countries-in-oval-office-meeting /2018/01/11/bfc0725c-f711-11e7-91af-31ac729add94_story.html?utm_term=.91ef 335ffb9a.

26. *Stinchfield*, "Dousing Fake News Wildfires."

27. *We Stand*, "Liberal Battle Plan," NRATV, March 29, 2018, https://www.nratv .com/series/we-stand/episode/we-stand-season-1-episode-18.

28. *Stinchfield*, "Sledgehammer of Truth."

29. *Commentators*, "How to Stop the Media from Inspiring Killers," NRATV, May 23, 2018, https://www.nratv.com/episodes/commentators-season-8-episode-6-how-to-stop -the-media-from-inspiring-killers.

30. "Colion Noir Gives the Media a Taste of Their Own Medicine," NRATV, accessed June 17, 2019, https://www.nratv.com/videos/colion-noir-gives-the-media-a-taste-of -their-own-medicine.

31. Stacy Washington, "Real Fearless Women," *America's 1st Freedom*, July 28, 2017, https://www.americas1stfreedom.org/articles/2017/7/28/real-fearless-women/.

32. *Stinchfield*, "AR-15 Most Popular Gun in America," NRATV, December 22, 2017, https://www.nratv.com/series/stinchfield/video/stinchfield-dan-gainor-ar-15-most -popular-gun-in-america/episode/stinchfield-season-1-episode-247.

33. National Rifle Association Institute for Legislative Action, "Fake News on Gun Confiscation," December 22, 2017, https://www.nraila.org/articles/20171222/fake -news-on-gun-confiscation.

34. *Freedom's Safest Place*, "Why the Media Is Failing."

35. Melzer, *Gun Crusaders*.

36. *Stinchfield*, "Media Hypocrisy."

8 Media Credibility before "Fake News": Interpreting an Antiabortion Activist Undercover Video

Colin Doty

Since the 2016 presidential election, President Donald Trump and his surrogates have used the term *fake news* to delegitimize news media,[1] yet the view of news media as untrustworthy predates the Trump administration. A 2014 Gallup poll finds that "Americans' confidence in the media's ability to report 'the news fully, accurately, and fairly' has returned to its previous all-time low of 40 percent."[2] Likewise, a Poynter Media Trust survey shows that overall trust in the news media has been declining steadily since the late 1970s (although trust has increased since 2016 among those who disapprove of Trump). However, the Poynter survey also finds that "a direct attack by the President on the media had limited effects on perceptions of the media."[3] This suggests that Trump's strategy of media criticism has not created *new* distrust of the media so much as it has harnessed and focused existing distrust.

This chapter explicates one case of how that existing media environment operated shortly before the election of Trump. During the campaign season in 2015, I worked with a colleague to analyze internet comments posted in response to news coverage of a covertly filmed video about Planned Parenthood (PP).[4] We found this to be a fruitful space to interrogate the antecedents to the contemporary "fake news" discourse. We observe, for example, not only a preexisting concern about media bias in our data, but also concern about what counts as legitimate, trustworthy journalism, especially given the video's status as alternative journalism in opposition to the mainstream sources that covered it. Understanding these antecedents can help us understand the contemporary fake news discourse as part of an ongoing cultural debate about media credibility.

The Video

On July 14, 2015, the Center for Medical Progress (CMP), a self-described medical ethics watchdog group run by antiabortion activists,[5] released the first in a series of videos of PP officials, who had no knowledge of the filming. The first video shows a PP official discussing the dispensation of postabortion fetal tissue with members of CMP, who are pretending to represent a company that serves as a broker between abortion clinics and researchers seeking fetal tissue. Although both a full-length and a shortened version of the video were released on the CMP website, the widely circulated version of the video was edited from nearly three hours to just under nine minutes, excising footage, repeating certain sequences for emphasis, and adding subtitles, ominous music, and explanatory intertitles. The CMP claims the videos prove that PP illegally sells fetal tissue for profit. PP of course disputes that claim, asserting that the tissue is donated, with only costs reimbursed. Subsequent investigations have supported PP's version of events.

The CMP characterizes these videos and its project as alternative journalism. On its website, the CMP describes itself as "a group of citizen journalists," and the press release accompanying the video describes it as resulting from an "investigative journalism study."[6]

Media organizations across the ideological spectrum covered both the release of the video and PP's response, with varying interpretations. Our initial study sought to capture general patterns in how news audiences made sense of the video. To study this, we purposively selected five ideologically diverse news websites. Two sites primarily publish content specific to abortion: *LifeSiteNews* (pro-life) and *RH Reality Check* (pro-choice, subsequently renamed *Rewire*). Two sites publish general news content but attract audiences of opposite partisanship: *The Blaze* (conservative) and *Mother Jones* (progressive). The fifth site, the *New York Times,* is a mainstream news source that attracts a large audience.

From each website, we selected the earliest news article that covered the video and received at least fifty reader comments. Each of the five articles reports about the video slightly differently.[7] *Rewire* identifies its article as "commentary," and the *Times* identifies its as an "editorial." Some of the articles (from *Rewire, Mother Jones,* and the *Times*) cite facts contrary to those presented in the video and emphasize different statements that appear in the full footage but not in the shorter version. *The Blaze* article reports the

CMP interpretation of the story with hedging phrases such as "claims" and "allegedly," and the *LifeSiteNews* article overtly adopts the CMP interpretation, describing the video as showing the "illegal" sale of "baby body parts."

Using inductive coding methods, we coded emerging themes in over three thousand comments across the five news sites.[8] Coding spanned October 2015 to July 2016, overlapping with the real-world shift in the usage of "fake news." For insight into that usage specifically, I conducted a secondary analysis of the data, which began with the review of excerpts related to discussions of "fake" (truth or falsity) and discussions of "news." This analysis identified 114 relevant excerpts, which were then subcoded, guided by concepts related to the contemporary fake news discourse, including bias, claims of journalism, and mainstream versus alternative news status. These themes emerged in comments about both the video itself and articles about the video.

Reader Comments

Evaluating the Video's Agenda and Status as Journalism

The comments on each article debate the video's intentions and its techniques using several criteria.[9] This section of the chapter focuses on comments expressing an evaluation of the video *as a source of news*. Common among such evaluations are comments about the political agenda of the video and its status as journalism.

Many commenters, for example, focus on the video's producer and the CMP's political stance toward abortion. For instance, a *Times* commenter questions the legitimacy of the video's purported investigation by characterizing the CMP itself as having a political agenda:

> This is anything BUT an independent investigation by a supposed third party. The so-called "Center for Medical Progress" ... are avowed anti-abortion religious zealots.

Here, by highlighting the producer's political position on abortion, the commenter suggests that the claims can be dismissed as biased. Other comments make similar claims, such as a commenter from *Mother Jones*, who ties political agenda to falsehood:

> The video is a complete invention by David Daleiden [of the CMP], a known solitary anti-choice crusader.

Other commenters tie the producer not to an antiabortion stance but to a broader political stance and use that association to impugn the trustworthiness of the video. As a commenter from *LifeSiteNews* argues:

> Would you prefer to believe the lying right wing nut jobs who put together this completely fake story?

By asserting that the video's creators are biased against abortion and simultaneously positioning that bias as discrediting, these commenters question the credibility of the video.

Some commenters take the concern with bias even further, asserting that it is inconsistent with traditional practices of journalism. For example, one *Times* commenter states:

> Their investigations are blatantly dishonest with an agenda to hurt people not expose any so called truth. ... Dishonesty. NOT investigative journalism.

This comment asserts motivations for the video (i.e., "to hurt people") other than uncovering truth and then distinguishes those from what "investigative journalism" does. This foregrounding of the status of journalism as conferring legitimacy is explicit elsewhere, as when a commenter from the *Times* argues:

> These folks are not journalists like ones employed by the NY Times and other news outlets.

This argument that the CMP is not producing journalism is used to suggest that the CMP is therefore not trustworthy.

Other comments evaluate the trustworthiness of the video based upon the techniques it employs. Some see the CMP as part of a tradition of undercover videos motivated by conservative causes, as in this *Times* comment:

> From the Breitbart School of Journalism. The most disturbing thing is that it works. The shameless video hit job on Shirley Sherrod ... [a]nd James O'Keefe's "stings" on ACORN, equally shameless and deceptive.

This comment itemizes examples of the history of conservative, politically motivated uses of undercover video, and explicitly situates the CMP video within that tradition. Furthermore, by calling such videos "shameless and deceptive," it depicts those uses, including by the CMP, negatively. This implies that the video's techniques are themselves what undermine its legitimacy, as demonstrated not only in this video, but also through a deceptive tradition of such tactics.

Other commenters, however, view these techniques positively, and place undercover video—and even the deception inherent in covert filming—squarely as a legitimate practice of journalism:

> This deception is also practiced by gotcha journalists. These "investigative jour-nalists" go undercover and pose as[,] for example, meat-handlers in supermarkets, in order to observe (and sometimes possibly stage) unsanitary practices. Appar-ently the Times is against deception only when its ox is gored by it.

For this *Times* commenter, since other journalists have used "deception" and "undercover" techniques to report on wrongdoing such as "unsani-tary practices," the techniques themselves are not inherently problematic. Another *Times* commenter says this explicitly:

> The technique of using video is just as valid when used by pro-life people as when it is used by progressives.

Comments such as these push back against the suggestion that the CMP video's undercover techniques invalidate it, instead asserting the video's validity and equivalence to other journalism. Such assertions deepen what qualifies as legitimate journalism by highlighting inconsistencies in how the label is applied.

Evaluating the Legitimacy of News Coverage of the Video

While many of the comments debate whether the video itself is trustwor-thy, other comments focus instead on whether the news sources covering the video—and particularly the *Times*—can be considered trustworthy. Using criteria similar to those used to evaluate the video, these comments regularly cite the *Times'* purported agenda and question whether its work constitutes legitimate journalism. In so doing, the comments contest the credibility of the *Times* article.

Many comments assert that the *Times* has a political bias, and this serves as a confounding factor in its credibility:

> The Times is failing its readers and what used to be its journalistic raison d'etre by acting like a political partisan instead of, and to the exclusion of, being an impartial investigator and reporter of facts.

This comment explicitly positions political partisanship in opposition to fact-finding, suggesting that the *Times* is partisan and therefore not "an impartial investigator and reporter of facts." That this bias is disqualifying for many is even more directly stated by a different reader, who explains:

The NYT's lack of objectivity, across the entire publication, makes it nearly an impossible proposition to support.

Comments such as these depict the *Times* as having a political bias, that bias as compromising its objectivity, and that lack of objectivity as making it an untrustworthy source of information about and evaluation of the CMP video. Notably, such criticisms are not limited to this single article, but situate the coverage within a preexisting distrust of the *Times* as a whole:

Wow, what an incredibly distorted representation of the videos by the NYT. ... But why should I be surprised.

This last observation, that the *Times'* "distorted representation" is not a surprise, suggests that this commenter's distrust of the *Times* predates the present article. Other comments imply the same thing, such as by a commenter who notes:

The facts should come before partisan demonization, but then again, this is the NYT.

These suggestions that the *Times* has a history of partisan bias are parallel to comments seeking to situate the video within an existing tradition of alternative journalism, inferring that the credibility of both the CMP video and the *Times* article depend upon the credibility of the tradition in which each is seen to operate.

Such parallels extend to evaluations of the *Times'* status as journalism. Just as some comments debate whether the video qualifies as legitimate journalism, so some comments criticize the journalistic legitimacy of the *Times*. One commenter states:

To defend Planned Parenthood's questionable practices is really beneath the standards of responsible journalism.

This commenter references a perceived universal standard of journalism and then asserts that the *Times* fails to meet it. This is, of course, a circular argument: such comments disqualify the *Times'* journalism *because* of the conclusions it draws. What is claimed to violate "the standards of responsible journalism" is the defense of PP. Disagreement is perceived as invalidating, as another commenter suggests:

Real news organizations would investigate the possibilities of poor governance at Planned Parenthood, instead the NYT rushes to its defense.

The contrast between this comment's category of "real news" and the Trumpian category of "fake news" is illuminating. Objectivity is essential to qualify as "real news," and therefore bias is disqualifying. The Trumpian redefinition of *fake news* first frames disagreement or criticism as bias, thereby disqualifying the story as "real news," and then declares that which is not "real news" to be "fake news."

Another essential precursor of this redefinition is that such criticisms are not limited to the *Times* or to news outlets supporting politically liberal positions. For example, some comments implicate Fox News as the dominant purveyor of ideologically partisan (conservative) news:

> The problem with the story is that FOX News [took] the story and ran with it. The NYT editorial although useful cannot compete with willful deception by the Republican Party and its powerful network of disinformation.

Again, a political agenda is invoked as a confounding factor, but with regard to a news platform other than the one (the *Times*) on which this commenter is commenting. That such charges against Fox News echo those leveled at the *Times* depicts a larger media environment where biased agendas are a concern on all sides. Such a media environment, where both sides of the political spectrum are concerned with bias and journalistic integrity, could afford—and even enable—a "fake news" discourse like the one that later emerged with Trump. The Trumpian use of "fake news" takes the standards upon which both sides agree—that objectivity and legitimate journalistic techniques are essential—and reappropriates them as a weapon against journalism it dislikes.

Media Credibility before "Fake News"

This analysis finds that comments on articles from five ideologically diverse sources about the CMP's covertly filmed video of a PP official frequently engage in claims and debate about bias, legitimacy, and what constitutes journalism. They do so in specific ways that offer insight on the rhetorical landscape into which the Trumpian "fake news" discourse emerges. In particular, commenters engage in evaluations of the various sources of news—both the video itself and the media coverage of the video—and whether those sources are trustworthy. In turn, these claims are used to build over-arching arguments that particular sources are generally illegitimate.

Importantly, although comments on all five sites engage with general debates about how to interpret the video,[10] most of the discussions about bias and journalistic legitimacy take place in the comment section of the *Times* (101 of 114 coded excerpts). This may be attributable partly to the higher volume of comments on the *Times* site, but it also may suggest that the *Times'* status as mainstream media, whether positive or negative, uniquely provokes such considerations.

Indeed, the concern with journalistic legitimacy may be enhanced by the fact that the story originated from an alternative media source. Commenters who trust the alternative source imply by that trust that the video's alternative status does not diminish its credibility. Similarly, distrust of the mainstream source implies that mainstream status does not ensure its credibility. (The reverse is true for those who trust the mainstream source more than the alternative one.) This long-standing debate over the trustworthiness and legitimacy of mainstream versus alternative media sources is another important aspect of Trump's adoption of the term *fake news*. As a report from the Data and Society Research Institute puts it:

> "Fake news" is used as an extension of well-worn critiques that the mainstream media feeds audiences false and untrustworthy narratives. As a result, this criticism serves as a justification for an alternative media network of hyper-partisan and conspiracy laden news sources that often spread disinformation and hoaxes.[11]

Put another way, preexisting debates about the trustworthiness of mainstream media sources, as amplified by the Trumpian use of "fake news," encourage the existence of organizations such as the CMP and the techniques it employs.

This is a useful case for understanding "fake news" because the news story relates to a highly partisan political topic and was initially released through alternative media and then covered in mainstream news outlets. Comments on these different sources suggest that audiences hold each kind of media to similar standards of objectivity and journalistic legitimacy, even though the audiences for each may be different. In so doing, they enable an environment where criticisms of those standards—even criticisms that are *themselves* highly partisan and of questionable legitimacy—can paint news stories as untrustworthy. If "real news" must be unbiased and legitimate, and disagreement is perceived as bias, then disagreement renders news "fake."

Acknowledgment

I wish to thank Katrina Kimport for her invaluable contributions to this chapter.

Notes

1. Robyn Caplan, Lauren Hanson, and Joan Donovan, *Dead Reckoning: Navigating Content Moderation after "Fake News"* (New York: Data and Society Research Institute, 2018).

2. Justin McCarthy, "Trust in Mass Media Returns to All-Time Low," Gallup, September 17, 2014, http://news.gallup.com/poll/176042/trust-mass-media-returns-time-low .aspx.

3. Andrew Guess, Brendan Nyhan, and Jason Reifler, "'You're Fake News!': Findings from the Poynter Media Trust Survey" (paper presented at the Poynter Journalism Ethics Summit, Washington, DC, December 4, 2017), https://poyntercdn.blob.core .windows.net/files/PoynterMediaTrustSurvey2017.pdf.

4. Katrina Kimport and Colin Doty, "Interpreting the Truth: How People Make Sense of New Information about Abortion" (unpublished manuscript, 2017).

5. Amanda Marcotte, "What Is the Center for Medical Progress, the Group behind the Latest Viral Abortion Video?," *Slate*, July 15, 2015, http://www.slate.com/blogs /xx_factor/2015/07/15/live_action_distributed_the_planned_parenthood_sting _video_why_aren_t_they.html.

6. Center for Medical Progress, "About Us," 2018, http://www.centerformedicalprogress .org/about-us/; Center for Medical Progress, "#PPSellsBabyParts Planned Parenthood's Top Doctor, Praised by CEO, Uses Partial-Birth Abortions to Sell Baby Parts," July 14, 2015, http://www.centerformedicalprogress.org/2015/07/planned-parenthoods-top-doc tor-praised-by-ceo-uses-partial-birth-abortions-to-sell-baby-parts/.

7. Becca Andrews, "GOP Candidates Pile on to Praise Planned Parenthood Sting," *Mother Jones*, July 15, 2015, https://www.motherjones.com/politics/2015 /07/planned-parenthood-video/; The Editorial Board, "Opinion: The Campaign of Deception Against Planned Parenthood," *The New York Times*, July 22, 2015, sec. Opinion, https://www.nytimes.com/2015/07/22/opinion/the-campaign-of-deception -against-planned-parenthood.html; Billy Hallowell, "Undercover Footage Captures Stunning Claim About Planned Parenthood," *The Blaze*, July 14, 2015, https://www .theblaze.com/news/2015/07/14/undercover-video-claims-planned-parenthood-uses -partial-birth-abortions-to-sell-baby-parts; Jodi Jacobson, "Profiting From Fetal Body Parts? The GOP Sure Is," *Rewire.News*, July 15, 2015, https://rewire.news/article/2015 /07/15/profiting-fetal-body-parts-gop-sure/; Ben Johnson, "BREAKING: Undercover

Video Catches Planned Parenthood Selling Baby Body Parts from Abortions," *LifeSite-News*, July 14, 2015, https://www.lifesitenews.com/news/undercover-video-planned
-parenthood-uses-illegal-partial-birth-abortions-to.

8. For more detail about the methods, see Kimport and Doty, "Interpreting the Truth."

9. Ibid.

10. Ibid.

11. Caplan, Hanson, and Donovan, *Dead Reckoning*, 27.

III Law and Policy: Part Introduction

All of the chapters in this part explore the role of government regulation in addressing online misinformation, or lack thereof. The authors of this part explore timely questions: Do we need radical regulatory reform to hold social media platforms accountable and support journalism? Do nation-states need to intervene to protect vulnerable groups against the violence resulting from the circulation of hate propaganda? Or do we need to preserve—or even increase—the openness of our communication channels by preventing governments from interfering? Ultimately, the authors of this part disagree on the best strategy, with three authors making the case that policies—rather than continued industry examples of "self-regulation"—are necessary for addressing misinformation, while one author pushes us to consider the drawbacks of government meddling in matters of speech.

The first chapter in this part is by media studies scholar Victor Pickard, "Confronting the Misinformation Society: Facebook's 'Fake News' Is a Symptom of Unaccountable Monopoly Power." Pickard's chapter begins by examining the structural nature of the fake news phenomenon, and it concludes with suggestions for radical reform. According to Pickard, various forms of misinformation and propaganda, whether hatched by governments or the likes of Fox News, have been circulating through media for decades, if not centuries. But the profound media power residing in one monopolistic platform, namely, Facebook, arguably presents a unique challenge to democratic societies. Even as Facebook comes under increased public pressure to be held accountable for the misinformation it purveys and profits from, a core problem is often overlooked: the proliferation of fake news is *symptomatic* of an unregulated news monopoly that is governed solely by profit imperatives. Thus, Pickard argues that solutions will remain elusive until we adequately diagnose this underlying problem.

The second chapter in this part is by communication scholar Stephanie Ricker Schulte, "Fixing Fake News: Self-Regulation and Technological Solutionism." Schulte's chapter places solutions to the fake news problem in two historical contexts: American media self-regulation and technological solutionism. First, Schulte argues that mechanisms deployed by internet platforms for self-regulating fake news content—including flagging, fact-checking, and content moderation—"make sense" in part because the history of media regulation in the United States has been one dominated by self-regulation. Time after time, through internal mechanisms—organizations such as the National Association of Broadcasters and industry agreements such as the Hays Code—media producers, distributors, and outlets walked back content deemed problematic or outrageous, shifting content on radio channels, film screens, and television broadcasts to diminish public and political outrage.

Second, Schulte tracks the history of "solutionism," the idea that technology can solve humanity's problems and make life "frictionless." Technological solutionism plays heavily in the fake news regulation conversation in part because fake news is understood as a technological problem or, at the very least, as a social problem solvable by technology. Ultimately, Schulte argues that, inserted into these two contexts, self-regulatory efforts put forward by internet platforms "make sense" only because these solutions continue the pattern of market (not government) regulation and because they perpetuate the illusion that technology is the best solution to humanity's problems.

Cherian George, a journalism and media studies scholar, contributes the third chapter in this part, "The Scourge of Disinformation-Assisted Hate Propaganda." According to George, probably no genre of fake news is more dangerous than disinformation campaigns that target socially marginalized communities. There is nothing new about such hate propaganda; it has been central to the communication strategy of groups engaged in territorial conquests, genocides, pogroms, and other crimes against humanity throughout history. In less extreme cases, groups using identity politics as a means to accumulate power deploy it to scapegoat "politically dispensable" minorities. In this chapter, George analyzes recent elections in India and Indonesia to understand how these disinformation campaigns work. To combat such propaganda, George contends that news media need to trace the interests behind them, in much the same way that investigative journalists follow the money to uncover corruption. Ultimately, though, George argues that addressing propaganda requires the protection of an activist state that intervenes to uphold people's rights to live free of discrimination and violence.

The final chapter in this part is by communication scholar Paul Levinson, "Fake News and Open Channels of Communication." Levinson argues that the ultimate antidote to fake news is the myriad sources we have to check any news sources, whether newspapers, cable news, or somewhere online. Levinson cautions us that the well-meaning (and not so well-meaning) attempts of governments to address misinformation problems like fake news through the regulation of social media will undermine sources of legitimate news. To Levinson, the best defense we have against misinformation is keeping all of our channels of information wide open, not only to the dissemination of fake news, but to the dissemination of truthful reporting.

Suggested Reading

Wajeeha Ahmad, "Dealing with Fake News: Policy and Technical Measures" (Internet Policy Research Initiative, Massachusetts Institute of Technology, Cambridge, MA, 2018), https://internetpolicy.mit.edu/wpcontent/uploads/2018/04/Fake-news-recommendations-Wajeeha-MITs-IPRI.pdf.

Daniel Funke, "A Guide to Anti-Misinformation Actions around the World," Poynter, accessed June 17, 2019, https://www.poynter.org/ifcn/anti-misinformation-actions/.

Philip M. Napoli, "What If More Speech Is No Longer the Solution? First Amendment Theory Meets Fake News and the Filter Bubble," *Federal Communications Law Journal* 70, no. 1 (2018): 57–103, http://www.fclj.org/wp-content/uploads/2018/04/70.1-Napoli.pdf.

9 Confronting the Misinformation Society: Facebook's "Fake News" Is a Symptom of Unaccountable Monopoly Power

Victor Pickard

Various forms of misinformation and propaganda have plagued societies for centuries. However, today's profound media power residing in one monopolistic platform arguably presents a unique challenge to democratic governance. Even as Facebook comes under increased public pressure to be held accountable for the misinformation it purveys and from which it profits, a core problem is often overlooked: the proliferation of so-called fake news is symptomatic of an unregulated news monopoly that is governed solely by profit imperatives. Facebook is not evil; it is merely the natural outgrowth of an information system governed by such an unaccountable, commercial logic.

Until we adequately diagnose the structural roots of the misinformation problem, potential solutions will remain elusive. Moreover, history shows us that expecting good corporate behavior simply by shaming information monopolies is a dubious proposition at best. Confronting the structural roots of this problem now will help prevent information monopolies from emerging in the future. This chapter will begin such a project by examining the systemic nature of what I refer to as the "misinformation society," and it concludes with suggestions for radical reform.[1]

A Moment of Reckoning

Donald Trump's election exposed structural pathologies in the American media system. Mono-causal explanations of Trump's ascendance that blame "fake news" are clearly insufficient—indeed, mainstream media contributed as much, if not more, to the lack of high-quality information leading up to the election—but widespread misinformation disseminated via Facebook is nonetheless a significant threat to democratic self-governance.[2]

As an algorithm-driven global editor and news gatekeeper for over 2 billion users, Facebook has tremendous power over much of the world's information system. In the United States, where news is increasingly accessed through its platform, Facebook's role in the 2016 presidential election has drawn well-deserved scrutiny. Reports suggest that fake news was widely circulated during the weeks before the election.[3]

Exacerbating the misinformation problem is a decreasing supply of reliable news media. Because Facebook (along with Google) is devouring the lion's share of digital advertising revenue, institutions that provide quality news and information—the same struggling news organizations that are expected to help fact-check against fake news—are further weakened. Journalism in general, and local news in particular, is increasingly threatened by the Facebook-Google duopoly, which takes a combined 85 percent of all new U.S. digital advertising revenue growth, leaving only scraps for news publishers.[4] According to one study, these two companies now control 73 percent of the total online advertising market.[5]

Thus far, technocratic discourses have dominated the discussion about misinformation. Suggested remedies typically involve a combination of media literacy and user responsibility; technological fixes such as new algorithms and policing specific ad networks; and crowdsourcing to the public or outsourcing to third parties like Snopes and other fact-checking organizations the responsibility of flagging fake news. Thus far, Facebook has taken few meaningful actions to address the problem, though this might change as the company continues to receive fines and threats, especially from Europe.

Meaningful competition to Facebook is unlikely in the near term, and allowing it to be governed solely by unfettered profit motives has created a number of social problems. Addressing these problems requires several steps. Facebook must be treated as a media company and held to norms of social responsibility. Thus far, Mark Zuckerberg has refused to even acknowledge that Facebook is anything more than a technology company.[6] In the meantime, the repercussions of Facebook's profit-driven control over the world's media will likely only worsen. This is an untenable situation; democratic societies must challenge Facebook's monopoly power on multiple fronts.

While no silver-bullet policy solution will likely present itself, the proliferation of misinformation is a serious social problem, and any social problem should be seen as a policy problem. Now is a rare—and, most likely, fleeting—opportunity to hold a public debate about what policy interventions are best suited to address the problem. Government, driven by social pressures from below and informed by public consent, has the power and responsibility to intervene. Ultimately, fake news is a structural problem; it will take structural reforms to fix it.

Confronting the Facebook Problem

Facebook's sudden fall from grace has loosened long-held verities. Regulating such firms was once unfathomable. Now even Republicans in Congress believe digital monopolies are too powerful and must face government intervention. The Cambridge Analytica scandal in the spring of 2018 helped kick-start a long overdue conversation about unaccountable monopoly power, its pernicious effects on society, and government's role in stopping it. With implications far beyond Facebook, this could be a pivotal moment and a rare opportunity for structural reform.

But how can society seize it? As part of his apology tour, Zuckerberg himself conceded (at least publicly) an openness to regulation. So the real question becomes *what kind* of regulation? Do we repeat old mistakes and impose self-regulation requirements that will erode over time? Or do we subject Facebook's monopolistic power to real public oversight and implement redistributive measures? Thus far, discussions have focused mostly on user privacy, which is vitally important. But we should consider a broader, bolder vision for what Facebook owes society in return for the incredible power we've allowed it to accumulate.

Journalism's ad-revenue dependency has always been deeply flawed,[7] but now the model is decimated—with devastating effects. Fewer revenues support fewer journalists, leaving newsrooms gutted and shuttered across the country. The newspaper industry has seen over half its workforce reduced over the past fifteen years. Entire regions of the country and severe social problems are barely covered in the news. This systemic market failure is not caused by Facebook alone, but the platform monopoly is certainly exacerbating and accelerating it.[8]

Although a post-newspaper future is becoming a distinct possibility, these struggling institutions still provide most of the original reporting for the entire news media system. A healthy fourth estate is needed now more than ever. It's tragically ironic that Facebook and Google are starving the very institutions they expect to help fact-check against misinformation.

Facebook Economics

Historical precedent and mainstream economics justify aggressive regulation,[9] especially in dealing with "natural monopolies." This assumes that specific industries, especially networks such as communication systems, tend toward one large centralized entity. Thus, it's socially optimal for one firm to invest in and maintain these services. Instead of breaking up such firms, regulatory incentives and penalties can prevent them from exploiting their market power.

Similar to that of a public utility, such firms often offer core services or infrastructures—like electricity, transportation systems, and water. Because they're expensive to maintain but essential for the public good, many societies shield these services from unmitigated market forces. Regardless of how we categorize it, Facebook is a core digital infrastructure upon which society has granted a special status with enormous privileges.

Historically, the American government has deployed various laws and policies to contain monopoly power. But Facebook has managed to escape this arrangement. It isn't under close government regulation or oversight. Nor is it expected to provide deliverables in return for being a state-sanctioned monopoly.

A counterexample involves AT&T (also called the Bell System), whose phone network attained a similarly dominant position in the early twentieth century. To forestall government regulation (including a threatened government takeover of its network), AT&T agreed to exit from a related market (telegraphy), interconnect with most non-AT&T systems, invest heavily in research and development (Bell Labs), maintain reasonable rates (especially for local calls), and help promote universal service.

It isn't a perfect analogy—AT&T was a common carrier that controlled the actual telephone wires—but it's instructive to consider what concessions a looming threat of antitrust litigation might bring (ultimately AT&T was broken up in the 1980s), including divestment of key components, radically changing business practices, and offsetting social costs / negative externalities. This approach to confronting monopoly power requires reframing key policy debates and broadening the political imagination of what's possible within the regulatory realm.

Make Facebook (and Google) Pay for Public Service Journalism

Google, which has a dominant market position in search, and Facebook, which similarly dominates social media, are together greatly contributing to the evisceration of journalism.[10] At the same time, they play an outsize role in proliferating misinformation. To help offset some of the damage they are causing, these firms should help fund local news, investigative journalism, policy reporting, and the kinds of coverage that doesn't always yield clicks, but democracy requires. Thus far, Google and Facebook have offered only what amounts to public relations initiatives.

Google has pledged $300 million over three years toward journalism-related measures for its News Initiative, but this is insufficient (on a three-year average, it represents less than 1 percent of its 2017 profits). It also doesn't directly fund the kinds of journalism the market fails to support. For its part, Facebook has launched a $3 million journalism "accelerator" (about 0.007 percent of 2017 revenues) to help ten to fifteen news organizations build their digital subscriptions using Facebook's platform.[11] These efforts are woefully insufficient. Current losses demand direct support for the journalism that Google and Facebook are actively defunding.

These two seemingly unrelated problems—unaccountable monopoly power and the loss of public service journalism—could be addressed through one policy intervention that redistributes revenue as part of a new regulatory approach to digital monopolies. Facebook (and also Google, which owns YouTube) should help fund the very industry that it simultaneously profits from and eviscerates. These firms should pay a "public service tax."

A nominal tax of 1 percent on Facebook's and Google's earnings would generate tremendous funds for a journalism trust fund. Based on their 2017 net income, Facebook would yield $159.34 million and Alphabet, which is the parent company of Google, would yield $126.62 million. Together, 1 percent of Alphabet's and Facebook's 2017 net income is $285.96 million, which would go far toward seeding an endowment for independent journalism, especially if combined with other philanthropic contributions that accumulate over time.

Shielded from powerful interests, this public media trust should be publicly operated, remain autonomous from government, and able to receive charitable contributions from other entities such as foundations. However, all donations must be severed from any institutional or personal attachments to ensure independence from any single funder or government entity. A well-funded national—and, ultimately, international—journalism service could help guarantee universal access to quality news.

Facebook could certainly afford such an expenditure since it currently pays preciously little in taxes, which is being increasingly scrutinized.[12] The European Commission reportedly wants a new tax of between 1 and 5 percent on digital companies' revenues, including Google, Facebook, and Amazon. The idea of a public media tax is gaining traction abroad as well as in the United States.[13]

In Great Britain, the Media Reform Coalition and the National Union of Journalists have proposed taxing digital intermediaries specifically for public service journalism. In 2016, they tried to amend the Digital Economy Act to levy a 1 percent tax on such firms to fund nonprofit reporting. They were unsuccessful, but nonetheless policy makers increasingly are seeing connections between digital monopolies' accumulation of wealth, the continuing degradation of journalism, and the rise of misinformation.

While some American and British proposals consider whether commercial news publishers receive a fair share of advertisement revenue from search engines and social media platforms, funding specifically for *public* media would decommercialize news and help ensure its integrity—and restore public trust.

Increasingly, governments are concluding that nonmarket support is journalism's last, best hope. The Canadian government has pledged $50 million (U.S.$39 million) to local journalism, and others are considering similar options. But taxing digital monopolies and subsidizing journalism requires reframing key policy debates, especially in the United States.

The Road Ahead

Over the past year, Facebook has been charged with mishandling users' data, abusing market power, and proliferating misinformation. Such negative externalities to society as Facebook extracts profound wealth across the globe should necessitate greater social responsibilities as a partial payback for Facebook's many benefits. It's time for a new social contract.

Financial support for public service journalism is just one piece of this contract, which could emerge from tackling these digital behemoths. But first we must broaden the discursive boundaries for what's possible in terms of regulating digital monopolies. Beyond historicizing this problem to consider what policy interventions have been deployed in the past, it's always a worthwhile exercise to consider other democratic nations' reform efforts.

For example, the Europeans are trying to compensate for policy failures that allowed Facebook to set terms to its own advantage. Going beyond already-existing fines and proposed taxes, the European Union (EU) is currently implementing its General Data Protection Regulation (GDPR). The GDPR ensures that internet users in the twenty-eight EU countries understand and consent to the data collected about them regardless of where it's stored and processed. This will affect companies based outside of Europe, especially Facebook and Google. The GDPR also guarantees a "right to be forgotten" that allows EU citizens to permanently remove online personal data and "data portability" that allows users to download their data and move it elsewhere.

Some may argue that since we receive social media services for free, we should resign ourselves to the bargain to which we agreed. But we actually pay dearly by providing content, data, and our attention. However, many users are simply ill informed about the true nature if this exchange. As the old saw goes, "If you're getting something for free, most likely *you* are the product." But while it's tempting to simply quit Facebook and delete one's account, such an individualistic, consumer-based reaction doesn't encourage institutional change. Many groups of people around the world depend on Facebook for basic communications. Given its tremendous network effects (the network's increasing size makes it more indispensable), it's unreasonable to expect a mass exit from Facebook—more likely its expansion will continue. If we're serious about systemic reform and reining in corporate power, we must commit to collective action and policy intervention.

Reining in Facebook will most likely require a well-equipped toolbox of regulatory instruments beyond safeguarding users' privacy. These may include a wide-ranging set of interventions, among them antitrust measures like divesting specific components such as WhatsApp, Messenger, and

Instagram; banning political advertising from dark money groups and foreign governments; reforming section 230 of the Communications Decency Act, which shields websites from legal liability; implementing radical transparency of algorithms and data collection; and promoting data portability and interoperability.

Facebook's power doesn't stem from magical technology or the market's genius. Rather, governance over communication infrastructures is a political decision that all societies must face. By dismantling antitrust laws, we've permitted Facebook to abuse its power. Too many were seduced by Silicon Valley's "move fast and break things" ethos. Too many stood silent when told that the internet was beyond the realm of regulation, that it was inherently and inevitably democratic, and that benevolent corporations were the best arbiters of this vital communication system. Policy decisions and indecisions have consequences, and we now reap what was sowed. But it isn't too late to fix things.

Facebook's technology isn't inviolable. Algorithms are human-made things—as demonstrated when Facebook adjusted its algorithms to privilege friends' and family's posts over those from news publishers. Nor is Facebook some kind of Frankenstein monster that is beyond social control. Humans can and must intervene. With its massive profits, Facebook should commit money to journalism, but also hire legions of human screeners and—dare we say it—editors.

Ultimately, however, this problem isn't simply Facebook's to solve and self-regulation is insufficient. Democratic societies must decide what Facebook's social responsibilities should look like and how they should be enforced. Public governance from international grassroots groups and watchdog institutions made up of independent experts should determine these measures and help monitor Facebook's actions, pressuring it to be more transparent and accountable. This bottom-up discussion must be held publicly and internationally, with the participation of diverse constituencies. At the very least, an independent press council should help monitor and audit Facebook's actions.

Facebook (and Amazon, Google, and Apple) simply has too much power over the world's media and politics. This power must be checked. The American political imaginary is too often limited to individual freedoms and consumer rights. But we can transcend this impoverished vision to draw from social democratic traditions—a paradigm that sees news and information as public goods that shouldn't be left solely to the corrosive commercialism of unregulated monopolies.[14]

A new social contract for digital media must assert public control over communication systems, and provide funding for the public infrastructure that democracy requires, especially journalism that can focus on local issues and hold concentrated power (like Facebook) to account. Any new arrangement should protect content creators and individual users (i.e., those who actually produce the labor upon which Facebook profits). Most importantly, this new contract must privilege society's democratic needs over Facebook's sole objective of profit maximization. Doing so is a necessary step toward restructuring our global media system and preventing unaccountable information monopolies from ever arising again.

Notes

1. On the "misinformation society," see Victor Pickard, "Media Failures in the Age of Trump," *Political Economy of Communication* 4, no. 2 (2017): 118–122. Sections of this chapter draw from Victor Pickard, "Break Facebook's Power and Renew Journalism," *The Nation* 306, no. 15 (2018): 22–24.

2. On the election's coverage, see Pickard, "Media Failures in the Age of Trump"; Thomas E. Patterson, "Harvard Study: Policy Issues Nearly Absent in Presidential Campaign Coverage," The Conversation, September 20, 2016, https://theconversation .com/harvard-study-policy-issues-nearly-absent-in-presidential-campaign-coverage -65731. On Facebook's threat to democracy, see Victor Pickard, "The Big Picture: Misinformation Society," *Public Books*, November 28, 2017, http://www.publicbooks.org /the-big-picture-misinformation-society/.

3. See Craig Silverman, "This Analysis Shows How Viral Fake Election News Stories Outperformed Real News on Facebook," BuzzFeed News, November, 16, 2016, https://www.buzzfeed.com/craigsilverman/viral-fake-election-news-outperformed -real-news-on-facebook.

4. Mike Shields, "CMO Today: Google and Facebook Drive 2017 Digital Ad Surge, *Wall Street Journal*, March 14, 2017, https://www.wsj.com/articles/cmo-today-google -and-facebook-drive-2017-digital-ad-surge-1489491871.

5. Tiernan Ray, "Google, Facebook Approaching 'Saturation' of Ad Budgets, Says Pivotal," *Barron's*, December 20, 2017, http://www.barrons.com/articles/google-facebook -approaching-saturation-of-ad-budgets-says-pivotal-1513804634.

6. Mathew Ingram, "The Media Today: Facebook Tosses a Dime at Local Journalism," *Columbia Journalism Review*, February 28, 2018, https://www.cjr.org/the_media_today /facebook-local-news-funding.php.

7. Victor Pickard, *America's Battle for Media Democracy: The Triumph of Corporate Libertarianism and the Future of Media Reform* (New York: Cambridge University Press, 2015).

8. For a historical analysis of this market failure and its implications for the future of journalism, see Victor Pickard, *Democracy without Journalism: The Structural Roots of the Misinformation Society* (New York: Oxford University Press, forthcoming).

9. Ibid.

10. Sally Hubbard, "Fake News Is a Real Antitrust Problem," Competition Policy International, December 19, 2017, https://www.competitionpolicyinternational.com /fake-news-is-a-real-antitrust-problem/.

11. Ingram, "The Media Today."

12. Scott Galloway, "Silicon Valley's Tax-Avoiding, Job-Killing, Soul-Sucking Machine, *Esquire*, February 8, 2018, https://www.esquire.com/news-politics/a15895746/bust-big -tech-silicon-valley/.

13. For earlier articulations of this idea, see Victor Pickard, "Yellow Journalism, Orange President," *Jacobin*, November 25, 2016, https://www.jacobinmag.com/2016 /11/media-advertising-news-radio-trump-tv/; Emily Bell, "How Mark Zuckerberg Could Really Fix Journalism," *Columbia Journalism Review*, February 21, 2017, https:// www.cjr.org/tow_center/mark-zuckerberg-facebook-fix-journalism.php.

14. For an elaboration of this social democratic logic, see Victor Pickard, "A Social Democratic Vision of Media: Toward a Radical Pre-history of Public Broadcasting," *Journal of Radio and Audio Media* 24, no. 2 (2017): 200–212.

10   Fixing Fake News: Self-Regulation and Technological Solutionism

Stephanie Ricker Schulte

After the 2016 presidential election, Barack Obama and Donald Trump did not agree on much, but they agreed on this: fake news threatened American democracy.[1] By the end of 2017, fake news was a "fixture of contemporary politics" and a "profitable business."[2] While some ambiguity existed about what the term actually meant and what these leaders meant by the term, the majority of Americans agreed it was a problem.[3] Despite these complications and incoherencies, it had become a "national common sense,"[4] something everyone just knew, and a dominant cultural framework through which Americans understood the relationship between media and government and assessed the health of their democracy. Under public scrutiny, policy makers, news organizations, and social media platform leaders proposed a variety of solutions—such as flagging, content moderation, and news consumer guides—aimed at controlling content and empowering consumers.[5]

This piece historicizes both the fake news crisis and these proposed solutions. As Victor Pickard wrote, "Historicizing current media debates allows us to reimagine the present and reclaim the alternative trajectories."[6] This piece, then, maps the field of what was thinkable about the fake news problem by charting the often-unacknowledged assumptions that led us to the current moment. Indeed, neither concerns about fake news nor the proposed solutions emerged in a cultural vacuum. Long-standing American cultural beliefs, or national common senses, about technology, about news, and about government are at play, ideas with the power not only to actively shape the ways Americans understood fake news as problematic, but also to shape the range of solutions. In an effort to understand why the problem and solutions emerged as they did (and did not), this chapter inserts the fake news into two cultural histories—*media self-regulation* and *technological solutionism*.

The History of Nonfactual Information

First, important to this conversation is the recognition that the exchange of nonfactual information has played a central role in human history.[7] During the formation of the United States, for example, printed rumors or outright lies were not just commonplace, they were key strategies for drumming up support for the American Revolution.[8] The fakeness of information was of little concern at the time. In 1731, Benjamin Franklin, then *Pennsylvania Gazette* editor, "expressed a widely-held sentiment" that "when Truth and Error have fair Play, the former is always an overmatch for the latter."[9] Clearly, much has changed since Franklin's era. Chief among those changes are evolutions in media technology, including the creation of the internet. This technology ramped up cultural ambivalence stemming back to the printing press about the promiscuous spread of information.[10] The ability of international computer networking systems and the platforms operating on them to facilitate the potentially global, instantaneous, and anonymous circulation of information struck a nerve in popular and scholarly circles in the decades after the technology's popularization. For decades, the internet was predominantly understood as a destabilizing agent, as a "disrupter," as a technology that challenged established systems of power and distributions of power.[11] Since the 1980s, the internet has caused Americans considerable anxiety.[12] Contemporary scholars focus on the ways the internet preys on human cognition to disrupt fact gathering and verification practices. Social media scholar Kate Starbird described information networks online as "almost perfectly designed to exploit psychological vulnerabilities to rumor" because information mirrored in multiple places online reaffirms its validity.[13] She said, "Your brain tells you 'Hey, I got this from three different sources,' but you don't realize it all traces back to the same place and might have even reached you via bots posing as real people." For Starbird, this could have deep consequences, bringing forth "the menace of unreality—which is that nobody believes anything anymore."[14] With the evolution of communication technologies, Franklin's "widely held sentiment" lost its dominance; the era of public faith in the "fair play" between truth and error is over.

News media often cited communication technologies as creating, worsening, or enabling the fake news problem. In 2017—for the first time in its sixty-four-year history—*The Associated Press Stylebook* included the term *fake news*. This definitive guide for American journalists applied the term to "deliberate falsehoods or fiction masked as news circulating on the internet."[15] News industries marked *fake news as primarily an internet problem*, a problem caused by the promiscuous circulation of information through online platforms, and not a problem of news itself. One important exception to this "internet problem" narrative is President Donald Trump, who also applied the term to legacy print and television news institutions such as the *New York Times* and CNN.[16] For President Trump, fake news was an *internet problem* and a *news problem*. As this illustrates, the debate about fake news engaged historical American narratives that presumed antagonism between news industries and government, which positioned news media as the primary agents of government accountability.[17] Americans had lost faith in the fourth estate and the state itself as cynicism took hold.[18] The fake news debate positioned the internet as a powerful piece in the ongoing chess match.

Media Self-Regulation

Part of this chess match has involved media regulation, or at least the specter of regulation. Historically, Americans and American media companies have valued self-regulation, or "governance without government," a model in which industries self-regulate, that is, "establish agreements, standards, codes of conduct or audit programs that address all firms of a particular industry with varying degrees of formalization and bindingness."[19] Self-regulation is a form of "private government" in that industry insiders retain control by enacting "self-imposed and voluntarily accepted rules of behavior," thereby preventing the loss of control to an external agent, in this case the government.[20] Self-regulation shielded the government from criticisms about news manufacturing and suppression American leaders so often lobbied at fascist and communist regimes, especially during the Cold War.[21] Although self-regulation may result from governmental regulatory threats, it is important to note that self-regulation is "never fully controlled by public authorities." Self-regulation is driven by private industry's "interest in shaping the rules that they depend on and by the public-sector's interest in delegating or leveraging regulatory powers in the face of formidable regulatory challenges."[22] In other words, industry executives like self-regulatory practices because they can set their own rules; legislators like it because it allows them the power to enact change, but relieves them of the responsibility or accountability for those changes.

The history of American media is an excellent example of this history of self-regulation.[23] Government has historically raised the specter of direct media regulation during moments of moral panic about the corruptibility of citizens.[24] Time after time, through internal mechanisms media producers, distributors, and outlets walked back content deemed problematic or outrageous, shifting content on radio channels, film screens, and television broadcasts to diminish public and political outrage. The film industry, for example, faced public concern in the 1920s and 1930s about "the effect movies might have on public morals" and corrupt "political attitudes."[25] William Harrison Hays, an industry trade group leader, created an industry agreement nicknamed the Hays Code, which restricted the content of films to within culturally normed bounds and "avoided social and political issues"; Hays and others "feared that, unless the trend in pictures was curbed, the federal government would step in to censor the movies or break up the industry."[26] In the 1960s, the industry replaced the Hays Code with the Motion Picture Association of America (MPAA) film rating system, a citizen empowerment mechanism designed so consumers could self-select content. The film industry, thus, effectively staved off government regulation through self-regulating content and through empowering citizens to make informed choices.

The fake news panic was heavily influenced by similar fears of citizen corruptibility surrounding the 2016 presidential election, questions about the potential influence of Russian online disinformation campaigns,[27] questions about how (or if) citizens might vet information, and questions about how (or if) platforms might control information online. Social media and search engines like Google were singled out in particular because their "proprietary 'black box' technologies, including opaque filtering, ranking, and recommendation algorithms, mediate access to information at the mass (e.g., group) and micro (e.g., individual) communication levels."[28] Up to 126 million Facebook users could have viewed content created by Russian agents; Twitter identified 2,752 accounts under Russian control; Google found 1,108 suspicious videos.[29] One study showed that between February and November 2016, "fake news items received 8.7 million 'engagements'" on Facebook while "'real news' received 7.3 million."[30] Political leaders judged the agents as responsible for solving the problem because social media and search companies controlled the black box systems that in turn controlled the "misinformation ecosystems."[31] At the same time, only about 20 percent of the accounts spreading fake news were animated bot accounts, meaning that most of the accounts appeared to belong to humans."[32] Fake news was presented as an *internet problem* and a *news problem*, but also a *human* problem. Indeed, as media scholar Jonathan Albright wrote, "social interaction is at the center of the 'fake news' debate."[33] In the fake news debate, familiar fears about citizen corruptibility mixed with long-standing cultural anxieties about the internet.

Fake News as a National Security Challenge

Following historical patterns, public outrage caused concerned political leaders to investigate fake news, in particular where it came from and how it spread. Members of Congress took their job seriously, presenting their investigation as high-stakes. In his opening remarks at the Senate judiciary subcommittee investigation, Senator Lindsey Graham said, "This is the national security challenge of the 21st Century."[34] These and other investigations resulted in calls for regulation, most of which focused on internet technologies.[35] And, following historical patterns, industries began to self-regulate. Legacy news industries and social media industries reacted differently. Legacy news agencies focused on defending their news products through transparency initiatives and on promoting media literacy. Transparency initiatives informed the public about the news-gathering process. For example, in January 2016, the *Washington Post* published "Policies and Standards," which detailed the organization's seven principles for conduct, ethics policy, fact-checking standards, and source and attribution policy, with the goal of "clarity in our dealings with sources and readers."[36] Literacy initiatives included the development of websites to help news consumers self-regulate their information diets. The *New York Times*, for example, rolled out a guide to citizens to help them protect themselves from fake news, to "determine the reliability of sources."[37] Such initiatives received support from scholars advocating for the integration of media literacy training into educational curricula, such as those who wrote that fake news in particular made media literacy "vital to the future of democracy in the United States" if expanded to take into account the nature of online economics and the "emerging spreadable ecosystem for information."[38]

These self-regulation, transparency, and citizen empowerment strategies made sense in that these solutions follow a path similar to that of the film industry. Legacy news industries self-regulated their content by making the process of news gathering more vigilant and transparent and by deploying citizen empowerment measures. Leveraging these market solutions has thus far shielded them from government regulation. These solutions also allowed legacy news agencies to mark the fake news problem as not a problem with news industries themselves and thereby push back at Trump's accusations. These solutions allowed news industries to mark the fake news problem as a problem of noise in the news ecology. This solution also worked to drive traffic back to legacy news. As an article in the *Seattle Times* in 2017 noted, "Infowars.com alone is roughly equivalent in visitors and page views to the *Chicago Tribune*."[39] But, like the self-regulation of the film industry, these solutions served regulators as well. Government regulators could present themselves as having pushed but not regulated news media industries, an important distinction since regulation in general, but especially media, remained taboo in the above-mentioned American watchdog narratives. Instead, regulators could be "change makers" who sparked market solutions that empowered citizens. And legislators understood the value of transparency as a regulatory mechanism. As legal scholar Cass Sunstein noted, transparency regulation, or "regulation through disclosure," has been "one of the most striking developments in the last generation of American law."[40]

Social media outlets were slower than legacy news organizations to react. Mark Zuckerberg's initial reaction to charges that fake news on Facebook influenced the election was to name it a "crazy idea."[41] Still, by November 2016, the founder of Facebook posted on his Facebook page that his company would "take misinformation seriously" and was working on plans for, among others, "stronger detection," "easy reporting," and "disrupting fake news economics."[42] Shortly thereafter, in December 2016, Facebook announced that it would allow users to report fake news by clicking the story and choosing "It's a fake news story."[43] In August 2017, it announced that it created a new algorithm to flag stories and divert them to third-party fact-checkers.[44] Companies such as Google also funded an initiative to "flag fake news online and remove posts if they are found to violate the companies' terms of use or local laws."[45] These flagging methods were also a type of transparency initiative, one called "participatory transparency," a system in which a "community of third parties" acts as "an autonomous body."[46] They addressed concerns about the role of internet technologies in the fake news problem by creating a new algorithm, providing a technological solution to the technological problem, and addressed concerns about the role of users in the process by providing a system of flagging.

Facebook's plan met mixed reviews. One the one hand, the plan received accolades for using crowdsourcing techniques to empower users and for using external evaluation systems for transparently judging the materials.[47] On the other hand, some claimed the system worked too slowly and questioned Facebook's motives in creating these systems, which were critiqued as more about solving the publicity problem than the actual problem.[48] One former operations manager, Sandy Parakilas, wrote in the *New York Times* that when he was at Facebook, "the typical reaction" was to "try to put any negative press coverage to bed as quickly as possible, with no sincere efforts to put safeguards in place or to identify and stop abusive developers" because the company "just wanted negative stories to stop." Parakilas remarked that "lawmakers shouldn't allow Facebook to regulate itself. Because it won't. ... The company won't protect us by itself, and nothing less than our democracy is at stake."[49]

Technological Solutionism

These platform self-regulation solutions engaged by Facebook made sense given the cultural history of what media scholar Evgeny Morozov has called "solutionism," the idea dominating Silicon Valley that "recasts" complex problems either as "neatly defined problems with definite, computable solutions" or as "transparent and self-evident processes that can be easily optimized—if only the right algorithms are in place."[50] In short, it is the idea that technology can and should solve humanity's problems. Technological solutionism played heavily in the fake news regulation conversation in part because fake news was understood as a technological problem or, at the very least, as a social problem solvable by technology.

These technological solutions emerged in American cultural and historical contexts, explaining why they contrast with the solutions that emerged elsewhere. In Europe, government emerged as a solution to the problem. In Brussels, the East StratCom team "serves as Europe's front line against this onslaught of fake news"; this team of diplomats, former journalists, and government employees "tracks down reports to determine whether they are fake," researches them, and then "debunks the stories for hapless readers."[51] Similar European Union state agencies emerged in Finland and the

Czech Republic.[52] In Germany, legislators discussed the option of fining American technology companies such as Google and Facebook for allowing "false stories to be quickly circulated."[53] These kinds of solutions did not make common sense in the United States, where the federal government had a public approval rate of 25 percent and technology companies had an approval rate of 71 percent.[54] Fixing this problem directly with government agencies or initiatives was not a viable option for political leaders. A direct government solution as emerged in Europe was not what Paul Pierson and Theda Skocpol would call the "path not taken" in the United States.[55] It was the path not even considered.

Conclusion

This chapter illustrated the ways that the U.S. fake news crisis found its roots in larger American cultural understandings of news media, government, and technology. These cultural understandings helped shape the fake news problem as primarily an internet problem that would result in the corruption of citizens. Solutions such as flagging, content moderation, and news consumer guides were put forward as solutions only because the problem was defined as primarily a technological one and because the history of media in the United States has been one dominated by self-regulation and reliance on market solutions to problems over government intervention. Longer historical and cultural contexts of self-regulation and technological solutionism illustrated that the self-regulatory efforts put forward by internet platforms and legacy news industries "make sense" because these solutions continued the pattern of market (not government) regulation and because they perpetuated the illusion that technology is the best solution to humanity's problems, in particular when contrasted with government. Ultimately, the fake news crisis was both a point of historical disjuncture and continuity, although generally understood as only the former. It was embedded in the conflicting history of American faith in and fear of technology.

Notes

1. Olivia Solon, "Barack Obama on Fake News," *The Guardian*, November 17, 2016, https://www.theguardian.com/media/2016/nov/17/barack-obama-fake-news-facebook -social-media; Jordan Taylor, "Why Trump's Assault on NBC and 'Fake News' Threatens

Freedom of the Press—and His Political Future," *Washington Post*, October 12, 2017, https://www.washingtonpost.com/news/made-by-history/wp/2017/10/12/why-trumps -assault-on-nbc-and-fake-news-threatens-freedom-of-the-press-and-his-political-future/.

2. Uri Friedman, "The Real-World Consequences of 'Fake News,'" *The Atlantic*, December 23, 2017, https://www.theatlantic.com/international/archive/2017/12 /trump-world-fake-news/548888/; Tom Standage, "The True History of Fake News," *The Economist*, June/July 2017, https://www.1843magazine.com/technology/rewind /the-true-history-of-fake-news. Also see John Corner, "Fake News, Post-Truth and Media-Political Change," *Media, Culture and Society* 39, no. 7 (2017): 1100–1107.

3. Among Americans surveyed, 62 percent view fake news as a serious problem with significant impacts on America. Amy Mitchell, Jesse Holcomb, and Michael Barthel, "Many Americans Believe Fake News Is Sowing Confusion," Pew Research Center, December 15, 2016, http://www.journalism.org/2016/12/15/many-americans-believe -fake-news-is-sowing-confusion/. Survey data show that 47 percent of respondents said fake news was "sloppy or biased reporting," 39 percent said it was "an insult being over-used to discredit news stories," and 15 percent called it "a Russian weapon to disrupt democracies" or a "political dirty trick." Friedman, "The Real-World Conse-quences." For a summary of conflated terms, see Caroline Jack, "Lexicon of Lies," Data and Society, August 9, 2017, https://datasociety.net/output/lexicon-of-lies/.

4. Karma Chavez, "Common Sense, Conservative Coalitions and the Rhetoric of the HIV+ Immigration Ban" (keynote presented at the Southern Colloquium on Rheto-ric, Fayetteville, AR, October 5, 2017).

5. Elizabeth Dwoskin, "Twitter Is Looking for Ways to Let Users Flag Fake News," *Washington Post*, June 29, 2017, https://www.washingtonpost.com/news/the-switch /wp/2017/06/29/twitter-is-looking-for-ways-to-let-users-flag-fake-news/; Casey Newton, "Facebook Is Patenting a Tool That Could Help Automate Removal of Fake News," The Verge, December 7, 2016, https://www.theverge.com/2016/12/7/13868650/facebook -fake-news-patent-tool-machine-learning-content; Alicia Shepard, "A Savvy News Consumer's Guide: How Not to Get Duped," *Moyers and Company*, December 9, 2016, http://billmoyers.com/story/savvy-news-consumers-guide-not-get-duped/.

6. Victor Pickard, "Media Reform as Democratic Reform," in *Strategies for Media Reform*, ed. Des Freedman, Jonathan Obar, Cheryl Martens, and Robert McChesney (New York: Fordham University Press, 2016), 211.

7. Joanna Burkhardt, "Combating Fake News in the Digital Era," *Library Technology Reports*, November/December 2017, 10–13. For more contemporary examples, see Edward Herman, "Fake News on Russia and Other Official Enemies," *Monthly Review*, July–August 2017, 98–111.

8. Taylor, "Trump's Assault."

9. Ibid.

10. Leo Marx, *The Machine in the Garden* (Oxford: Oxford University Press, 2000).

11. Stephanie Ricker Schulte, "United States Digital Service: How 'Obama's Startup' Harnesses Disruption and Productive Failure to Reboot Government," *International Journal of Communication* 12 (2018): 131–151; Michael X. Delli Carpini and Bruce Williams, "Let Us Infotain You: Politics in the New Media Age," in *Mediated Politics: Communication in the Future of Democracy*, ed. by W. Lance Bennett and Robert Entman (Cambridge: Cambridge University Press, 2001), 160–181.

12. Stephanie Ricker Schulte, *Cached: Decoding the Internet in Global Popular Culture* (New York: New York University Press, 2013).

13. Danny Westneat, "The Information War Is Real, and We're Losing It," *Seattle Times*, March 29, 2017, https://www.seattletimes.com/seattle-news/politics/uw-professor-the-information-war-is-real-and-were-losing-it/.

14. Starbird, quoted in ibid.

15. Laura Hazard Owen, "Fake News Might Be the Next Issue for Activist Tech-Company Investors," Nieman Lab, June 2, 2017, http://www.niemanlab.org/2017/06/fake-news-might-be-the-next-issue-for-activist-tech-company-investors/.

16. Yen Nee Lee, "Trump and GOP Attack CNN, New York Times and Washington Post in 'Fake News Awards,'" CNBC, January 17, 2018, https://www.cnbc.com/2018/01/17/fake-news-awards-by-donald-trump-gop-cnn-new-york-times-washington-post.html.

17. Christian Christensen, "WikiLeaks and 'Indirect' Media Reform," in Freedman et al., *Strategies for Media Reform*, 58–71.

18. Priscilla Meddaugh, "Bakhtin, Colbert, and the Center of Discourse: Is There No 'Truthiness' in Humor?," *Critical Studies in Media Communication* 27, no. 4 (2010): 376–390.

19. Reinhard Steurer, "Disentangling Governance: A Synoptic View of Regulation by Government, Business and Civil Society," *Policy Sciences* 46, no. 4 (2013): 395.

20. Jean Boddewyn, "Advertising Self-Regulation: True Purpose and Limits," *Journal of Advertising* 18, no. 2 (1989): 20.

21. Doris Graber and Johanna Dunaway, *Mass Media and American Politics* (Los Angeles: Sage, 2015).

22. Tony Porter and Karsten Ronit, "Self-Regulation as Policy Process: The Multiple and Criss-Crossing Stages of Private Rule-Making," *Policy Sciences* 39, no. 1 (2006): 67.

23. Pickard, "Media Reform."

24. Clayton Koppes and Gregory Black, *Hollywood Goes to War: How Politics, Profits, and Propaganda Shaped World War II Movies* (Berkley: University of California Press, 1987).

25. Ibid., 12–13.

26. Ibid., 14.

27. Jim Rutenberg, "RT, Sputnik and Russia's New Theory of War," *New York Times Magazine*, September 13, 2017, https://www.nytimes.com/2017/09/13/magazine/rt -sputnik-and-russias-new-theory-of-war.html.

28. Jonathan Albright, "Welcome to the Era of Fake News," *Media and Communication* 5, no. 2 (2017): 87–88; Albright cites Frank Pasquale, *The Black Box Society: The Secret Algorithms That Control Money and Information* (Cambridge, MA: Harvard University Press, 2016).

29. Hamza Shaban, Craig Timberg, and Elizabeth Dwoskin, "Facebook, Google and Twitter Testified on Capitol Hill," *Washington Post*, October 31, 2017, https://www .washingtonpost.com/news/the-switch/wp/2017/10/31/facebook-google-and-twitter -are-set-to-testify-on-capitol-hill-heres-what-to-expect/.

30. Corner, "Fake News," 1102.

31. Ibid.

32. Rutenberg, "RT, Sputnik."

33. Albright, "Era of Fake News," 87.

34. Shaban, Timberg, and Dwoskin, "Facebook, Google and Twitter."

35. Elizabeth MacBride, "Should Facebook, Google Be Regulated? A Groundswell in Tech, Politics and Small Business Says Yes," *Forbes*, November 18, 2017, https:// www.forbes.com/sites/elizabethmacbride/2017/11/18/should-twitter-facebook-and -google-be-more-regulated/; Edward Herman, "Fake News on Russia and Other Official Enemies," *Monthly Review*, July–August 2017, 109.

36. Washington Post Staff, "Policies and Standards," *Washington Post*, January 1, 2016, https://www.washingtonpost.com/policies-and-standards/.

37. Katherine Schulten, "Skills and Strategies: Fake News vs. Real News; Determining the Reliability of Sources," *New York Times*, October 2, 2015, https://learning.blogs .nytimes.com/2015/10/02/skills-and-strategies-fake-news-vs-real-news-determining -the-reliability-of-sources.

38. Paul Mihailidis and Samantha Viotty. "Spreadable Spectacle in Digital Culture: Civic Expression, Fake News, and the Role of Media Literacies in 'Post-Fact' Society," *American Behavioral Scientist* 61, no. 4 (2017): 450.

39. Westneat, "The Information War."

40. Cass Sunstein, "Informational Regulation and Informational Standing: Akins and Beyond," *University of Pennsylvania Law Review* 147 (1999): 613 and 635.

41. Shaban, Timberg, and Dwoskin, "Facebook, Google and Twitter."

42. Zuckerberg, Facebook, November 18, 2016, https://www.facebook.com/zuck /posts/10103269806149061.

43. Bill Chappel, "Facebook Details Its New Plan to Combat Fake News Stories," NPR, December 15, 2016, https://www.npr.org/sections/thetwo-way/2016/12/15 /505728377/facebook-details-its-new-plan-to-combat-fake-news-stories.

44. Andrew Bloomberg, "Facebook Has a New Plan to Curb 'Fake News," *Fortune*, August 3, 2017, http://fortune.com/2017/08/03/facebook-fake-news-algorithm/.

45. Mark Scott and Melissa Eddy, "Europe Combats a New Foe of Political Stability: Fake News," *New York Times*, February 20, 2017, https://www.nytimes.com/2017/02 /20/world/europe/europe-combats-a-new-foe-of-political-stability-fake-news.html.

46. Stephan Dreyer and Lennart Ziebarth, "Participatory Transparency in Social Media Governance: Combining Two Good Practices," *Journal of Information Policy* 4 (2014): 533.

47. Davey Alba, "Facebook Finally Gets Real about Fighting Fake News," *Wired*, December 15, 2016, https://www.wired.com/2016/12/facebook-gets-real-fighting-fake-news/.

48. On the system's slowness, see Madison Kircher, "Facebook's Tactics to Stop Fake News Work (After It's Already Been Spreading for 3 Days)," *New York*, October 12, 2017, http://nymag.com/selectall/2017/10/facebook-fake-news-flag-works-but-takes -3-days.html.

49. Sandy Parakilas, "We Can't Trust Facebook to Regulate Itself," *New York Times*, November 19, 2017, https://www.nytimes.com/2017/11/19/opinion/facebook-regu lation-incentive.html.

50. Evgeny Morozov, *To Save Everything, Click Here: The Folly of Technological Solutionism* (New York: Public Affairs, 2013), 5.

51. Scott and Eddy, "Europe Combats a New Foe."

52. Ibid.

53. Ibid.

54. Pew Research Center, "Beyond Distrust: How Americans View Their Government," November 23, 2015, http://www.people-press.org/2015/11/23/11-how-govern ment-compares-with-other-national-institutions/.

55. Paul Pierson and Theda Skocpol, "Historical Institutionalism in Contemporary Political Science," in *Political Science: State of the Discipline*, ed. Ira Katznelson and Helen Milner (New York: W. W. Norton, 2002), 693–721.

11   The Scourge of Disinformation-Assisted Hate Propaganda

Cherian George

In early 2017, the governor of Jakarta, Indonesia, was ousted with the aid of disinformation-fueled hate propaganda, a practice that has become an alarmingly common feature of democratic politics. Assailed by accusations that he had insulted Islam, Basuki Tjahaja Purnama not only was defeated in an election that he had been expected to win, but also was convicted of blasphemy and sentenced to two years in jail. Basuki, an ethnic Chinese Christian, had long been dogged by opponents' carping that he should not be in charge of the predominantly Muslim country's capital city. In September 2016, the plain-speaking politician retorted that voters were welcome to vote against him if they believed his opponents' lies that the Quran prohibits Muslims from electing non-Muslims. This impetuous remark was swiftly twisted by his opponents to make it seem as if the governor had claimed that the Quran itself was deceiving the people. This incendiary mischaracterization was aided by a genuine video of Basuki with crucial words omitted from the subtitles, posted online with a provocative caption. Hardliners seized on the episode to mobilize major protests that culminated in Basuki's defeat in April 2017 and his conviction the following month.

Governor of a city of 10 million in the world's third-largest democracy, Basuki's is possibly one of the biggest scalps to have been claimed by disinformation-aided hate propaganda, a particularly distressing genre of what is loosely called "fake news." Here, the term *disinformation* refers to falsehoods that are deliberately manufactured and circulated with an intent to mislead.[1] Hate, in the sense used here, refers to expression that disparages a whole community of people based on identity, such as race, religion, nationality, immigrant status, caste, gender, sexual orientation, and so on.[2] I am referring here to hate not as a psychological state, but as a strategy of political contenders who, while certainly exploiting individual-level emotions of their followers, are themselves guided by cold calculation.[3] Hate campaigns are a communication strategy of groups engaged in territorial conquests, genocides, pogroms, and other crimes against humanity and have been used throughout history. In less extreme cases, they scapegoat vulnerable minorities in order to activate fear and harness identity politics as a means to accumulate power. Hate campaigns invariably incorporate disinformation—deliberately deceptive content ranging from outright lies and fabrications to the use of misleading frames, selectivity in the presentation of facts, and misrepresenting context to show people and events in a false light.

Few speech situations cry out more strongly for public intervention than hate propaganda. When dealing with such expression, liberal faith in the marketplace of ideas tends to be misplaced. The communities targeted by such campaigns are often politically, economically, and culturally weak; they suffer historical handicaps that prevent them from protecting their rights in open competition with opponents who wish them harm. This structural imbalance is acknowledged in international human rights law and most democratic constitutions. The International Covenant on Civil and Political Rights, in article 20, requires states to prohibit by law "[a]ny advocacy of national, racial or religious hatred that constitutes incitement to discrimination, hostility or violence."[4] Even American First Amendment doctrine, which tolerates almost no government-imposed limits on public discourse, permits regulation of direct incitement to immediate violence.[5] In the so-called media trial following the 1994 Rwandan genocide, an international tribunal found that a radio station and newspaper had inflamed hatred and instigated mobs to massacre Tutsis.[6] No major free speech advocacy group objected to the criminal convictions handed down to three executives.

While the legal and moral philosophical case for strong regulation of extreme and dangerous forms of hate speech is relatively uncontroversial, it is difficult to formulate effective policy responses to the much broader challenge of disinformation-assisted hate propaganda. There are two major conundrums to deal with: first, hate propagation is conducted through amorphous, distributed campaigns that are practically impossible for regulators to come to grips with, and, second, the most sophisticated campaigns symbolically exploit attacks against them, thus making legal challenges backfire to their advantage.[7] While this is not to say that law should not be used, it does suggest that legal prohibitions and penalties are never sufficient. Policy attention needs to shift from the supply side of hate-propagating disinformation to the demand side: how to reduce the demand for simplistic, exclusionary, and intolerant rhetoric and cultivate publics that value diversity and protect equality.

The Structure of Hate Campaigns

Unfortunately, an analyst of disinformation in hate campaigns has no shortage of historical and ongoing cases to dissect. Anti-Semitic propaganda leading up to the Holocaust included the hoax *The Protocols of the Elders of Zion*, fabricated to lend credence to the conspiracy theory about a Jewish plan for global domination. American history is replete with examples of hateful untruths disseminated in the service of power. The physical subjugation of Native Americans and then Africans required their symbolic dehumanization by politicians, scientists, theologians, writers, and artists.[8] The success of the American Revolution depended in part on the vilification of the British, including through "fake news": a 1770 skirmish in which British soldiers killed half a dozen civilians while under physical attack by a mob was transformed into the "Boston Massacre" by radical pamphleteers and lithographers to whip up public outrage.[9] Contemporary politics the world over is filled with more examples. Elaborate and influential conspiracy theories have been manufactured in the United States by the Islamophobia industry about the incursion of sharia law; in India, by the Hindu Right about Muslim men mounting "love jihad" on Hindu women and girls; in Indonesia, by Muslim hard-liners about a resurgent communist threat; and in Europe, by anti-immigrant groups against sexual predators or "rapefugees."[10]

Our attention tends to be drawn to speech that is extreme—either using language that violates social norms, such as openly racist epithets, or containing explicit calls to action, such as incitement to violence. But such expression forms only a small part of a hate campaign and does not work in a vacuum. Instead, hate campaigns comprise multiple, layered, loosely interlocking messages, disseminated by different actors over years or decades.[11] Master narratives, which usually emphasize the in-group's noble characteristics and often hark back to some mythical golden age that demonstrates the community's true potential, provide the backdrop.

Past traumas may also be highlighted, to heighten the community's sense of victimization and impending danger. A complementary master narrative portrays a particular out-group as inherently untrustworthy because of certain irredeemable cultural, religious, or ideological traits. The effect of these grand narratives is to cultivate an exclusive primary identity, a sense of belonging to a community that is both exceptionally valuable and uniquely vulnerable.

These master narratives are regularly refreshed with contemporary examples, largely from the news but also from popular culture and even scientific research. The examples are often drawn from faraway places and contexts that have little to do with the community, but they are appropriated and framed in ways that keep the group in a heightened state of anxiety. The final step is a call to action, in the form of voting for a populist leader or joining a riot against a minority, for example. Such incitement is usually pegged to a particular event in the here and now, such as a government announcement deemed as disadvantaging the in-group or the appearance of a cultural product seen as deeply offensive. The perceived provocation is treated as the last straw, requiring members of the community to rise up in defense of their values and way of life.

Structured thus, hate campaigns pose intractable regulatory conundrums. First, any attempt to police falsehoods (through fact-checking, for example) would find that much of the content of the hate propaganda is not wholly fabricated. For example, newspapers and websites intent on promoting the "rapefugee" myth can do so simply by playing up every report of an immigrant or refugee suspected of a sexual offense, each of which may be factually accurate. These stories are curated in a highly selective and often malicious manner, thus creating a distorted picture of the world; but they are not all falsifiable. Their master narratives may be even harder to contest, since they draw on myths and legends, poems and songs. Second, most of the messages making up a hate propaganda campaign do not cross the conventional threshold for hate speech (as applied by internet platforms' community standards, for example). They neither amount to direct incitement nor contain extreme language. Many statements are innocuous in isolation but inflammatory when read in context. Hindu nationalists' matter-of-fact references to population trends, for instance, are designed to dovetail with conspiracy theories about Muslims trying to take over India by marrying four wives and outproducing Hindus. It is usually not possible to hold speakers accountable for these campaigns because the messaging work is distributed across a wide network. There is a division of labor, with the most extreme language usually left to minor politicians and anonymous trolls, while the movement's leaders keep their hands clean. Think tanks and experts use pseudo-intellectual and even pseudoscientific language to give the movement's ideology a veneer of reasonableness.

A third complication is that modern hate campaigners are adept at turning the tables on any attempt to counter them. Regardless of whether the intervention succeeds in restricting their speech, they can milk the episode to demonstrate to followers that the community is under siege and in need of the kind of committed leadership that only they can provide. One example concerns the anti-Muslim hate propagandist Robert Spencer and his Jihad Watch disinformation website. When Google quite reasonably adjusted its search algorithms to promote more authoritative sites over Jihad Watch, Spencer issued statements with headlines such as "Google Bows to Muslim Pressure, Changes Search Results to Conceal Criticism of Islam and Jihad." Civil rights organizations' classification of Jihad Watch as a hate group was condemned on Fox News as an example of left-liberal bias. The calculated taking of offense in this manner is now a standard strategy of hate propagandists. Classic hate speech, openly instigating harms against a target community, is both legally and socially unacceptable in many societies. Instead of going on the attack, therefore, hate propagandists often play the victim, whipping up indignation and outrage at perceived—and often manufactured—symbolic injustices.[12]

Intervening in the Ecosystem of Hate

Societies already have at their disposal a range of possible responses to disinformation used as vehicles of hate. Criminal sanctions include laws against incitement to hatred, which exist in most democracies. Under civil law, defamation suits are sometimes an option. Self-regulation within the news media and advertising industries usually includes codes against deceiving audiences. Internet intermediaries' terms of use and community standards disallow hate speech. Fact-checking organizations flag prominent falsehoods propagated in the public arena. More resources are being poured into such efforts as a result of heightened concern about how disinformation has undermined democratic processes. Internet companies, in particular, are under pressure to modify their algorithms and protocols to reward more authoritative information providers and disincentivize the deliberate circulation of falsehoods through their platforms.

While many of these moves are necessary, it is important to recognize their limitations. They tend to treat disinformation as discrete messages that can be picked off, sniper-style, by lawyers, moderators, fact-checkers, and other gatekeepers and regulators.

But, the most powerful "fake news" deceptions are not usually made up of neatly self-contained messages. For example, the well-documented misperception among most Americans that crime has been rising cannot be attributed solely to election candidates' "pants-on-fire" lies, but is also due to selective but factual reporting by news media as well as fictional depictions of violence in entertainment media.[13] Similarly, hate campaigns comprise disaggregated collections of historical narratives, tropes about being and belonging, stereotypes about the other, and curated streams of news and opinion that reinforce favored ideologies. Viewed singly, most of these messages may not cross any regulatory threshold; it is in the audience's heads that they combine to harmful effect.

If this is what societies are up against, much more attention needs to be paid to the demand side of hate campaigns. From a psychological perspective, the behavioral sciences are shedding light on people's observed preference for untruths, even after their falsity is objectively exposed. Among the reasons is people's need to protect their identities,[14] which in turn raises the question of why certain identities—race, language, and religion, in particular—seem much easier to activate than others, such as class and, ultimately, humanity. From a political perspective, it is the relative ease with which leaders can mobilize collective action around tribal loyalties that helps explain why would-be demagogues opt for identity politics over appeals to reason. The human species has millennia's worth of practice in caring for members of one's family, village, or tribe; but the idea that a duty of care should be extended to all strangers since everyone has inalienable human rights is barely a century old.[15] At the core of most situations in which disinformation-assisted hate propaganda is causing havoc is this lag in societal conscience. Even democracies founded on modern civic nationalism, where citizenship is based on this shared principle and not identity, have found themselves pressured to revert to more primitive racial or religious nationalisms. The battle to combat hate propaganda is part of this much larger contest between competing visions of nationhood and constitutional order.

Notes

1. Claire Wardle, "Fake News. It's Complicated," First Draft, February 16, 2017, https://firstdraftnews.org/fake-news-complicated/.

2. Cees J. Hamelink, *Media and Conflict: Escalating Evil* (Boulder, CO: Paradigm Publishers, 2011); Jeremy Waldron, *The Harm in Hate Speech* (Cambridge, MA: Harvard University Press, 2012).

3. Ria Kirk Whillock, "The Use of Hate as a Stratagem for Achieving Social and Political Goals," in *Hate Speech*, ed. Rita Kirk Whillock and David Slayden (Thousand Oaks, CA: Sage, 1995), 28–54.

4. United Nations Office of the High Commissioner for Human Rights, International Covenant on Civil and Political Rights, 1996, http://www.ohchr.org/en/profes sionalinterest/pages/ccpr.aspx.

5. Robert Post, "Hate Speech," In *Extreme Speech and Democracy*, ed. Ivan Hare and James Weinstein (Oxford: Oxford University Press, 2009), 123–138.

6. Article 19, *Broadcasting Genocide: Censorship, Propaganda and State-Sponsored Violence in Rwanda 1990–1994* (London: Article 19, 1995), http://www.article19.org /pdfs/publications/rwanda-broadcasting-genocide.pdf.

7. Cherian George, *Hate Spin: The Manufacture of Religious Offense and Its Threat to Democracy* (Cambridge, MA: MIT Press, 2016).

8. Alexander Tsesis, *Destructive Messages: How Hate Speech Paves the Way for Harmful Social Movements* (New York: New York University Press, 2002).

9. Peter Messer, "'A Scene of Villainy Acted by a Dirty Banditti, as Must Astonish the Public': The Creation of the Boston Massacre," *New England Quarterly* 90, no. 4 (2017): 502–539, https://doi.org/10.1162/tneq_a_00639.

10. Katherine Lemons and Joshua Takano Chambers-Letson, "Rule of Law: Sharia Panic and the US Constitution in the House of Representatives," *Cultural Studies* 28, nos. 5–6 (2014): 1048–1077, https://doi.org/10.1080/09502386.2014.886486; Mohan Rao, "Love Jihad and Demographic Fears," *Indian Journal of Gender Studies* 18, no. 3 (2011): 425–430, https://doi.org/10.1177/097152151101800307; Stephen Miller, "Zombie Anti-Communism? Democratization and the Demons of Suharto-Era Politics in Contemporary Indonesia," in *The Indonesian Genocide of 1965*, ed. Katharine McGregor, Jess Melvin, and Annie Pohlman, Palgrave Studies in the History of Genocide (Cham, Switzerland: Palgrave Macmillan, 2018), 287–310, https://doi.org/10.1007/978-3-319-71455-4_15; Der Spiegel Staff, "Fact-Check: Is

There Truth to Refugee Rape Reports?," *Spiegel Online*, January 17, 2018, http://www
.spiegel.de/international/germany/is-there-truth-to-refugee-sex-offense-reports-a
-1186734.html.

11. George, *Hate Spin*.

12. Ibid.

13. John Gramlich, "Voters' Perceptions of Crime Continue to Conflict with Reality," Pew Research Center, November 16, 2016, http://www.pewresearch.org/fact
-tank/2016/11/16/voters-perceptions-of-crime-continue-to-conflict-with-reality/.

14. Dan M. Kahan, "The Politically Motivated Reasoning Paradigm, Part 1: What
Politically Motivated Reasoning Is and How to Measure It," in *Emerging Trends in
the Social and Behavioral Sciences*, ed. Robert Scott and Stephen Kosslyn (Hoboken,
NJ: John Wiley and Sons, 2017), 1–16, https://doi.org/10.1002/9781118900772
.etrds0417.

15. Eric Posner, *The Twilight of Human Rights Law* (New York: Oxford University
Press, 2014).

12 Fake News and Open Channels of Communication

Paul Levinson

The destruction on the Weimar Republic (1919–1933) at the hands of the Nazis is a well-known and tragically significant story. Beset by a de facto alliance of Nazis, Communists, and monarchists—unlikely bedfellows whose only commonality was a loathing of democracy—the republic (the official name of which was Deutsches Reich, or German Realm) didn't stand a chance.

The television series *Babylon Berlin* (2017–2018) presents a dramatically accurate snapshot of this state of affairs in 1929. The bedrocks of democracy, including freedom of speech, were present, if not well established, in the Weimar Republic. Article 118 of its constitution provided that "no censorship will take place," though motion pictures were exempted from this protection (mirroring *Mutual Film Corporation v. Industrial Commission of Ohio*, 1915, in which the United States Supreme Court held that motion pictures were not protected by the First Amendment—a decision not overturned by the Supreme Court until *Joseph Burstyn, Inc. v. Wilson* in 1952). The Nazis attained a plurality (33 percent) in the Reichstag in 1932, President Paul von Hindenburg appointed Hitler chancellor a year later, and in 1934 Hitler declared himself führer and assumed absolute power. Fundamental to the Nazi ascension of power and subsequent governing was an all-out attack on all media, especially conveyors of news. The attack began in the 1920s with shouts of *Lügenpresse*—"lying press"—at Nazi rallies.[1] Undermining the public's confidence in a foundation of democracy proved to be an effective first step in removing it completely.

Hitler's hatred of the press was also expressed in his preference for radio, which allowed him to address the German people without journalistic intermediaries, who, he was sure, deliberately distorted his message.[2] In the United States beginning in 2016, Donald Trump has apparently found the same freedom from journalistic interpretation in Twitter, and has used it the same way as Hitler used radio.[3]

And since January 2017, Trump has also denounced the press as "fake," every chance he gets. We have no monarchists here in the United States. Communist and radical-left adherents are relatively small in number. Nazis and white supremacists are more numerous, but neither are likely, even combined, to topple our republic. But Trump's attack on the press as fake news, from his powerful position as president, may be one of the greatest threats to democracy our nation has ever encountered, and needs to be taken seriously.

Real Fake News

Before looking at how Trump has adopted the fake news moniker as a weapon to undermine reporting of real news, we need to understand what fake news really is.

To begin with, it's not just news reports that are factually incorrect or in error. That happens all the time, in all news media, and is why the *New York Times* has a "corrections" column (which used to be called "errata"). The *New York Times* publishes errors all the time—usually here and there in one or more articles, sometimes systematically, as in Jayson Blair's years of concocted articles replete with made-up interviews, revealed in 2003. But does this mean, then, as Trump has often bellowed, that the *New York Times* is "fake news"? (For example, "The failing @nytimes does major FAKE NEWS China story saying 'Mr. Xi has not spoken to Mr. Trump since Nov.14.' We spoke at length yesterday!").[4] Not unless we believed that the newspaper deliberately published Blair's fabrications, and every other news story with errors, knowing full well they were errors.

But some people apparently do believe this. A recent survey reports that 17 percent of Americans "strongly agree" that the "*New York Times* regularly reports made up or fake news about Trump and his administration," in contrast to 17 percent who "strongly disagree," 27 percent with "no opinion," and the rest in the middle.[5] Bill O'Reilly, in a recent interview with me, explained that the *New York Times* "couldn't care less about seeking the truth. They take their orders from their corporate masters"[6]—in other words, nothing, according to O'Reilly, is worthy of belief in the *New York*

Times, and the errors are deliberate, that is, distortions dictated by "corporate masters."

The notion that nothing is reliable in the news media is as extreme—and, to some people, as self-evident and even comforting as a guide to political life—as the other end of the continuum, the naive view that everything we read in a newspaper or see on a TV news show is true. Yet how do we combat these views with a recognition that some of the news we receive is incorrect, but most of it is not deliberately deceitful, which is the hallmark of fake news?

Combating the Extremes

I've often said that the famous tagline of the *New York Times*—"All the news that's fit to print"—is a deliberate distortion. No news medium, including the *New York Times*, ever publishes all of the news, or has any way of intrinsically identifying what news is "fit to print" and what news is not. Instead, the news editors make decisions about what to print, where to place the story in the newspaper (front page or wherever), how long the article should be, and other considerations. A more truthful logo for the *New York Times* would therefore be "All the news that we deem fit to print." Similarly, the iconic newscaster Walter Cronkite ended his nightly news reports on CBS-TV with a gravitic "And that's the way it is," but he would have been truthful had he concluded with something along the lines of "And that's the way a small group of editors here at CBS thought you should think it was." But acknowledging such distortions does not mean that nothing reported in the *New York Times* or on the *CBS Evening News* is true. How, then, can we ascertain whether a given story is true or not?

I first thought about this problem a long time ago, when John F. Kennedy was assassinated in 1963 and I was sixteen years old. How did I know that JFK had really been killed? The answer seemed obvious and clear back then, and still does today: consult other media. If every newspaper and radio newscast and TV newscast is reporting the same thing, then that makes it likely that the reports are true. To believe otherwise would be to posit that all media were in some sort of conspiracy to deceive us. Back in 1963, I reasoned that maybe that was so in the Soviet Union, but not here in the United States, or in any free, democratic society.

Note, however, that the number of media that report the same thing
need to be more than just a handful—they should be myriad and legion
as evidence of truth. When I received the final page proofs for my novel
The Plot to Save Socrates, the proofreader had a query for me: was I sure that
Charles Darwin had actually visited the home of William Henry Appleton
in New York (as I had mentioned offhand in the novel). Yes, I said to myself,
I was sure. I knew I had seen that online. I then confirmed it on at least
half a dozen sites. But something about the query bothered me. So I looked
in one of the books I had about Darwin in my home library, and, lo and
behold, it said there in plain English on page 94 that Darwin had never
been to the United States.[7] I checked several other biographies of Darwin on
my bookshelf, and they concurred. The proofreader had been right!

But why, then, did so many online sites say otherwise? I discovered that
the error had originated with the Wave Hill website (Wave Hill, now a public garden, had been Appleton's home), and the other sites had simply copied the wording from the Wave Hill site, without verifying the information.
There was nothing controversial about Darwin visiting America, so none of
these other sites thought they had any reason to check the Wave Hill site's
facts.

Today, we have vastly more sites where facts can be checked on the internet, and they're much more easily reached.

Where We Go from Here

The plethora of online news and information sites, reachable twenty-four
hours a day, from almost anywhere in the world, via any laptop or smart-
phone, provides access not only to accurate news reporting but also to
incorrect reporting due to accident, corporate bias, or just plain deliberate
falsehood born of politics or a malicious desire to mislead, also known as
fake news. But it would be an error to say that the myriad of sources is both
a blessing and a curse, and leave it that, because the ability to check any
news story, in as many places as you like, is the ultimate antidote to fake
news, whether it appears in newspapers, on cable news shows, or somewhere online.

But this in turn means that we must take special precautions to make
sure that these sources of legitimate news are not undermined, whether
by Trump's and O'Reilly's denunciations or, much more insidiously, by

well-meaning (and not so well-meaning) attempts of government to address the problem of fake news by regulation of social media.

As I've written in many places, we are fortunate in the United States to have a First Amendment that flatly prohibits any government regulation of speech and press.[8] Unfortunately, this prohibition has all too often been ignored (as in the 1978 United States Supreme Court case *Federal Communications Commission v. Pacifica Foundation*, in which government threatening of WBAI-FM Radio was upheld). But its value has never been more paramount than in this, our age of fake news. Even O'Reilly and Trump don't allege that all media are engaged in a conspiracy to report false information. But were our government to any way control news reporting in social media, the source of so much of our news today, the government in that one fell swoop would be enacting a conspiracy to shape the information we receive.

In the end, the best defense we have against the United States succumbing to what happened to the Weimar Republic is not that we have no monarchists in the United States or even that we in America are somehow more rational than the denizens of the Weimar Republic (because we are not— evolution does not move that quickly). The best defense is keeping all of our channels of information wide open, not only to the dissemination of fake news, but to the dissemination of truthful reporting, which, as John Milton argued in his *Areopagitica* nearly four hundred years ago, is the most reliable way of defeating falsity in the marketplace of ideas.[9]

Note that, in this schema, a prevalence of falsity in the marketplace is not an insurmountable problem. As long as truth exists somewhere, in a place where people can find it, that one true statement will be recognized as such by our rationality. This persistence of rationality in the face of fake news was experimentally demonstrated by John G. Bullock, Alan S. Gerber, Seth J. Hill, and Gregory A. Huber, who found that subjects identified truthful news reports as such even when these reports contradicted the subjects' political biases, if a small financial incentive was provided for identifying the truth.[10] This suggests that belief in fake news is a lazy luxury that can be easily cracked.

To return to Milton's point, the ultimate threat would then be not too much fake news and falsity, but too little truth available to refute it. We all, therefore, must make our best efforts to ensure that truthful news reports, also known as honest journalism, are never limited or extinguished, by intention or well-meaning accident.

Notes

1. See Victoria Saker Woeste, "The Anti-Semitic Origins of the War on 'Fake News,'" *Washington Post*, September 5, 2017, https://www.washingtonpost.com/news/made-by-history/wp/2017/09/05/the-anti-semitic-origins-of-the-war-on-fake-news/.

2. See Paul Levinson, *The Soft Edge: A Natural History and Future of the Information Revolution* (New York: Routledge, 1997).

3. See Paul Levinson, *McLuhan in the Age of Social Media* (White Plains, NY: Connected Editions, 2018).

4. Donald Trump (@realDonaldTrump), "The failing @nytimes does major FAKE NEWS," Twitter, February, 10, 2017, https://twitter.com/realDonaldTrump/status/830047626414477312.

5. "How much do you agree that *The New York Times* regularly reports made up or fake news about Donald Trump and his administration?," Statista, November 2017, https://www.statista.com/statistics/784088/nyt-fake-news-trump/.

6. Paul Levinson, interview by Bill O'Reilly, *No Spin News*, May 29, 2018, https://youtu.be/Ry6bnZyRaIM.

7. Hans Schwarz, *Creation* (Grand Rapids, MI: Eerdmans, 2002).

8. See Paul Levinson "Government Regulation of Social Media Would Be a 'Cure' Far Worse than the Disease," The Conversation, November 28, 2017, https://theconversation.com/government-regulation-of-social-media-would-be-a-cure-far-worse-than-the-disease-86911; Paul Levinson, "The First Amendment in the Post-Truth Age," *The Digital Life* (blog), Garrison Institute, May 15, 2018, https://www.garrisoninstitute.org/blog/the-first-amendment-in-the-post-truth-age/.

9. John Milton, *Areopagitica* (London, 1644), https://www.bl.uk/collection-items/areopagitica-by-john-milton-1644.

10. John G. Bullock, Alan S. Gerber, Seth J. Hill, and Gregory A. Huber, "Partisan Bias in Factual Beliefs about Politics," *Quarterly Journal of Political Science* 10, no. 4 (2015): 519–578. See Paul Levinson, *Fake News in Real Context* (White Plains, NY: Connected Editions, 2018).

IV Social Media: Part Introduction

Although fake news and misinformation more generally are not new, they have the potential to spread much further thanks to social media. Each of the authors in this part looks at how ideological and political information spreads and shapes our understandings of different stories, events, public figures, or journalism itself. More specifically, the first two chapters in this part consider how platforms enable misinformation to circulate both through the way they are set up and their moderation practices. The second two chapters look at how small "bits" of information, specifically memes and Instagram posts, shared on social media shape our social and political discourses.

The first chapter in this part, "Fake News Fingerprints," is by social media scholar Dan Faltesek, who uses computational methods to look at the diffusion of fake news across two tweet-swarm case studies: accusations of Hillary Clinton's Satanism and the WikiLeaks Democratic National Committee e-mail release. Through these two case studies, Faltesek differentiates between types of misinformation—and producers of misinformation—and the ways that they operate. Faltesek ultimately concludes that preventing these kinds of bot swarms, and the misinformation they circulate, will require changes to Twitter's platform.

The second chapter in this part is by communication scholar Adrienne Massanari, "Reddit's Alt-Right: Toxic Masculinity, Free Speech, and /r/The_ Donald." Massanari examines how Reddit's culture and politics support the creation and dissemination of reactionary memes and fake news. This chapter traces specific moments in Reddit's history that have cultivated a large alt-right community welcoming to movements like #Gamergate and #Pizzagate. Massanari argues that Reddit's support of "unrestricted free speech" and its "democratic" voting system result in the normalization of fringe right-wing and antifeminist communities that spread misinformation while simultaneously undermining news organizations.

The third chapter in this part, "Fake Memetics: Political Rhetoric and Circulation in Political Campaigns" by media studies scholar Benjamin Burroughs, looks at politically charged memes and fake news during the 2016 U.S. presidential campaigns. While much debate in the wake of these campaigns has dealt with the sources of fake news and even how those stories are manufactured, little attention has focused on what makes these narratives both salient within social networks and easily digested by people. Burroughs argues that political memes are a unique site of study for the weaving of fake news and misinformation into the fabric of political discourse and, ultimately, political deliberation. By looking at how memes "stitch together" both information and social media platforms, Burroughs examines the rhetoric surrounding the employment of memes designed to create "meme magic," and looks at how political memes turn complex arguments into easily consumable mimetic bites.

The final chapter of this part, "Weaponizing #fakenews in a Visual War on Journalism: Seeing a Big Picture through Instagram," is by Leslie-Jean Thornton, who researches journalism and is a former news editor. This chapter explores Instagram posts to the wildly popular hashtag #fakenews and the delegitimation of credible news sources through emotionally appealing images, memes, and slogans targeting news organizations. Thornton traces how the Instagram #fakenews feed started out narrowly focused, but as the volume of traffic increased so did the range of #fakenews perspectives. Increasingly, the feed became the site of partisan sniping, outright propaganda, trolling, and anti-news information. Thornton argues that the combination of imagery, texts, and mode of distribution gives content published using the Instagram platform a high degree of persuasiveness in destabilizing public perceptions of news organizations.

Suggested Reading

Yochai Benkler, Robert Faris, and Hal Roberts, *Network Propaganda: Manipulation, Disinformation, and Radicalization in American Politics* (New York: Oxford University Press, 2018).

Tarleton Gillespie, *Custodians of the Internet: Platforms, Content Moderation, and the Hidden Decisions That Shape Social Media* (New Haven, CT: Yale University Press, 2018).

Kate Starbird, "Examining the Alternative Media Ecosystem through the Production of Alternative Narratives of Mass Shooting Events on Twitter" (paper presented at the International Conference on Web and Social Media, Montreal, May 15, 2017), http://faculty.washington.edu/kstarbi/Alt_Narratives_ICWSM17-CameraReady.pdf.

Siva Vaidhyanathan, *Antisocial Media: How Facebook Disconnects Us and Undermines Democracy* (New York: Oxford University Press, 2018).

Soroush Vosoughi, Deb Roy, and Sinan Aral, "The Spread of True and False News Online," *Science* 359, no. 6380 (2018): 1146–1151, http://science.sciencemag.org/content/359/6380/1146.

13   Fake News Fingerprints

Dan Faltesek

Is Chelsea Clinton a Satanist? What about Hillary Clinton, for that matter? As Susan Faludi recalled in an editorial advocating for Senator Clinton in the *New York Times*, the idea of the Clinton family, particularly Hillary Clinton, as being in league with the Devil is not new: it was among the many conspiracies floated around the 1996 Republican National Convention.[1] In the days leading up to the 2016 election, accusations of Satanism against the Clintons again appeared. The satanic canard even makes an appearance in the Robert Mueller indictment.[2] It is not surprising that thousands of tweets also made the accusation and it is even a point worthy of further investigation.

But why would someone go to the trouble of flooding an entire network with false content of moderate interest? The Satanism story has some shock value, but is easily dismissed by all but the most ardent of Clinton haters. There is a strategic purpose to the deployment of this content, and the networks that make these floods possible are detectable. This would seem to be the heart of the fake news crisis: not the confusion that one might feel on seeing a really convincing article on ClickHole or The Borowitz Report, but particularly strategic action that manipulates the formation of publics.[3]

In this chapter, I consider the dynamics of two distinct fake news stories and the networks that promoted them: the WikiLeaks Democratic National Committee (DNC) e-mail release and the accusation of Satanism. These are two distinct data sets that are useful for different reasons. WikiLeaks intervened in the election at a key point just a week before the vote; the goods it brought to the table were the e-mails of DNC chairman John Podesta. From pasta sauce to strategy, the e-mails were his.[4] Dumped en masse, this effort to intervene in the election was repeated in France during the race between Emmanuel Macron and Marine Le Pen.[5] As an example, this speaks to a standard coordinated playbook that relies on the campaign itself as an argument, with the hope that actors sifting through the data produce individual claims. The satanic data set is tiny by comparison, but useful, as the insights we can take from it are so clear, and the story itself is absurd.

To understand the fingerprints of a fake news network we need to distinguish between the types of fake news organizations and the ways that they operate. The literature reviewed in this chapter ranges from early journalism research into the meaning of fake news to election strategy, information theory, and computational work in social media. A broad view is important, as this chapter considers the decision to deploy a fake news network and the ideas necessary in that moment. After the literature review, the computational methods used in this study are documented. Each individual case is considered in an independent section, one for WikiLeaks, another for Satanism. The conclusions for the study for fake news follow.

The Fake Game

There are many ways of distinguishing between fake news, propaganda, and simple errors. Fake news is an extremely broad category. Edson C. Tandoc Jr., Zheng Wei Lim, and Richard Ling reviewed thirty-four articles, finding that the term was used to describe forms ranging from satire to advertising.[6] Better and worse fake news items were then distinguished by the propensity for a source to be based on facts or to be intentionally deceptive. As much as the strength of the archive is appreciated, the typology starts one step too far into the definition: it accepts that all material studied under the sign fake news must be fake news. A rich, internally consistent satire is not fake news, nor is an advertisement for a sale on socks. This is to say, not that a tipped news article should not be studied as fake, but that many different and platform-specific strategies are needed in this area.

Similarly, models of exposure effect prediction, as demonstrated by Hunt Allcott and Matthew Gentzkow, who rely on assumptions about the exposure to the feed producing reliable results.[7] The model of effects supposed in this research depends on the alignment of messaging. This research is important, as it is ultimately the public that votes, but it is still too far downstream, as it depends on resonance with individual voters and their fragile memories. If we look at the texts shared, rather than user perceptions, the story becomes more complicated. Considering the diffusion of stories is also important. Soroush Vosoughi, Deb Roy, and Sinan Aral use experimental methods to demonstrate that false information spreads more quickly than the truth and that botnets tend to amplify false and true stories at a similar rate.[8] The implication is that humans have an important role in amplifying falsehood. Fake news as a category is too broad, the analysis of the effects is too difficult, and the distinction between robots and people is overrated.

Rather than attempt to analyze material that would be coded as fake or non-fake, we should turn to the structure of the games that shape the maneuvers of the producers of fake news. After all, we cannot simply call the staff of the Concord Catering Company; we can only evaluate the structure in which they made critical decisions.[9] What kinds of games do they think they are playing? How do you win? What are the rules? Are there scores or pieces? It would seem reasonable to object to this line of analysis as trivializing something so important as democracy itself. The metaphor at the heart of game theory is intended, not to make light of important decisions, but to reveal how people play strategic games in everyday life. It would be difficult to imagine a campaign manager not having a game framework for his or her decision making. In the next section, I consider how information games are played and how these plays dovetail with what we already know about social media strategy.

Information Theory and Election Strategy

Elections are a powerful tool, as they produce a single winner. It is all or nothing; we can't both win. Elections in the United States amplify these dynamics with a combination of candidate-specific ballot access, winner-take-all counting, regularly scheduled elections, and two parties. In these games, players work to minimize losses. This is different from a non-zero-sum game, where players work to maximize their payoff.[10] Most important, any strategy that can prevent an adversary from winning becomes an opportunity for offense, a place to score and win the game.

To win an election, your candidate must receive the largest number of votes. This is a deceptively simple statement. It may not be entirely clear how to vote or how to interpret the documents or electronic impressions created by a voting system. There are two distinct plays, those that seek to maximize the number of voters for a candidate and those that seek to minimize votes for the other side; Donald Trump > Hillary Clinton is derived from the totals for each side of the Electoral College. Campaigns are playing both sides and often looking for strategies that have the highest probability of effect. "Get out the vote" (GOTV) operations are expensive and labor-intensive ways to secure a vote among those already with a propensity to vote.[11] Much of the strategy in this area depends on delivering reliable votes at a high yield. General efforts to turn out new or low-propensity voters are not a core strategy. Voter suppression strategies have a very high probability of effect and may appear as a key strategy for those who would seek to decrease votes for the other side. Dynamics of suppression can unfold both through formal structures and through the imaginary collectivity we call the public.

Publics form ad hoc and likely invisibly. Michael Warner's insight is critical here—members of counterpublics are engaged by attention alone.[12] The public sphere is not the collection of interest groups that would engage institutions, but the groups of people or people who imagine themselves to be a part of groups considering how they might take action. It would be much easier to research publics if we limited our studies to formal interactions, but the loss would be in the complexity of information. This perspective has been important for communication research, as it emphasizes the ephemerality of public life and the emergence of counterpublics. It is conceivable, then, that a communication strategy could be formed that would preclude the formation of rival counterpublics by flooding the channel with information for one side or that would make it impossible for a transient signal to appear. An overlooked dimension of this theory as it relates to Twitter is the emphasis on the synthetic temporality of now. Publics are magical because they are both very real and imaginary at the same time.

During media events, when publics become more literal, tweeters become retweeters: Yu-Ru Lin, Brian Keegan, Drew Margolin, and David Lazer find that during media events, the total production of new content by tweeters decreases.[13] Swarms of retweeters amplify already powerful voices. In terms of theorizing diffusion, Yini Zhang, Chris Wells, Song Wang, and Karl Rohe demonstrate the power of clusters of voices to amplify communication within Trump's network.[14] Networks have a powerful role in intermedia agenda setting: clusters, waves, cascades, and hoards that appear in the networks are likely newsworthy. Circularity ensues when the legacy coverage of the event drives social circulation. Democratization of the media seems in reach, as new voices, if attached to a cascade, could drive legacy coverage. They describe research in this area as developing a new paradigm for the study of amplification, and this chapter could be read as a contribution to such a project. This study employs a similar approach to the analysis of clusters and social network contributions. Users act increasingly as swarms and those swarms can be detected. Publics become bots.

Claude Shannon's information theory is important for understanding these games.[15] This signal/noise relationship is the basis of digital communication and at times an oversimplification of communication, but a useful simplification for understanding channels in operation. For Shannon, the problem of communication involves the translation of all meaning into discrete units, rather than the contiguous flows of human experience. Entropy is the tendency of a signal to become disorderly. All information sources have a dimension of entropy; only those that appear in toy games or examples are perfect. In the example of an automatic text-generating machine, it became clear that a cybernetic process could, when driven by the seed of regular use tables and a number generator, produce meaningful yet meaningless strings of text. The randomness would naturally introduce some entropy, but there would still be enough signal. It is entirely possible that a receiver accessing this text could mistake the nonsense for a message. This depends on framing, as not all finite character groups assembled in this way are semantically meaningful. On a more basic level, Shannon demonstrates that the capacity of a channel depends on the clearing of noise. As message complexity increases, vulnerability to noise also increases.

For the purposes of this study, the channel is the material that is organized within a single hashtag. This presumes that those users deploying a hashtag are attempting to produce some kind of meaningful message with that hashtag. Users would be recirculating (and occasionally creating) tweets to lead to a vote for their particular candidate.

Retweeting may serve an adaptive role, as it would appear that an overconverged swarm would have lower entropy than a more personal message. Matthew Brashears and Eric Gladstone argue that error correction is a key capacity of social networks and that corrected errors increase the variety of messages diffusing across a network.[16] Error correction and variation are features of real communication, not flaws. The need for error correction is mitigated by the diffusion of low-entropy messages. Decreased risk of error explains the seductive danger of over-convergence: if everyone tweets the same thing, the messenger is more likely to be lost, but that messenger is also less credible.[17] The problems of extremely similar messages are well known in crisis and risk communication: over-convergence can swamp a good idea. Conversely, in the world of victim selection, the use of an utterly ridiculous, low-entropy classifier can quickly parse publics.[18] Game and information metaphors unlock new possibilities for the study of the public sphere.

Countdown to Election Day

This data set includes 1,210,031 directed links scraped nightly via the Twitter application programming interface (API) with the text string "ImWithHer," perhaps the most popular Clinton campaign–related hashtag during the week preceding the election. Initial analysis of this data set revealed that the fifth-highest degree among nodes was Rihanna's endorsement of Senator Clinton. However, Rihanna's original tweet was not within the time window of the study. This is a powerful example of information entropy: even seemingly friendly noise can overwhelm the signal.

Tweets were recorded using the twitteR package for R and analyzed using a combination of packages for R and Gephi.[19] Users who are not major public figures will remain nameless. Celebrities tweeting endorsements of Senator Clinton would surely not presume that they would remain unknown. Of interest in this analysis are both the network structures among the tweeters and the semantic content of their tweets. The graphical representation of clusters and structures can be helpful for understanding the dynamics of the moment. Graphics presented here are drawn in Gephi, using a force-directed algorithm.[20] This is not an aesthetically pleasing strategy—but one that reveals structure of the @ network related to a particular hashtag. This was chosen, as it would minimize the number of assumptions in the analysis. The following are the analyses of the WikiLeaks and Satanism data sets.

WikiTweets

Initially, the network appears sparse, with minimal original content. Of the 1,210,031 tweets, 1,027,860 are retweets. The highest prestige node is WikiLeaks.[21] WikiLeaks tweets are almost entirely identical. Of the 115,544

Figure 13.1
Wiki network.

tweets about WikiLeaks in this data set, 113,346 are retweets. First, we should look at the WikiLeaks network for structure. The measure of kurtosis for the kcores calculated for both the full data set and then the restricted WikiLeaks data set is revealing: in the context of the entire network, the kurtosis of the distribution is 34.47 with a skewness of 4.19, while in the WikiLeaks distribution it is 189.65 with a skewness of 7.50.[22] What does this mean?[23] When the data set is filtered for the network around a single story/flare, the relief of the kcores sharpens. The cone and magnet of the amplifier become visible. At the same time, the core detection method reveals not that a single community drove the WikiLeaks story—but that a few communities were far more involved in the story.

The pendanting in this data set is clear. When users with a single interaction are removed, the actual scaffolding of conversation is revealed. It is also important to see the core node of this plot—WikiLeaks itself. Consider the three graphics in figure 13.1. This is a ForceAtlas-directed graph of tweets using the word *WikiLeaks*. There are three graphics in the panel: the first is a full map of all interactions in the data set; the second requires five interactions to be visible, and the third requires fifteen. It also becomes clear that a few nodes were central to the entire network. If you cleave out either the center or the margins, the structure of users involved in ongoing conversation is scant.

Homogeneity is also a key feature in the texts distributed through this network. Of entries, 89 percent include the stem "RELEASE," which is a key indicator of a retweet storm about the Podesta e-mails, and 98 percent are retweets. The absent center reveals the gravity well structuring the public sphere—the attempt to articulate Clinton to WikiLeaks. This is a relatively clear way to detect cascades directed at a particular node with

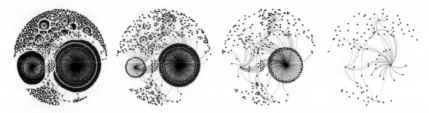

Figure 13.2
They smell of sulfur.

the potential for jamming these interactions. Detecting and labeling these networks could allow for efficient advertising targeting or the deployment of countermeasures.

As we can see in figure 13.2, there are clearly two very large cores present; both are organized around the twitter handles of existing celebrities. On the left, we see the full network related to the Satanism accusation, then the nodes of the network are progressively filtered for degrees of two, three, and, finally, five. It should be clear that there is very little underlying organic conversation here. At the same time, we have established that there are thin relational networks created by fake news networks. These would allow core nodes in an ecosystem, such as those spreading the satanic tweet, to appear important and thus to appear more frequently than others. Even more than the WikiLeaks example, it is apparent here that there is not a sustained conversation about Satanism, but rather an organized effort to make it appear that Satanism is an issue, even as satirical use of the story would trigger a low-entropy messenger strategy—the story connects Clinton to WikiLeaks via Podesta.

The texts shared by the networks identified with WikiLeaks or Satanism are remarkably similar. Taking direction from an old, but important, source, Shannon's mathematical theory of information, we can utilize the common use tables of information from the data set to produce a model of the relationship between the possible messages provided in a corpus and the possible effects of those messages.[24] Intermedia agenda setting thus allows the deployment of a dissimilar low-entropy message about the same issue to have the effect of making the issue real. Bots are not the real source of impact here: people choosing not to recognize the work of bots give the story life.

If we think of this list in categories, it would not be beyond the scope of possibility to construct an algorithm that would produce messages seemingly at random utilizing the contents of the frequency tables. It would appear that the vast majority of the WikiLeaks posts follow a template similar to this: RT @wikileaks: RELEASE: The Podesta Emails Part 24 #PodestaEmails #PodestaEmails24 #HillaryClinton #ImWithHer. Typically, a shortened link follows. The message here contains ideas: WikiLeaks, Podesta, and Clinton. There is no other semantic content to get in the way. The satanic example makes this clear as well, as the base tweet of the largest core presented in the graph relates to a single joke: "#ImWithHer—Satan."[25]

The Fingerprint

In the context of this study, we can see constellations of nodes and edges that form the prints of different networks. These networks may not be an easily read signature, but they are an important indicator. What has come across in this research is that there are swarms of users to interact with a key story or actor in a network once; these swarms tend to have very low levels of linguistic innovation.

The fingerprint of a fake news network would be the deployment of semantically similar content along a shallowly linked network. The goal of a fake news operation in a zero-sum game would be to disrupt the signal of democratic deliberation (the low goal) and replace the signal of the other side (the high goal). Even if the legacy media did not fall for the effort, agenda setting onto the question of Satanism was marginally effective in the effort to articulate WikiLeaks and Clinton, and the effort to inspire the image of corruption was successful. When considered through Warner's counter-publicity, the fleeting referent is a part of the circulation of publicity and counter-publicity: tiny messages in fleeting moments have a profound impact. Echoes may resonate as a new voice. Communication research should not allow a preference for high-entropy strategies by sophisticated interest groups to replace the study of real publicity in actually existing games. Practitioners should take care that they address publics that exist and that they pay attention to the level of entropy in real debates.

Returning to information theory, we can begin to restage Shannon's conjecture: that a machine employing a regular usage table for human writing could produce text reliably. In our context today, the elements of the proto-typical tweet could become a tweet generator. The generator would assign direct addresses, deploy a short message (which could easily be created with frequency tables in an existent data set), followed by three hashtags, and a link to some other site. As a formula: Sock puppets (2) + Text (8) + Hashtags (3) + (1) Link = a low-entropy masterwork. It is not difficult to imagine doz-ens or more different political tweets produced by this algorithm. In the context of our fingerprints, and the agenda setting they drove, it would be enough to simply roll through a list of sock puppet accounts to produce the appearance of a network.

To build a machine that produces text would only require a list of Twitter account names, which would drive enough entropy and address structure to make a nearly identical message look at least somewhat authentic. When the referenced account names or hashtags are included, the noise sounds like a voice. Unlike a pure retweet, the bot-produced directed cascade has a more realistically networked appearance.

There are three distinct practical implications. First, in a zero-sum game, a noising operation could effectively introduce enough entropy into a chan-nel to overwhelm it. Feeds have inherent scarcity. Second, the noise intro-duced would not be random, but be a strategic form designed to work at the lowest possible level of entropy. The counterargument introduced into a hashtag channel would only need a few words. Similarly, low-entropy mes-sages, such as seen in the Satan data set, would inspire intermedia agenda setting, driven by their extremely low entropy and high affective poten-tial. Beyond simply overwhelming a channel, a counterargument can be delivered as the noise. Third, swarms can be organized around realistic-looking webs of users to form a pseudo-event; when real users encounter these events, they may over-converge their messaging, enhancing the effect of the noise.

Prevention is critical. Individual users are not equipped to manage swarms of bots. Distinguishing between a swarm and a public is tricky, but necessary. The election itself may be a zero-sum game; social network firms should reimagine the feed to challenge this assumption. At the same time, as Warner's counterpublics suggest, individual actors in the public sphere system could react to the swarm by retweeting their own information and building their own counterpublics. This is more likely with smaller swarms. Counter-publicity alone is not enough: affective resources are not evenly distributed; easily translated, highly affective meanings are likely reactionary. Messages we see circulating in this data set are simple: Hillary is Satan, WikiLeaks releases Clinton e-mails, and other three- and four-word wonders. This is not the stuff of technical public policy. Simple, direct, black-and-white alignments like "bad people should be punished," "good people should be praised," will beat shades of gray. Symmetrical or reciprocal plays are not available. Campaigns need swarms of candidate-specific, positive, low-entropy messaging to continuously flow through the feed. This strategy would be best after a significant change in platform-level policies such as cascade suppression and the removal of bot accounts.

Without platform-level change, it would not be difficult to imagine a future campaign where multiple fake news networks deploy increasingly low-entropy, highly converged messages across the platforms. These new low-entropy messages could become something of a new poetics. The question would become—what do we do with mass-mediated politics when the height of strategy is a two-word growl?

Notes

1. Susan Faludi, "How Hillary Clinton Met Satan," *New York Times*, October 29, 2016, https://www.nytimes.com/2016/10/30/opinion/sunday/how-hillary-clinton-met-satan.html.

2. The specific accusation in the indictment is that "Hillary is a Satan," which is interesting given the context. United States of America v. Internet Research Agency LLC et al. (District Court for the District of Columbia, February 16, 2018), https://www.justice.gov/file/1035477/download.

3. These are particularly well-known satire sites. ClickHole, https://resistancehole.clickhole.com/; The Borowitz Report, *New Yorker*, https://www.newyorker.com/humor/borowitz-report.

4. Gregor Aisch, Jon Huang, and Cecilia Kang, "Dissecting the #PizzaGate Conspiracy Theories," Business Day, *New York Times*, December 10, 2016, https://www.nytimes.com/interactive/2016/12/10/business/media/pizzagate.html.

5. This timing did not work, as election law in France is designed to suppress news related to last-second updates or October surprises. "WikiLeaks Publishes Searchable Archive of Macron Campaign Emails," Reuters, July 31, 2017, https://www.reuters.com/article/us-france-politics-wikileaks/wikileaks-publishes-searchable-archive-of-macron-campaign-emails-idUSKBN1AG1TZ.

6. Edson C. Tandoc Jr., Zheng Wei Lim, and Richard Ling, "Defining 'Fake News': A Typology of Scholarly Definitions," *Digital Journalism* 6, no. 2 (2017): 137–153.

7. Hunt Allcott and Matthew Gentzkow, "Social Media and Fake News in the 2016 Election," *Journal of Economic Perspectives* 31, no. 2 (2017): 211–236.

8. Soroush Vosoughi, Deb Roy, and Sinan Aral, "The Spread of True and False News Online," *Science* 359, no. 6380 (2018): 1146–1151, http://science.sciencemag.org /content/359/6380/1146.

9. The Concord Catering Company was one of many names used by the Internet Research Agency in the United States. United States of America v. Internet Research Agency LLC et al.

10. This central theoretical construction for game theory has up to this point been woefully underemployed in communication research. In this context, I am referencing Ken Binmore's description of the construct, as it both is adequately robust and provides the relevant context for the use of the ideas in this context. Ken Binmore, *Game Theory: A Very Short Introduction* (New York: Oxford University Press, 2007).

11. GOTV is effective; at the same time, it is important to note that these methods may increase inequality. The research in this area emphasizes the difficulty in producing meaningful mobilization. Ryan D. Enos, Anthony Fowler, and Lynn Vavreck, "Increasing Inequality: The Effect of GOTV Mobilization on the Composition of the Electorate," *Journal of Politics* 76, no. 1 (2014): 273–288, https://doi.org/10.1017 /S0022381613001308.

12. Michael, Warner, "Publics and Counterpublics," *Quarterly Journal of Speech* 88, no. 4 (2002): 413–425.

13. Yu-Ru Lin, Brian Keegan, Drew Margolin, and David Lazer, "Rising Tides or Rising Stars? Dynamics of Shared Attention on Twitter during Media Events," *PLoS ONE* 9, no. 5 (2014): e94093, https://doi.org/10.1371/journal.pone.0094093.

14. Yini Zhang, Chris Wells, Song Wang, and Karl Rohe, "Attention and Amplification in the Hybrid Media System: The Composition and Activity of Donald Trump's Twitter Following during the 2016 Presidential Election," *New Media and Society* 20, no. 9 (2018): 3161–3182.

15. Claude Shannon, "A Mathematical Theory of Communication," *Bell System Technical Journal* 21 (1948): 379–423, 623–656.

16. Matthew Brashears and Eric Gladstone, "Error Correction Mechanisms in Social Networks Can Reduce Accuracy and Encourage Innovation," *Social Networks* 44, no. 1 (2016): 22–35.

17. Kathryn E. Anthony, Timothy L. Sellnow, and Alyssa G. Millner, "Message Convergence as a Message-Centered Approach to Analyzing and Improving Risk

Communication," *Journal of Applied Communication Research* 41, no. 4 (2013): 346–364.

18. Cormac Herley, *Why Do Nigerian Scammers Say They Are from Nigeria?* (Redmond, WA: Microsoft Research, 2012), http://research.microsoft.com/pubs/167719/WhyFromNigeria.pdf.

19. The critical packages for this project include twitteR, for data collection, and dplyr and stringr, deployed through R studio. Hadley Wickham, *Stringr*, version 1.3.1 (R, 2018); Hadley Wickham et al., *Dplyr*, version 0.75 (R, 2018).

20. Mathieu Jacomy et al., *ForceAtlas2* (Gephi, 2015).

21. Calculated via the Eigenvector mode, this is adequate but not ideal. There are other methods for calculating centrality that call for additional exploration in this context in particular.

22. The implementation of kcores used here is the base in the SNA package. This was done because it is a well-regarded package for network analysis, other studies have used this function, and the function could be implemented with this data set with the resources available to the researcher. Carter Butts, *SNA*, version 2.4 (R, 2016). Kurtosis and skewness were calculated using the moments package. Lukasz Komsta and Fredrick Novomentsky, *Moments*, version 0.14 (R, 2015).

23. There are important issues at play here. First, networks like these are obviously non-normal, meaning that any test that relies on a normal distribution would be inappropriate. There are other statistical methods that could be applied to determine if the change was significant. A qual-quant mix could also be a profitable strategy. It is important to note that both Wiki and Satan are relatively small subsets and that a few cores have dramatically larger representation in the data set. Further, these cores could be effectively segmented repeatedly to reveal the structure within the structure. This is likely an important future method for increasing the resolution of a network scan for bots.

24. Shannon, "A Mathematical Theory of Communication."

25. This is a common joke that could be attributed to the data set as a whole.

14   Reddit's Alt-Right: Toxic Masculinity, Free Speech, and /r/The_Donald

Adrienne Massanari

Reddit is the fourth most visited site in the United States (and seventh globally).[1] Anyone can create a community, called a subreddit, on the open-source platform, and each Reddit member (Redditor) can vote on content and subscribe to subreddits of interest. In addition to being a hub for geek culture and fandom, it is also playing a less savory role in mainstreaming the "alt-right." The "alt-right"—a loose collection of white ethnonationalists, misogynists, Islamophobes—has gained national attention in the United States with the ascendance of Donald Trump, and mirrors far-right sentiment globally.[2] While these sorts of movements are not a new phenomenon, nor is their presence on the web,[3] a definite shift is happening in spaces like Reddit and on other social media. Previously marginal groups are gaining a foothold, often using memetic logics to radicalize and spread their message of hate. Unfortunately, Reddit administrators seem unwilling to intervene in any meaningful way, instead suggesting that outright bans of many objectionable communities will not effectively address the issue. This counters research which suggests that banning hate speech and subreddits that traffic in harassing others improves discourse across the platform.[4]

In this chapter, I outline the reasons for the "alt-right's" outsize presence on Reddit. I contend that this is due both to toxic "geek masculinity" that permeates many of the most popular subreddits and to specific technical affordances of the platform. Underlying both the technical and the social realities of Reddit is a valorization of techno/cyberlibertarian values,[5] and in particular an unrestricted version of free speech that normalizes and amplifies sexist and racist discourse. Reddit's origins as a hub of geek masculinity often mean that women and women of color are viewed as interlopers or objects to be critiqued and sexualized.

Toxic Geek Masculinity

Reddit has long been home to geek fandom and niche interests. Since each Reddit user can subscribe to subreddits of interest, there is no *one* Reddit experience. However, examining the most popular subreddits is telling, with the top twenty-five focusing mostly on science, technology, engineering, and mathematics (STEM); video games; and popular culture.[6] Redditors are a technically savvy group, who tend to spend lots of time online and often work in/around industries in information technology and technology. Reddit has also become a hub for breaking news and current events coverage, with the Pew Research Center suggesting that almost 80 percent of Redditors get news from the site.[7] Redditors are mostly men under thirty years old who have some amount of college, and they tend to be more liberal than the general U.S. population.[8] Perhaps it is not surprising, therefore, that Reddit's dominant culture represents a kind of "geek masculinity."[9]

Geek or nerd masculinity is often positioned in opposition to hegemonic masculinity.[10] As Lori Kendall argues, the "nerd" stereotype often resists many notions of hegemonic masculinity, as nerds are not interested in pastimes coded as "masculine," such as sports, and are often portrayed as sexually frustrated.[11] The nerd or geek also embodies a particular social category: white, cisgendered, heterosexual, middle-class, and able-bodied.[12] And this creates a conundrum, as, "confronted with his cultural centrality and white, masculine privilege—geeks are most frequently represented as white males—the geek seeks a simulated victimhood and even simulated ethnicity in order to justify his existence as a protagonist in a world where an unmarked straight white male protagonist is increasingly passé."[13] Therefore, geek masculinity embodies both elements of marginality and unrecognized privilege. As Joseph Reagle notes, the narrative often becomes one of "geek triumphalism," in which geeks experience a deep sense of marginalization and insecurity because of their unique, niche interests, but may also view themselves as being successful (and superior) precisely because of these same factors.[14] This triumphalism often makes them unwilling to accept critique—as they may see themselves as above reproach or bias because of their past experiences as "outsiders." Concomitantly, geek culture often champions meritocratic logics that tend to view success or failure as the result of individual effort rather than of systems or cultures that might support or impede a person's progress. As Christopher Paul argues,

"By individualizing people, meritocracy has the impact of making people judgmental and rude, while making individuals more likely to attribute their status in life to their own efforts or lack thereof, which makes us less sensitive to others."[15]

On Reddit, this kind of meritocratic logic is mirrored by the platform's technological affordances. The voting system, for example, is designed to demonstrate the relative worth of a given submission or comment. While on the surface this appears democratic, suggesting that each Redditor has an equal voice in shaping conversations, it is not entirely the case. First, Reddit's algorithm weights earlier votes more heavily than later votes, meaning that those individuals (usually moderators) who spend a significant time on the site are more likely to shape the platform's overall conversation. Second, power law dynamics shape the likelihood of the most popular content becoming more popular, with more-upvoted content being more likely to be voted up by others (and appearing first given the site's default sorting mechanism). Third, voting is easily gamed, by bot accounts designed to shift the conversation in a particular direction through mass upvoting, by individuals using multiple accounts to vote on content, or by groups of Redditors banding together to "brigade" other subreddits. In addition, studies suggest that many Reddit users do not read submitted content before voting on it, instead merely basing their votes on the title or headline of the piece.[16] This kind of voting behavior can transmit fake news, conspiracy theories, and rumors across subreddits with ease.

Conspiracies Welcomed: #Gamergate

As articulated above, geek masculinity/triumphalism champions a kind of superiority based on intellect and esoteric knowledge. This manifests in several ways on Reddit. In other work, I have noted that Redditors tend to prize rationality, authenticity, and accuracy.[17] At the same time, there is a tendency for rumors, fake news, and conspiracy theories to spread quickly across subreddits, particularly during crisis moments. For example, after the Boston Marathon bombing in 2013, members of the /r/bostonbombing subreddit wrongly identified several individuals as suspects, including a Brown University student who was later found to have died by suicide. This interest in crowdsourcing intelligence around crisis moments is driven in part by a general skepticism of the ability of government agencies and law enforcement. It is also in keeping with a kind of techno/cyberlibertarianism that permeates Reddit, which has manifested in large-scale political activism around such things as net neutrality, surveillance, and online piracy.[18]

Redditors have also demonstrated a tendency to engage and support conspiracy theories, especially if they relate to geek fandom or if it furthers their own vision of geek masculinity. Most notably, this includes #Gamergate, an anonymous hashtag activist movement. It started in late 2014 when a woman game developer (Zoe Quinn) was accused of cheating with a games journalist and other industry leaders in an effort, her ex-lover alleged, to gain positive support and reviews for her work. This led to a large-scale harassment campaign against women game developers, critics, and industry professionals. While #Gamergate proponents claimed that they were concerned with the lack of "ethics in games journalism" that Quinn's alleged infractions represented, their actions looked suspiciously motivated by other factors.

While much of the harassment campaign was Twitter-based, Reddit served (and continues to serve) as the public hub for conversation about #Gamergate through /r/KotakuInAction (KIA). KIA's name references both the *Gawker*-owned gaming blog *Kotaku* (which is seen as the foremost hub of "politically correct" games journalism) and another subreddit, /r/TumblrIn-Action, dedicated to sharing and making fun of posts gathered from Tumblr (seen as the anti-Reddit given its user base).[19] Like the larger #Gamergate movement, posts to KIA often have little to do with video games. This may be due in part to a natural ebb and flow of #Gamergate, which peaked between August and November 2014 (according to Google search trends), but I would argue that it also points to the reality of #Gamergate, which was more about railing against social justice and political progressiveness than it was about games.[20] While KIA still discusses #Gamergate proper, it also regularly features content related to the men's rights movement, the suppression of free speech on college campuses by so-called social justice warrior (SJW) activists, anti-affirmative action polemics, and stories about vaunted members of the so-called intellectual dark web.[21]

Ultimately, #Gamergate activists are angry at the diversifying audience for video games, and viewed increasing representations of marginalized groups within gaming content as somehow "political correctness" gone amok.[22] One group, SJWs, are particular targets. For #Gamergate supporters, SJWs represent an insidious other: simpering liberals who are intent on destroying video games (and culture) and the "gamer" identity with their insistence that every game (or any other cultural product) conform to their sanitized version of reality. This feeds into a larger conspiracy theory that SJWs are embedded in multiple places of power within not just the games industry, but also Hollywood, Silicon Valley, and Washington, D.C. Unsurprisingly, many within the alt-right became outspoken #Gamergate supporters (most notably Milo Yiannopoulos and #Pizzagate conspiracist Mike Cernovich), and many of the tactics used by #Gamergate activists were later refined by the "alt-right" during the U.S. presidential election campaign of Trump.[23]

/r/The_Donald Conundrum

By far the most difficult community for Reddit administrators and users has been /r/The_Donald (TD). While Pew data suggested that many Redditors supported primary candidate Bernie Sanders during the 2016 U.S. presidential campaign,[24] by late 2016 /r/SandersforPresident was outpaced significantly by TD subscribers (and both subreddits had far more subscribers than /r/HillaryClinton). TD is still wildly popular, currently ranking number 188 with over 620,000 subscribers, according to Redditlist.[25] Research suggests that throughout the election cycle, incivility and negative partisanship were particularly high in TD[26]—and this spilled over to other spaces on Reddit as well.

TD continues to be somewhat different from other political subreddits on the platform (such as /r/Libertarian, /r/Conservative, /r/Democrats, for example), featuring far more memes than actual news and a lingua franca that is almost impenetrable to outsiders. It is also extremely effective in pushing far-right ideas and racist speech through memetic content. Researchers have argued that while 4chan's /pol (politically incorrect) board creates an outsize number of memes given its size, TD is actually more efficient in spreading them to other spaces online.[27] These also easily spread across Reddit. For example, in 2016 TD postings was overrepresented on /r/all (the listing of top-rated content across Reddit) because of a loophole in Reddit's algorithm. This bug was later fixed, but it's possible that this act introduced many Redditors to the "alt-right" ideas TD peddles.

Unlike other political subreddits, TD is for supporters only, with moderators regularly banning individuals with impunity. Questioning Trump's policies or even asking for clarification about them is a bannable offense. This is somewhat ironic given that Trump supporters also decry public spaces and college campuses as being overrun with SJW "snowflakes" who cannot tolerate having their ideas challenged. And, despite significant evidence of the community breaking voting rules by brigading other subreddits, calling for violence against certain individuals, and doxing journalists, Reddit administrators have still not rid the platform of /r/The_Donald.[28] CEO Steve Huffman recently told Redditors that banning the subreddit "probably won't accomplish what you want. However, letting them fall apart from their own dysfunction probably will. Their engagement is shrinking over time, and that's much more powerful than shutting them down outright."[29] But this stance is not tenable given the significant part that TD, other reactionary subreddits, and bots played in spreading fake news from Russian trolls across the platform during the 2016 election cycle.[30] A number of observers have suggested that the real reason TD and other troubling (but popular) subreddits are not banned outright is because the company generates significant revenue from them.[31]

"We're Banning Behavior, Not Ideas"

In keeping with the techno/cyberlibertarian ethos that underpins Silicon Valley culture, Reddit administrators have long championed an unrestricted approach to free speech on their platform. Former interim CEO Ellen Pao, when announcing the ban of troublesome fat-shaming harassment subreddit/r/fatpeoplehate in June 2015, said, "We're banning behavior, not ideas."[32] This seems to be the general approach of Reddit's administrators: rather than directly take a stand against sexist, racist, transphobic, and misogynistic speech, simply wait for subreddits where hate speech festers and spills over into harassing "behavior." After the ban, Pao was subjected to a large-scale harassment campaign, leading her to suggest in an op-ed that the "trolls" were winning the internet.[33]

Reddit's administrators have long championed a "hands-off" approach to content, typically requiring volunteer moderators to police their own subreddits as they see fit. Prior to 2012, Reddit had few limitations on content, dealing with the most egregious of these on a case-by-case basis. In February 2012, following a media exposé of Reddit's child pornography "problem," administrators explicitly banned content featuring sexualized images of minors. This followed several months in which popular subreddits such as /r/jailbait (which featured sexualized images of clothed minors stolen from other social media sites) flourished—in part because of the powerful status of their moderators. Since moderating subreddits is an unpaid, onerous position, moderators of problematic subreddits often gain outsize influence. For example, *Gawker's* Adrian Chen argued that part of the reason infamous moderator Violentacrez's odious subreddits (which included /r/jailbait, /r/incest, /r/chokeabitch, /r/Jewmerica, among others) were allowed on the platform is that he would also regularly report child pornography to administrators so they could report it to the appropriate authorities.[34]

This becomes a double bind for administrators. On the one hand, they are dependent on unpaid labor to manage the site and deal with spam and other troubling content, as Reddit has few paid community managers given the size of its user base. On the other hand, it is often the most powerful moderators/users who post objectionable content in the first place. After Chen published Violentacrez's identity, many subreddits banned *Gawker* postings in retaliation, calling it "a breach of ethics and integrity."[35] And despite their dependence on moderators to ensure the platform's success, the relationship between moderators and administrators remains tense—with moderators often frustrated by the lack of tools and support from admins.[36]

Despite these realities, Reddit administrators tend to quarantine troublesome subreddits, preventing them from appearing in /r/all or on its front page, rather than removing them entirely. Visitors to these subreddits must also explicitly opt in, and these subreddits do not generate ad revenue (although they are implicitly supported by ad revenue generated by other subreddits). The quarantine policy was announced soon after Pao left the company in mid-2015. At the same time, a number of subreddits affiliated with the racist community /r/coontown were finally banned. Unfortunately, /r/coontown was banned not because it broke any new or existing rules, or because it was virulently racist (which it most definitely was), but rather because it represented, according to one user, part of "a handful of communities that exist solely to annoy other redditors, prevent us from improving Reddit, and generally make Reddit worse for everyone else."[37] Many users were chagrined, some because they felt these actions did not go far enough (asking, for example, why other racist and misogynistic subreddits were not banned), while others argued that it was censorship and limited their "free speech" rights.

This becomes part of a troubling pattern wherein Reddit administrators introduce new content rules only when forced (usually by unfavorable media coverage), and often the rules are vague and not applied consistently. There is also the troubling reality that by not allowing advertisers to monetize quarantined subreddits, the rest of Reddit essentially bankrolls their existence through advertising on other subreddits. And quarantining a subreddit does nothing to prevent those users from interacting in other subreddits, and creating a toxic atmosphere across the platform.

Conclusion

Toxic geek masculinity pervades Reddit, from activist movements like #Gamergate to the "manosphere" and its undercurrent of violent misogyny, to the "alt-right" organizing of /r/The_Donald.[38] While reflective of larger cultural dynamics, Reddit has created a space where individuals affiliated with these groups not only feel welcome, but have a platform to recruit and spread fake news, conspiracies, and rumors. Under the guise of supporting unrestricted "free speech," administrators refuse to take a stand against these toxic elements and continue to suggest that if they are ignored, they will go away. This despite numerous examples of these groups breaking Reddit's own (very minimal) conduct and content rules. Unfortunately, the platform's technical affordances serve only to weaponize their speech under the guise of a "democratic" voting system that is easily gamed. And waiting for harassing speech to spill over into "behavior" works to create a platform where marginalized populations feel increasingly unwelcome.

Notes

1. Alexa, "Top Sites in United States," 2018, http://www.alexa.com/topsites/countries /US.

2. Southern Poverty Law Center, "Alt-Right," 2018, https://www.splcenter.org/fight ing-hate/extremist-files/ideology/alt-right.

3. Jessie Daniels, *Cyber Racism: White Supremacy Online and the New Attack on Civil Rights* (Lanham, MD: Rowman and Littlefield, 2009).

4. Eshwar Chandrasekharan, Umashanthi Pavalanathan, Anirudh Srinivasan, Adam Glynn, Jacob Eisenstein, and Eric Gilbert, "You Can't Stay Here: The Efficacy of Reddit's 2015 Ban Examined through Hate Speech," *Proceedings of the ACM on Human-Computer Interaction* 1, no. 2 (2017): 1–22.

5. Nathan Jurgenson and P. J. Rey, "Liquid Information Leaks," *International Journal of Communication* 8 (2014): 2651–2665; Paulina Borsook, "Cyberselfish: Ravers, Guilders, Cyberpunks, and Other Silicon Valley Life-Forms," *Yale Journal of Law and Technology* 3, no. 1 (2001), http://digitalcommons.law.yale.edu/yjolt/vol3/iss1/1.

6. Redditlist, "All Subreddits | Redditlist.com—Tracking the Top 5000 Subreddits," 2018, http://redditlist.com/all.

7. Alex Leavitt and Joshua Clark, "Upvoting Hurricane Sandy: Event-Based News Production Processes on a Social News Site" (paper presented at the Special Interest Group on Computer-Human Interaction [SIGCHI] Conference on Human Factors in Computing Systems, Toronto, April 26–May 1, 2014); Michael Barthel, Galen Stocking, Jesse Holcomb, and Amy Mitchell, "Nearly Eight-in-Ten Reddit Users Get News on the Site," Pew Research Center, 2016, http://assets.pewresearch.org/wp-content/uploads/sites/13/2016/02/PJ_2016.02.25_Reddit_FINAL.pdf.

8. Barthel et al., "Nearly Eight-in-Ten Reddit Users."

9. Adrienne Massanari, *Participatory Culture, Community, and Play: Learning from Reddit* (New York: Peter Lang, 2015).

10. R. W. Connell and James W. Messerschmidt, "Hegemonic Masculinity: Rethinking the Concept," *Gender and Society* 19, no. 6 (2005): 829–859.

11. Lori Kendall, "Nerd Nation: Images of Nerds in US Popular Culture," *International Journal of Cultural Studies* 2, no. 2 (1999): 260–283; Lori Kendall, "'White and Nerdy': Computers, Race, and the Nerd Stereotype," *Journal of Popular Culture* 44, no. 3 (2011): 505–524.

12. I am using the terms *nerd* and *geek* interchangeably for convenience.

13. Kim Kunyosying and Carter Soles, "Postmodern Geekdom as Simulated Ethnicity," *Jump Cut*, no. 54 (2012), https://www.ejumpcut.org/archive/jc54.2012/SolesKunyoGeedom/.

14. Joseph Reagle, "Nerd vs. Bro: Geek Privilege, Idiosyncrasy, and Triumphalism," *First Monday* 23, no. 1 (2017), http://firstmonday.org/ojs/index.php/fm/article/view/7879/6629.

15. Christopher A. Paul, *The Toxic Meritocracy of Video Games: Why Gaming Culture Is the Worst* (Minneapolis: University of Minnesota Press, 2018), 14.

16. Maria Glenski, Corey Pennycuff, and Tim Weninger, "Consumers and Curators: Browsing and Voting Patterns on Reddit," *IEEE Transactions on Computational Social Systems* 4, no. 4 (2017): 196–206.

17. Massanari, *Participatory Culture, Community, and Play*.

18. arabscarab, "(Orange)Red Alert: The Senate is about to vote on whether to restore Net Neutrality," Reddit, 2018, https://www.reddit.com/r/announcements

/comments/8i3382/orangered_alert_the_senate_is_about_to_vote_on/?st=jiuh32ev
&sh=5fc5c6c5; trevorEFF, "One year ago today, you help us beat SOPA. Thanks
Reddit. This is Eff, Ask Us Anything," Reddit, 2013, https://www.reddit.com/r
/IAmA/comments/16tu47/one_year_ago_today_you_help_us_beat_sopa_thanks/?st
=jiuh2imb&sh=6e3bea51.

19. Gawker Media has since collapsed, due in significant part to the bankruptcy
caused by a lawsuit brought up by former wrestling star Hulk Hogan, which was
secretly backed by billionaire Facebook investor (and Trump supporter) Peter Thiel.
Kotaku is now owned by Univision Communications. Andrew Ross Sorkin, "Peter
Thiel, Tech Billionaire, Reveals Secret War with Gawker," *New York Times*, May 25,
2016, https://www.nytimes.com/2016/05/26/business/dealbook/peter-thiel-tech-billio
naire-reveals-secret-war-with-gawker.html.

20. Adrienne Massanari, "#Gamergate and the Fappening: How Reddit's Algorithm,
Governance, and Culture Support Toxic Technocultures," *New Media and Society* 19,
no. 3 (2017): 329–346.

21. Bari Weiss, "Meet the Renegades of the Intellectual Dark Web," *New York Times*,
May 8, 2018, https://www.nytimes.com/2018/05/08/opinion/intellectual-dark-web
.html.

22. Shira Chess and Adrienne Shaw, "A Conspiracy of Fishes, or, How We Learned to
Stop Worrying about #Gamergate and Embrace Hegemonic Masculinity," *Journal of
Broadcasting and Electronic Media* 59, no. 1 (2015): 208–220; Torill Elvira Mortensen,
"Anger, Fear, and Games: The Long Event of #GamerGate," *Games and Culture* 13,
no. 8 (2018): 787–806.

23. Katherine Cross, "We Warned You about Milo and You're Still Not Listening,"
The Establishment, October 9, 2017, https://theestablishment.co/we-warned-you
-about-milo-and-youre-still-not-listening-947dad4a8400.

24. Barthel et al., "Nearly Eight-in-Ten Reddit Users."

25. Redditlist, "All Subreddits," 2018.

26. Rishab Nithyanand, Brian Schaffner, and Phillipa Gill, "Online Political Discourse in the Trump Era" (preprint, submitted November 14, 2017), https://arxiv
.org/pdf/1711.05303.

27. Savvas Zannettou, Tristan Caulfield, Jeremy Blackburn, Emiliano De Cristofaro,
Michael Sirivianos, Gianluca Stringhini, and Guillermo Suarez-Tangil, "On the Origins of Memes by Means of Fringe Web Communities" (preprint, last revised September 22, 2018), https://arxiv.org/abs/1805.12512.

28. DubTeeDub, "Reddit admins have confirmed they are comfortable with T_D
and other altright subs engaging in a harassment campaign attacking survivors of
the Parkland school shooting," February 22, 2018, Reddit, https://www.reddit.com

/r/AgainstHateSubreddits/comments/7zgo1c/reddit_admins_have_confirmed_they
_are_comfortable/?st=jixmxa4o&sh=9efae7f0.

29. spez, "In response to recent reports about the integrity of Reddit, I'd like to share our thinking," Reddit, 2018, https://www.reddit.com/r/announcements/comments /827zqc/in_response_to_recent_reports_about_the_integrity/dv824bf/?context=5 &st=jixne4wl&sh=9a183ffb.

30. Issie Lapowsky, "Russian Propaganda Remains on Reddit," *Wired*, March 9, 2018, https://www.wired.com/story/reddit-russian-propaganda/.

31. Tim Squirrell, "Opinion: Reddit's Advertising Strategies Still Hide Hate Speech," *Quartz*, April 6, 2018, https://qz.com/1246087/opinion-reddits-advertising-strategies -still-hide-hate-speech/.

32. Reddit, "Removing harassing subreddits," 2015, https://www.reddit.com/r/anno uncements/comments/39bpam/removing_harassing_subreddits/cs21aj4/?st=jixkz3fk &sh=e52f8c2f.

33. Ellen Pao, "Former Reddit CEO Ellen Pao: The Trolls Are Winning the Battle for the Internet," *Washington Post*, July 16, 2015, https://www.washingtonpost.com /opinions/we-cannot-let-the-internet-trolls-win/2015/07/16/.

34. Adrian Chen, "Unmasking Reddit's Violentacrez, the Biggest Troll on the Web," *Gawker*, October 12, 2012, http://gawker.com/5950981/unmasking-reddits -violentacrez-the-biggest-troll-on-the-web.

35. Rebecca Greenfield, "Redditors Stand Up to Gawker to Protect Child Pornog-raphy," *The Atlantic,* October 11, 2012, https://www.theatlantic.com/technology /archive/2012/10/redditors-stand-gawker-protect-child-pornography/322479/; /r/politics moderator, "An Announcement about Gawker Links in /r/politics," Reddit, October 10, 2012, https://www.reddit.com/r/politics/comments/119z4z/an _announcement_about_gawker_links_in_rpolitics/?st=jivtz3kk&sh=91f7f751.

36. Nathan J. Matias, "Going Dark: Social Factors in Collective Action against Plat-form Operators in the Reddit Blackout," in *Proceedings of the 2016 CHI Conference on Human Factors in Computing Systems* (New York: ACM Press, 2016), 1138–1115.

37. spez, "Content Policy Update," Reddit, 2015, https://www.reddit.com/r/announce ments/comments/3fx2au/content_policy_update/.

38. Debbie Ging, "Alphas, Betas, and Incels: Theorizing the Masculinities of the Manosphere," *Men and Masculinities*, May 10, 2017, http://journals.sagepub.com/doi /abs/10.1177/1097184X17706401.

15   Fake Memetics: Political Rhetoric and Circulation in Political Campaigns

Benjamin Burroughs

Memes were once the stuff of 4chan /b/ boards and insider internet culture and humor,[1] but they now occupy an emergent space within political communication and the dissemination of political imagery. Memes operate as stitching devices, which meld platforms, ideology, and geopolitics within social networks and political campaigns, making them an important site of study for the weaving of fake news and misinformation into the fabric of political discourse and, ultimately, political deliberation.

Nominally, internet memes are defined as image macros with text on the top or bottom, generally in a sans serif font. Early examples of internet memes include Grumpy Cat, Success Kid, Rickrolling, and Scumbag Steve. Limor Shifman provides the clearest definition on internet memes defining them as "units of popular culture that are circulated, imitated, and transformed by individual Internet users, creating a shared cultural experience in the process."[2] Stemming out of remix and participatory culture, internet memes have been studied in a variety contexts ranging from popular culture to Occupy Wall Street, YouTube, LOLCats, and religion.[3] This chapter delves into the political rhetoric surrounding the employment of memes designed to create "meme magic."[4] Memes are increasingly the battleground of politics. In reference to the 2012 U.S. presidential campaign, memes were theorized as part of an "agonistic politics" where "memes, deception, and affective play" are central to "understanding discursive political identities and broader cultural values within networked popular culture."[5] This intensified during the 2016 presidential campaign and will likely continue to in the future. Political memes can act as ideological gatekeepers, reinforcing political division by being "in the know."[6] Political memes can also boil down complex arguments, for better or worse, into easily consumed memetic bites, operating as metonyms. This can make political memes extremely articulate and very poignant as they cut through the clutter of social media and the messiness of political campaigns to both inform and subvert. Memes are about connecting the political to the popular, the political to emotionally charged, affective media.

Memes and Political Slogans

From "binders full of women," a phrase uttered by Republican presidential candidate Mitt Romney that became a meme during the 2012 election cycle, to #BirdieSanders," a meme that captured a moment where a bird landed onstage with presidential candidate Bernie Sanders in the 2016 election cycle, political memes inject themselves into the spectacle of political discourse and political campaigns. As Asaf Nissenbaum and Shifman argue, memes can be wielded as "discursive weapons," which move beyond "trivial humor" and constitute "significant social functions."[7] Memes (as a media form) can keep pace with the speed and circulation of popular culture and contemporary social networking practices. The rapid pace of circulation also fits within the contemporary political landscape and its accompanying journalism and media news cycles, which intensify during political campaigns. Within political campaigns, the desire to reduce broad policy discussion into a sound bite or slogan works in conjunction with the popularity of memes.

Political campaigns have long attempted to offer slogans to voters, from "Tippecanoe and Tyler too" to "I like Ike" or Barry Goldwater's "In your heart, you know he's right" countered by Lyndon Johnson with "In your guts you know he's nuts." This continued during the 2016 election cycle. For example, the phrase "Make America great again" and the hashtag #MAGA acted as a narrative framing, which incorporated many of Donald Trump's campaign ideas on immigration, trade, and security. The chant "Lock her up" served to paint Hillary Clinton as embroiled in scandal and unfit for office. The term *fake news* itself, popularized and repeated by Trump, served to rebut and delegitimize criticism directed at the candidate by traditional media sources. However, what is different about contemporary political campaigns is the increasing ability for audiences to engage in the unfolding of political messaging and political speech.

Memes as Stitching Device

Memes are central to that process of citizen engagement in politics (both positively and negatively) because they act as a stitching device. Memes stitch in several ways. First, memes stitch together different media platforms. The form of a meme means it can easily migrate across media platforms, traversing between sites such as Reddit, Tumblr, Facebook, Twitter, and many others.[8] This means that memes are easily woven into political narratives, adding poignant political messaging to social networks. Based on the affordances of memes and their iterating and reciprocating potential, a larger political and ideological narrative can be stitched between platforms.

Second, memes stitch together narrative and ideology. Memes, as metonym, make salient and intensify political discourse. As a part standing for the whole, memes can provide jolts of affect resulting in cohesion around political ideology in the most efficient of ways, thus solidifying the political. This often happens through capitalizing on everyday, emergent digital vernacular adapted to politics, which Cole Stryker calls "visual vernacular" as the "language of memes."[9] When placed in the context of political campaigns and when serving the interests of candidates or political ideology, memes amass a political vernacular—a shared cultural register to stoke and weaponize memetic fires.

In the lead-up to the 2016 election, for example, some of the memetic cultural vernacular that emerged around candidate Trump included "Pepe Trump," being "redpilled," or "Can't stump the Trump."[10] Memes are "strands of populist discourse,"[11] but within the context of campaigns those strands are stitched together into calcified, weaponized political ideology. Memetic politics were so mainstream and part of the 2016 campaign that candidates and their families responded and propagated memes during the course of the campaign themselves. For example, Donald Trump Jr. posted a meme to his Instagram page in response to Clinton's "basket of deplorables" comment.[12]

This political meme (figure 15.1) is doing the work of signaling to an audience of campaign supporters an understood cultural vernacular laced with political ideology. Notice the usage of a "friend" and the humor / popular culture referencing of the image as a form of "plausible deniability" to shield from potential blowback, while fully embracing "Pepe Trump" next to then candidate Trump. When humor is added to memes, citizens can spread

Figure 15.1

memes by hiding behind the humor as a form of plausible deniability—in a way other mediated forms of ideology or campaign messages wouldn't as easily spread (such as a campaign speech or policy position statement).

Third, and lastly, memes stitch geopolitically, allowing different countries and global ideology and politics to enter national boundaries through social networks. The trafficking in memes is no longer a national phenomenon. Memes operating through bursts of affective, ideological punch are subject to a global audience. This means that state and non-state actors recognize the potency of memes and their ability to influence and destabilize, to cultivate discord in a foreign country. In 2016, this was made apparent after it was shown that Russian bots attempted to influence the election through Facebook and Twitter, primarily through memetic communication. Social media makes it cheap to micro-target audiences despite distance. This trend of geopolitical encounters through memes is unlikely to stop as we move forward into future campaigns.

A meme from the Facebook group "Army of Jesus" (figure 15.2) is one of the three thousand ads lawmakers disclosed as part of Russian efforts to influence the campaign.[13] The majority of these political ads on Facebook and Instagram are presented in the form of political memes.[14] The question of authorship arises with the review of memes related to purported Russian interference in the 2016 campaign. Memes, such as the Army of Jesus, are largely anonymous with regard to authorship, part of the larger cultural

Figure 15.2

vernacular due to their iterability. This anonymity allows for the spread of "fake" memetics because the focus bubbling from the meme is about the connection to narrative or ideology. The meme in figure 15.2 connects the election and Trump to a broader religious discourse pitting good and evil against each other, Satan and Jesus. Despite the meme excusing Trump's past indiscretions and impropriety by stating that he "isn't a saint by any means," Hillary is cast as Satan with "her crimes and lies." The "crimes and lies" connect with the larger campaign messaging about "Crooked Hillary" being morally bankrupt because of her e-mails and the Clinton Foundation allegations. The connection to a religious system of belief does the stitching work to cement the jolts of affect from the meme with the emergent political narrative.

Figure 15.3

Another image (figure 15.3) does the work of connecting to religious ideology, but through anxieties related to "illegals" and border security. The meme concocts a story about "an illegal alien from Honduras that had previously been deported and convicted of Rape Second Degree." The meme cites Barack Obama and Hillary Clinton as the culprits for "illegals" and the distance of politicians from the border as evidence of a government out of touch. The meme parrots Trump's campaign speeches about Mexicans as a rationale for rejecting "amnesty," stating that "rapists, drug dealers, human traffickers, and others" are crossing the border. The meme is tapping into a deeper ideological fear of difference, racial politics, and immigration, while propping up the border patrol of law and order as "always guided by God." Memes are incredibly potent during the election cycle, but they are also seeping into an emergent social media vernacular combining activism and ideology, making racist incidents more visible with memes like "BBQ Becky" and "Permit Patty."[15] This wielding of memes can push back against misinformation and racist ideology as a form of social activism.

The Democratic primary also used political memes as the staging grounds for political clashes. The Sanders campaign, for example, strategically capitalized on social media in 2016, creating its own "social media machine."[16] Beyond the effective #FeeltheBern hashtag and the myriad other official organizing tools and messages, average citizens participated in the crafting of Sanders as a candidate and the surge of support for him online. One site of creative participation is the Facebook group page Bernie Sanders' Dank Meme Stash (BSDMS). As of May 2016, the group had more than four hundred thousand members, a substantive jump from just five thousand members in January 2016. Part of the rapid growth came in conjunction with Tumblr and Reddit/Imgur posts around the "Bernie or Hillary?" meme (figure 15.4), which depicted (mostly) fictitious contrasts between the candidates on issues ranging from "sleeping" and "Star Wars" to "Radiohead" and "Carly Rae Jepsen."[17]

Sanders is depicted as "dank" (deriving from "stoner" or "hippie" slang for potent or high-quality), with a deep understanding of issues and cultural nuance, whereas Hillary is portrayed as trying too hard and as unrelatable.

This is not to say that memes cannot be extremely problematic forms of political engagement that squelch larger debates and reinforce stereotypes. Certainly, ardent Sanders supporters and "Bernie Bros" have been accused of misogyny and sexism through their memetic practices during the campaign (including within the "Bernie or Hillary?" meme example). The memetic form, however, speaks in a language that many, especially the constructed category of "millennial," have grown up with on social media. Memes are an important part of the "dank" articulation of Sanders as a candidate.

Conclusion

Memes are an increasingly important part of political speech. Social media provides the tools directly to citizens for dissemination and spread of

Figure 15.4

messages through memes. What was once the prerogative and purview
of campaigns and candidates competing with news cycles acting as gatekeepers has now become enmeshed in the participatory elements of social
media and the apparatus of citizen journalism. This imbues memes with a
grassroots authenticity within social networks juxtaposed against corporate media gatekeepers or media elites who have traditionally used op-eds
or town hall debates to invite particular kinds of public participation in
political spectacle. Memes serve as stitching agents that weave together
platforms, ideology, and geopolitical discourse. As memes have expanded
beyond popular culture and humor, they become the grounds for social
activism, merging the political and the social. While "LOLitics" will continue to playfully merge humor and politics,[18] memes are increasingly the

site of blunt ideological force, intensifying political division. The memes are "fake," but the ideological ramifications are tangible and potent.

Notes

1. Whiney Phillips, "The House That Fox Built: Anonymous, Spectacle, and Cycles of Amplification," *Television and New Media* 14, no. 6 (2013): 494–509.

2. Limor Shifman, "Memes in a Digital World: Reconciling with a Conceptual Troublemaker," *Journal of Computer-Mediated Communication* 18, no. 3 (2013): 367.

3. On the origins of internet memes, see Lawrence Lessig, *Remix: Making Art and Commerce Thrive in the Hybrid Economy* (New York: Penguin, 2008); Lev Manovich, "The Practice of Everyday (Media) Life: From Mass Consumption to Mass Cultural Production?," *Critical Inquiry* 35, no. 2 (2009): 319–331. For the varied contexts in which internet memes have been studied, see Michele Knobel and Colin Lankshear. "Online Memes, Affinities, and Cultural Production," in *A New Literacies Sampler*, ed. Michele Knobel and Colin Lankshear (New York: Pete Lang, 2007), 199–227; Ryan M. Milner, "Pop Polyvocality: Internet Memes, Public Participation, and the Occupy Wall Street Movement," *International Journal of Communication* 7 (2013): 2357–2390; Limor Shifman, "An Anatomy of a YouTube Meme," *New Media and Society* 14, no. 2 (2012): 187–203; Kate M. Miltner, "'There's No Place for Lulz on LOLCats': The Role of Genre, Gender, and Group Identity in the Interpretation and Enjoyment of an Internet Meme," *First Monday* 19, no. 8 (2014), http://dx.doi.org/10.5210/fm .v19i8.5391; Benjamin Burroughs and Gavin Feller, "Religious Memetics: Institutional Authority in Digital/Lived Religion," *Journal of Communication Inquiry* 39, no. 4 (2015): 357–377.

4. Milo Yiannopoulos, "Meme Magic: Donald Trump Is the Internet's Revenge on Lazy Elites," Breitbart, May 4, 2016, http://www.breitbart.com/milo/2016/05/04/meme -magic-donald-trump-internets-revenge-lazy-entitled-elites/.

5. Benjamin Burroughs, "Obama Trolling: Memes, Salutes and an Agonistic Politics in the 2012 Presidential Election," in "Trolls and the Negative Space of the Internet," *Fibreculture Journal*, no. 22 (2013): 260.

6. Ryan M. Milner, "The World Made Meme: Discourse and Identity in Participatory Media" (Ph.D. diss., University of Kansas, 2012).

7. Asaf Nissenbaum and Limor Shifman, "Internet Memes as Contested Cultural Capital: The Case of 4chan's /b/ Board," *New Media and Society* 19, no. 4 (2017): 497.

8. On Reddit, see, for example, Ioana Literat and Sarah van den Berg, "Buy Memes Low, Sell Memes High: Vernacular Criticism and Collective Negotiations of Value on Reddit's MemeEconomy," *Information, Communication and Society* 22, no. 2 (2017): 232–249.

9. Cole Stryker, *Epic Win for Anonymous: How 4chan's Army Conquered the Web* (New York: Overlook Duckworth, 2011).

10. For discussion of how the Pepe Trump meme was leveraged through memes and sites like Reddit, as "internet folklore" to make "meme magic," "Kek," and "memetic warfare," see Paul Spencer, "Trump's Occult Online Supporters Believe 'Meme Magic' Got Him Elected," *Motherboard*, November 18, 2016, https://motherboard.vice.com /en_us/article/pgkx7g/trumps-occult-online-supporters-believe-pepe-meme-magic -got-him-elected; "Redpilled" builds from popular culture, using imagery of the pills from Morpheus in *The Matrix*, presenting an alternative to the perceived overreach of "PC culture" and feminism. See Amelia Tait, "Spitting out the Red Pill: Former Misogynists Reveal How They Were Radicalised Online," *New Statesman*, February 28, 2017, https://www.newstatesman.com/science-tech/internet/2017/02/reddit-the -red-pill-interview-how-misogyny-spreads-online; Comrade Stump, "You Can't Stump the Trump (Volume 4)," YouTube video, October 13, 2015, https://www.youtube .com/watch?time_continue=8&v=MKH6PAoUuD0.

11. Milner, "Pop Polyvocality," 2363.

12. Donald Trump Jr., Instagram, September 10, 2016, https://www.instagram.com /p/BKMtdN5Bam5/?utm_source=ig_embed.

13. U.S. House of Representatives Permanent Select Committee on Intelligence (HPSCI), HPSCI Minority Exhibit A, Army of Jesus, https://democrats-intelligence .house.gov/uploadedfiles/6053177352305.pdf.

14. Methodologically, this research reviewed the three thousand Russian political ads released by the HPSCI and used these ads for textual and semiotic analysis. These memes were combined with the researcher's own review of memes related to the 2016 presidential campaign.

15. Jessica Guynn, "BBQ Becky, Permit Patty and Why the Internet Is Shaming White People Who Police People 'Simply for Being Black,'" *USA Today*, July 18, 2018, https://www.usatoday.com/story/tech/2018/07/18/bbq-becky-permit-patty-and -why-internet-shaming-white-people-who-police-black-people/793574002/.

16. Michael Grothaus, "Inside Bernie Sanders's Social Media Machine," *Fast Company*, April 11, 2016, https://www.fastcompany.com/3058681/inside-bernie-sanders -social-media-machine.

17. "Bernie or Hillary?—Sleeping." Know Your Meme, http://knowyourmeme.com /photos/1074782-bernie-or-hillary.

18. LOLitics are defined as "popular culture products that exist within the intersection between pleasure-driven 'play' and (arguably) genuine political discourse." Geniesa Tay, "Binders Full of LOLitics: Political Humour, Internet Memes, and Play in the 2012 U.S. Presidential Election (and Beyond)," *European Journal of Humour Research* 2, no. 4 (2014): 46.

16   Weaponizing #fakenews in a Visual War on Journalism: Seeing a Big Picture through Instagram

Leslie-Jean Thornton

When CNN reporter Jim Acosta broadcast live from a rally for Donald Trump in Tampa, Florida, the sight of an angry, threatening crowd yelling insults his way while waving fists and antipress signs made news worldwide.[1] It was no surprise to those who had watched the highly charged "enemy of the people" rhetoric grow on social media, particularly in visual posts hashtagged #fakenews and distributed on Instagram. For them, this was an enactment of the potentially explosive antagonistic discourse they saw rationalized again and again in images they scrolled on their phones and computers. The possibility of a violent outcome targeting a member of the press is troubling, but for some, at least if #fakenews posts before and after the rally are to be believed, violence is viewed as a desirable and even deserved outcome.

Video clips and photographs of that event circulated online and were viewed by millions. On Instagram, where hashtags aggregate posts together, there were more than 210 posts to #fakenews during the time of this event. Many of the posts also contained additional hashtags, pushing them to other hashtag publics where they could be seen.[2] For example, 422 individuals clicked the heart-shaped "like" button on just one post (out of many) of Acosta warily eyeing someone giving him the finger, an obscene gesture (figure 16.1). "They are scared," the caption states, referring to journalists. The popular image itself was incorporated into multiple memes, including one featuring a fake "cover" of *Time* magazine (figure 16.2). But possibly the most significant post chronicling that event and posted to #fakenews was one from President Trump himself, which was viewed a million times in just one day.

The thriving world of Instagram's #fakenews feed, more than 637,700 posts strong and growing as of July 4, 2018, is one of conspiracies, crisis actors, duplicity and deception, depictions of violent or punitive acts,

docs_red_hat • Follow

docs_red_hat They are scared.
We have Awaken!
POWER TO THE PEOPLE!
SHEEP NO MORE.
His Face says it All... 😆 😆 😆
#QAnon #wwg1wga #FakeNews #CNN
#JimAcosta

gigisblueiz CNN are not news and do
represent the American people

red_american_mama Best 📷 picture 📷
ever 👏 👏 👏 👏

realjzg 😆 😆 😆 😆 😆 🇺🇸 🇺🇸 🇺🇸 🇺🇸 I Love
it!!!!!

themysteriousnomad ACOSTA...a Liberal
girly man

_q_anon_1 He looked like he shit himself

gardenmaestro Priceless!!!

gardenmaestro @_q_anon_1 he should of

♡ ○   🔖

422 likes

23 HOURS AGO

Add a comment...   ...

Figure 16.1

provocative mockery, partisan sniping, memes,[3] misunderstandings passed off as wisdom, and directed anger and outrage. In the first half of 2018, the forum became increasingly global as other countries faced fake-news incursions and interested parties began posting to the hashtag.[4]

In the mix, there is occasional guidance about how to detect actual fake news (deliberately false information) or posts debunking rumors and allegations, but overwhelmingly, it is an insult-rich zone with the legitimate press, not false information, as the primary target. A significant and thriving aspect of the platform's #fakenews forum is a steady stream of posts attempting to undermine the credibility and legitimacy of journalists and journalism organizations in the United States. How that plays out in a visual social media forum, where repetition, public pressure, and the immediacy and emotionality of visual cognition combine to make a strikingly powerful delivery system,[5] is the focus of this chapter.

The political weaponization of the phrase *fake news* arose primarily from then president-elect Donald Trump's appropriation of the term to denounce the press. Although he criticized journalists and news organizations frequently during his campaign, Trump used "FAKE NEWS!" in his tweets and

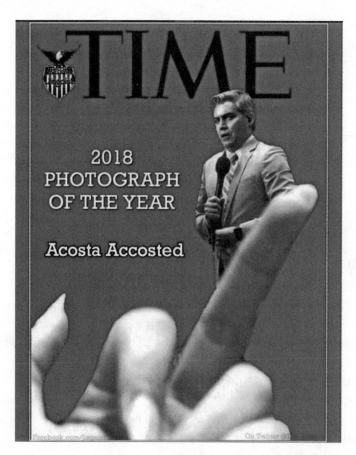

Figure 16.2

public statements through early January 2017 as a way to label what he deemed false or unflattering information.[6] However, his use of "fake news" changed when he started using it to describe whole news organizations as well as stories and reports, resulting in a muddied definition. During a televised press conference on January 12, 2017, then president-elect Trump thundered, "You are fake news!," from behind the Trump Tower lectern while pointing dramatically at CNN reporter Jim Acosta and the assembled corps.[7] Images from that moment, photographed from television screens and computer monitors, turned into internet memes, many of which carried the #fakenews hashtag. This redefinition was famously cemented on February 17, 2017, when Trump tweeted, "The FAKE NEWS media (failing

@nytimes, @NBCNews, @ABC, @CBS, @CNN) is not my enemy, it is the enemy of the American people!"[8] Screenshots of the tweet went viral on social media and were voluminously posted to #fakenews.

#fakenews on Instagram

Acceleration of posts on Instagram's #fakenews feed began around the time of the you-are-fake press conference. By mid-January 2017, the hashtag had approximately 20,000 posts. A year and a half later, it has attracted in excess of 617,700 more. Beginning in November 2016 and continuing through August 1, 2018, I monitored the feed on a weekly, sometimes daily, basis. Posts representative of viewpoints about journalists, journalism, and fake news were archived contemporaneously during that time. Analysis of the posts reveals four distinct content stages that may help us better understand journalism's role in American life during a time of heightened political friction. The first stage begins with Trump's recharacterization of the term *fake news* to refer to journalists and their organizations. After that key polarity is established, the second stage shows why they should not be trusted. In the third stage, the posts show there can be consequences to being enemies of the American people. In the fourth stage, there are cautions and reminders that the threat from so-called fake-news journalists is dangerous and pervasive. The images chosen as illustrative were analyzed following visual analysis guidelines;[9] the observations contributed to the overall analysis, but full descriptions were beyond the scope of this essay.

Creating an Other

The first stage creates a basis for arguments that follow by breaking the original "fake news" binary opposition (fake versus actual news). Here, Trump's January 2017 accusation making journalists "fake news" appears to be seminal, with multiple iterations serving as visual testament. This foundational image establishes "us versus them" in a classic binary opposition, encouraging identity formation and setting the framework of a constructed reality. The image aligns Trump with truth and the United States—he wears the colors of the flags behind him, visually and symbolically identifying this president with the nation. He is strong, sure of himself, clearly in charge. The "you" in his accusation refers to journalists, but also to anyone who is not

Figure 16.3

Figure 16.4

on his and the nation's side, facing down news and news reporters not of his liking. Memes, in many iterations, were posted to #fakenews (figure 16.3).

Visually, these images call to mind another historic image, the iconic Uncle Sam poster created by James Montgomery Flagg for the government during World War I. The allusion was not lost among posters using #fakenews; both the U.S. Army poster and various spinoffs were popular (figure 16.4). The visual message is clear: Trump stands for America and he wants to rally an army. In this case, though, it is against the people toward whom he was pointing—the people he placed in opposition to himself—when he said, "You are fake news": journalists.

Don't Trust Journalists, Don't Trust These Journalists

The second stage builds on the first, but identifies journalists more granularly, both by organization and individually. The memes—and there are thousands of them—give reasons why journalists should not be trusted and encourage non-journalists to keep their distance. Insults and mockery play into this stage, with popular targets chosen largely from the ranks of broadcast journalists, and mostly from CNN (figure 16.5). Occasionally, a Trump administration hero is shown, as in one image where White House press secretary Sarah Huckabee Sanders is shown with a mop and bucket. The

Figure 16.5

mop has the face of the CNN reporter from the "you are fake news" press conference. She refers to him in the image, saying, "I don't always enjoy mopping up the floor. But when I do, it's with Jim Acosta." In other memes, she is depicted as belittling reporters in White House press conferences. In something of a double whammy, MSNBC anchor Brian Williams, who lied repeatedly about his whereabouts and involvement for a story and was, as a result, fired from his job as an NBC anchor in 2015, is shown purportedly delivering the message that journalists make up news. The overall message: "fake news" journalists do not deserve civility, respect, or trust.

The use of branding logos is a popular symbolic device in visual messages for several reasons: they are designed for immediate recognition, as they do not depend on language to understand them or to connect them with the organizations they represent. And in the context of this hashtag community, they serve as shorthand messaging to announce "fake news," an association that would likely carry over to when the logos were seen outside of the #fakenews forum as well. In that sense, the organizations' own branding is weaponized along with the phrase *fake news*. An example: "WARNING," intones big, white-on-red, all-cap letters across the top of one post in this category, "THE FOLLOWING MEDIA OUTLETS PROMOTE FAKE NEWS." Below (figure 16.6) are brand logos for eighteen well-known journalism organizations, including CNN, the *New York Times*, the *Washington Post*, NBC, ABC, *USA Today*, *Politico*, and *Time*. Hundreds of iterations of this meme play on the same theme.

The top middle image of figure 16.6 signals that the news media are "whorish" in an unquestioning obedience to former president Barack Obama, a reference to Trump's deep state conspiracy charges as well as an accusation of media bias mirroring statements made by Trump. Next to it is a cautionary tale reinforcing an assessment of the moral depravity of journalists, in general, and of CNN reporters, in particular. Following it, four advisories offer direct, if blanket, identification of journalist organizations one should disbelieve and why.

The left image in the top row of figure 16.7 is based on a pictorial maxim dating back centuries. The three wise monkeys (slightly out of traditional order here) stand for "say no evil, see no evil, and hear no evil"—generally shortened to mean, "turning a blind eye." This is another image that would convey meaning across cultures without relying on words. The two images referencing Facebook rely on wide-eyed expressions of credulity, with the

Figure 16.6

Figure 16.7

underlying message implying that Facebook is complicit in publishing "fake news" journalists, playing on Facebook's stated intent of eliminating actual fake news. Anyone who believes otherwise, the visuals imply, is either a baby who does not know better or an overly trusting adult. The last image speaks for it itself in the most dyadic color scheme possible: contrasting the reflection of all light (white) with the total absorption thereof, which shows as black.

Enemies and Consequences

Having established journalists as untrustworthy others, and having identified them by affiliation and likeness, the visual rhetoric in the third stage again establishes a foundational image—a screengrab of Trump's "enemy of the American people" tweet. That accusation provides justification for exploring potential consequences enemies of the nation may face. Positioning journalists as enemies, in this context, provides a rationale for visually insulting, mocking, shunning, punishing, and even killing them. Although no connection has been documented, the last is especially chilling after five journalists were fatally shot at the *Capital Gazette* newspaper in Maryland on June 28, 2018.[10]

One post (figure 16.8) shows five hanged bodies, nooses around their necks, suspended from the word "TIME" displayed as if it were *Time* magazine's cover (it is not) and the (presumed) corpses were cover art. Nineteen brand logos are placed on the bodies, including CNN, the *New York Times*, MSNBC, the *Washington Post*, and CBS. Toward the bottom of the post, where one would find teases for that issue's articles had this been an actual cover, the words "High Treason" are displayed in white against *Time*'s signature blood-red background. The "assembly required" post suggestive of lynching refers to a T-shirt worn at a Trump rally the day before the 2016 presidential election. Reuters photojournalist Jonathan Ernst captured the image and it went viral on social media, inspiring graphics such as this one. A year and a half later, after the *Capital Gazette* shootings, the shirt again made news because it was still being sold.[11]

The first image in figure 16.9 has the appearance of having been made on a typewriter, harking back to precomputer news days. In the second image, bullet holes mark what appears to be glass separating the shooter

Figure 16.8

from journalists on the other side. "Trump 2018" suggests that this might be part of an agenda. The third image appeared on July 4, 2018. It was a topical cookout post, drawn by a skilled cartoonist but not carrying any attribution or credit (later identified as the work of Antonio Branco): Trump is dressed for a celebratory barbecue; he wears a "commander in chef" apron and an Uncle Sam stars-and-stripes top hat. He holds a flipper. Next to him is a grill, smoke rising, with hamburgers labeled CNN, NBC, ABC, *WAPO*, CBS, NPR, and *NYT* sizzling away.

Figure 16.9

Huge Threat

In the fourth stage, another category of images argues how threatening journalists are to "us"—that they're the bad guys even if they insist they're not. (Many posts mock CNN's motto: "The most trusted name in news," for example.) As one of the "threat" posts suggests, the very fabric of our nation is being ripped apart by their fakery (figure 16.10). In another post typical of the subtheme, you (non-journalists) have no control over how you perceive the world. While you are asleep and vulnerable, they (the journalists and their corporate owners) are busy creating your reality. The head in the meme, showing Caucasoid features and seen reflecting what could be the blue glow of a television or computer screen, shows how journalists have lodged in the host of this presumably white human's brain. Journalists ("aliens"?) exist both within and without, godlike, and unsusceptible to a need for sleep.

Keeping with the theme of defenseless complicity, one of the top posts on Independence Day 2018 proclaimed, "In North Korea, people are forced to listen to propaganda. IN THE USA PEOPLE DO IT WILLINGLY" (figure 16.10). At the top of the meme is a photograph of loudspeakers mounted on a pole. There is a small photo of the American flag next to it, a rallying image for patriots. To the right of the "willingly" statement, there are brand logos for NBC, ABC, CBS, CNN, and MSNBC. Unspoken message: the named news organizations are propagandists, and you should be smarter than to heed their broadcasts. Visually, the loudspeakers evoke jail yards and captive areas, and the flag insert effectively transports what is allegedly North Korea to the United States. The common tie? Propaganda. Journalists, in this meme, are equated with a dictator's propaganda mouthpieces.

Another popular perspective in this category suggests that hackers, working outside the system, are reliable sources of truth, not journalists. An anti-Semitic strain, long seen in anti-media protests, is evident in #fakenews. Many memes draw on cultural references, such as the image of mild-mannered reporter Clark Kent, also known as Superman, here on Earth to protect the planet from evildoers (figure 16.11). Alas, he's also an alleged illegal immigrant, so be warned. In another image, Macaulay Culkin from *Home Alone* (1990), a popular movie series about a young boy mistakenly left behind from family vacations, gains topical association with the border separations taking place and in the news when this (and other memes like it) are posted. A meme featuring a scene from *Kindergarten Cop* (1990), a movie starring former two-term California governor Arnold Schwarzenegger, incorporates a recurring "But the liberal media…" memetic theme. Those who do not know the film references might assume the memes refer to actual news reports; those who do get it could interpret this as mockery, meaning that journalists conflate fact and fiction.

Finally, two images (bottom row) refer to media framing with a more sophisticated illustration than generally seen in the #fakenews feed. In the graphic, which dates back to at least 2010 and appears often on social media, a cameraman is shown broadcasting a scene in such a way that the

Figure 16.10

attacker becomes the attacked, a perspective that might resonate with both sides of the us versus them construction.

Counter-Memes and Conclusions

The preceding images represent visual rhetoric supporting the delegitimization of the press in the United States. The #fakenews feed, however, is not homogeneous in viewpoint. There are occasional counter-posts. These

Figure 16.11

memes, and others in the same vein, appeared soon after Trump's "fake news" press conference and "enemy of the American people" charges. The first four (figure 16.12) make sharp connections between Hitler's and Trump's treatment of the press. The fifth image rebuts: the connection's only there if you're seeing through CNN's blood-colored glasses.

The casting of journalists as not only un-American but anti-American, as Trump did when he called them enemies of the American people, is a particularly significant charge for people who derive their professional calling as public servants from the Constitution's First Amendment. To be labeled "fake news media" harms their credibility, whether that's the intended purpose or not. The repeated use of the phrase *fake news* makes it familiar, normal—less likely to be parsed for exact meaning. Whether these anti-journalism posts persuade anyone or not, they damage journalistic standing, even if only by validating a dangerous worldview. In short, any journalistic use of the words *fake news* normalizes them as well, making them more familiar and easier to slide into one's brain uncontested. How can anyone, the reasoning goes, believe anything journalists report when they, themselves, are fake?

Within the visual world of #fakenews, everyone agrees that fake news is bad. No less an authority than the current president of the United States has told them so repeatedly and with great passion. Right-leaning voters and

Figure 16.12

politicians assign blame to left-leaners and tie the rise of fake news to what they perceive as multiple social ills. Journalists and social media companies deploy experts to combat it. When one looks at what each group means, however, contradictions appear. When one follows visual rhetoric for the Trumpian logic, the depicted way to fight fake news is to punish or eliminate journalists, suggesting a troubling Big Picture indeed. The stages of thought I present in this chapter show how a hateful viewpoint might grow with continued exposure to the #fakenews feed. One might begin noticing the posts out of curiosity, then buy into some of them, and then into more until it makes perfect sense to mock (or worse) a so-called enemy of the American people. Newcomers to the feed can find a plethora of posts from which to choose, tuning in to their existing perspective but awash in material politically and emotionally charged and intended to validate or persuade.

Days before the Tampa rally in which CNN was targeted, *New York Times* publisher A. G. Sulzberger asked President Trump to stop his "enemy of the people" rhetoric, fearing it would lead to violence.[12] Days after, human rights appointees from the United Nations and the Inter-American Commission on Human Rights condemned Trump's treatment of news media: "We are especially concerned these attacks increase the risk of journalists being targeted with violence."[13] Instagram's #fakenews feed amplifies those attacks, raising challenges involving freedom of speech, political manipulation, and safety. Although the platform blocks or removes offensive accounts or content (this is clear from occasional complaints in comments), all the images included in this chapter remained online as this chapter was written, some well more than a year after being posted. There are difficulties, as well, in knowing where the posts originate. Facebook, which owns Instagram, was used extensively as a tool of foreign influence in the 2016 campaign, and the interference continued. It seems likely #fakenews was a prime arena. As account purges continue, change may occur, but experts extend little encouragement.[14] Traffic ebbs and flows, but spikes in positing around political events or controversies provide a pattern of sorts. Journalists can hardly be expected to cover news as well as post corrective counterarguments into the #fakenews fray, but one wonders what might happen if public service–minded volunteers began practicing a bit of hashtag activism, strategically seeding the feed with support.

Notes

1. Tom Embury-Dennis, "Trump Supporters Filmed Hurling Sustained Abuse at Journalists following Make America Great Again Rally," *The Independent*, August 1, 2018, https://www.independent.co.uk/news/world/americas/trump-florida-rally-supporters-cnn-jim-acosta-tampa-maga-a8472436.html.

2. Nathan Rambukkana, *#Hashtag Publics: The Power and Politics of Discursive Networks* (New York: Peter Lang, 2015).

3. Embury-Dennis, "Trump Supporters."

4. Jon Henley, "Global Crackdown on Fake News Raises Censorship Concerns," *The Guardian*, April 24, 2018, https://www.theguardian.com/media/2018/apr/24/global-crackdown-on-fake-news-raises-censorship-concerns; Anya Schiffrin, "How Europe Fights Fake News," *Columbia Journalism Review*, October 26, 2017, https://www.cjr.org/watchdog/europe-fights-fake-news-facebook-twitter-google.php.

5. On visual cognition, see Paul Messaris and Linus Abraham, "The Role of Images in Framing News Stories," in *Framing Public Life: Perspectives on Media and Our Understanding of the Social World*, ed. Stephen D. Reese, Oscar H. Gandy Jr., and August E. Grant (Mahwah, NJ: Lawrence Erlbaum, 2001), 215–226.

6. On Trump's criticism of the press during his campaign, see Nick Corasaniti, "Partisan Crowds at Trump Rallies Menace and Frighten News Media," *New York Times*,

October 14, 2016, https://www.nytimes.com/2016/10/15/us/politics/trump-media
-attacks.html. On Trump's use of "fake news" to label information as false, see Adam
Gabbatt, "How Trump's 'Fake News' Gave Authoritarian Leaders a New Weapon,"
The Guardian, January 25, 2018, https://www.theguardian.com/us-news/2018/jan
/25/how-trumps-fake-news-gave-authoritarian-leaders-a-new-weapon.

7. Maxwell Tani, "Trump Battles CNN Reporter in Heated Exchange at Press Conference: 'You Are Fake News,'" Business Insider, January 11, 2017, http://www.business
insider.com/cnn-fake-news-donald-trump-cnn-jim-acosta-question-press-conference
-2017-1.

8. Donald Trump (@realDonaldTrump), Twitter, February 17, 2017, https://twitter
.com/realdonaldtrump/status/832708293516632065.

9. Paul M. Lester, *Visual Communication: Images with Messages*, 7th ed. (Dallas, TX:
WritingForTextbooks, 2017); Gillian Rose, *Visual Methodologies: An Introduction to
Researching with Visual Methods*, 4th ed. (London: Sage, 2016).

10. Sabrina Tavernise, Amy Harmon, and Maya Salam, "5 People Dead in Shooting
at Maryland's *Capital Gazette* Newsroom," *New York Times*, June 28, 2018, https://
www.nytimes.com/2018/06/28/us/capital-gazette-annapolis-shooting.html.

11. John Bonazzo, "'Rope. Tree. Journalist.' T-Shirt Shows Need for Online Moderators," Observer, July 2, 2018, http://observer.com/2018/07/ccafepress-rope-tree
-journalist-site-moderators/.

12. Mark Landler, "New York Times Publisher and Trump Clash over President's
Threats against Journalism," *New York Times*, July 29, 2018, https://www.nytimes
.com/2018/07/29/us/politics/trump-new-york-times-sulzberger.html.

13. United Nations Office of the High Commissioner for Human Rights, "Trump
Attacks on Media Violate Basic Norms of Press Freedom, Human Rights Experts Say,"
August 2, 2018, https://www.ohchr.org/EN/NewsEvents/Pages/DisplayNews.aspx
?NewsID=23425&LangID=E.

14. Matt O'Brien and Ryan Nakashima, "Social Media Plays Whack-a-Mole with
Russia Interference," *Seattle Times*, August 1, 2018, https://www.seattletimes.com/busi
ness/social-media-plays-whack-a-mole-with-russia-interference/.

V Reception: Part Introduction

All of the chapters in this part explore the complexities of how individuals make sense of fake news and other kinds of false information. Too often public debates about fake news fail to consider why or how individuals engage with a variety of types of information, the psychological processes involved in how we assess information, or how technologies may influence the ways we think.

The first chapter in this part, "Mental Shortcuts, Emotion, and Social Rewards: The Challenges of Detecting and Resisting Fake News," is by media effects scholars Nicholas David Bowman and Elizabeth Cohen. In this chapter, Bowman and Cohen argue that even though "spot fake news" tools are given to individuals to help them make sense of online information, there are a variety of reasons individuals may choose not to use them. Using mass communication and media psychology theories, Bowman and Cohen discuss fake news in relation to emotion, confirmation bias, cognitive dissonance, and other factors influencing both the ways we engage with news content and whether we believe it. Finally, this chapter presents several explanations for why audiences might both mistrust and misunderstand news content, which make accepting and believing fake news all the easier.

The second chapter in this part, "Source Credibility and Belief in Fake News: I'll Believe You If You Agree with Me," is by Danielle Polage, who researches false belief from a psychological perspective. In her chapter, Polage discusses an experiment looking at the effects of false information exposure on individuals. She explores how our perceptions of source credibility, our existing knowledge frameworks, and the repetition of messages influence whether we believe false information. More specifically, results of Polage's research support the idea that exposure to false information makes the information seem truer and more plausible and that increased familiarity can also lead people to misattribute where they heard about the false information. Polage concludes her chapter by discussing our collective responsibilities to stop the spread of fake news.

The final chapter in this part is by computer scientist Panagiotis Takis Metaxas, "Technology, Propaganda, and the Limits of the Human Intellect," examines how technology relates to the ways people think, how we believe what we believe, and how we can be fooled. Metaxas argues that the blame we assign to social media and web technologies for the circulation of fake news as well as other types of online misinformation actually serve to manage *our own* intellectual limitations. Metaxas argues that we are "thinking lazy," and while regulatory and technology changes will be necessary to address online misinformation, no solution will be complete without widespread epistemological education and the active engagement of citizens in democratic societies.

Suggested Reading

Alice Marwick, "Why Do People Share Fake News? A Sociotechnical Model of Media Effects," *Georgetown Law Technology Review* 2, no. 2 (2018): 474–512, https://georgetownlawtechreview.org/wp-content/uploads/2018/07/2.2-Marwick-pp-474-512.pdf.

Brendan Nyhan, "Why Fears of Fake News Are Overhyped," *Medium*, February 4, 2019, https://medium.com/s/reasonable-doubt/why-fears-of-fake-news-are-overhyped-2ed9ca0a52c9.

Francesca Polletta and Jessica Callahan, "Deep Stories, Nostalgia Narratives, and Fake News: Storytelling in the Trump Era," *American Journal of Cultural Sociology* 5, no. 3 (2017): 392–408.

17 Mental Shortcuts, Emotion, and Social Rewards: The Challenges of Detecting and Resisting Fake News

Nicholas David Bowman and Elizabeth Cohen

London-based *Channel 4 News* (via its *FactCheck* blog) released a video on Facebook titled "Stopping Fake News." The video provides viewers with three "quick tips" to detecting fake news online. In just over two minutes, the video explains to viewers how to more critically process content by scrutinizing the sources (confusing "abc.com with abc.com.com") as well as images and sources used in an article (by searching for the original materials)—a skill known as *lateral reading* in media literacy circles.[1]

Such literacy efforts are well-intentioned and no doubt helpful in making citizens more critical and effective media consumers.[2] Yet, even if individuals are given the tools to vet information online, there are a variety of psychological or social reasons they may not. This chapter reviews a number of potential reasons—explicit and implicit, intentional and unintentional, or informed or ignorant—for why news consumers might actively engage with fake news, through the lens of mass communication and media psychology scholarship. First, the psychological mechanisms of cognitive dissonance and confirmation bias are introduced, as well as other cognitive shortcuts that audiences might engage in when listening to, reading, or viewing news content that they might not believe in. Then, the chapter will shift to discussions of the role that emotions play in what audiences choose to believe from the news, as well as other social influences that might explain why people read and share fake news. From this, the chapter presents several explanations for why audiences might both mistrust and misunderstand news content, which make accepting and believing fake news all the easier.

Cognitive Dissonance and Confirmation Biases

People may not be equally likely to believe all fake news they encounter, but we all possess a confirmation bias that tends to make us less critical of and more likely to believe news and information that supports or confirms our preexisting opinions and beliefs. Leon Festinger's (1957) theory of cognitive dissonance posits that exposure to information that challenges a person's perspective creates a discrepancy between his or her own views and the one being presented, which in turn elicits psychological discomfort. To avoid this discomfort, people tend to seek out information that confirms their existing attitudes and beliefs, and avoid information that conflicts with these. Even when blatantly false beliefs are corrected, people have a tendency to reinterpret the information in a way that makes their initial beliefs seem justified—Festinger, Henry Riecken, and Stanley Schachter (1956) demonstrated this effect when studying cult members' increased devotion to their belief system after a failed "doomsday date" prophecy led them to reinterpret the world's survival as evidence that their devotion to the cult had saved the world.[3] Hence, when it comes to news, people are prone to believe information that resonates with their existing beliefs, and they tend to be more critical of information that contradicts their point of view, whether the information is true or not.

Cognitive Shortcuts to Processing Fake News

Beyond confirmation biases, oftentimes people will not exert the effort to scrutinize news and information simply because doing so requires too much effort. The so-called *cognitive miser* approach suggests that people tend to treat cognitive energy as a valuable resource, often reserved for situations in which cognition is thought to be critical.[4] Given the number of decisions people are required to make in daily life, and the vast amounts of information people could use to inform those decisions, it simply is not practical, efficient, or feasible for them to carefully scrutinize all available pieces of information before drawing conclusions. Instead, people rely on more heuristic "cognitive shortcuts" to judge the quality of information.[5] For instance, to determine whether an article is credible, readers may base their decision on heuristics (cues) such as the attractiveness of the layout or the familiarity of the source, rather than devote effort to weighing the logic and veracity of the article's content—if nothing else, as a way to quickly sort seemingly endless information flows.

One such heuristic relevant to social media is social endorsement, or the extent to which we think other people are supporting and sharing the content. Indeed, these bandwagon effects have been found to override people's initial concerns about dubious message sources, and such a finding might in part explain why the most popular stories shared during the 2016 U.S. presidential election were verifiably fake news.[6] According to the cognitive miser approach to information processing, people rely on these types of mental shortcuts not because they are unconcerned with truth and accuracy, but because human brains simply do not have the capacity to apply the maximum amount of mental effort in every situation.

Emotion and Fake News

Up until this point, we have focused on how our perceptual restrictions and biases make us sitting ducks for absorbing misinformation, but cognitive limitations are not the only trap. The reasons that fake news often resonates with people is rooted in how they *feel* about it as much as—if not more than—how they think about it. Studies have rather consistently found that people are more drawn to news and information if it packs an emotional punch. For instance, an analysis of seventy thousand online news articles reveals that articles that were associated with more extreme emotions were more likely to be clicked on.[7] Purveyors of fake news and "clickbait" capitalize on this attraction to the emotional by fabricating or exaggerating headlines, stories, and images that capture people's attention by engaging intense affective reactions.[8] The more emotions that news content elicits, the more likely it is to be remembered as well, as (a) humans are hardwired to commit emotionally charged information and events to memory and (b) emotionally charged examples in media content tend to be more cognitively accessible.[9] Fortunately, even highly emotional misinformation is not immune to retraction.[10]

Emotions also explain why misinformation spreads. Jonah Berger and Katherine L. Milkman demonstrate that news content evoking highly arousing emotions such as awe or anger is more likely to be shared with others.[11] Likewise, a study of political messages on Twitter finds that emotionally charged tweets are retweeted more often and spread more quickly than more neutral content.[12] More recently, another study finds that fake news and misinformation spreads faster than true information on Twitter and evokes more emotional replies.[13] From this, we surmise that fake news and information is more emotionally evocative and therefore more likely to prompt people to share it, regardless of how accurate it is. Collectively, these findings demonstrate that much of the success of fake news lies in its ability to tap into our emotions.

Social Gratifications of Sharing Fake News

Beyond psychology, there are also a number of social reasons for reading, believing, and sharing news, regardless of whether it's accurate or not. To some extent, news has always provided opportunities for social bonding. Other evidence suggests that consuming tragic news coverage allows audiences to form a feeling of connection with others who are following the same story.[14] Sharing news with others also allows people to socialize and feel a sense of status within their peer groups.[15] Indeed, people who treasure their roles as social opinion leaders are more apt to share information than to evaluate it, and social status is one of the motivators that drive this effect.[16] Precisely because fake news, urban legends, and conspiracy theories are more novel than the run-of-the-mill truth, users are driven to share them on a platform where social status is often determined by how quickly one posts new and relevant content. On Twitter, novelty and speed is valued over convention and validation. Although the social benefits of consuming and sharing novel news should be attainable regardless of whether the information is true or false, verified or unverified—for some, subscribing to unsubstantiated, fringe ideas can be particularly gratifying.

On one hand, belief in conspiracy theories has been found to satisfy a need of uniqueness—a desire to distinguish oneself from the crowd.[17] On the other hand, belief in conspiracy theories is also associated with greater feelings of alienation and reduced feelings of belongingness.[18] Although these findings could indicate that subscribing to conspiracy theories is detrimental to people's social well-being, scholars have instead suggested that embracing conspiracy explanations helps people feeling disconnected to tap into fringe groups with like-minded people.[19] In other words, beyond reducing a sense of uncertainty,[20] the draw of many conspiracy theories could be the feeling of belonging to a special group of seemingly independent-minded others "in the know." In fact, there's some evidence to suggest that people don't mind being associated with conspiracy theories. Michael J. Wood finds that labeling something a conspiracy does not make people less likely to endorse it.[21] This finding is attributed to the romanticized image of conspiracy theories in popular media, featuring protagonists who stick to their guns to fight conspirators in spite of others' doubts, and to the overuse of the terminology in political rhetoric, which has inoculated the public against the social stigma of subscribing to and sharing these ideas. Much like the term *fake news*, as more political actors use the term to refer to any news that contradicts their interests, if everything is "fake news" or "a conspiracy theory," then nothing is.

Mistrust in the Media

Yet another reason for the belief in and sharing of fake news might be the perception of a media environment that lacks clear information authorities. Research by Yariv Tsfati and Regina Marchi finds that with younger audiences in particular, alternative, satirical, and nonmainstream sources (mostly all online sources) are seen as more credible than legacy news, and Gallop polls have found that public trust in the media "to report the news fully, accurately and fairly" has been declining for decades—particularly among younger people and those who identify as Republicans.[22]

The reasons for this decline in trust are numerous. Political actors have attacked the credibility of mainstream media sources for years. Accusations of news bias from political elites (such as candidates running for office or prominent members of the political system) during presidential campaigns can be traced to public belief in media bias.[23] Although there was no evidence of bias in the press, elite conversation about the issue brought media attention to it, and in turn, influenced public perceptions. Current U.S. president Donald Trump, for instance, declared that several mainstream news outlets were "the enemy of the American people"—in May 2018, Trump tweeted from @realDonaldTrump:

> The Fake News is working overtime. Just reported that, despite the tremendous success we are having with the economy & all things else, 91% of the Network News about me is negative (Fake). Why do we work so hard in working with the media when it is corrupt? Take away credentials?[24]

Many media outlets, such as the *Washington Post*,[25] interpret this as further conflation of "fake news" and "disagreeable news," and no doubt this type of rhetoric exacerbates public mistrust in journalism.

Simultaneously, the line between "news" and "entertainment" has been steadily blurring. While twenty-four-hour news channels such as Fox, CNN, and MSNBC pass off emotionally charged partisan editorial content as news content, it is becoming increasingly common for satire news and talk show hosts to set the mainstream media agenda. Related to this, we allege that the state of the press itself is a factor in the declining public trust in media. Some of this is likely associated with the erosion of local reporting industries. Local news sources are typically seen as being the trustworthiest,[26] yet these are the sources that are in the most financial jeopardy. But as Alice Marwick and Rebecca Lewis note, high-profile "missteps" from otherwise reputable sources have also fueled public skepticism toward the media.[27] For instance, the *New York Times* has been rightly criticized for its flawed reporting based on unsubstantiated information that Iraq possessed weapons of mass destruction.[28] Likewise, by paying undue attention to unconfirmed claims, the media has also been blamed for fanning the flames of conspiracy theory movements (such as claims that former U.S. president Barack Obama was not a natural-born citizen).[29] Even if these controversies are relatively rare in the greater scheme of the U.S. press, they leave an indelible mark on public perception of the news media establishment.

Misunderstanding Media Systems

One more explanation for why individuals might not be so savvy toward fake news is a general misunderstanding about the motives and intentions that drive this sort of "journalism." As end consumers, few media users are acutely aware of the comparatively complex processes involved in news production.[30] In fact, a larger issue of media production might be the conflation of news coverage with editorial content—the latter of which often has entertainment (and related) outcomes.[31] While research has challenged the extent to which so-called soft news programs influence political knowledge, high-conflict news programs (programs common on cable networks such as CNN and MSNBC that usually feature pundits on opposite sides of political issues in direct confrontation with each other) can erode watchers' views of larger political systems.[32] Put another way, audiences tend not to distinguish between objective reporting and subjective editorial, categorizing both under the larger heuristic of "the news" and, as a result, paradoxically engaging editorial content as newsworthy, while rejecting objective news content as "biased." Such effects are particularly relevant when news is shared via social media, as often times headlines are shared and framed as news reports when, in actuality, the content being shared might be opinion articles and blog posts from activists and political pundits.

In this conflation of editorial style is a misunderstanding of where information originates from, or even the ultimate goals of fake news—in many cases, goals that are more financial than political, and more economic than altruistic. Journalist Craig Silverman demonstrated this with two highly partisan sides of a story about Kellyanne Conway, who ran Trump's successful 2016 election campaign.[33] Amid speculation that Conway was taking a reduced role in the White House, one source, Liberal Society, claimed that the White House was upset with her performance; another source, Constitution 101, claimed that the "mainstream liberal media" was responsible for the speculation.[34] Silverman was able to track down the source of both stories (the "left-spun" former and the "right-spun" latter) as having come from the same media company: American News LLC. Companies such as American News LLC and other "fake news" factories, including those based overseas, engage the practice because it is remarkably profitable.[35]

Conclusion

The public discourse around fake news is heartening in that media audiences seem more aware of the potential that the news delivered to them might not always be objective and free from agenda. At the same time, simply being aware of fake news is only one step in overcoming our very human (and thus very natural) flaws associated with understanding what to do with it. We are exposed to fake news every day—much of which probably confirms how we wish to see the world—and because these stories resonate with us, it can take a great deal of effort to become aware of our own biases, to be cognizant of our emotions, and to be savvy about each source we encounter in the vast seas of information in which we swim. We contend that media literacy efforts designed to make media consumers more critical about the information they encounter is a worthy pursuit. Interventions that make people more self-aware about how they are inclined to process that information—the psychological factors outlined in this chapter—may be even more effective. However, any literacy effort is unlikely to completely snuff out engagement with fake news. The downside of living in an information-rich era, where we have access to more knowledge and information than anyone could ever hope to process, is that we cannot carefully process it all. We are only human. We will always be attracted to those stimuli that appeal to our passions, save us time, validate us, connect us to others, and (seemingly) help us make sense of the world. Understanding our processing limits and being aware of the implications of those limits is helpful, but it does not completely inoculate us from the trappings of sensationalism. In fact, purveyors of fake news are also intuitively aware of many of the cognitive, affective, and social forces that we have outlined in this chapter, and they leverage them in order to sew an environment fertile for fake news to thrive. If our psychological predispositions are what lead us to fall for fake news, then it is unlikely that we can alter those heuristics—the idealized media literate is a desired-yet-lofty goal. As such, we realize that this chapter offers few answers, but we hope that it brings an awareness of the psychological and social reasons why we are so inclined to believe the sensational. As they say, knowing is half the battle.

Notes

1. See Sam Wineburg and Sarah McGrew, "Lateral Reading: Reading Less and Learning More When Valuating Digital Information," Stanford History Education Group Working Paper no. 2017-A1 (Stanford University, Stanford, CA, 2017), https://papers .ssrn.com/sol3/papers.cfm?abstract_id=3048994.

2. Cf. Jennifer Fleming, "Media Literacy, News Literacy, or News Appreciation? A Case Study of the News Literacy Program at Stony Brook University," *Journalism and Mass Communication Educator* 69, no. 2 (2013): 146–165.

3. Leon Festinger, Henry Riecken, and Stanley Schachter, *When Prophecy Fails: A Social and Psychological Study of a Modern Group That Predicted the Destruction of the World* (Minneapolis: University of Minnesota Press, 1956).

4. Susan T. Fiske and Shelley E. Taylor, *Social Cognition: From Brains to Culture*, 2nd ed., (Los Angeles, CA: Sage, 2013).

5. Richard E. Petty and John T. Cacioppo, "The Elaboration Likelihood Model of Persuasion," *Advances in Experimental Social Psychology* 19 (1986): 123–205.

6. Miriam J. Metzger, Andrew J. Flanagin, and Ryan B. Medders, "Social and Heuristic Approaches to Credibility Evaluation Online," *Journal of Communication* 60, no. 3 (2010): 413–439; Hunt Allcott and Matthew Gentzkow, "Social Media and Fake News in the 2016 Election," *Journal of Economic Perspectives* 31, no. 2 (2017): 211–236.

7. Julio Reis, Fabrício Benevenuto, Pedro O. S. Vaz de Melo, Raquel Prates, Haewoon Kwak, and Jisun An, "Breaking the News: First Impressions Matter on Online News" (paper presented at the 2015 International AAAI Conference on Web and Social Media, Oxford, England), https://arxiv.org/pdf/1503.07921.pdf.

8. Bryan Gardiner, "You'll Be Outraged at How Easy It Was to Get You to Click on This Headline," *Wired*, December 18, 2015, https://www.wired.com/2015/12/psychology-of-clickbait/.

9. On memory, see Larry Cahill, Bruce Prins, Michael Weber, and James L. McGaugh, "β-Adrenergic Activation and Memory for Emotional Events," *Nature* 371 (1994): 702–704. On cognition, see Dolf Zillmann, "Exemplification Theory: Judging the Whole by the Some of Its Parts," *Media Psychology* 1, no. 1 (2009): 69–94.

10. Ullrich K. H. Ecker, Stephan Lewandowsky, and Joe Apai, "Terrorists Brought Down the Plane!—No, Actually It Was a Technical Fault: Processing Corrections of Emotive Information," *Quarterly Journal of Experimental Psychology* 64, no. 2 (2011): 283–310.

11. Jonah Berger and Katherine L. Milkman, "What Makes Online Content Go Viral?, *Journal of Marketing Research* 49 (2012): 192–205.

12. Stefan Stieglitz and Linh Dang-Xuan, "Emotions and Information Diffusion in Social Media—Sentiment of Microblogs and Sharing Behavior," *Journal of Management Information Systems* 29, no. 4 (2014): 217–248.

13. In the case of Twitter, see Soroush Vosoughi, Deb Roy, and Sinan Aral, "The Spread of True and False News Online," *Science* 359, no. 6380 (2018): 1146–1151, http://science.sciencemag.org/content/359/6380/1146.

14. Cynthia A. Hoffner, Yuki Fujioka, Jiali Ye, and Amal G. S. Ibrahim, "Why We Watch: Factors Affecting Exposure to Tragic Television News," *Mass Communication and Society* 12 (2009): 193–216.

15. Chei Sian Lee and Long Ma, "News Sharing in Social Media: The Effect of Gratifications and Prior Experience," *Computers in Human Behavior* 28, no. 2 (2012): 331–339.

16. On social opinion leaders, see Elihu Katz and Paul Lazarsfeld, *Personal Influence* (New York: Free Press, 1955). On social status, see Vosoughi, Roy, and Aral, "The Spread of True and False News Online."

17. Roland Imhoff and Pia Karoline Lamberty, "Too Special to Be Duped: Need for Uniqueness Motivates Conspiracy Beliefs," *European Journal of Social Psychology* 47, no. 6 (2017): 724–734.

18. On alienation, see Richard Moulding, Simon Nix-Carnell, Alexandra Schnabel, Maja Nedeljkovic, Emma E. Burnside, Aaron F. Lentini, and Nazia Mehzabin, "Better the Devil You Know than a World You Don't? Intolerance of Uncertainty and Worldview Explanations for Belief in Conspiracy Theories," *Personality and Individual Differences* 98 (2016): 345–35. On belonging, see Jan-Willem van Prooijen, "Sometimes Inclusion Breeds Suspicion: Self-Uncertainty and Belongingness Predict Belief in Conspiracy Theories," *European Journal of Social Psychology* 46 (2015): 267–279.

19. Marius H. Raab, Stefan A. Ortlieb, Nikolas Auer, Klara Guthmann, and Claus-Christian Carbon, "Thirty Shades of Truth: Conspiracy Theories as Stories of Individuation, Not of Pathological Delusion," *Frontiers in Psychology* 4 (2013): 1–9.

20. Moulding et al., "Better the Devil You Know."

21. Michael J. Wood, "Some Dare Call It Conspiracy: Labeling Something a Conspiracy Theory Does Not Reduce Belief in It," *Political Psychology* 37 (2015): 695–705.

22. Yariv Tsfati, "Online News Exposure and Trust in Mainstream Media: Exploring Possible Associations," *American Behavioral Scientist* 54, no. 1 (2010): 22–42; Regina Marchi, "With Facebook, Blogs, and Fake News, Teens Reject Journalistic 'Objectivity,'" *Journal of Communication Inquiry* 36, no. 3 (2012): 246–262; Art Swift, "Americans' Trust in Mass Media Sinks to New Low," Gallup, September 14, 2016, http://news .gallup.com/poll/195542/americans-trust-mass-media-sinks-new-low.aspx.

23. Mark D. Watts, David Domke, Dhavan V. Shah, and David P. Fan, "Elite Cues and Media Bias in Presidential Campaigns: Explaining Public Perceptions of a Liberal Press," *Communication Research* 26 (1999): 144–175.

24. Donald Trump, (@realDonaldTrump), Twitter, May 9, 2018, https://twitter.com /realdonaldtrump/status/994179864436596736.

25. Philip Bump, "Trump Makes It Explicit: Negative Coverage of Him Is Fake Coverage," *Washington Post*, May 9, 2018, https://www.washingtonpost.com/news/politics /wp/2018/05/09/trump-makes-it-explicit-negative-coverage-of-him-is-fake-coverage.

26. Morning Consult and Politico, National Tracking Poll #170806, August 10–14, 2017, https://morningconsult.com/wpcontent/uploads/2017/08/170806_crosstabs_Politico _v2_TB.pdf.

27. Alice Marwick and Rebecca Lewis, *Media Manipulation and Disinformation Online* (New York: Data and Society Research Institute, 2017), https://datasociety.net/pubs /oh/DataAndSociety_MediaManipulationAndDisinformationOnline.pdf.

28. Jack Shafer, "The Times Scoops That Melted," *Slate*, July 25, 2003, http://www
.slate.com/articles/news_and_politics/press_box/2003/07/the_times_scoops_that
_melted.html.

29. David Folkenflik, "Obama Chides Media over Role in the 'Birther' Controversy,"
NPR, April 27, 2011, https://www.npr.org/2011/04/27/135778712/role-of-media-in
-the-birther-controversy.

30. Jihii Jolly, "News Literacy vs. Media Literacy," *Columbia Journalism Review*, September 4, 2014, http://archives.cjr.org/news_literacy/news_literacy_vs_media_literac
.php.

31. Anthony Sampson, "The Crisis at the Heart of Our Media," *British Journalism
Review* 7, no. 3 (1996): 42–51.

32. Markus Prior, "Any Good News in Soft News? The Impact of Soft News Prefer-
ences on Political Knowledge," *Political Communication* 20, no. 2 (2010): 149–217.
The findings related to high-conflict news programs are similar to those in Marchi,
"With Facebook, Blogs, and Fake News."

33. Craig Silverman, "This Is How Your Hyperpartisan Political News Gets Made,"
BuzzFeed, February 27, 2017, https://www.buzzfeed.com/craigsilverman/how-the
-hyperpartisan-sausage-is-made.

34. Ibid.

35. See Andrew Higgins, Mike McIntire, and Gabriel J.x. Dance, "Inside a Fake News
Sausage Factory: 'This Is All about Income,'" *New York Times*, November 25, 2016,
https://www.nytimes.com/2016/11/25/world/europe/fake-news-donald-trump
-hillary-clinton-georgia.html.

18   Source Credibility and Belief in Fake News: I'll Believe You If You Agree with Me

Danielle Polage

In 2016, the website PolitiFact named fake news "the lie of the year."[1] There were so many fake news stories circulating online that it was hard for Politi-Fact to pick just one. Fake news has been blamed for everything from disbelief in global warming and #Pizzagate to Brexit and swinging the 2016 U.S. presidential election.

Although spin and evasion in politics are almost expected, fake news has been described as more pernicious than typical political bias, as it is intended to mislead the public in systematic ways. If voters base their political views on false information, fake news is a real threat to democracy since the democratic process depends on informed voters. This chapter presents research demonstrating that people do believe fake news and that information coming from credible sources—as long as it does not contradict existing knowledge—will become more believable as a result of repetition. The chapter concludes with potential ways to counteract fake news and avenues of future research.

According to statistics from a research study conducted by Andrew Guess, Brendan Nyhan, and Jason Reifler, approximately one in four Americans visited a fake news website between October 7 and November 14, 2016, the critical last weeks of the presidential campaign.[2] Through their analysis of web traffic from a nationally representative sample, they find that the most likely place where people accessed fake news was Facebook. It is estimated that fake news was shared millions of times through this platform. Clearly, people are exposed to fake news, so it is important to understand whether exposure to fake news will increase belief in it.

Belief in False News

In one of the first studies conducted on belief in fake news, I presented forty-four undergraduate university students with fake and true news stories.[3] Participants were asked to read these stories and then provide titles for them. An example of a fake news story included in the study claims that tomato paste causes male infertility. A sample true story describes the many health benefits of drinking green tea. Half of the participants were exposed to one set of true and false news stories during the first session of the experiment; the other group read a different group of true and false stories. Five weeks later, participants rated the likelihood of both old and new stories. Participants rated the false stories they had previously read as more truthful and more plausible than did participants who had not read those stories. Simply reading the stories one time made them seem more likely to be true. Participants also believed that they had heard about the repeated fake news stories from a source other than the experiment, even though it was not possible, since the fake stories had been experimenter-generated. This increased belief is a result of simply exposing half of the participants to each set of stories a single time. It is likely that participants were using familiarity as a basis for truth. If a story seems familiar, participants assume it is more likely to be true.

Many studies demonstrate that simply repeating a statement makes it seem truer. This illusory-truth effect was first observed by Lynn Hasher, David Goldstein, and Thomas Toppino and has just recently been applied to contemporary fake news.[4] Gordon Pennycook, Tyrone D. Cannon, and David G. Rand used fake news headlines that had actually been posted on Facebook to demonstrate that a single exposure to the fake news increases its perceived truth.[5] In general, when presented with information, people tend to believe it. This so-called truth bias demonstrates that our default is to believe what we are told. The truth is the most efficient way of communication, and most people tell the truth most of the time.[6] Thus, it is our default to tell the truth and to expect to hear the truth from others. We usually lack the time and means necessary to determine the veracity of everything we hear. Therefore, we default to believing that others are generally being honest, unless there is a reason not to believe them. If we trust the source of the information, we will typically believe the information as long as it does not contradict information that we know to be true.

Belief in Contradictory Information

If new information can be rejected simply based on its contradiction to accepted truths, the statement will not be accepted, even if it is repeated. When Pennycook, Cannon, and Rand presented participants with statements that were clearly false, such as "the earth is a perfect square," participants did not increase their belief in those statements even when viewing them for the second time.[7] It seems that, when new information contradicts knowledge that we already have, we use our knowledge, and not the feeling of familiarity, to assess truthfulness. It is important to note that the incompatibility between the old and new information must be apparent and that the previous knowledge must render the novel statements implausible. If the contradiction to fact is not apparent, information that is known to be false might still increase in believability with repetition. For example, Lisa K. Fazio, Nadia M. Brashier, Keith B. Payne, and Elizabeth J. Marsh demonstrate that participants rated statements, such as "a date is a dried plum," as more likely to be true after they are repeated, even though it was assumed that participants knew that a prune, not a date, is a dried plum.[8] The authors suggest that the statement may have been similar enough to the truth to go undetected. They argue that a statement, such as "a grapefruit is a dried plum," would likely have made the contradiction more obvious and should not result in that statement being believed. On one hand, these data suggest that it is possible to believe false information, even when it contradicts known information, as long as the contradiction is not noticed. On the other hand, information that clearly violates known facts is unlikely to be believed, even if it is repeated.

One potential way that news consumers might counteract belief in fake news is by increasing their knowledge base. However, news, almost by definition, involves the presentation of information that is relatively unknown to the general public. Fake news, therefore, is not likely to be debunked simply by reliance on contradictory knowledge, because the public often lacks the relevant information to dispute the claims. Take, for example, the birther conspiracy, which alleges that Barack Obama is not a natural-born citizen of the United States and was therefore ineligible to be president. Democrats find it shocking that some Republicans do not believe that Obama was not born in the United States. Yet it is unlikely that the location of Obama's birth would be counteracted by direct knowledge of members of the general population. The statement itself is not really preposterous; the United States is made up of individuals who have immigrated to the country from all over the world. To process the veracity of the statement, however, one needs to have information about which the public lacks access, namely, a legal birth certificate. Yet even after Obama's birth certificate was produced, a *Newsweek* story cited data from a YouGov poll in 2017 showing that more than half of Republicans surveyed still believed that Obama was born in Kenya.[9] Why would that be? They likely did not believe the source of the information to be credible.

Source Credibility

As mentioned previously, people will believe information to be true if it is repeated, if it does not contradict previously stored knowledge, and if the source has not been discredited. Even if the public had access to that original document, the average person would not have the expertise necessary to determine whether it was a legitimate copy. To believe that Obama was born in the United States requires a person to believe the experts who analyzed the documents. Thus, without any knowledge to contradict the claim, the credibility of the source becomes an important component of whether or not the information will be accepted. So how do we decide what is a trustworthy source? It turns out that people determine the credibility of the source based on whether or not the source espouses beliefs that support people's preexisting opinions.

Dan M. Kahan, Hank Jenkins-Smith, and Donald Braman conducted a study looking at how perceived credibility of a so-called expert can change depending on whose side of a debate the expert is on.[10] If the participants share the same views on a topic with the expert, participants perceive the expert as credible. However, if the expert does not validate the participants' position, the expert is discounted. Participants in this study were given the credentials of a scientist with a Ph.D. in climate studies. The expert's degree was from Harvard University, and he held a current professorship at the Massachusetts Institute of Technology. Both groups of participants received the same description of the scientist, but half of the participants were told that the expert said that it was undoubtable that humans were causing climate change, whereas the other half of participants were told that the expert said it was premature to claim that humans were causing global warming. Even though the credentials of the scientist were impressive and held constant across conditions, people only agreed that the expert was a credible source on climate change when he agreed with their opinions of the cause of climate change. Very conservative, committed Republicans tended to accept the scientist as a credible expert when he claimed that it was premature to claim that global warming was caused by human activity. Very liberal, committed Democrats dismissed his opinion unless he claimed that human activity caused global warming. These data suggest that the expert's perceived credibility is not a reflection of his education and experience, but rather a reflection of whether or not his opinion matches the opinions of his audience.

Elizabeth E. Housholder and Heather L. LaMarre show that perceived credibility of a political figure also depends on the perceived similarity between the politicians and their constituents.[11] The authors of this study created fake Facebook pages for fictitious senatorial candidates. Their Facebook pages included information that expressed views on a variety of issues. Half of the participants saw a candidate who held traditional Republican views, and half viewed the page of a candidate holding traditional Democratic views. Participants rated the credibility of the two candidates in terms of honesty and competence in addition to other factors. Participants also rated the credibility of the information posted on the fictitious candidates' Facebook pages. Finally, participants indicated how similar they thought their beliefs were with the politicians' beliefs. The results showed that the more similarity that viewers perceive between themselves and the candidate, the more credible they think the candidate is and the more credible they perceive the information provided by the candidates. This study supports the idea that source-credibility judgments are based on whether the source espouses information with which the individual agrees.

These studies suggest that viewers determine the credibility of a source based on whether the source supports views similar to the viewer's own. If news sources do not align with a viewer's preconceived beliefs, they will be viewed as less credible. Interestingly, mainstream news is losing credibility, and partisan-biased coverage of news stories may be one of the reasons why. In 1976, 72 percent of respondents to a Gallup poll said that they trusted the news, whereas in 2016, that number sank to 32 percent.[12] Although a recent meta-analysis indicates that both liberals and conservatives show a similar partisan bias to accept information that confirms their beliefs,[13] the Gallup poll shows a higher distrust of mainstream media among Republicans. Fifty-one percent of Democrats and 14 percent of Republicans expressed "a fair amount" or "a great deal" of trust in mass media as a news source.[14] This decline in trust in mainstream media could also be a reason that belief in fake news is growing. The number of fake news stories targeting Republicans is higher than those targeting Democrats. It is possible that Republicans' skepticism of mainstream media might lead them to seek alternative news that they feel is less biased against their positions.

Source Credibility and Belief in Fake News

Briony Swire, Adam J. Berinsky, Stephan Lewandowsky, and Ullrich K. H. Ecker show that people evaluate the veracity of information based on who says it.[15] Participants were presented factual and false campaign statements that Donald Trump made prior to the 2016 presidential election. Those statements were either attributed to Trump or presented without an identified source. Participants were then given an explanation as to whether the statements were true or false. Participants were asked either immediately or after a one-week delay to rerate the statements in addition to rating their feelings toward the candidate. As expected, Republican supporters of Trump were more likely to believe both true and false information when it was attributed to Trump. Democrats were less likely to believe both true and false statements when they were attributed to Trump. Republicans who did not support Trump were less likely to accept facts spoken by Trump as true, but were not more likely to accept his false statements. In summary, the results show that participants' opinions of Trump colored their perceptions of the accuracy of his statements. Respondents who supported Trump believed what he said, whereas those who did not support Trump did not believe him, even when what he was saying was true.

The default with sources believed to be credible is to expect to hear the truth from them. This can lead to increasingly polarized views if people are more likely to believe people who agree with them. Eytan Bakshy, Solomon Messing, and Lada A. Adamic find that the majority of people's friends on Facebook share their political views: 80 percent for liberals and 82 percent for conservatives.[16] Sources that are perceived to be reliable are also less likely to be fact-checked. This dynamic creates an echo chamber in which people's own views are shared back with them, validated, and repeated.

Ways to Counteract Fake News

So, how can fake news be counteracted? Since fake news will be believed if it does not contradict previously stored knowledge and does not come from a discredited source, the first line of defense against belief in false information is a deeper knowledge base. One suggestion is to increase general knowledge in a nonbiased way *before* people are exposed to fake news. The more people know about a topic, the less likely they are to believe false information about it.

Another possibility is to use source credibility as a way to counteract fake news. Those with perceived low credibility are less likely to be believed, whereas increased source credibility increases the likelihood that presented information will be believed. Source credibility is not necessarily based on the source's experience or credentials, but is based on a perceived match between the opinions of the listener and the source. Fake news is typically targeted toward groups that are most likely to believe it. If a source that seems credible to members of the target group discounts the fake news, it might be possible to decrease the members' belief in the fake news. For example, Berinsky looked at attempts to counteract rumors surrounding Obama's Affordable Care Act.[17] One such rumor was that people would be required to consult "death panels" when making decisions about end-of-life care. Berinsky's study found that when a Republican involved in drafting the relevant legislature debunked the death panel story, all respondents, regardless of partisanship, were more likely to reject the rumor. It was assumed that a Republican who supported a Democratic plan would be perceived as a credible source. This study suggests that politicians can help reduce belief in fake news if they are willing to make statements based on truth, regardless of their personal political interests.

The same logic could apply to friends who are discussing issues, both in person and online. Facebook users, for example, could "like" posts that are truth-based, whether or not they support the posts. They could be open to challenging others on political facts, not just emotional rhetoric. Social media users could avoid echo chambers by surrounding themselves with intelligent and well-informed individuals who do not share their point of view. In addition, although difficult, social media users should reconsider unfriending those who disagree with them. This chapter discusses how the credibility of strangers is based on shared beliefs and opinions; however, it is likely that the credibility of a familiar person is based on other factors, such as shared experiences and interests. Exposure to repeated information from friends and family may increase receptivity to facts that challenge previously held beliefs, but only as long as the source is perceived to be credible. Trust is part of credibility. Everyone should attempt to maintain credibility in conversations by presenting facts with cordiality and respect and avoiding shame tactics and name-calling. Friends on social media look to each other as valued sources of information; therefore, individuals should not be a source of fake news. They should not "like" or repost something without reading and verifying it, even if it validates their opinion. Twitter users should not retweet stories when they have only glanced at the headline. All users of social media should report suspected fake news and ask that it be removed. Social media consumers cannot avoid fake news, but everyone has a responsibility to help prevent the spread of it.

In summary, it is hard to counteract fake news that does not contradict information known to be true, that comes from a source considered to be reliable, and that espouses claims that the person already believes. Fake news will continue to be posted online; the goal, then, should be to decrease the spread of fake news. Future research should continue to explore the limits of belief in fake news and to more clearly examine the effects of belief in fake news. Does belief in fake news translate into changes in behavior? Do people believe fake news that contradicts previous knowledge if it comes from a perceived credible source? The presence of fake news is unlikely to decrease; however, it is everyone's job to fact-check and limit the spread of fake news before it is read by others.

Notes

1. Angie Drobnic Holan, "Lie of the Year: Fake News," PolitiFact, December 13, 2016, http://www.politifact.com/truth-o-meter/article/2016/dec/13/2016-lie-year-fake -news/.

2. Andrew Guess, Brendan Nyhan, and Jason Reifler, "Selective Exposure to Misinformation: Evidence from the Consumption of Fake News during the 2016 U.S. Presidential Campaign" (working paper, January 9, 2018), https://www.dartmouth .edu/~nyhan/fake-news-2016.pdf.

3. Danielle Polage, "Making Up History: False Memories of Fake News Stories," *Europe's Journal of Psychology* 8, no. 2 (2012): 245–250.

4. Lynn Hasher, David Goldstein, and Thomas Toppino, "Frequency and the Conference of Referential Validity," *Journal of Verbal Learning and Verbal Behavior* 16, no. 1 (1997): 107–112.

5. Gordon Pennycook, Tyrone D. Cannon, and David G. Rand, "Prior Exposure Increases Perceived Accuracy of Fake News," *Journal of Experimental Psychology: General* 147, no. 12 (2018): 1865–1880, http://dx.doi.org/10.1037/xge0000465.

6. D. T. Gilbert, "How Mental Systems Believe," *American Psychologist* 46 (1991): 107–119; Timothy R. Levine, "Truth-Default Theory (TDT): A Theory of Human Deception and Deception Detection," *Journal of Language and Social Psychology* 33, no. 4 (2014): 378–392.

7. Pennycook, Cannon, and Rand, "Prior Exposure."

8. Lisa K. Fazio, Nadia M. Brashier, Keith B. Payne, and Elizabeth J. Marsh, "Knowledge Does Not Protect against Illusory Truth," *Journal of Experimental Psychology: General* 144, no. 5 (2015): 993–1002.

9. Julia Glum, "Some Republicans Still Think Obama Was Born in Kenya as Trump Resurrects Birther Conspiracy Theory," *Newsweek*, December 11, 2017, http://www.newsweek.com/trump-birther-obama-poll-republicans-kenya-744195.

10. Dan M. Kahan, Hank Jenkins-Smith, and Donald Braman, "Cultural Cognition of Scientific Consensus," *Journal of Risk Research* 14, no. 2 (2011): 147–174.

11. Elizabeth E. Housholder and Heather L. LaMarre, "Facebook Politics: Toward a Process Model for Achieving Political Source Credibility through Social Media," *Journal of Information Technology and Politics* 11, no 4 (2011): 368–382.

12. Art Swift, "Americans' Trust in Mass Media Sinks to New Low," Gallup, September 14, 2016, http://www.gallup.com/poll/195542/americans-trust-mass-media-sinks-new-low.aspx.

13. Peter H. Ditto, Brittany Liu, Cory Clark, Sean P. Wojcik, Eric Chen, Rebecca Grady, and Joanne Zinger, "At Least Bias Is Bipartisan: A Meta-Analytic Comparison of Partisan Bias in Liberals and Conservatives," *Perspectives on Psychological Science* 14, no. 2 (2019): 273–291, https://doi.org/10.1177/1745691617746796.

14. Swift, "Americans' Trust in Mass Media."

15. Briony Swire, Adam J. Berinsky, Stephan Lewandowsky, and Ullrich K. H. Ecker, "Processing Political Misinformation: Comprehending the Trump Phenomenon," *Royal Society Open Science* 4, no. 3 (2017), https://doi.org/10.1098/rsos.160802.

16. Eytan Bakshy, Solomon Messing, and Lada A. Adamic, "Exposure to Ideologically Diverse News and Opinion on Facebook," *Science* 348, no. 6239 (2015): 1130–1132.

17. Adam J. Berinsky, "Rumors and Health Care Reform: Experiments in Political Misinformation," *British Journal of Political Science* 47, no. 2 (2017): 241–262.

19 Technology, Propaganda, and the Limits of the Human Intellect

Panagiotis Takis Metaxas

"Fake news," or online falsehoods that are formatted and circulated such that a reader might mistake them for legitimate news articles,[1] is a relatively recent phenomenon born out of the financial attractiveness of "clickbait"—capturing users' attention online to generate revenue through advertisements. It has expanded into new forms of propaganda, bullshit (as defined by Harry Frankfurt),[2] and financial scams, all of which have existed since the creation of early human communities. Since ancient times, people have been exposed to lies, misinformation, and falsehoods. Believing lies can come at grave personal and social costs. In some extreme cases, communities, religions, and cultures were destroyed due to misplaced belief in falsehoods. Even the end of the first democracy came when the Athenian citizens, led by the charismatic populist leader Alcibiades, believed reports that their Syracusan enemies were cowards and Sicilian city-states would support them as allies, and entered in a disastrous war they could not win.[3]

Today, we are exposed to "fake news," a newer phenomenon in the ever-widening genre of deception. We faced and overcame challenges throughout our history, but I argue that this time is different. The volume of (mis) information reaching us comes at speeds and levels that we, as a species, have not evolved to handle. Technology, ethical policies, laws, regulations, and trusted authorities, including fact-checkers, can help, but we will not solve the problem without the active engagement of educated citizens. Epistemological education, the recognition of our own biases, and the protection of our channels of communication and trusted networks are all needed to overcome the problem and continue our progress as democratic societies.

Personal Perspective

I first became curious about the question of identifying truth as an under-graduate majoring in mathematics at the University of Athens, in Greece. A trusted friend, fluent in Russian, informed me that Soviet mathematicians had devised a model by which one could determine the facts in news announcements. I tried to find more information about the model, but during the Cold War there was not much scientific communication between East and West, there was no internet, and I could not read Russian. It took me years to realize that I had encountered an early instance of "fake news."

In 1994, when the first search engine appeared, I became interested in the phenomenon of online propaganda. As an educator, my concern developed when I realized that my students were using search engines to retrieve and use information without an understanding of how it was produced. Until the advent of search engines, print information generally had greater validity over information gathered in other ways, so conducting quality research involved discovering printed sources—something that was quite hard, generally requiring hours spent poring over library books. For something to get published meant that it had been successfully scrutinized by professional editors, and challenged in ways that other forms of communication were not. But with the advent of the World Wide Web, in a sudden twist equal parts liberatory and dangerous, achieving publication became trivially easy. Barriers to authorship crumbled; in the internet era virtually anyone can be an author of content, and with the help of search engines, virtually any content authored can be found.

Google Search successfully presented itself as being able to objectively measure information quality using its famous PageRank algorithm. Its Page-Rank algorithm was listed among the ten best algorithms of data mining,[4] and its reputation was transferring to its search results. If you find an article in the top-ten search results, the thinking goes, it must be good. Sure, you could encounter a bad search result, but you would think that it was due to the lack of your searching skills and you would try again with different keywords. But when you were searching for things for which you had no prior knowledge, there was no way of recognizing misinformation. In fact, in one study, "'Of Course It's True; I Saw It on the Internet!,'" my coauthor and I found that more technically competent students were more likely to be fooled by unreliable search results because they trusted their ability to find information using this technological tool and, thus, applied less critical thinking.[5] Most people do not know (even today) that search engines can be gamed to promote the page of an experienced manipulator, or web spammer. "Search Engine Optimization," a $65 billion industry born in the early 2000s, was making a living by fooling Google and the other search engines on particular search queries. Now, search engines are under continuous attacks to promote the agenda of propagandists, advertisers, fanatics, or conspiracy theorists.[6]

And while Google has been successful in defending itself from attacks against electoral candidates since 2008, Twitter and Facebook have become the new battleground. We observed the first Twitter bomb during the 2010 Massachusetts special senatorial election, and we observed that the same technique was employed on Facebook during the 2016 U.S. elections.[7] Propagandists create fake accounts, then infiltrate and lurk in political groups until the appropriate time to promote their "fake news" to the group and watch it spread throughout the political echo chamber. Afterward, the fake accounts can delete themselves, making it difficult to determine the identity of the propagandist.[8]

Avoiding this manipulation has to be a coordinated effort. In particular, both social media platforms and citizens need to do a better job of recognizing "fake news" online. Our first collective reaction was to demand the deployment of fact-checking procedures. We want fact-checkers that will reliably determine the truth behind any online rumor and will notify us immediately. We want our social networks to inform us of what is reliable and what is not. We want policies that will enforce trustworthy information and laws that will punish those who violate them. And we want magical technologies to apply immediately, automatically, and correctly every time. In other words, we demand benevolent censorship.

Unfortunately, this cannot happen. There is no universal agreement on what is true and what is not. One person's spam can be another person's treasure. Laws are likely to be outdated before they even pass by the advances of technology. Policies can be a weapon against the public in the authoritarian regimes, which we see appearing around the world these days, as the new Malaysian Anti-Fake News Bill 2018 demonstrates.[9] Deep learning technologies are as likely to help as to hurt, as the so-called deep fake videos already demonstrate.[10] Moreover, machine learning technologies that do not give evidence on how they make decisions can only learn and imitate biases and injustices we already have in our communities.[11]

This does not mean we should not deploy dependable, independent, experienced, and educated smart crowds to help evaluate "fake news." We should. We should encourage academic librarians to take the role of overseeing fact-checking organizations. Social networks and search engines should diminish the financial incentives that drive the "web spam" and "fake news" producers. User interfaces need to be clearer to help us detect "clickbait." But nothing will succeed, unless we, the consumers of information, take more responsibility. We cannot avoid it any longer.

Epistemological Education

How easy is it for people to recognize "fake news"? How do we know what we know? This is one of the fundamental questions that we need to answer to evaluate the performance of any fact-checking system, whether operated by humans or machines. There is a whole branch of philosophy, called epistemology, that deals with the establishment of knowledge. Briefly, we know things due to our own experiences, our trust in reliable authorities, and our personal skill in handling logical reasoning, which is also known as critical thinking. Each of these three sources of knowledge (intrinsic, extrinsic, and derivations) is challenged by our technologies today.

We hold some beliefs for extrinsic reasons: because we trust the entity that is providing or supporting the information. Our whole educational system is based on this premise. Our systems of governance are also based on this, especially the "fourth estate," the press.[12] We also hold some beliefs for intrinsic reasons, that is, based on our own experiences realized through our senses and interpreted with our mind. We consider our experiences fundamental, and we rarely question whether what we learn from them is ever in doubt. "I saw it with my own eyes" is an expression that exists in most, if not all, languages. Trusting our eyes is considered equivalent to having absolute confidence, since seeing is the most powerful of all our senses. But it rarely is the case that we can make sense of what we see or hear without some thought process that interprets and establishes the factual aspects of our experience. Here is where we need the support of critical thinking skills that will help us determine the validity of our thoughts and observations. And for that, we also want the aid of a sound mind.

Even though in daily conversations we use the term *critical thinking* as a synonym to *common sense*, they are quite different, as Duncan Watts explains in the book *Everything Is Obvious (Once You Know the Answer)*.[13] Critical thinking means to use mathematical logic and rigor, to combine things that you already know, to derive new knowledge. By rigor, we mean to apply the scientific method in the derivation, and it starts with carefully writing down a hypothesis. Committing the hypothesis on a fixed medium is a crucial step because, without it, our thoughts may drift and we may end up evaluating something quite different. Then, we need to search for evidence, both supporting the hypothesis *and* discrediting it. Looking for both types of evidence is essential, because searching only for confirming evidence and ignoring discrediting evidence is the basis of most fallacies and conspiracy theories.

Of course, we need to apply mathematical logic in making sense of the evidence we have collected. This technical part of evaluating the hypothesis is hard, as it requires both education and practice. Unfortunately, not all educational systems prepare people for this step. Logic rules can be confused. A common logical mistake often used in conspiracy theories is to consider lack of evidence against a hypothesis as proof of correctness. If I cannot see why something could be wrong, the erroneous thinking goes, it must be true. For example, Facebook used flags to denote that some news articles had been fact-checked as true.[14] But flagged articles are few, and most articles are not checked. Someone mistakenly may derive that an article without a flag is false. However, it could be that no one has checked that second article.

Unfortunately, applying the scientific method all the time is not easy for three reasons. The first reason relates to effort and education. It is mentally tiring, and it requires training to think critically. The good news here is that the more you practice critical thinking, the less tiring it becomes, and you can even come to enjoy it. The second reason relates to prejudices: we need to be aware of our own biases. We need to have what ancient Greek philosophers termed γνωθι σ'αυτον, or self-knowledge. We are not, by default, the objective judges we may wish to be. There are many cognitive biases we carry along, and they are all transparent to us. One of the more commonly used is confirmation bias: when we are presented with facts, it is easier to cherry-pick those that agree with what we already believe—and discredit those that do not—than change our opinion.[15] The longer we think in a certain way, the more we reinforce the existing neural connections, the harder it is to change them. Changing our thinking requires effort and time.

The third reason is related to false information we have already accumulated over the years. Not everything we were taught as children by parents, teachers, and communities is true. Some of the "facts" we learned were made-up stories easy to comprehend or provide comfort for our worries. Belief in astrology is just one such example. Even though it is relatively easy for people to see it as invalid, many choose to believe in it and have it guide some of their actions.

We also know "facts" that are related to the brain's limitations, for example, "facts" that we misunderstood, misheard, or remember incorrectly. The brain is not a reliable database of information that can be accessed accurately and on demand every time. Early efforts to understand the brain were comparing it to computer memory, but this metaphor is misleading. Every time we remember something, we are reconstructing the memory through an inexact and unreliable process. For example, sometimes police detectives and lawyers are successful in implanting "memories" to unsuspected witnesses by describing in detail the events. Witnesses may end up "remembering" these "memories."

We may also know "facts" because we applied the wrong pattern trying to make sense of something. Our brain is a pattern-matching machine. On the one hand, finding similarities and patterns is fundamental to creativity. We develop solutions by recognizing similarities between a situation we are familiar with and another that is new to us. But, on the other hand, our pattern-matching ability can fail us sometimes: we can see the image of a face on a rock in New Hampshire or on the surface of the moon the moment someone points it out.

We also know "facts" that we have observed under emotional stress, such as fear, anger, and passion, as we often feel during important political elections. And, of course, we sometimes know "facts" that we derived upon when our brain was not working reliably. This could be due to the influence of alcohol or other chemical substances, due to lack of sleep, due to mental illnesses, or even due to extreme focus, as with the famous case of missing the gorilla appearing in a video of people passing a basketball.[16] I am sure we can add more such examples that we have observed in others. It is always far easier to observe such behavior in others because, well, if we realize that they are happening to ourselves, we could try to correct them, assuming we have enough mental power for that.

Our brain is impressive, but it is not perfect, and it does not work well every time or at every phase of our life. Our brains are the products of evolution. They are not perfect or complete; they are works in progress. Neuroscientists describe the evolutionary process that started with the so-called reptilian brain, the smaller component that responds immediately to the basic instincts: fear, hunger, sexual desire.[17] On top of that we have the mammal brain, then the primate brain, then the human brain occupying much of the neocortex.

Our brain is affected by construction limitations and errors. Our feelings, our senses, our environment challenge our perception of reality. We need to feel that we are in control of our environment to survive. The natural world around us is full of randomness, but we do not readily accept randomness in phenomena; we want to "discover" reasons explaining randomness. Again, this desire for control and for an explanation that discounts randomness is a powerful source for conspiracy theories.

We are not stupid; we are thinking lazy. Our brain has a hard time staying focused for too long.[18] When we sit down to study intensely for an hour or two, we end up feeling exhausted, though we did not move from that chair. Thinking critically is very taxing to the brain. We try to avoid it unless we have to, like when we take a test in school. In most other cases, we try to create shortcuts to avoid using all of it. We adopt heuristics, stereotypes, personal ways of "thinking" that most of the time serve us well— but not always.[19]

It is counterintuitive, but even binary logic does not always help. From a young age, we practice with statements that are either true or false, because they are easier to understand. We are so accustomed to the process of understanding our world through a "closed world" assumption: we often assume that if something cannot be shown to be true, it must be false. Well, it may be impossible to determine its validity under the accepted assumptions.[20]

We have been dealing with this situation for hundreds of years. Our technologies have helped us make progress in controlling the world around us, but they have also challenged us. Consider one of the most impressive technologies of all times, the technology of writing. Using little drawings to form phonemes, words have been one of the more profound technologies of all times. We spend a good time of our lives training to recognize words, form sentences, compose arguments. Writing enables us to transmit ideas and information across generations. Every time we make it more efficient, as with the invention of the printing press, it has a profound effect on human history. But up until the spread of the interconnected networks of social media, we had few books to read. Few, of course, compared to the tsunami of words we read these days on Facebook, online newspapers, and, well, fake newspapers produced both by humans and by artificial intelligence. The amount of information that reaches us has exploded. Censorship used to be the act of hiding information from the public. In our new world, overwhelming noise can also function as censorship.[21] Our social media are shifting our attention constantly between issues and topics with such speed and volume that we lose track of what is important.

Conclusion

The past couple of years have seen a massive rise in interest in "fake news." But although many researchers, politicians, lawmakers, and laypeople are trying to address this issue, it remains an immensely complex problem, challenging the limits of our human intellect. What can we do?

Technology can certainly help, primarily if it is used to discover valid evidence that diverges from what we are casually aiming to locate, and to inform us when we find ourselves in an echo chamber. Wiki technology maintaining evidence considered by fact-checkers and librarians can also help. It can help them to manage and the rest of us to monitor the process that led to their decisions. Interfaces that give comparable exposure to a claim and its refutation would also help, so that, for example, the comments refuting a claim appearing in a social medium are also visible.

But other things will help: laws limiting the financial incentives that draw pranksters, propagandists, and advertisers in producing misinformation to draw our attention and clicks; regulations that restrict the collection and exchange of personal information, such as the recent European General Data Protection Regulation (GDPR); ethical policies that protect our limited attention capital so that we do not sink in the constant wave of information that covers us every day. Policies, laws, regulations, trusted authorities, and technology will help, but they will not solve the problem of propaganda, misinformation, and "fake news" if we rely just on them. No solution will be complete without active engagement of the citizen, epistemological education, and an active democratic society. We need to be aware of why we believe what we believe and of our own biases. We need to listen to those outside our echo chambers. And we need to apply critical thinking habitually so that we enjoy practicing it on a daily basis. Mastery of (most of) these skills is necessary for a successful life in the twenty-first century and beyond. It is not easy, because we need to change ourselves, but that's what education has always been about.

Notes

1. As others have pointed out, some politicians, populists, and dictators misuse it to describe opinions they dislike; this co-opting of terminology is commonly done, as with other terms such as *patriotism* and *the people*. Angie Drobnic Holan, "The Media's Definition of Fake News vs. Donald Trump's," PolitiFact, October 18, 2017, http://www.politifact.com/truth-o-meter/article/2017/oct/18/deciding-whats-fake -medias-definition-fake-news-vs/; Panagiotis Takis Metaxas, "Separating Truth from Lies," interview by Alison Head and Kirsten Hostetler, Project Information Literacy, Smart Talk Interview no. 27, February 21, 2017, http://www.projectinfolit.org/takis -metaxas-smart-talk.html.

2. Harry Frankfurt, *On Bullshit* (Princeton, NJ: Princeton University Press, 2005).

3. Mary Lefkowitz, "Do Facts Matter? Redefining Truth Is a Tried and True Method of Taking Control," *The Spoke* (blog), Albright Institute for Global Affairs, February 24, 2017, https://www.wellesley.edu/albright/about/blog/3261-do-facts-matter.

4. Xindong Wu, Vipin Kumar, J. Ross Quinlan, Joydeep Ghosh, Qiang Yang, Hiroshi Motoda, Geoffrey J. McLachlan, Angus Ng, Bing Liu, Philip S. Yu, Zhi-Hua Zhou, Michael Steinbach, David J. Hand, and Dan Steinberg, "Top 10 Algorithms in Data Mining," *Knowledge and Information Systems* 14, no. 1 (2008): 1–37, http://www.cs .uvm.edu/~icdm/algorithms/10Algorithms-08.pdf.

5. Leah Graham and Panagiotis Takis Metaxas, "'Of Course It's True; I Saw It on the Internet!': Critical Thinking in the Internet Era," *Communications of the ACM* 46, no. 5 (May 2003): 71–75, http://bit.ly/oMjgnw.

6. Panagiotis Takis Metaxas and Joseph DeStefano, "Web Spam, Propaganda and Trust" (paper presented at the Adversarial Information Retrieval [AIRWeb] World Wide Web Conference, Chiba, Japan, May 10, 2005), http://airweb.cse.lehigh.edu /2005/metaxas.pdf.

7. Panagiotis Takis Metaxas and Eni Mustafaraj, "From Obscurity to Prominence in Minutes: Political Speech and Real-Time Search" (paper presented at Web Science Conference, Raleigh, NC, April 26–27, 2010), http://bit.ly/Twitter-Bomb; Eni Mustafaraj and Panagiotis Takis Metaxas, "The Fake News Spreading Plague: Was It

Preventable?" (paper presented at Web Science Conference, Troy, NY, June 2017), http://bit.ly/2sehUCv.

8. The infamous #Pizzagate conspiracy is an example of such behavior. See Panagiotis Takis Metaxas and Samantha Finn, "The Infamous 'Pizzagate' Conspiracy Theory: Insights from a TwitterTrails Investigation," (paper presented at Computation and Journalism Symposium, Northwestern University, Evanston, IL, October 13–14, 2017), http://bit.ly/2xEfIKU.

9. Marc Lourdes, "Malaysia's Anti-Fake News Law Raises Media Censorship Fears," CNN, April 3, 2018, https://www.cnn.com/2018/03/30/asia/malaysia-anti-fake-news -bill-intl/index.html.

10. Kevin Roose, "Here Come the Fake Videos, Too," *New York Times*, March 4, 2018, https://www.nytimes.com/2018/03/04/technology/fake-videos-deepfakes.html.

11. Julia Angwin and Jeff Larson, "Bias in Criminal Risk Scores Is Mathematically Inevitable, Researchers Say," ProPublica, December 30, 2016, https://www.propublica .org/article/bias-in-criminal-risk-scores-is-mathematically-inevitable-researchers-say.

12. "Of course it's true, I saw it in the newspaper!" was an expression that people in my home country used to use when they wanted to support a claim they believed as true. Graham and Metaxas, "'Of Course It's True.'"

13. Duncan Watts, *Everything Is Obvious (Once You Know the Answer): How Common Sense Fails Us* (New York: Crown Business, 2011).

14. Jason Silverstein, "Facebook Will Stop Labeling Fake News Because It Backfired, Made More Users Believe Hoaxes," *Newsweek*, December 21, 2017, http://www .newsweek.com/facebook-label-fake-news-believe-hoaxes-756426.

15. D. J. Flynn, Brendan Nyhan, and Jason Reifler, "The Nature and Origins of Misperceptions: Understanding False and Unsupported Beliefs about Politics," *Advances in Political Psychology* 38, no. S1 (2017): 127–150.

16. Christopher Chabris and Daniel Simons, "The Invisible Gorilla," 1999, http:// www.theinvisiblegorilla.com/gorilla_experiment.html.

17. Daniel Kahneman, *Thinking, Fast and Slow* (New York: Farrar, Straus and Giroux, 2011). Kahneman's "System 1" may have its headquarters in that part of the brain. See Lea Winerman, "A Machine for Jumping to Conclusions," *Monitor on Psychology* (American Psychological Association) 43, no. 2 (2012): 24.

18. Ferris Jabr, "Does Thinking Really Hard Burn More Calories?," *Scientific American*, July 18, 2012, https://www.scientificamerican.com/article/thinking-hard-calories/.

19. Cathy O'Neil, *Weapons of Math Destruction: How Big Data Increases Inequality and Threatens Democracy* (New York: Penguin Books, 2016).

20. This is a belief that mathematicians had until the early twentieth century, when Kurt Gödel proved that axiomatic mathematical systems containing basic arithmetic are incomplete. They contain many mathematical statements that one can neither prove they are correct nor prove incorrect. In our educational systems, however, we are never given exercises for which we cannot have a definite answer.

21. Yuval Noah Harari, *Homo Deus: A Brief History of Tomorrow* (New York: Harper-Collins, 2017).

VI   History: Part Introduction

The following part widens the scope of fake news to provide more historical context for many of the issues that have been discussed thus far. This group of chapters suggest that the sorts of partisan deceptions, conspiracy theories, and related contemporary phenomena are not all that new and have been deeply ingrained within Western societies. Taken together, the authors provide both cautionary tales and critical road maps that can help us navigate our tricky media landscape—so that we won't get fooled again, and again, and again.

The first chapter in this part, "A Prehistory of Fake News in America," is written by coeditor Kembrew McLeod, a media scholar and media practitioner who has produced documentaries and published pieces within popular press outlets, including the *New York Times*. Beginning with Benjamin Franklin and the early days of newspaper publishing in America, this chapter traces the evolution of journalism from the partisan press that flourished during the eighteenth and nineteenth centuries and concludes in the early twentieth century with the emergence of new codes of journalistic professionalism and objectivity. During this later period, at a time when there was mounting faith in empirical facts and social scientific inquiry, newspapers were being reimagined as instruments that could foster a healthy democratic society. This understanding of mainstream news outlets held sway throughout the following century, but in retrospect this "objective" school of journalism may have been just an anomalous blip, one that was bookended by the fake news age of today and the sorts of deceptions that had previously proliferated for three centuries.

In the second chapter in this part, "Beware the Theory in Conspiracy Theories," media historian Benjamin Peters unpacks the concept of conspiracy theories, with a focus on both conspiracy and theory. In many discussions of conspiracy theories, *theory* is often left uninterrogated, when, he argues, it is perhaps the most significant ingredient that helps them spread. The cognitive appeal of conspiracy theories is their sweeping explanatory powers that can account for a wide array of phenomena, which in turn highlights the weakness of theory in general, especially when theories are divorced from evidence. Using examples from the ancient past (Philolaus) and the present (#Pizzagate), Peters argues that theory allows us to see beyond what is directly in front of us, something that is "both a telltale weakness in modern inquiry and part of the tall tales informing conspiracy theories."

In the third chapter in this part, "'The Intel on This Wasn't 100 Percent': Fake News and Concerns over the Modern Democratic Project," media scholar Mark Brewin uses one of the examples that Peters focuses on— #Pizzagate—as a jumping-off point to historicize many of the themes that run through present-day conspiracy theories. Contemporary confusion over how to determine what is real and what is not, Brewin observes, did not begin with the rise of social media memes such as #Pizzagate (which prompted a true believer to open fire inside the Washington, D.C., pizza hangout at the center of the conspiracy theory). Instead, Brewin turns our attention back to the seventeenth century, when an alleged Catholic plot to kill the English king Charles II was uncovered by two Protestant ministers. Belief in this "plot" relied on the use of the same cognitive tics that drove #Pizzagate, just as today's fake news contains echoes of a different case study Brewin examines from the nineteenth century: the famous Great Moon Hoax, perpetrated by the *New York Sun*. This "penny press" newspaper often published sensationalistic news stories—if it bled, it led—that were designed more to sell copies than to uncover the truth. Well over a century later, as we currently swim in a sea of clickbait, it is clear that some things never change.

Suggested Readings

David Aaronovitch, *Voodoo Histories: The Role of the Conspiracy Theory in Shaping Modern History* (New York: Riverhead Books, 2010).

James Carey, *Communication as Culture: Essays on Media and Society* (New York: Routledge, 1988).

James W. Cook, *The Arts of Deception: Playing with Fraud in the Age of Barnum* (Cambridge, MA: Harvard University Press, 2001).

Karen Halttunen, *Confidence Men and Painted Women: A Study of Middle-Class Culture in America, 1830–1870* (New Haven, CT: Yale University Press, 1982).

Richard Hofstadter, *The Paranoid Style in American Politics* (New York: Vintage Books, 2008).

Elise Lemire, *"Miscegenation": Making Race in America* (Philadelphia: University of Pennsylvania Press, 2002).

Kembrew McLeod, *Pranksters: Making Mischief in the Modern World* (New York: New York University Press, 2014).

20 A Prehistory of Fake News in America

Kembrew McLeod

Deception has long been part of America's media landscape. When Benjamin Franklin emerged as a public figure as the publisher of the *Pennsylvania Gazette*, he used it to plant ironic satires, partisan potshots, and other false stories. The line between fact and fiction has been blurry since the early days of journalism. Throughout the eighteenth and nineteenth centuries, it was common for newspapers to print straight news alongside hoaxes, tall tales, and real events told through the eyes of fictional characters—a literary form known as a sketch. Today, it is not uncommon for people to mistake satirical news stories for real events—credulously reposting them on their social media accounts—and there is no evidence that our predecessors were any wiser.

Satirists like Mark Twain, who hatched several surreal hoaxes as a newspaper writer, eventually pushed the industry to more clearly define the limits of journalism, and by the beginning of the twentieth century this tricky tradition largely came to an end. New codes of ethics and standards of professionalism moved tall tales, sketches, and hoaxes to the margins of the page, or eliminated them altogether. Today, people lament the decline of journalistic standards and pine for an idealized past, but we should remember that fake news is as American as apple pie. Even the popular story about George Washington—who could not tell a lie about chopping down the cherry tree—was a fiction invented by his biographer to boost book sales.

Franklin got his start working for his brother James Franklin's *New England Courant*. It often displaced news from the front page with items, according to Nelson Keyes's 1956 biography *Ben Franklin: An Affectionate Portrait*, intended to be "entertaining and opinion-forming, rather than dully matter-of-fact."[1] During this time, Benjamin Franklin developed a love of pseudonyms that were used to stir up his ideological opponents, a practice that predated anonymous internet trolls by three centuries. He penned at least one hundred items under fake names throughout his life: Ephraim Censorious, Patience, the Casuist, the Anti-Casuist, Anthony Afterwit, Silence Dogood, and, his most famous, Richard Saunders, the Richard of *Poor Richard's Almanack*.[2]

"Just published for 1733: *Poor Richard: An Almanack*," announced an ad in the December 19, 1732, edition of Franklin's *Pennsylvania Gazette*, "containing the lunations, eclipses, planets motions and aspects, weather, … [and the] prediction of the death of his friend Mr. Titan Leeds." Saunders not only narrowed down Leeds's time of death to the date and time—October 17, 1733, at 3:29 p.m.—but also the exact moment when two worldly bodies aligned: "at the very instant of the conjunction of the Sun and Mercury."[3] Franklin was a rationalist product of the Enlightenment, a cynic who valued science over superstition and heaped scorn on astrologers such as Leeds. More crucially, Leeds was a business rival, and the printer's way up the ladder of wealth was often achieved by stepping on his competitors.[4]

When Leeds did not die on that date, Franklin/Saunders bemoaned the fact that he couldn't attend to his best friend during his final moments on earth. This infuriated the astrologer, who was not in on the joke and ranted in his not-quite-posthumous 1734 almanac about this "false Predictor," "conceited Scribbler," "Fool," and—last but not least—"Lyar."[5] Poor Richard was shocked by these rude utterances, and noted that there was absolutely no doubt Leeds had died, for it was "plain to everyone that reads his last two almanacks, no man living would or could write such stuff."[6] Franklin owned and operated the printing house that churned out Leeds's almanac, giving him a crucial advantage in this war of words. This inside knowledge allowed Franklin to read his attacks and respond to them in *Poor Richard's Almanack* before Leeds's publication even went to press. The astrologer's ongoing protests continued to pour fuel on the fire, which by now had captivated much of the colonies' reading public and turned *Poor Richard's* into a best seller. (After he actually did die, Franklin published a letter from Leeds's ghost admitting that Saunders was right all along.)[7]

Franklin executed several hoaxes, pranks, and satires over the course of his life, and readers who were not in the know often mistook his often-anonymous or often-pseudonymous stories for real events. However, he saved his most meaningful deception for last. Weeks before Franklin died in 1790, he wrote a pseudonymous newspaper editorial arguing that

Muslims should be allowed to enslave Christians—inverting the ideology of Christian pro-slavery advocates. Filled with fake citations and an elaborate backstory, the goal of the piece was to make them see the errors in their ways—or at least to ridicule their hypocritical beliefs.

In it, Franklin/Historicus quoted a speech that had allegedly been given by a Muslim leader a century earlier: "Who are to perform the common labors of our city," he asked, "and in our families? Must we not then be our own slaves? And is there not more compassion and more favor due to us Mussulmen, than to these Christian dogs?"[8] He enthusiastically piled on reasons for maintaining the status quo, including the fact that the labor pool enjoyed by Muslims would be annihilated if slavery ended. Property values would drop, as would tax revenues. And what on earth would be done with all those slaves if they were released from bondage? You can't trust those shifty Christians to stay out of trouble!

Franklin/Historicus further needled anti-abolitionists by arguing that slavery actually uplifted those Jesus-loving infidels: "They have an opportunity of making themselves acquainted with the true doctrine, and thereby saving their immortal souls."[9] There was the added benefit, he claimed, that Muslim slave masters treated their slaves with more humanity than how "free" laborers were handled in Christian nations. Also, slaves couldn't slit the throats of other warlike Jesus-lovers—just as European savages had done for centuries. Franklin signed off in his usual deadpan style, "I am, Sir, your constant Reader and humble Servant, Historicus."[10]

A political hoax timed for the U.S. presidential election season of 1864 served an entirely different purpose, anticipating some of the racially charged fake news that circulated during the 2016 elections. *Miscegenation: The Theory of the Blending of the Races, Applied to the American White Man and Negro* was a seventy-two-page pamphlet that is most notable for coining the word *miscegenation*, unleashing it on the public imagination.[11] It caused an immediate sensation by claiming that it was the Caucasian man's "noble prerogative to set the example of this rich blending of blood."[12] Predictably, white supremacists went into apoplectic fits.

David Goodman Croly, an editor at the *New York World* and an avowed racist, surreptitiously wrote *Miscegenation* with George Wakeman, a reporter at the same paper (which regularly stirred up white working-class racial anxieties). "And now, behold!," announced the authors, who posed as anti-slavery crusaders, "the great Republican party has merged into the little abolition party. The drop has colored the bucket-full."[13] From a contemporary vantage point, *Miscegenation* reads like an ideologically confusing game of Mad Libs: *Look at those antiwhite Republicans and their progressive agenda! Who will they vote for next, a black president with a white mother?* The pamphlet stoked passions on both ends of the political spectrum; it was embraced by prominent abolitionists, while at the same time passages were read in the halls of Congress in an attempt to obstruct the Freedman's Bureau bill, which was meant to assist former slaves.[14]

Croly and Wakeman expertly managed the hoax like a public relations campaign, sending abolitionist tastemakers advance copies along with a warm letter soliciting their opinions.[15] Parker Pillsbury, the editor of the *National Anti-Slavery Standard*, published a glowing review of the *Miscegenation* pamphlet, hoping that "there will be progressive intermingling and that the nation will be benefited by it."[16] Pro-slavery newspapers happily expanded on the hoax by making up their own fictions. The *New Hampshire Patriot* concocted an article titled "Sixty-Four Miscegenation," which implausibly claimed that sixty-four pro-abolitionist teachers in New England's Port Royal school gave birth to "mulatto" babies.[17] The Democrats also circulated an inflammatory leaflet aimed at the white working class titled "Miscegenation and the Republican Party," and reiterated the false claim that Abraham Lincoln advocated race mixing (he most certainly did not).[18]

Miscegenation successfully turned interracial marriage into one of the central campaign issues of the 1864 elections, a time when the electoral tide was turning against Lincoln. His campaign was in shambles, and the president privately believed it was "exceedingly probable" he would lose the election.[19] Croly and Wakeman's hoax had long legs, and it helped shape racial history in twentieth-century America. Within a year after the publication of the *Miscegenation* pamphlet, this newfangled word was in widespread use, and for decades it remained a powerful rhetorical tool used to police color lines.[20] It took until 1967, in the *Loving v. Virginia* decision, for the United States Supreme Court to rule that laws banning interracial marriage were unconstitutional.

Deception in journalism thrived throughout the 1800s, when news outlets regularly mixed fact and fiction. Of particular note was the *New York Sun*, which specialized in crime—if it bled, it led—as well as other eye-popping articles that were geared toward the working masses. It entertained people with huge headlines, slang-filled prose, sensational stories, and several bald-faced hoaxes.[21] During the summer of 1835, *Sun* reporter Richard Adams Locke published a series of stories about shocking new astronomical discoveries made from a South African observatory.[22] The sightings were attributed to a famous astronomer named Sir John Herschel, who allegedly scanned the moon with his telescope and came across a field of poppies, a red-hilled valley, and moon animals with horns! Locke named this area "the Valley of the Unicorn."[23]

The surreal sight grew weirder when the scientific team observed a group of man-bats, or *Vespertilio-homos*, who apparently enjoyed active sex lives. (Their "improper behavior," Locke intoned, would "ill comport with our terrestrial notions of decorum."[24]) The *Sun*'s circulation soon topped eighteen thousand—transforming it into the biggest newspaper in the world.[25] This story made an impression on P. T. Barnum, who was launching a career in the deceptive arts the very same year. "The sensation created by this immense imposture, not only throughout the United States, but in every part of the civilized world," Barnum noted, "will render it interesting so long as our language shall endure."[26] Eventually, Locke confessed his deception to a colleague at a competing newspaper, and news of the ruse rippled around the globe.[27]

Four decades later, the *New York Herald* whipped the city into a frenzy when it published a story on November 9, 1874, about a Central Park Zoo animal riot that killed forty-nine people and injured more than two hundred. New York governor John A. Dix reportedly arrived with a gun in hand, and several other prominent New Yorkers took part in an animal hunt on Broadway.[28] Because of the slow speed at which news traveled back then—there was no telephone or radio, for instance—many city residents lived in fear until the following morning.[29] Readers locked themselves indoors, and even some journalists fell for the story. Dr. George W. Hosmer—a celebrated war correspondent—appeared in the *Herald*'s offices with two large navy revolvers, shouting, "Well, here I am."[30] Even James Gordon Bennett, the paper's owner, collapsed in his bed after reading the story and remained there all day.[31] Like many of his own paper's readers, Bennett didn't make it to the article's final paragraph, which began: "Not one word of it is true."[32] Its stated goal was supposedly to "test the city's preparedness to meet a catastrophe," though selling lots of papers was likely the hoax's main goal.[33]

Before the twentieth century, pulling a hoax was considered as much a badge of honor as, say, getting an exclusive today.[34] It was not uncommon for newspapers to print rumors and tall tales, which were sometimes marked with the preamble "IMPORTANT, IF TRUE." Many of the yarns published in the American West were obviously preposterous, such as a story about a bird that hid from its enemies by swallowing itself. In the South, newspapers printed similar folktales, which were typically provided by readers.[35] The sketch was another familiar form for unreliable narrators. It was essentially a report that used many of the literary tropes of fiction writing, but was based on a real event. In the early eighteenth century, Daniel Defoe, Benjamin Franklin, and contributors to *The Spectator* routinely published sketches.

This slippery journalistic style thrived into the nineteenth century, when Mark Twain got his start writing for newspapers. The fledgling humorist moved with his brother to Nevada, where he worked for the Virginia City *Territorial Enterprise*.[36] His most significant literary hoaxes were of a regional nature, like an 1862 tale about a hundred-year-old "petrified man" who was found embedded in a cliff, sitting pensively.[37] "I was a brand-new local editor in Virginia City, and I felt called upon to destroy this growing evil," Twain said of a fad that was sweeping the area, where people obsessed over all things fossilized. "I chose to kill the petrifaction mania with a delicate, a very delicate satire."[38] The *Enterprise*'s editors noted, "Truth is not an indispensable requisite in the local columns of a newspaper," adding, "the more outrageous the hoax, the greater the evidence of talent."[39] Throughout the nineteenth century, newspaper articles were not judged solely on their "truthfulness." The quality of their wit and storytelling was important in their reception, but by the early twentieth century that changed. New codes of professionalism, combined with economic and technological transformations, wiped out this strain of journalism.

By the turn of the twentieth century, newspapers were being reimagined as an instrument that could foster a healthy democracy—an ideal that coincided with a mounting faith in empiricism and social-scientific inquiry. There were these things called "facts," and it was the role of the journalist to transparently transmit that information to citizens. This approach conflicted with more colorful literary styles, pushing reporters to write in particular ways, and only about certain subjects.[40] Additionally, news stories were increasingly compartmentalized into different sections of the newspaper: local news, entertainment, sports, political opinion, and other offerings. These demarcations, which separated one interest area from the other, changed the way reporters understood and described the world.

The more emotional and imaginative forms of journalism—like hoaxes and sketches—were relegated to sections that weren't explicitly marked as "news," or they were left out completely. This further standardized news writing.[41] Technological, cultural, and economic transformations changed the face of journalism. Information became something that could be measured and sorted, and the organization of the newsroom grew increasingly factorylike. The massive volume of data flowing through the wires required news to be treated like a commodity, in part because long-distance transmissions were expensive. This demanded a spare economy of language, forcing reporters to write sentences that were lean and unadorned—something that further standardized writing and ironed out regional quirks of language. Publishers that sought greater profits through mass advertising could now appeal to wider audiences.

"If the same story were to be understood in the same way from Maine to California, language had to be flattened out," media scholar James Carey writes. "The telegraph, therefore, led to the disappearance of forms of speech and styles of journalism and story telling—the tall story, the hoax, much humor, irony, and satire."[42] These changes were also prompted by hoaxers like Mark Twain and P. T. Barnum. Not only did they use media to make their mischief; their actions *remade* newspapers by pushing them to adopt new norms of professionalism by the 1900s. Nevertheless, America's contemporary media landscape reflects its nineteenth-century predecessors in some important ways, from the more frivolous moon and zoo hoaxes to the racially charged fake news of the 1864 presidential elections *and* the 2016 campaign season.

Acknowledgment

Elements of this chapter previously appeared in my column in *Little Village* and my book, Kembrew McLeod, *Pranksters: Making Mischief in the Modern World* (New York: New York University Press, 2014).

Notes

1. James N. Green and Peter Stallybrass, *Benjamin Franklin: Writer and Printer* (Philadelphia: Oak Knoll Press, 2006), 3; Walter Isaacson, *Benjamin Franklin: An American Life* (New York: Simon and Schuster, 2003), 22.

2. Green and Stallybrass, *Benjamin Franklin*, 7–8.

3. Benjamin Franklin, *Fart Proudly: Writings of Benjamin Franklin You Never Read in School*, ed. Carl Japikse (Berkeley, CA: Frog, 2003), 37.

4. Green and Stallybrass, *Benjamin Franklin*.

5. Franklin, *Fart Proudly*, 39.

6. Isaacson, *Benjamin Franklin*, 96.

7. Douglas Anderson, *The Radical Enlightenments of Benjamin Franklin* (Baltimore: Johns Hopkins University Press, 1997), 100.

8. Benjamin Franklin, *A Benjamin Franklin Reader*, ed. Walter Isaacson (New York: Simon and Schuster, 2003), 373.

9. Fred Fedler, *Media Hoaxes* (Ames: Iowa State University Press, 1989), 12.

10. Ibid., 13.

11. Leslie M. Harris, "From Abolitionist Amalgamators to 'Rulers of the Five Points': The Discourse of Interracial Sex and Reform in Antebellum New York City," in *Sex, Love, Race: Crossing Boundaries in North American History*, ed. Martha Hodes (New York: New York University Press, 1999), 208.

12. Sidney Kaplan, "The Miscegenation Issue in the Election of 1864," *Journal of Negro History* 34, no. 3 (1949): 279.

13. *Miscegenation: The Theory of the Blending of the Races, Applied to the American White Man and Negro* (New York: H. Dexter, Hamilton, 1864), 50.

14. Elise Lemire, *"Miscegenation": Making Race in America* (Philadelphia: University of Pennsylvania Press, 2002), 116.

15. Kaplan, "The Miscegenation Issue," 280, 284.

16. Lemire, *"Miscegenation,"* 137.

17. Kaplan, "The Miscegenation Issue," 309–310.

18. Ibid., 319.

19. Paul Collins, *The Trouble with Tom: The Strange Afterlife and Times of Thomas Paine* (New York: Bloomsbury, 2005), 164; Kaplan, "The Miscegenation Issue," 275–276.

20. Kaplan, "The Miscegenation Issue," 277–278.

21. Paul Maliszewski, *Fakers: Hoaxers, Con Artists, Counterfeiters, and Other Great Pretenders* (New York: New Press, 2008), 104.

22. Herma Silverstein and Caroline Arnold, *Hoaxes That Made Headlines* (New York: Julian Messner, 1986), 76; Fedler, *Media Hoaxes*, 57.

23. Matthew Goodman, *The Sun and the Moon: The Remarkable True Account of Hoaxers, Showmen, Dueling Journalists, and Lunar Man-Bats in Nineteenth-Century New York* (New York: Basic Books, 2008), 172.

24. Benjamin Reiss, *The Showman and the Slave: Race, Death, and Memory in Barnum's America* (Cambridge, MA: Harvard University Press, 2001), 147.

25. Fedler, *Media Hoaxes*, 63.

26. Goodman, *The Sun and the Moon*, 12.

27. Ibid., 218.

28. Fedler, *Media Hoaxes*, 89–91.

29. Ibid., 96.

30. Curtis D. MacDougall, *Hoaxes* (New York: Dover, 1958), 232.

31. Silverstein and Arnold, *Hoaxes That Made Headlines*, 74.

32. Michael Farquhar, *A Treasury of Deception* (New York: Penguin, 2005), 39.

33. Paul Collins, *Sixpence House: Lost in a Town of Books* (New York: Bloomsbury, 2003), 157.

34. N. H. Sims, "The Chicago Style of Journalism" (Ph.D. diss., University of Illinois, 1979), 34.

35. Fedler, *Media Hoaxes*, xvi–xvii.

36. Sims, "The Chicago Style of Journalism," 29–32.

37. Silverstein and Arnold, *Hoaxes That Made Headlines*, 80.

38. Fedler, *Media Hoaxes*, 44.

39. Silverstein and Arnold, *Hoaxes That Made Headlines*, 82.

40. Sims, "The Chicago Style of Journalism," 20–21.

41. Ibid., 26–28.

42. James Carey, *Communication as Culture: Essays on Media and Society* (New York: Routledge, 1988), 210–211.

21 Beware the Theory in Conspiracy Theories

Benjamin Peters

Conspiracy theories are no joke. They ruin lives and poison public trust in legitimate inquiry. More destructive than conspiracy theory, however, are its two component parts—actual conspiracies, on the one hand, and the work of theory itself, on the other. I take the first point as well understood and uncontroversial: many modern institutions—ranging from the state investment in the intelligence community to the press in investigative journalism, public education in critical thinking, and knowledge industries in science—share a common commitment to rooting out real-life conspiracies. However, the second point—the sweeping power of theory itself—often goes less carefully considered. Perhaps the greatest danger of conspiracy theory is its significant cognitive appeal, which, upon closer reflection, reveals the end weakness of theory, namely, its separation from evidence. Using examples from ancient Greek science and modern U.S. politics, I argue that theory, especially when separated from evidence, permits humans to see beyond what is already there. Theory, which, at its best, *limits* its boldest claims with evidence, is discussed as both a telltale weakness in modern inquiry and part of the tall tales informing conspiracy theories.

The Misuses of Theory from Philolaus to #Pizzagate

Philolaus, a noted Pythagorean, saw a little further than his peers in ancient Greece. Unlike others, he set aside the then popular geocentric models of the cosmos and centered the earth's orbit around what he called "Hestia," the great fire. He also gave contour to the continuous flows of sound, discovering wave ratios in musical intervals such as the octave (2:1), the fifth (3:2), and the fourth (4:3). These empirically verifiable insights sped his theorizing about the whole of the cosmos, which he claimed consists of only two different classes of things: *unlimited* (continuums, flows) and *limiters* (structure, thresholds, breaks). Unlimited and limiters combined in ratios so completely that, for him, all nature revealed itself in the harmonies of numbers: "All things that are known have number," he declared, "for without this nothing whatever could possibly be thought of or known."[1] Philolaus was no conspiracy theorist, but he was also dead wrong about most of these details. In other words, his theories let him, like all theorists, see beyond what was actually there. It is simply not true that "all things that are known have number" (nowhere does or must there exist a *Durchmusterung* of, say, all the lilies, the clouds, or the connections among lovers). Nor does the inverse hold that "all things with numbers are known" (consider the vast oceans of unprocessed data upon which the modern media environment floats). So, too, is his model of the solar system at odds with modern astronomical observation: there are *not* ten planets (a cosmic number for him) in the solar system, the moon is *not* inhabited by massive animals, and there is *no* counter-earth circulating on the other side of the sun. Still, Philolaus deserves credit for being wrong in ways that other Pythagoreans could later correct. His contributions lie in the fact that his theories were not true or false, but falsifiable by evidence. Today most theories are verifiable, some are even falsifiable; by contrast, most conspiracy theories are not. Still, they share something in common: *all* theorists, including the conspiracy theorist, use theory to see past the evidence. Theory, in short, is a way to see beyond what is there. The term *theory*—derived from the Greek θεωρία for the action of viewing, contemplation, and spectacle—is a way of seeing the world anew, even if the world itself (or *Ding an Sich*, as Kant called it) remains always partly hidden. While empiricism would ask that theorists check their vision against new fact patterns, theory itself has no necessary relationship to facts. To *theorize* is to see farther than the facts permit.

Now let us fast-forward to a puzzle recently circulating in U.S. politics: Which U.S. president, does the reader imagine, is most likely to have been variously accused online of being an antichrist, Kenyan-born, secret Muslim reptilian Martian who murdered his Pakistani husband in a gay orgy before marrying his transvestite wife—and why? All these details are obviously utter nonsense: a future historian will find no evidence to indicate any grounds for leveling these claims against any U.S. president, let alone former president Barack Obama, as they have been in various unnamed online forums. Nevertheless, a future *theorist* may be able to see that what remains *unseen* in this list of claims conspiring against this president's actual religion (Christian), nationality (American), sexuality (straight), sex (male), morality (non-murderous), species (human), and planet of origin (terrestrial) is the very feature that publicly marks his minority status— namely, his race (African American). In other words, while future historians will find ample damning evidence of racism in the United States, it will take a future *theorist* to see what remains unstated in these outrageous claims: by deploying these theories, the opponents of Obama sidestep the taboo confession that they do not trust black people in power. Instead, they sound out claims for why they do not trust *this* particular person, who happens to be black, for any other reason they might theorize—and theory is endlessly creative in its self-justifications. The superpower of theory precipitates and reveals its core weakness: again, theory lets us see so far that we eventually see what is not there.

What can we learn from such ancient and modern overseeing? Conspiracy thinking does not need to be true or false in order to flourish—rather, it simply needs to motivate and confirm our favorite cognitive biases. Philolaus, a fan of ratios, found them littering the heavens, just as political contenders battle the very demons they identify in and promise to exorcise from their opponents: in Russia, for example, a common strategy among businesspeople seeking public office is to claim that all politicians are corrupt, thus making it easier for outsiders, like themselves, to wrest profitable seats from incumbent contenders.[2] Such claims about conspiracies about hiding evidence often flourish best in the uncertainty they create: in the run-up to the 2016 U.S. presidential election, the #Pizzagate conspiracy held that the Democratic National Party supported child sex trafficking in the basement of a pizza parlor. While there is no evidence to support this claim, it is a morally motivating position precisely because it works *in theory* whether or not it is true:[3] Who, after all, could ever elect to power a child trafficker? *If true*, it *would* be morally reprehensible to support a public official guilty of such charges. The danger of #Pizzagate is that its perverse charge is most persuasive in the hypothetical—no one could dare to oppose such an obvious position in theory, *if true*.

How much reasonable disbelief is suspended in that powder-keg phrase "if true"! A single "if" may pack enough explosive possibility to ruin the world. The hypotheticals spin themselves out: *What if* President Donald

Trump, drunk on power and nursing his massive and fragile ego, were to reach for the nuclear football in his feverish dreams at night? *What if* the bulk of the blame for the corrupt secret heart of America could be shifted onto Russian meddling in the election? *What if it were true?* The extraordinary power of theory is that it blurs, for the motivated mind, the line between the thinkable and the desirable; and, of course, in politics (or what Richard Hofstadter calls "an arena of angry minds"[4]), as in identity construction, it remains troublingly desirable to oppose one's opponents. Many scholars—in and beyond the media and communication field—have written about the troubled sorting of individuals into porous community sociopsychological orders and disorders. While conspiracy thinking is not necessarily pathological, it is often represented as paranoiac in its reasoning since the Enlightenment attempt to separate public reason and private madness. The most prominent case study is, of course, that of *Memoirs of My Nervous Illness*, the 1903 autobiography of Daniel Paul Schreber, whose reasoned madness appealed to Sigmund Freud, Michel Foucault, Elias Canetti, Walter Benjamin, and Friedrich Kittler. Still other (often midcentury) theorists—Gregory Bateson, R. D. Laing, Gilles Deleuze and Félix Guattari, and, more recently, Amit Pinchevski—have shown how representations of mental illness, and the schizophrenic in particular, cannot help but reveal that normal standards for social behavior often contain and are subverted by the abnormal.[5] This insight applies to the social sciences as well: Richard Hofstadter's iconic essay, "The Paranoid Style in American Politics" and Hadley Cantril's famous study both normalize and criticize the panicked American public as paranoid.[6] Jefferson Pooley and Michael J. Socolow, however, convincingly argue that Cantril overstated the effect and degree of panic to the infamous radio broadcast of Orson Welles's *War of the Worlds* in 1938.[7] The point, of course, is not whether certain subjects should or should not ever be called "crazy" or "paranoid" or "panicked" or "conspiratorial": rather, the point, examined below, is that doing so, even justifiably, does not always have the effect it intends. The simple fact is that conspiracy theories are encountered only in public accusations, not private belief. Instead of separating legitimate and illegitimate claims, mass accusations of any kind—especially of psychosocial abnormality—often depreciate the role of counterintuitive theory-making so central to modern inquiry. The next section, in search of firmer ground on which to rest such public judgment, seeks a shortcut through the rocky waters that separate the limits of theory and limited theories.

On the Weakness of Strong Theories

Theory is only as good as the evidence that limits its boldest claims. Conversely, theories that prosper in the absence of evidence are cognitively so powerful precisely because the claim is structured to make it hard to convince otherwise. But this power is of course also its corrosive weakness, for theory alone cannot distinguish conspiracy theory from actual conspiracy. If acquaintances were to claim, for example, that they are so smart that no external test can measure it, so beautiful that only those with more refined senses can observe it, or so powerful that they can hide their influence from detection, their statement would amount to nonsense except as a preemptive protest against those who might deem them dumb, ugly, or impotent. Or, consider the circular assertion that the U.S. government popularized the phrase *conspiracy theory* to discredit those who seek to expose its many actual conspiracies: if this were true, there should be little or no evidence to support it. Like this very statement, no nonfalsifiable claim can mean what it says—it always means less and more. One is tempted to repeat the empiricist's creed: do not believe that which cannot be tested.

Such hard-nosed empirical realism has a certain commonsensical appeal, but alas, it, too, is insufficient to chill the boiling brew that is the theory behind conspiracy theory. Conspiracy theories do much more than pose untestable claims: rather, conspiracy theory functions as fashionable modern folklore, the linguistic cloth out of which one weaves the scientific-sounding garb for a group identity narrative based on opposing other groups. In this tapestry of talk, one group prizes its knowledge of its enemies' secret knowledge that endlessly pits "us" versus "them" (the use of the universal "we" in this essay is both intentional *and* problematic). Groups that exist at the expense of other groups imagine in-group experts as knights of knowledge poised to battle against some foreign threat that can approach from any of the four directions that commentator Jesse Walker lists: the "Enemy Above" (e.g., King George taxing the colonies to death), the "Enemy Below" (e.g., paupers attempting to assassinate the king), the "Enemy Outside" (e.g., Soviet spies), and the "Enemy Within" (e.g., Communists in Joseph McCarthy's U.S. government).[8] The truth is that there really *are* enemies in the world, just not the ones Walker names. Indeed, false claims about opponents, not the opponents themselves, must be recognized as the common enemy to all modern inquiry.

So if the label "conspiracy theory" is a bit of modern folklore for constructing opposing scholarly group identities, then the *theory* of conspiracy theory marks a signal contradiction in the mythologies of modern inquiry: calling a claim a "conspiracy theory" often has the unintended effect of perpetuating conspiracy theorizing. If conspiracy theorists are synonymous with those who espouse nonfalsifiable theories, then trying to delegitimize claims by castigating members of the believing community as "conspiracy theorists" actually *legitimatizes* the in-group belief that it alone bears certain secret (hence permissibly nonfalsifiable) insights. Instead of heightening suspicion against conspiracy theorists, outside calls for strict empiricism justifies the group's perception that its own beliefs are exceptional. Such insults poison the theory community's well, supply the very opposition the community needs to vindicate its own narratives of victimhood, and question the legitimacy of any counterargument before it can be made. At best an unfair power move, the label "conspiracy theory" renders its object—a theory community—prescientifically unscientific.

The resolution to this contradiction lies not in the empiricist's strict suspicion against theory, although falsifiability, verisimilitude, verification, and other standards remain necessary, if insufficient. Indeed, if falsifiability holds as the golden standard for distinguishing science from conspiracy theory, then scholars must hasten to shelve their favorite nonfalsifiable theoretical frameworks as well, no matter how much useful interpretive insight they bring. For example, much about Marxist false consciousness, Freudian psychoanalysis, and Lacanian deconstruction takes openly nonfalsifiable approaches to critical reading. The qualia that attend the experience of poetry, the arts, and other sources of vital inspiration fare no better against this strict standard. Discarding all nonfalsifiable sources is surely too high of a cost for scholars in the humanities and social sciences, among others committed to the flourishing and legitimation of the human sciences.

Instead, let us reflect on the slivers of light that sometimes sneak through critical cracks in the methods of modern inquiry. Many conspiracy theorists cannot easily be distinguished from the most devoted, even obsessive, scientific inquirers: scientific empiricists and conspiracy theorists alike gather and pore over highly complex and detailed records, explore and draw out unexpected causal relationships, and unearth potent meaning from seemingly innocent details. Neither group knows whether its favorite theory will experimentally fail for being too simple or too complex (conspiracy theories are often dismissed for proposing explanations in turn too parsimonious or too ornate). Both groups congratulate themselves for being, unlike the other group, open-minded: conspiracy theorists are convinced they are virtuously open only to the possibility that their pet theory is right; while falsifiable empiricists pride themselves on being open only to claims that evidence could challenge—and in so doing, both groups consider themselves open-minded and the other close-minded. Not only do conspiracy theorists label other groups as outside the truth, but the label "conspiracy theory" does that very thing itself as well. Like the other double-edged term *fake news* and much else in the distorting fun house mirrors of online trolling culture, a strange loop results: any group that ostracizes another group for ostracizing others will stumble in persuasively claiming either the methodological or moral high ground.

Conclusion: Hearing out the Siren Song of Theory

Of course, the call to set aside conspiracy theory accusations is no call to pass on the need for critical judgment. Indeed, if anything, it heightens the need to be able to call out nonsense where one sees it. To do so can be both justifiable and necessary. Setting aside accusations of conspiracy theory must not ease the burden of critical evaluation—rather, it simply instructs scholars and students to not mirror the very cardinal sin that it accuses conspiracy theorists of taking against a world of evidence. Theory communities that hurl conspiracy theory slings and arrows rehearse the brittle and reductive identity politics so often encountered around questions of gender and race in the echo chambers and filter bubbles online and off.[9] Perhaps community identities, whatever else they may be, grow best in the soil of experience.

Instead of calling conspiracy theorists by that label, perhaps we may ask the theorists in question to recount their own best attempts to disprove their most potent theories. So, too, may we acknowledge that modern inquiry rests on the tautological belief that any other belief that can benefit from the absence of evidence is illegitimate—and yet it does so, as philosophers of science as different as Karl Popper and Paul Feyerabend have clarified, without satisfactorily justifying the grounds of that same belief. It is precisely this fundamental limitation in modern inquiry—*truth tends to follow evidence that limits theory, not theory that limits evidence*—that gives grounds for hope: for this limitation also witnesses that the appetizing feast that is modern inquiry has many courses before it concludes. The antidote to conspiracy theory is not just hard-minded empiricism. It is rather, as Josiah Royce suggests, self-consciously limited theorists who acknowledge that, even as not every so-called conspiracy theorist is a tinfoil-hat nut job, the larger purpose of theory making remains the sustenance of communities of inquiry committed to shared standards of critical evaluation and judgment.[10]

In closing, the theory in conspiracy theory is any theory set apart from such a world of evidence—a world that must be larger than, and thus capable of limiting, its own worldview. If the extraordinary promise of theory is to let us see beyond what is there, then perhaps the sustainable practice of theory is to let us see, through its weakening and weighing with evidence, *less, not more,* than the theory lets us see at first. To let theory flow freely, from Philolaus to #Pizzagate, will surely steep us in the septic waters of our own unchecked biases. "Conspiracy theory" is not only the label modern humans use to insult someone else for taking theory too seriously—it is a vista onto the shipwrecked coast that bedevils any modern inquirers who orient their craft too closely to the siren song of theory. Beware the theory in conspiracy theories, for the astronomical summits of theory alone are vertiginous and dangerous, and it is precisely our modern tendency to believe our own theories, without acknowledging that we may already be on the wrong side of history, that renders such theory—in the full splendor of its immodest isolation from evidence, in folkloric bias confirmation dressed up in the garb of modern science—among the most dangerous and powerful tall tales the modern world tells itself.

Acknowledgment

This essay has benefited from the critical comments of Joli Jensen, Mark Brewin, Seth C. Lewis, Kembrew McLeod, Sebastian Vehlken, and two anonymous reviewers. I acknowledge and thank them all.

Notes

1. Carl Huffman, "Philolaus," in *The Stanford Encyclopedia of Philosophy*, Summer 2016 Edition, ed. Edward N. Zalta, https://plato.stanford.edu/archives/sum2016/entries/philolaus/.

2. David Szakonyi, "Renting Elected Office: Why Businesspeople Become Politicians in Russia" (Ph.D. diss., Columbia University, 2016).

3. Cecilia Kang, "Fake News Onslaught Targets Pizzeria as Nest of Child-Trafficking," *New York Times*, November 21, 2016, https://www.nytimes.com/2016/11/21/techno logy/fact-check-this-pizzeria-is-not-a-child-trafficking-site.html.

4. Richard Hofstadter, "The Paranoid Style in American Politics," *Harper's Magazine*, November 1964.

5. A small selection of the literature on pathology and media includes Sigmund Freud, "Psycho-Analytic Notes upon an Autobiographical Account of a Case of Paranoia (Dementia Paranoides)," in J. Strachey, *The Standard Edition of the Complete Psychological Works of Sigmund Freud* Volume XII (1911–1913) (London, England: The Hogarth Press and Institute of Psycho-analysis, 1958), 3–82; Michel Foucault, *Madness and Civilization: A History of Insanity in the Age of Reason*), trans. Jean Khalfa (New York: Vintage Books, 1995) (originally published as *Folie et déraison: Histoire de la folie à l'âge classique*, 1961); Elias Canetti, *The Conscience of Words*, trans. Joachim Neugroschel (London: Andre E. Deutsch, 1986); Walter Benjamin, "Books by the Mentally Ill: From My Collection," in *Walter Benjamin: Selected Writings Volume 2, Part 1 (1927–1930)*, ed. Michael William Jennings, Howard Eiland, and Gary Smith and trans. Rodney Livingstone et al. (Cambridge, MA: Belknap Press of Harvard University Press, 1999), 123–130; Friedrich Kittler, "Flechsig—Schreber—Freud. Ein Nachrichtennetzwerk der Jahrhundertwende, " *Der Wunderblock. Zeitschrift für Psychoanalyse* 11, no. 12 (1984): 56–68. See also Friedrich Kittler, *Aufschreibesysteme 1800/1900* (Berlin: Wilhem Fink, 1985), 194–195; Gregory Bateson, "Toward a Theory of Schizophrenia," *Behavioral Science* 1, no. 4 (1956): 251–254; R. D. Laing, *The Divided Self: An Existential Study in Sanity and Madness* (New York: Penguin, 1960); Gilles Deleuze and Félix Guattari, *Anti-Oedipus: Capitalism and Schizophrenia* (Minneapolis: University of Minnesota Press, 1983); Amit Pinchevski, "Bartleby's Autism: Wandering along Incommunicability," *Cultural Critique* 78 (Spring 2011): 27–59; Amit Pinchevski and John Durham Peters, "Autism and New Media: Disability between Technology and Society," *New Media and Society* 18, no. 11 (2016): 2507–2523.

6. Richard Hofstadter, "The Paranoid Style in American Politics"; Hadley Cantril, *The Invasion from Mars: A Study in the Psychology of Panic* (1940; repr., New York: Harper Torchbooks, 1966).

7. Jefferson Pooley and Michael J. Socolow, "The Myth of the *War of the Worlds* Panic," *Slate*, October 28, 2013, https://slate.com/culture/2013/10/orson-welles-war-of -the-worlds-panic-myth-the-infamous-radio-broadcast-did-not-cause-a-nationwide -hysteria.html.

8. Jesse Walker, *The United States of Paranoia: A Conspiracy Theory* (New York: Harper, 2013), 14.

9. Wendy Hui Kyong Chun, "Queerying Homophily: Muster der Netzwerkanalyse," *Zeitschrift für Medienwissenschaft*, no. 18 (2018): 131–148.

10. Josiah Royce, *The Problem of Christianity* (1913; repr., Washington, DC: Catholic University of America Press, 2001).

22 "The Intel on This Wasn't 100 Percent": Fake News and Concerns over the Modern Democratic Project

Mark Brewin

On December 4, 2016, Edgar Maddison Welch, a twenty-six-year-old community college dropout and sometime actor from Salisbury, North Carolina, walked into a Washington, D.C., pizzeria called Comet Ping Pong and began firing an assault rifle into the walls of the restaurant. Welch would later tell police and newspaper reporters that he had made the six-hour trip from his home to Washington in order to investigate the possibility of a child sex-trafficking ring operating out of the restaurant, an unbelievable story made even more so with the added claim that Democratic presidential candidate Hillary Clinton was involved in the conspiracy.[1] Welch had become aware of the ring from personal discussions, and also various online posts, listservs, and websites.[2]

Disturbed individuals are driven to commit desperate and seemingly illogical acts, and this might easily have seemed to be the case with Welch. But in the wake of a dramatic presidential election that highlighted important divisions in what Americans thought about themselves and their place in the world, in what they saw as important and nonnegotiable, Welch's act took on greater significance. Perhaps most alarmingly, what was rapidly dubbed #Pizzagate illustrates the mutual incomprehension that had obviously developed between conservative Americans like Welch and the type of liberal city-dweller who lived in places like Washington, D.C.

That discussion was largely ignored, however, in favor of a more fashionable and more easily digestible one: the rise of so-called fake news. A widely cited study conducted in the fall of 2016, sponsored by the news site BuzzFeed, suggests that "fake" news stories on Facebook were more likely to be shared than stories from reputable news organizations like the *New York Times* or the *Washington Post*.[3] Within this environment the #Pizzagate controversy could be taken as symbolic of some deeper and more serious political sickness. "It's tempting to think of fake news as a political dirty trick devised by partisan mischief-makers that caters to ignoramuses in election season," read an editorial in the *Post* two days after Welch's arrest. "But the Comet Ping Pong incident is a reminder that fake news isn't only a distortion of public events." Those who spread fake news, the editorial added, "are complicit in fouling the public discourse and in the incitement that led to Sunday's attack."[4] Evidence not simply of stupidity, but stupidity wedded to malice, in other words.

What are we to make of fake news, and its pernicious effects on individuals like Welch? Since the fall of 2016, that question has occasioned analyses from a number of different perspectives. The one taken here will be historical in nature. I consider the current debate over fake news in light of two much earlier instances of mendacity within the popular media. The first of these is the "Popish Plot," an imagined political conspiracy promoted by a seventeenth-century English adventurer and scoundrel named Titus Oates. The second is a series of humbugs published by the *New York Sun* in 1835, now known to journalism historians as the Great Moon Hoax. By placing fake news within a longer narrative of public lying, I hope to provoke some critical reflection on what exactly it is that we are worried about when we discuss the problem of fake news.

The Debate over Fake News

Different people mean different things by the term *fake news*. My focus is on the sort of news that *New York Times* reporter Sabrina Tavernise defined in her 2016 article on the topic: "a made-up story with an intention to deceive, often geared toward getting clicks."[5] Tavernise's notion that fake news is geared toward getting "clicks" implies that it is somehow distinctive to internet culture and perhaps even to social media. It suggests moreover that there is something unique to our current moment—in this case, our technology, or at least our use thereof—that has allowed fake news to flourish in a way not previously possible.

There are two elements that make fake news distinctive. The first is the way that it regards facts: with a cynical disdain. If we take a narrow compass of the issue, fake news fits into a political culture that has been defined as "post-truth," one that finds a place for what are now sneeringly referred to as "alternative facts"—or what an earlier age might have called "lies."[6]

This in turn derives from a more sustained and more intellectually serious debate over the status of facts: scientific facts, moral facts, historical facts.[7] After all, how, in a postmodern world, do we decide what is true or not?

The second important aspect to fake news is that it arises within a specific media regime—that is to say, a specific conjunction of practice and technology—that promotes the splintering of audiences into narrower and narrower information streams. Unlike the shared experiences and interpretations provided to citizens in a mass-mediated public sphere, individuals in an age of "mass individualized media" have little if any sense of shared values or shared reality.[8] Thus what seems nonsensical or ridiculous to one portion of the population—the idea that the Democratic candidate for president would take time out of her campaign schedule to help her friends run a child prostitution ring—can seem entirely plausible to another section. What we are investigating, in other words, is what journalist and media commentator Brooke Gladstone calls our "trouble with reality."[9]

Here's the thing, though: to the extent that we do indeed have trouble determining what is real and what is not, this did not begin with the rise of reality TV, or with social media memes.

Plotting Papists in Seventeenth-Century London

In the late summer of 1678, two English Protestant ministers, Israel Yonge and Titus Oates, uncovered a plot to kill Charles II, then king of England and Scotland. The authors of the plot were a group of Catholics, including a number of Jesuit priests. But there were problems with this supposed conspiracy. Both Yonge and Oates were dubious characters. Yonge was a fanatical anti-Papist and by this point in his life probably mad. Oates had already demonstrated a decided proclivity to perjury and dissembling. His evidence, though dramatic, was so dodgy that government officials prosecuting the cases against the accused plotters in court tried to keep him off the witness stand if at all possible.[10]

Nevertheless, Oates's claims, published by himself and supporters in numerous pamphlets, led to a print war and something approaching mass hysteria, as well as the deaths of more than a dozen Catholics. Eventually he was charged and convicted of perjury, although, somewhat amazingly, he did not receive a death sentence for the very considerable discord that he had created.

The plot dreamed up by Oates, Yonge, and their numerous enablers is important not merely as an early example of journalistic chicanery: a Restoration version of fake news, as it were. It is also one of the most dramatic examples of the emerging power of the press in modern society and, not unrelated to this last point, an early lesson for the English ruling class of the role that public opinion was to play in this new age.[11] The Marquess of Halifax was famously reported to say of the plot: "It must be handled as if it were true, whether it were so or not."[12] In 1687, English society had been dealing with religious strife and the violence that often accompanied it for over a century, and religious debates had infiltrated into almost every locality in the country.[13] People had been burned at the stake for their beliefs. The country had suffered a civil war at least in part provoked by differences in faith. All members of the dispute were disposed to believe the worst of their opponents, and with a good deal of justification. Hence the country's rulers realized at a certain point that, whatever they might have thought personally of Oates and his cockamamy stories, they needed to be seen as *doing* something. This was perhaps most obviously the case for the king himself, who was widely and popularly believed to be too friendly to the Catholics.

The people needed to be managed, but would not be managed. Their enthusiasm, particularly in the cause of persecuting Catholics (who composed at this point only about 2 percent of English residents), was unreserved, and their mob-like behavior, combined with their credulity as regards Oates's fantastic tales, fit with the more general fears of many members of elite society that ordinary people could not be trusted to discern truth from lies.[14] Roger L'Estrange, who operated at times as a kind of propagandist for the king, when he was not busy hunting down troublesome opponents as the government's censor, noted:

> Truth and falsehood have chang'd place; and according to the mode of the times the very quality of it is inverted too … and what was this [popish] plot at last but a blasphemous slanderous imagination, made up of lies and contradictions? … the [people] were never cut out for the judging or the understanding of things; but plausible disguises and appearances, have with them the force and value of certain truths and foundations.[15]

But L'Estrange had never trusted the people, nor, despite the fact that he was himself a practicing journalist, did he trust the press. He did not need the example of Titus Oates to conclude that public opinion was a danger to the nation. With that bias in mind, it is worth pointing out that while the plot itself was fiction, the notion that many well-connected Catholics would dearly have loved to put a Catholic king on the English throne and bring the nation back into the welcoming arms of Mother Rome was not at all imaginary. They already had the candidate for sovereign at hand: Charles's brother James, who eventually did become king, an event that in turn provoked the century's second revolution.

To put it another way: the Popish Plot was about more than simply the potential threat posed to the public peace by a few ill-meaning, scheming fellows capable of using the press and rumor to manipulate the people into believing outrageous and implausible conspiracies. That it is often framed in such terms suggests not only that we have simplified the plot, but that we have done so because of certain concerns we continue to have over the way that the media works on the public mind.

The Discovery of Men on the Moon

The Popish Plot was not the first, and would not be the last, journalistic fraud perpetrated on the British public. In the century to come, journalistic falsehoods would course through London's coffeehouses and news exchanges with regularity, where they were then picked up and spread into the general population by print reporters. Indeed, the fakery was prevalent enough that journalists themselves remarked upon it, Daniel Defoe once characterizing the denizens of the city's Exchange Alley as being "as dangerous to the public safety as a magazine of gun powder is to a populous city.[16] Things were no better in the colonies, nor later in the early American republic. Newspaper editors often owed their livelihood either directly or indirectly to party and faction, and regularly printed outlandish and thinly sourced calumnies of their political opponents. These fake news stories, especially common during campaign season, owed what plausibility they could garner more or less to the partisan biases of the readership.[17]

It is within this general culture of a laxity toward matters of fact that we must place the most famous newspaper hoax of the nineteenth century. In late August 1835, the *Sun*, one of the first examples of the penny press, published a series of stories on the scientific observations made by famed astronomer Sir John Herschel. The most fantastic of these was the discovery of a number of animals living on the moon: a species of unicorn, two-legged beavers, and a kind of winged humanoid who resembled a bat. Herschel was a real person, but the rest of the *Sun's* reporting was pure fiction. The setup was uncovered rather quickly by the paper's competition, although its editor, Benjamin Day, never did own up to printing manufactured news—that is to say, fake news—and the paper did not seem to suffer a falloff in readership when the whole affair was laid out for public critique.[18]

The Great Moon Hoax has been analyzed from any number of different angles: for example, as an instance of showmanship and brazen pranks in an age where public truth-telling was not always the highest priority, or as an illustration of the power of appeal to objective "science" in the nineteenth century, or, most recently, as a parable of the country's obsession over race.[19] According to the purported author of the piece, Richard Adams Locke, however, the Great Moon Hoax had originally been conceived as satire. In a long letter to a different penny paper several years later, Locke claimed that his real intent in writing and publishing the fiction had been to call attention to what he considered the disreputable, confused, and evidence-free theories concerning life on other planets, especially those made by presumptuous theologians such as the popular author Thomas Dicks.[20] The ultimate aim of the whole business was to illustrate the absurdity of mixing theological speculation with scientific investigation, a style of thinking that Locke feared "would rapidly emasculate the minds of our studious youth."[21]

As with almost all the other participants in the affair, Locke assumed that the Great Moon Hoax had managed to fool large numbers of contemporary readers into believing the stories of the discoveries to be true. This may not have been correct. Most of the accounts of widespread gullibility were made secondhand: a widely circulated story about the students and faculty at Yale College was strongly disputed by some of those who were reputedly bamboozled.[22] Many readers were no doubt in the position of Philip Hone, onetime mayor of New York: "In sober truth, *if this account is true*, it is most enormously wonderful.[23] The sensational nature of the stories may have been more important to the audience than an immediate decision on their veracity. Given the rapid advances in scientific knowledge, given the rampant speculation by reputable voices on the question of life on other planets, the possibility that there was life on the moon was not as outrageous to readers in 1835 as it is to us.[24] At the same time, in a culture that produced P. T. Barnum and other famous tricksters, that same audience probably also realized the somewhat pliable nature of truth in Jacksonian America. Enjoyment of the story could very well have been more important than debating its veracity.

Summary

Fake news is not new. It is not a product of our postmodern disdain for the Truth, nor the "slivercast" audience strategies afforded by modern social media, nor some blend of the two.[25] The history of modern journalism's lies is roughly coextensive with the history of modern journalism. Made-up news was very nearly a tradition by the time that Titus Oates started passing around tales of meddling Jesuits. Indeed, already in the early part of the sixteenth century, the popular press's reputation as a fountain of untruth was so well established that Ben Jonson was able to use it as a subject for a play.[26]

So why did fake news so suddenly become such a "problem" for modern Americans? A search of the term of *fake news* on EBSCOhost turns up twelve stories in October 2016. The next month, the same search turns up more than five hundred such stories. Something happened to cause such a dramatic rise in concern.

What happened was the election of Donald Trump to the presidency of the United States. That a B-rated celebrity, a reality TV star and real estate developer, a man with no political experience and few discernible skills of any sort save an ability to promote his own personality, could become the leader of the most powerful nation on earth suggested to many members of the knowledge class that something had gone terribly wrong. The ultimate governor of modern liberal democracy—the People—did not seem capable of exercising the judgment and wisdom demanded of it. An explanation had to be found.

Roger L'Estrange would have understood the sentiment. So, too, would have Richard Adams Locke. At various points in the history of modern democratic culture, public opinion has seemed a tenuous peg to place our hopes upon. Sometimes the populace fails to behave in a responsible manner—it goes running after Papists or gullibly swallows tall tales about moon-men or elects an idiot to run the country. The most ardent defenders of democracy then find themselves in the uncomfortable position of calling into question the very basis of democracy. Norms of public discourse in such a situation require that an alternative plan of rhetorical attack be found: not the people but conspiracy theorists, foreign agents, unscrupulous journalists, or "fake news" are responsible for the ills that plague the regime. It is worth remarking that new media forms—the popular pamphlet press, the penny paper, or social media—often seem to play an especially malignant role in this confusion of the public mind.

Such a reframing of the issue, while understandable, may lead us to strategically misdiagnose whatever is ailing the body politic. Lies are always lies, but some lies are believed and some are not. It was ridiculous for Welch to believe that Comet Ping Pong was the center of a child prostitution ring. It was somewhat less ridiculous for him to believe that his understanding of American culture and history, of basic moral distinctions between right and wrong, may have been so radically at odds with many of the people who voted for Hillary Clinton, or indeed ate at establishments like Comet Ping Pong, that a workable compromise was not in the cards: best just shoot up the place. This is a troubling possibility, in part because within a diverse society that requires some basic unifying beliefs but that also bases its identity on the ability to accommodate widely differing opinions on fundamental matters, there is no easy resolution to the puzzle it presents. Worrying over the machinations of mischievous Macedonian teenagers is not going to get us any closer to solving it.

Notes

1. Faiz Siddiqui and Susan Svrluga, "N.C. Man Told Police He Went to D.C. Pizzeria with Assault Rifle to 'Self-Investigate' Election-Related Conspiracy Theory," *Washington Post*, December 5, 2016.

2. Adam Goldman, "Comet Ping Pong Gunman on Motive, and Fake News," *New York Times*, December 9, 2016.

3. Craig Silverman, "This Analysis Shows How Viral Fake Election News Stories Outperformed Real News on Facebook," BuzzFeed News, November 16, 2016, https://www.buzzfeed.com/craigsilverman/viral-fake-election-news-outperformed-real-news-on-facebook.

4. "Trump Has Made a Safe Zone for Fact-Free Discourse, and 'Pizzagate' Proves It," The Post's View, *Washington Post*, December 6, 2016, https://www.washingtonpost.com/opinions/dc-pizzeria-is-a-casualty-of-trumps-safe-zone-for-fact-free-discourse/2016/12/06/b68708ba-bb1f-11e6-ac85-094a21c44abc_story.html.

5. Sabrina Tavernise, "As Fake News Spreads Lies, More Readers Shrug at the Truth," *New York Times*, December 6, 2016, https://www.nytimes.com/2016/12/06/us/fake-news-partisan-republican-democrat.html.

6. Olivia Ward, "Have Donald Trump's Lies Pushed U.S. into a 'Post-Truth' Universe?," *Toronto Star*, May 24, 2016, https://www.thestar.com/news/world/2016/05/24/have-donald-trumps-lies-pushed-us-into-a-post-truth-universe.html; Solomon Jones, "Alternative Facts Are Lies, and We Must Point This out Every Time," *Philadelphia Inquirer*, January 25, 2017, https://www.postguam.com/forum/alternative-facts-are-lies-and-we-must-point-this-out/article_c447cae8-e392-11e6-909d-77131efe0b7e.html.

7. See, e.g., Ian Hacking, *The Social Construction of What?* (Cambridge, MA: Harvard University Press, 2000); Christopher Norris, *Reclaiming Truth: Contributions to a Critique of Cultural Relativism* (Durham, NC: Duke University Press, 1996).

8. Manuel Castells, *Communication Power* (Oxford: Oxford University Press, 2009), 55.

9. Brooke Gladstone, *The Trouble with Reality: A Rumination on Moral Panic in Our Time* (New York: Workman Publishing, 2017).

10. John Kenyon, *The Popish Plot* (London: Heinemann, 1972), 168–176.

11. Arthur Asa Briggs and Peter Burke, *A Social History of the Media: From Gutenberg to the Internet* (Cambridge, UK: Polity Press, 2002), 92–93; Jonathan Scott, "England's Troubles: Exhuming the Popish Plot," in *The Politics of Religion in Restoration England*, ed. Tim Harris, Paul Seaward, and Mark Goldie (Oxford, UK: Basil Blackwell, 1990), 107–131.

12. Kenyon, *The Popish Plot*, 166.

13. Dan Beaver, "Conscience and Contest: The Popish Plot and the Politics of Ritual, 1678–1682," *Historical Journal* 34, no. 2 (1991): 297–327.

14. On England's Catholics, see Scott, "England's Troubles," 113. On the political culture of the period, see Mark Knights, *Representation and Misrepresentation in Later Stuart Britain: Partisanship and Political Culture* (Oxford: Oxford University Press, 2005).

15. Cited in Knights, *Representation and Misrepresentation*, 208.

16. Cited in Juraj Kittler, "The Enlightenment and the Bourgeois Public Sphere (Through the Eyes of a London Merchant-Writer)," in *The International Encyclopedia of Media Studies*, ed. Angharad N. Valdivia, vol. 1, *Media History and the Foundation of Media Studies*, ed. John Nerone (Malden, MA: Wiley-Blackwell, 2013), 227.

17. See Mark Brewin, *Celebrating Democracy: The Mass-Mediated Ritual of Election Day* (New York: Peter Lang, 2008), esp. chaps. 3 and 4.

18. David A. Copeland, "A Series of Fortunate Events: Why People Believed Richard Adams Locke's 'Moon Hoax,'" *Journalism History* 33, no. 3 (2007): 140–150.

19. On analysis of the Great Moon Hoax as showmanship, see Matthew Goodman, *The Sun and the Moon: The Remarkable True Account of Hoaxers, Showmen, Dueling Journalists, and Lunar Man-Bats in Nineteenth-Century New York* (New York: Basic Books, 2008); as objective science, see Dan Schiller, *Objectivity and the News: The Public and the Rise of Commercial Journalism* (Philadelphia: University of Pennsylvania Press, 1981), 76–80; as a parable on race, see Kevin Young, *Bunk: The Rise of Hoaxes, Humbug, Plagiarists, Phonies, Post-Facts, and Fake News* (Minneapolis: Graywolf Press, 2017), 16–18.

20. Richard Adams Locke, "Mr. Locke's Moon Story," *New World* (New York City), May 16, 1840.

21. Ibid.

22. Goodman, *The Sun and the Moon*, 182.

23. Ibid., 180 (italics mine).

24. Copeland, "A Series of Fortunate Events."

25. On slivercasting, see William Uricchio, "Contextualizing the Broadcast Era: Nation, Commerce, and Constraint," *Annals of the American Academy of Political and Social Science* 625, no. 1 (2009): 71.

26. Ben Jonson, *The Staple of News*, ed. Anthony Parr (Manchester: Manchester University Press, 1988). Jonson's play was first performed in 1625. See Stuart Sherman, "Eyes and Ears, News and Plays: The Argument of Jonson's *Staple*," in *The Politics of Information in Early Modern Europe*, ed. Brendan Dooley and Sabrina A. Baron (London: Routledge, 2001), 23–40.

VII   Media Hoaxes and Satires: Part Introduction

The meaning "fake news" took on a substantially different connotation in the wake of the 2016 U.S. presidential election, when the term developed quite negative connotations. Just a few years before, the sorts of satirical, misleading techniques employed by *The Daily Show with Jon Stewart* and *The Colbert Report* (which featured two pretend fake news anchors/comedians) were often celebrated as media products that encouraged critical thinking.

The first chapter in this part, "An Oral History of the Yes Men," discusses how two prankster-activists use humorous deceptions to encourage critical thinking and get their political points across. The Yes Men demonstrate one of the many ways pranking and similar deceptions can shake people out of their daily routines and rewire taken-for-granted realities. By turning the world upside down—even for a brief moment—it can be seen from a new vantage point, a different perspective. This can spur people to imagine a better society and, occasionally, turn fantasy into reality through the hard work of community building and activism. For instance, one of the Yes Men's most successful mergings of grassroots political action and pranks, not covered in the following chapters, occurred at a conference held on the one-year anniversary of Hurricane Katrina's devastation of New Orleans.

On August 28, 2006, Yes Man Andy Bichlbaum stood onstage along-side the mayor of New Orleans and the governor of Louisiana, posing as "Rene Oswin"—an assistant undersecretary of the Department of Housing and Urban Development (HUD). Having tricked the conference organizers into believing he was a genuine government official, he announced a New Deal–like plan for the Gulf Coast that included requiring oil companies to set aside some of their profits for wetland renewal (the lack of which exacer-bated flooding during the storm). Bichlbaum/Oswin emphasized that HUD's mission was to provide affordable housing, but admitted that it failed. To correct this problem, he announced that the agency was going to halt plans to demolish five thousand residential housing units that former occupants desperately wanted to move back into. These apartment complexes received only minor damage from the storm, but because of their close proximity to valuable downtown-area real estate, they were condemned. However, soon after Bichlbaum left the podium, reporters discovered his imposture, and a HUD spokesperson denounced it as a "sick" hoax. Survivors Village, a tent-city protest group that collaborated with the Yes Men, didn't share that opinion, noting that their lie was told to reveal a larger truth. An essential part of the Yes Men's method has always been "the big reveal," in which they publicly announce their deception and explain to reporters the purpose behind it (a concern that is certainly not employed by fake news click-bait sites).

The second chapter in this part, "An Interview with the Yes Men," calls into question the continued efficacy of satirical tactics. Tracing the duo's history from the 1990s to the present, interviewer Kembrew McLeod discussed with Mike Bonanno and Andy Bichlbaum the strategies behind some of the Yes Men's actions. During their conversation, they also addressed how the shifting media landscape and changing technologies have altered the way they approach their humorous, deceptive campaigns. Many of the questions the Yes Men have asked themselves can also be generalized in ways that can help us all better understand the murky, mediated world we live in today.

The third chapter in this part, Sophia A. McClennen's "All 'Fake News' Is Not Equal," also reminds us that there was a time not so long ago when the "fake news" broadcast on *The Daily Show with Jon Stewart* was celebrated as a critique of, and corrective to, sensationalist news media. As she notes in the chapter, for example, Jon Stewart was even voted the most trusted journalist not long after Walter Cronkite's death. McClennen argues that *irony* is one of the key characteristics that distinguishes the "fake news" produced by *The Onion* (whose headlines sometimes seem plausible) from the sorts of "fake news" disseminated on social media (which is intentionally meant to fool people). Because those ironic news stories are meant to prompt readers or viewers to think critically, in ways that are complex and not literal, they encourage media consumers to think for themselves. "Ironic fake news teaches us to question the status quo," McClennen states; "unironic fake news teaches us to panic about everything."

Suggested Reading

Stephen Duncombe, *Dream: Re-imagining Progressive Politics in an Age of Fantasy* (New York: New Press, 2007).

Christine Harold, *OurSpace: Resisting the Corporate Control of Culture* (Minneapolis: University of Minnesota Press, 2007).

Andrea Juno and V. Vale, eds., *Pranks!* (San Francisco: RE/Search, 1987).

Leonard C. Lewin, *Report from Iron Mountain: On the Possibility and Desirability of Peace* (New York: Free Press, 1996).

Graham Meikle, *Future Active: Media Activism and the Internet* (New York: Routledge, 2002).

23   An Oral History of the Yes Men

Kembrew McLeod

The Yes Men have regularly made headlines using humorous deceptions to get their political points across since Jacques Servin and Igor Vamos joined forces in 1999. Their actions often follow a similar template: outrageously caricature an opponent's position, document the performance, reveal their trickery in a press release, and spark a public discussion. Their preferred tactic is "identity correction," impersonating businesses and government representatives in both online and interpersonal contexts using a variety of pseudonyms. (Oddly enough, Jacques's and Igor's given names sound more like pseudonyms than their primary Yes Men names, Andy Bichlbaum and Mike Bonanno.)

It all began with a book: *Pranks!* This edited volume, published in 1987 by the independent imprint RE/Search, served as an operator's manual for a generation of absurdist troublemakers, from the Yes Men to myself. "I had read that RE/Search *Pranks!* book," said Mike, recalling the true-life stories of subversion contained in this collection of interviews of various pranksters. "Those things sort of leapt out at me as being really interesting. At the time, I was doing this kind of guerrilla theater—we called it 'guerrilla theater of the absurd,' which was a group I founded where I used student activity money to do weird shit at Reed College. So we had done a couple of projects that were sort of weird public art interventions, like, we changed the name of a local street in Portland overnight into Malcolm X Street."[1] Andy followed a similar path that also began with that RE/Search book. "The *Pranks!* book was really seminal for me," he said. "In Louisiana, when I was a graduate student, I taught a freshman comp class, and I used it as the book that the kids had to read and write essays [on], based on things contained in it. I was a super fan of that book, and I knew all of the stories. Having read about Alan Abel and Joey Skaggs and all the others in it, *Pranks!*

was super formative for me. It's interesting to see how important a book can be. Probably without that book, I wouldn't have thought of doing any of this."

With this seed planted in his mind, Andy engaged in his first highly publicized act of mischief in the mid-1990s when he was working as a computer programmer for Maxis Inc.'s combat video game SimCopter. He reworked an animated segment in which the heroic helicopter captain was rewarded with the image of women fawning over him, which was typical of these sorts of military-themed games. Instead, it showed the victorious player an animated homoerotic sequence of two bare-chested men in swim-suits making out, something that went undiscovered by the company until after the game had shipped to stores. This alteration likely would have gone unnoticed by the wider public if Andy had not reached out to a journalist acquaintance, who was the first to write about his SimCopter hack.

At first, Andy did not lie to reporters about his motivations or any other details (that came later). "I never made up anything," he recalled. "I just said, 'This is what I did.' I put these kissing boys into a video game, and [a reporter] said, 'Why did you do it?' And I think I told him the truth, prob-ably? And he said 'Might there not be some kind of, like, you know, activist element to what you did? About gay content and how macho these video games are and how they're just like insanely stupid? And how they appeal to people's aggression?' I said, 'Well, *yeah.*' There was no lying, there was no making things up—until later when there was a bunch of press around it, and that was fun. And I was like, 'Wow, this is kind of powerful. This is an interesting thing.'" Andy's soon-to-be partner in crime had a similar experience: "It became clear that there's stuff that I should be doing," Mike said, "like writing press releases—standard PR stuff, media news releases and stuff."

Mike's first high-profile attempt at "cultural sabotage" was the Barbie Liberation Organization (BLO), launched in 1993 during the Christmas sea-son. He purchased multiple Barbie and G.I. Joe dolls, switched their voice boxes, and "reverse shoplifted" them back into stores. Holiday shoppers brought home Barbies that grunted, "Dead men tell no lies," while gender-bending G.I. Joes gushed, "I like to go shopping with you!" After the BLO sent out press kits to news organizations, the story broke nationally, and Mike learned through trial and error how to engineer stories that news organizations then spread far and wide. "At first, I said I was anonymous,"

Mike recalled, "and there were reporters who said, 'No, I can't do this story because I can't cover a story where the source is anonymous.' And so the next person I talked to, I made up a name. That kind of thing, where you realize, 'Oh you can just work within the rules and make all this up.'"

Mike quickly learned that the fictions he provided a journalist would often be picked up by wire services and repeated ad nauseam and legitimized as facts. "For the Barbie Liberation Organization, I remember quite distinctly a moment when a journalist asked me how many of these dolls have been altered across the country," he recalled. "In reality, I had done seventy-two actual surgical swaps of the toys, and maybe about sixty of them ended up on store shelves. When the journalist asked, I just thought, 'God, that number seems really too small.' I didn't want to overdo it, so I said three hundred, and that number just stuck and it became the number. In hindsight, I should have said a thousand or ten thousand or a hundred thousand." Mike added: "There was a local reporter in Albany where I lived who asked me, 'Well, what stores are they in?' Since I knew where he's from I said, 'the KB Toys store in Colony Center,' and he said, 'Oh great. I'll go there.' So I drove over there and I put one on the store shelf, and I saw him walk in the door, right afterwards."

This became a pivotal moment for Mike. "It was the type of story where you realized, 'Wow, you can make a lot of shit up.' It was just this realization of, 'Wow, there's a lot that's possible. You can take steps to ensure that the story that you're trying to tell has the best chance of getting out there with the help of the media.'" Andy, who was not yet working with Mike, had a similar epiphany after the mischief he made at the video game company. "At the point when the SimCopter hack started to die down," Andy recalled, "I sort of thought, 'Well, there is something there that's very interesting. I just accidentally created a media firestorm around something really, really stupid. Maybe there's a way that this can actually be meaningful in a bigger way?' And so I came up with a shadowy organization called RTMark.com that was supposedly funding sabotage of corporate products around the country en masse."

Andy created ®™ark during the late 1990s in order to entice journalists into covering his weird ideas, claiming the organization would provide a $5,000 grant to any programmer working on a violent and sexist video game who subverted the game's ideological message. "It had supposedly been around for a very long time on a BBS [bulletin board system] accessed by a dial-up modem," Andy laughed as he recalled the yarn he spun. "But then suddenly, for reasons unknown, the top levels of ®™ark management, in their hideaway, decided to go public with their manifesto. I thought it would be cool if we created a kind of phenomenon, you know." Andy and Mike were introduced to each other around this time, and they began working together on ®™ark projects, before morphing into the Yes Men by the end of the 1990s. "The RTMark.com website wasn't really working to attract donations. There were a few, but they were symbolic, or from people that we actually knew. But the idea that somebody would give money to attack corporations [by] using mischief was very exciting to the press. There were lots of stories. I think there was one year where we had about four or five prominent stories in the *New York Times* about individual projects from ®™ark, which was crazy."

The ®™ark project that got some of the biggest coverage was *Deconstructing Beck*. This CD contained thirteen collages based on the music of Beck, a musician who has been celebrated for his innovative use of digital sampling, particularly on 1996's *Odelay*. One piece on *Deconstructing Beck*, by Jane Dowe, cut up the song "Jackass" into twenty-five hundred segments, making the original only subliminally recognizable to the listener. *Deconstructing Beck* was released in 1998 on Negativland's Seeland record label in conjunction with the ®™ark-affiliated label Illegal Art and was sold on the internet for $5. Rather than quietly distributing this CD, ®™ark fired off e-mails and press releases announcing this work, making sure that Beck's publicist and attorney received a copy. Some corporate music industry sabers were rattled, but ultimately there was no legal action.

"There were these kind of kooky projects," Mike said. "*Deconstructing Beck*, it was just an album where a bunch of people sampled Beck illegally and made music. I can't imagine anybody covering that in the media today, much less the *New York Times*." The dynamic duo was learning on the job, so to speak, figuring things out as they went on about their business. "When it was decided that ®™ark was going public as this big shadowy organization," Andy said, "I sent a press release to the reporters at *Newsweek*. 'Okay, I guess that's what you do, you send out an announcement to people." Their learning curve ramped up when they began developing satirical websites that employed their "identity correction" tactic, in which they made the positions of their corporate adversaries even more explicitly clear.

One of the Yes Men's first projects involved registering the web domain name GATT.org in 1999. The General Agreement on Tariffs and Trade, or GATT, was a treaty governing international trade and was replaced in 1995 by the World Trade Organization (WTO). Mike and Andy set up a website that copied the graphic design and repeated the rhetoric used by GATT and the WTO—with a few glaring differences, of course. "The first major thing we did was copy the World Trade Organization's site and post a satirical version of it that took the basic logic of the WTO and just pushed it all the way," Andy said. "We never intended for people to be fooled for longer than a minute. We just wanted people to visit the WTO website and think they're reading some official WTO statement, and then kind of get queasy and realize how fucked up it is, and then realize it's a hoax. It was a trick to get them to experience the same queasiness about the WTO that *we* felt, and that all the antiglobalization people felt. That was our discovery of how it worked—when people didn't get the joke and started e-mailing us thinking we were actually the WTO, then sending invitations to conferences that we accepted, and then using all that to get press. That became the hook. It wasn't really like we were trying to fake out the news that much. We were trying to get people to think, and then it became a hook to generate news around the issue."

In their web pages and press releases, the Yes Men reappropriated corporate-speak—flipping familiar phrases in a deconstructive attempt to show how language conceals power, how bland-sounding expressions can hide unsettling ideas. When the organizers of the "Textiles of the Future" conference in Finland needed a WTO representative to deliver a keynote address, the merry pranksters flew to Tampere in August 2001. Posing as "Dr. Hank Hardy Unruh of the WTO," Andy delivered a speech that used terms such as *market liberalization* to favorably compare sweatshops to slavery. During a subsection of his speech, titled "British Empire: Its Lessons for Managers," Unruh dismissed Mohandas Gandhi as "a likable, well-meaning fellow who wanted to help his fellow workers along, but did not understand the benefits of open markets and free trade." As was recorded in the 2003 documentary *The Yes Men*, an assistant removed Unruh's tear-away business suit at the conclusion of his speech. Underneath was a gold bodysuit with a giant and shiny inflatable phallus containing a video screen that supposedly monitored workers in the Third World, illustrated in PowerPoint.

None of the international scientists, businesspeople, officials, and academics did much more than to blink; they just politely applauded.

When they were first starting to work together, Mike and Andy also developed a George W. Bush parody site, gwbush.com, in collaboration with a like-minded computer consultant. "Zack Exley, who still is doing awesome work, had somehow thought to register gwbush.com in advance of the 2000 election," Andy said. "He had seen our previous stuff with GATT.org and the WTO site, and so we had people write articles for it that were definitely not G. W. Bush's positions." They duplicated the layout of the Bush campaign site and filled it with slogans such as "Hypocrisy with bravado" and other absurd spins on political campaign slogans. The parallel-universe political page invited people to engage in acts of symbolic subterfuge, such as inserting "slaughtered cow" plastic toys into Happy Meals or jumping the fence into Disneyland and demanding political asylum. Candidate Bush was frighteningly candid when commenting on his doppelganger site: "There ought to be limits to freedom." This reaction demonstrates the pedagogical possibilities of pranks, because the Yes Men's little lie exposed Bush's true feelings not long before he began dramatically chipping away at civil liberties as president.

"It was a provocation that worked," Mike observed. "It caused Bush to lash out in a news conference. That spawned, I guess for us, a whole bunch more enthusiasm for making fake websites. Yeah, it's interesting thinking about that as a sort of proto–fake news thing. It was very easy to get into the game at that time. It was kind of like dirty tricks in politics that have been going on forever, and it was kind of like stuff that the PR industry was doing, except the internet made it possible for us bottom-feeders to do it at a scale that was compared to what they were doing. We had this outsize or disproportional ability to act in an arena that used to be reserved for these huge companies, or these very powerfully connected people, the Roger Ailes of the world. So, for a brief window, we had this possibility of being these really small fish, but having the effect of the bigger fish—at least in terms of the media."

The Yes Men's most controversial prank involved Dow Chemical and its subsidiary Union Carbide India Limited. In 1984, the Union Carbide pesticide plant negligently leaked poisonous chemicals in Bhopal, India. Hundreds of thousands of people were exposed, thousands died immediately, and the long-term effects on the population were disastrous. It remains the world's worst industrial accident, but the corporation's relief efforts were minimal. Three years after Dow purchased the company in 2001, the Yes Men leveraged the twentieth anniversary of the catastrophe to bring attention to this issue. They started by creating a fake Dow Chemical web page that many journalists mistook for the real deal. The site claimed Dow was going to sell off Union Carbide and use the billions of dollars to pay for medical care and the cleanup of the Bhopal site. BBC World, the British Broadcasting Company's global news network, invited a Dow spokesperson to discuss the announcement on air. Instead, it got a Yes Man. Andy appeared as "Jude Finisterra," and within two hours this news fanned out internationally, prompting celebrations in Bhopal. Before Dow had a chance to deny the story, the corporation's stock plummeted in value by $2 billion.

Even though the Yes Men are often referred to as pranksters, Andy prefers to use the term *clownery* for what they do, and he is uncomfortable with the word *prank*. "The thing that bothers me about the word *prank* is that it's something like what you would play on your kid brother." In other words, it's something you might do in a fun-loving way to someone you are close to, which is certainly not true of the Yes Men's targets—such as the WTO. "They're strictly our opponents. If we do something, like a 'prank' on the WTO, we're not trying to be nice or pleasant or friendly. We don't *ever* want to be friends with the WTO. They are our opponents, and we want to use this thing that we're doing—this bit of clownery—to draw the broader public's attention to the WTO so that we can build to a point where we can change things."

Note

1. This quote and those that follow are drawn from an interview Kembrew McLeod conducted with the Yes Men via phone on August 6, 2018.

24 An Interview with the Yes Men

Kembrew McLeod

I was introduced to Igor Vamos and Jacques Servin, a.k.a. Mike Bonanno and Andy Bichlbaum, through my friend Sarah Price, who codirected *The Yes Men*, the first feature-length documentary film about the duo (she also helped shoot their most recent documentary, 2014's *The Yes Men Are Revolting*). As a like-minded mischief maker, I bonded with them and we later ended up collaborating on a project that critiqued recent trends in higher education and what was then happening at the University of Iowa (UI), where I teach. On August 26, 2015, the Yes Men used their "identity correction" tactic during a satirical press conference we staged in Iowa City, where they impersonated two representatives from the firm Pappas Consulting. This firm had been hired by the Iowa Board of Regents to conduct a series of "efficiency reviews" for the purpose of cutting costs, and jobs. Using the pseudonyms Bert Schwingler and Morton Oorst—names they made up on the spot while we were rehearsing—the Yes Men announced several modest proposals: allowing the campus community to hold direct elections for the Iowa Board of Regents, opening up tenure-track lines to all adjuncts, and redistributing upper-admin salaries to create living wages for all university workers.

The Yes Men also announced that UI would adopt an open-border asylum policy for all Wisconsin university employees negatively affected by the actions of Wisconsin governor and Republican presidential candidate Scott Walker, who made headlines in 2015 by effectively eliminating tenure at state universities and slashing state university budgets. The Yes Men's fake press conference resulted in a visit by UI's Threat Assessment Team, though life on campus continued imitating the Yes Men's performance art. Eight days later, the Iowa Board of Regents unanimously voted former IBM and Boston Market executive Bruce Harreld as UI's next president—despite submitting an error-ridden résumé, having no university administrative experience, and giving a disastrous public job talk where he cited Wikipedia, among other things. It was later revealed that his presidency was engineered by the regents, who actively recruited him by holding highly questionable private meetings that skirted open records laws. To summarize: The Yes Men posed as fake representatives of a consulting firm and the Threat Assessment Team was called in, while at the same time other forms of chicanery resulted in Harreld being installed as the president of UI. I developed a better understanding of how the Yes Men operate after working with them on the faux press conference, sitting in during the planning stages of another one of their actions, and having several informal conversations with them over the years. Building on the previous "Oral History of the Yes Men" chapter, this Q&A examines the tactics they have used in the past, while also reflecting on the ways the media landscape has shifted since 2016.

Kembrew: *When was the first time you realized that you could engineer situations so that news media would disseminate your ideas?*

Andy: We had been playing around with fake websites and setting up websites for various entities we didn't like—Shell was the first one—and it was just kind of playing with the technology. It was 1998 or 1999, and the internet was pretty new. We never intended these things to actually fool anyone. It was more just like, "We want to fool people *briefly*." Sort of like satire, but it was really important that people believe it was the actual site, and then they read a little closer and they realize what it's actually saying. It wasn't really like we were trying to fake out the news that much. We intended to get people to think, and then we ended up accidentally giving the news something to play with so that they would cover those important issues.

Mike: This was right around the time when Yes Men was beginning, but Andy's SimCopter hack seemed to me like a big *a-ha* moment—like, "I can just make up anything I want now, you know?"

Andy: I e-mailed a journalist acquaintance an account of what happened, and he just said, "Oh my God, that's such a great story." An AP [Associated Press] reporter wrote about it, and it was all over, and on TV news, and so on and so forth. At the point when that started to die down, I sort of thought, "Well, there is something there that's very interesting. I just accidentally created a media firestorm around something really, really stupid. Maybe there's a way that this can actually be meaningful in a bigger way?"

Kembrew: Mike, what was the first eye-opening moment for you, when you realized a lone individual with a weird idea could engineer widespread media coverage?

Mike: I think it was sort of two steps, and one of the things that makes sense to mention is that I had read that RE/Search *Pranks!* book. You know the book. That had a chapter on Alan Abel, a chapter on Joey Skaggs that I remember really, really well. Those things sort of leapt out at me as being really interesting. ... So then a little bit later, I started the Barbie Liberation Organization project. With that, I was really just going for it in a much more focused way based on having read about what Alan Abel and Joey Skaggs did. And then I just started to figure out how PR works, trying to do it myself. You don't realize how far you can take it until you're really in it. I had sort of a gradual introduction to it.

Andy: Mike said he learned a bit how it works as he was doing it and figured things out while going along, and I kind of did too. I mean, basically I had figured how press releases worked, so I sent these messages out to reporters. I had a little list of them, especially the ones who had covered the SimCopter hack.

Kembrew: Can you just talk about how the media landscape and the technology has shifted over the two decades that you've been doing this, and what that has meant for the kinds of actions that you currently do?

Andy: When I did the SimCopter hack, I sent out e-mail press releases to people I knew, like, "Hey Lee, I know you work for the *L.A. Times*, what do you think of this?" Then it just took off; I started getting the e-mails from other journalists. There was no physical mailing of things, except we did package an ®™ark video press release as beta tapes, and dropped them off across the country in TV stations' mailboxes for journalists, because we were crossing the country anyhow. We had a very elaborate plan that totally didn't work at all. There was absolutely no effect. What did work was the online thing, the website, but we couldn't have known that. Talk about learning as you go. Websites were new. There weren't a lot of corporate sabotage websites, and you could publish it on the web and journalists would find it. Even if they kind of only half believed it, they would write about it.

Mike: There were lots of stories. I think there was one year where we had about four or five prominent stories in the *New York Times* about individual projects from ®™ark, which was crazy.

Andy: Keep in mind this was the 1990s, when the dot-com bubble was in full swing, and you had companies that delivered dog food raising enormous capital. There was all this nonsense that burst in 2000, but this was the time that people thought the web could do anything, and that was extremely important.

Kembrew: One last thing about the late-1990s. Can you talk briefly about the G. W. Bush campaign website, because that seemed like another significant turning point in the evolution of the Yes Men.

Mike: The critical difference with what we do is we're telling stories to reveal more information, not to obscure it. With the G. W. Bush website, the idea was to always reveal our real position in an interview with the press, as we do with all of the stuff we've done. There is a phase in which you reveal it, and then we get more attention and get to tell the whole story—you get to get the facts and information in that you want to. What we're doing is not really "fake news," although it uses trickery to get there. It fits in better with traditions of satire, where the goal of the satire is not to make people believe something that is false, but rather to get them interested in discovering the truth. Jonathan Swift didn't write *A Modest Proposal* so that more people would think that the Irish should eat their own babies. He wrote it to provoke a reaction and, through that reaction, reveal that the English were starving the Irish.

Andy: That example, by the way, is a really good way to get in to how things have changed since 2016. Talking about how the Irish should eat babies was sort of predicated on nobody thinking it was a good idea to eat babies. We're just assuming nobody in our audience really likes the idea of eating babies. That's kind of the premise of what we were doing with all of our fake websites and fake press releases. It was pushing the organizations that we were mocking to a really extreme version of their positions—like with the WTO [World Trade Organization], or G. W. Bush, or whatever it was. But I think now we're in a very different moment. Jonathan Swift depended on a belief in universal values that human life is important and that humans shouldn't be eaten, and they also shouldn't be enslaved. You couldn't say, "I want to enslave people" or "I want to imprison immigrants in concentration camps." You couldn't say those things, but now we're in a very different moment where fundamental, universal values are in question and not being respected. So [we're] pushing our targets to say an extreme example of what they think doesn't work anymore. It's not guaranteed that it will offend people, and you can't rely on universals like human rights.

Kembrew: *With that in mind, what space is there left for the kind of things that you two have been doing for a quarter century?*

Andy: Like everyone, we're having to reexamine what we're doing—it was like putting a Band-Aid on a severed head. In retrospect, it's clear if you're in a world where there seems to be an arc of improvement, a lot of things that used to make sense now no longer make sense. In labor history, unions in the 1970s really took a turn away from proper organizing—where you try to reach out to workers on the factory floor who don't necessarily agree with you at the beginning, but you need them. That's extremely power-ful, and that model really is responsible for all the gains of labor, starting in the 1930s. In the 1970s, unions took up a mobilizing model, which is what social movement organizations often do, like Greenpeace, Move On, et cetera, et cetera. All of them basically mobilize people who already agree with them to do things and get media attention and hopefully somehow pressure leaders. That works in smaller ways, but not nearly as well as actual organizing. Where we are now is, we have to look back at the drawing board. It's not a matter of doing the same things anymore.

Kembrew: *We've talked about the term* fake news, *but for clarity's sake, how do you define* fake news, *and how do the Yes Men's tactics fit into this concept?*

Mike: I guess I would say there are two versions of fake news: one is news that is intended to deceive, but the other is news that is simply untrue and it is spread without the intention of deceiving anybody. The other fake news can just be populist bullshit that people want to repeat, but it's simply untrue. I mean, Trump creates fake news all the time just by tweeting crazy shit. There has to be a distinction between what we do, which is to tell a few lies in order to reveal a bigger truth, and what this other fake news is doing.

Kembrew: *Because you have both taught in the college classroom, what do you do to try and instill better critical thinking skills when it comes to media consumption?*

Mike: I think that by teaching through examples of manipulating media—by talking about, by showing, or by showing [students] a documentary, for example, about how the PR industry basically helped start the Gulf War in

1991. Those kinds of things call into question their entire reality, because they go, "Oh, holy shit, this entire reality is being created. It's not just happening; there are people who are making it happen in a particular way and they're presenting selective facts to me."

Andy: I've used those examples too, like the PR industry is the biggest purveyor of fake news in history, with a budget of billions of dollars a year, things like that. But I think the real question is, "How do you actually blow the minds of people who don't agree with you?" We're no longer in a place where everybody kind of agrees on the same definition of reality at all, or the same definition of what is unacceptable or acceptable. I don't think that would [have been] the case ten years ago, so there's a different kind of work that has to be done now that has to do with communicating that there is a different reality besides the reality of hatred and fear and building walls and all that.

Mike: My feeling right now is that I don't really know what works anymore. It used to be that we were very, very successful with traditional journalism, where we could reach other journalists who would recognize this as a fun story and would write about it. With there being so many fewer journalists, and also having to find something that's sticky in social media, it almost necessarily requires it to be vastly simplified. We used to tell really complex stories, because journalists can distill a very complicated story and make it really great, but now it's like, "How do you get these hooks on social media?" It is kind of distasteful, because to do it, you're kind of catering to like the lowest common denominator. But that's one of the reasons that fake news works so well, because you can actually tell really simplistic, dumb, aggravating, annoying stories really easily and really quickly—really incendiary things that you target for a very specific audience that you know will spread it. I find it hard to understand how to do this stuff usefully and consistently; it's harder for me than it was, and I feel like an old codger saying this.

Andy: Yeah, yeah, me too. It's definitely harder. Yes, the technology makes it a little harder, but not impossible at all. The technology is sort of the least of the problems, but it does make it a little harder. I think it would still be possible to get on the BBC as a spokesperson for Dow Chemical, for example, because back then they could have googled just as easily as they can now. What is missing, I think, is the purpose and the effectiveness of what are essentially corporate campaigns. I think everything we've done is effectively a corporate campaign—maybe a more radical and interesting and funny version of it than you usually see, but not necessarily more effective, just different. I think something like the Dow thing we did was effective, and it generated media for it and helped to mobilize people and so on and so forth. It was fully ensconced in the realm of corporate campaigning, which I think is really a model that has proven its inability to really keep us safe. Once you lose sight of the question "Why are we doing this?" it becomes hard to do these things. It's not a technical problem, it's a "Why are we doing this?" problem. It did make perfect sense before 2016—or it seemed to, and I think it did, given what we knew—but now it has all blown up.

25 All "Fake News" Is Not Equal

Sophia A. McClennen

Shortly after the 2016 election of Donald Trump, the fake news hysteria happened. Could it have been possible that propaganda, hoax news, and other deliberate forms of misinformation swayed the election? Before long there were studies that showed that the rise of election fake news was not just a sign of a gullible electorate; it was also a sign of how false information combined with a culture of angry fear has become increasingly toxic.[1] The discovery of the extent of fake news further led many citizens to worry that they, too, had been duped by one of these pernicious websites. How-tos on avoiding fake news abound. Fingers were pointed at Facebook and Twitter. Fake news creators were being mocked and excoriated. And the "poor dupes" who bought into it were alternately considered victims and perpetrators. But here's the thing: There was once a time when we could prove that consumers of fake news were some of the smartest citizens in the country. How did fake news go from describing critically productive comedy to referring to mind-numbing, hysteria-provoking catastrophe?[2]

#Pizzagate, where a reader of a story suggesting Hillary Clinton was running a pedophile ring out of a pizza parlor decided to attack the place, was just one of the most notorious examples that indicated that fake news held considerable power to sway public opinion.[3] And yet, that story is in stark contrast to the pre-2016 version of fake news. In fact, it wasn't long ago that fake news was lauded as a much-needed corrective to sensationalist news media. When Jon Stewart announced he would be stepping down as host of *The Daily Show* in February 2015, a number of articles lamented the loss of the "fake news" man. For instance, *Time* ran a story with the headline "Jon Stewart, the Fake Newsman Who Made a Real Difference."[4] At the time, fake news was understood as a social positive. Stewart was even voted the most trusted journalist after Walter Cronkite's death.[5] And viewers of *The*

Daily Show and *The Colbert Report* consistently scored higher than viewers of mainstream news outlets on knowledge of current issues.[6]

It is important to recall this earlier version of fake news, because in the era of constant historical amnesia most stories about the negative effects of "fake news" have completely forgotten the days when we used to love it. From *The Onion* to *The Daily Currant* to the always-refreshing dispatches from Andy Borowitz at the *New Yorker*, fake news was one of the most important ways to stay informed, laugh, and hone our abilities at critical thinking.

In the years following 9/11, it was increasingly the satirical fake news that helped us all make sense of the world. *The Onion* halted its presses for one week after the attacks, only to come back with one of the best issues ever.[7] The cover read: "Holy Fucking Shit—Attack on America." Its lead article was "U.S. Vows to Defeat Whoever It Is We're at War With." Dubbing itself "America's finest news source," *The Onion* intensively lobbied to get a Pulitzer back in 2011.[8]

All of this history has been overshadowed by the current crisis, which has brought us four types of fake news purveyors: those in it for the money, those in it to mock the alt-right or rile them up, and those in it to promote propaganda. It is important to note that all of these efforts may amount to the "bad" types of fake news, but they aren't equivalent sorts of projects. The Macedonian teens who raked in cash catering to the alt-right have almost nothing in common with Alex Jones, for example.[9] While it is a mistake to lump all of these types of fake news together, it is important to note that they are all currently understood as a threat to the health of our democracy. If you search for "fake news" today, you will get a range of articles on its dangers, but only five years ago a search for "fake news" gave you *The Onion* as the top hit. The point is that we have a tale of two types of fake news: one has saved us from a declining news media, and the other has threatened the very idea of news media. Both types depend on exaggeration. When the hyperbole is satirical and ironic, it is funny. When the hyperbole aims at rabble-rousing, it is frightening. One uses "fake news" to get people to think. The other uses "fake news" to cut off any thinking whatsoever.

One of the key critical distinctions between "good" fake news, like that of Borowitz, whose headlines sometimes seem plausible, and "bad" fake news, like that found on Infowars, is irony.[10] While fake news stories can sometimes seem real, satirical ones eventually draw on the reader's ability to detect sarcasm and irony. Because sarcasm and irony require the mind to read in a way that is complex and not literal, it actually encourages critical thinking and boosts intelligence.[11] Meanwhile, fake news stories, like those found on Infowars or in the *National Enquirer*, appeal to emotion and encourage stupidity. Ironic fake news teaches us to question the status quo; unironic fake news teaches us to panic about everything.

It would be convenient if we could easily divide the bad fake news from the good. Mostly we can, but it isn't always straightforward since at times satirical fake news comes dangerously close to hoax news. That was the case with the fake news site run by Paul Horner, who later wondered if he might have had a role in helping elect Trump.[12] Horner seemed to both want to publish satirical fake news and dupe Trump supporters into sharing fake stories. His site was clearly satire, but most folks who shared his pieces weren't even reading past the headlines.[13]

The fact that his site looked as if it were CNN or ABC or another recognized outlet helped the hoax factor. But it wasn't always true that hoax sites were a big problem. Parody sites have long been a staple of satire. Remember, for example, the parody issue of the *New York Times* that the Yes Men and a team of writers produced back in November 2008 only days after Barack Obama was elected president.[14] That parody issue was welcomed as a satirical intervention meant to coax the real *New York Times* into doing better reporting.

As Will Oremus points out in a piece for *Slate*, today all news is being called fake.[15] The overuse of the term empties the phrase of any meaning. The problem, though, is the fact that the only reason why we have seen such a rise in fake news—both comedic and catastrophic—is because the so-called "real" news is often terrible. A postelection poll by the Pew Research Center showed that only 22 percent of U.S. citizens give the press an A or a B for its coverage, signaling the lowest public approval for the press ever.[16] A report from the Harvard Kennedy School's Shorenstein Center on Media, Politics and Public Policy analyzed news coverage during the 2016 general election and found that both Hillary Clinton and Donald Trump received coverage that was overwhelmingly negative in tone and extremely light on policy.[17] It also found that the media's lust to cover anything and everything Trump did turned him into the first media-created candidate in history.

Today's satirical and nonsatirical fake news consumers have a common enemy: the corporate, mainstream media. In fact, fake news satirist Lee Camp did an excellent bit on his show *Redacted Tonight* calling out the fact that the real fake news was CNN itself.[18] Meanwhile, right-wing News-Busters found it hilariously ironic that Brian Williams could say that "fake news played a role in this election and continues to find a wide audience."[19] Williams, who has his own credibility issues, seemed entirely unaware of how hard it was to interpret him as a voice of news integrity.[20]

There is no doubt that the rise in fake news is directly linked to the lack of trust in the mainstream news. The key difference, though, is what the viewer thinks is the problem. Those viewers who turn to satirical fake news like that of Camp, John Oliver, or Samantha Bee do so because they feel that the mainstream news is too sensationalist, too corporate, and too supportive of the status quo. They watch "fake news" because it gives them a better chance of getting at the truth. Those viewers who swallow up the drivel offered by Alex Jones or Rush Limbaugh do so because they have bought into the conspiracy theory that the news media is politically biased. They think that the mainstream news cannot be trusted, and they think that their conspiratorial or highly partisan "fake news" outlets offer them the truth. If you notice a pattern match, that is because there is one. Fake news consumers—whether seeking comedy or calamity—agree that the mainstream news media are untrustworthy.

And the 2016 election proved them right. Aside from the way that the news media promoted Trump, the e-mails of John Podesta revealed a number of disturbing shady deals between the Clinton camp and a number of mainstream news outlets.[21] The e-mail that showed CNN contributor Donna Brazile leaked a town hall question ahead of time just furthered suspicion that the news media couldn't be trusted.

The news media wasn't just falling down on the job; the politicians were actively supporting the fake news system and attempting to turn it to their advantage. Trump's constant whining about negative "fake" news, his tweeting of falsehoods, his cyber bullying and his advancement of cronies who have created the alt-right fake newsiverse are all troubling signs of the post-truth era. And yet, while Trump threw hissy fits any time he came under scrutiny, the Clinton camp wasn't much better. From the launching of the myth of the "Bernie Bro" to the internet trolling of Clinton supporting the political action committee Correct the Record, we have ample evidence that the promotion of "fake news" was not limited to only one party.[22]

Trump tapped into the long-standing right-wing practice of discrediting the news media as an agent of liberal elites. There's nothing new there; it's the bread and butter of Fox News (despite its status as the mainstream news). But Clinton also waged a campaign to sow distrust of the news among her supporters. Channeling Cold War anxieties, critics of Clinton were characterized as Russian propagandists. While it seems likely that some of the critical news about Clinton was connected to Russia, a piece by The Intercept shows that basically those critical of Clinton were lumped together as "routine peddlers of Russian propaganda."[23] It reported that the list of so-called Russian disinformation outlets "includes WikiLeaks and the Drudge Report, as well as Clinton-critical left-wing websites such as Truthout, Black Agenda Report, Truthdig, and Naked Capitalism, as well as libertarian venues such as Antiwar.com and the Ron Paul Institute."

The Democratic echo chamber cast criticism as conspiracy, just as the Trump camp does. The Intercept explains that for a long time, liberals heralded themselves as part of the "reality-based community" and derided conservatives as faith-based victims of "epistemic closure."[24] But that distinction became extremely blurred during the 2016 election, from misleading Occupy Democrat Facebook posts shared thousands of times to "alternative" government Twitter accounts promising insider information about "the resistance," and it has all led to more fake news. Trump's allies hawk fake news masquerading as truth. Clinton supporters condemned critical reporting as "fake" or propaganda. And the news media itself continues to be dominated by a ratings-driven corporate mentality that privileges clicks over meaningful critique.

And that brings me back to the "good" fake news—because alongside the watchdog reporting of sites like The Intercept, it is only thanks to satire news, like that of Camp, Oliver, or Bee, that we are getting any meaningful alternatives. Camp, Oliver, and Bee deliver satirical fake news meant to inform the public and offer information redacted or ignored by the news media. Their comedic fake news, in fact, offers viewers far more truth than they would typically get in any other news venue.

So before we panic about fake news, we would do well to remember that not all fake news is created equal. And before we go on a fake news witch hunt, we should recall the way that fake news saved us during the George

W. Bush years. As we attempt to understand a post-truth president who makes up his own reality and bullies anyone who disagrees, we have good reason to worry that the mainstream news media will continue to fall down on the job while the Breitbarts will gain in power. In the face of that fake news reality, we are going to need all of the ironic, satirical fake news we can get.

Notes

1. Amanda Marcotte, "With Fake News Spiraling out of Control, What Can Real People Do?," Salon, December 9, 2016, https://www.salon.com/2016/12/09/with -fake-news-spiraling-out-of-control-what-can-real-people-do/.

2. Andrew O'Hehir, "Fox News Is Half-Right about Jon Stewart: How the Brilliant Satirist of the Bush Years Has Been Undone by His BFF in the White House," Salon, August 6, 2015, https://www.salon.com/2015/08/06/fox_news_is_half_right_about _jon_stewart_how_the_brilliant_satirist_of_the_bush_years_has_been_undone_by _his_bff_in_the_white_house.

3. Andrew Breiner, "Pizzagate, Explained: Everything You Want to Know about the Comet Ping Pong Pizzeria Theory but Are Too Afraid to Search for on Reddit," Salon, December 10, 2016, https://www.salon.com/2016/12/10/pizzagate-explained -everything-you-want-to-know-about-the-comet-ping-pong-pizzeria-conspiracy -theory-but-are-too-afraid-to-search-for-on-reddit/.

4. James Poniewozik, "Jon Stewart, the Fake Newsman Who Made a Real Differ- ence," Time, last modified August 4, 2015, http://time.com/3704321/jon-stewart -daily-show-fake-news/.

5. Ronald E. Riggio, "Why Jon Stewart Is the Most Trusted Man in America," Psy- chology Today, July 24, 2009, https://www.psychologytoday.com/us/blog/cutting-edge -leadership/200907/why-jon-stewart-is-the-most-trusted-man-in-america.

6. Pew Research Center, "Public Knowledge of Current Affairs Little Changed by News and Information Revolutions," April 15, 2007, http://www.people-press.org/2007 /04/15/public-knowledge-of-current-affairs-little-changed-by-news-and-information -revolutions/.

7. Theodore Hamm, "Reading the Onion Seriously," In These Times, June 26, 2008, http://inthesetimes.com/article/3778/.

8. An Anonymous Man, "If the Onion Is Not Awarded a Pulitzer Prize within the Next Year, I Will Murder 50 People," The Onion, June 24, 2011, https://www .theonion.com/if-the-onion-is-not-awarded-a-pulitzer-prize-within-the-1819584742.

9. Craig Silverman and Lawrence Alexander, "How Teens in the Balkans Are Duping Trump Supporters with Fake News," BuzzFeed News, November 3, 2016,

https://www.buzzfeed.com/craigsilverman/how-macedonia-became-a-global-hub-for-pro-trump-misinfo; Amanda Marcotte, "The Dangerous Rise of Alex Jones: How Austin's Pet Conspiracy Kook Conquered the Republican Party," Salon, November 3, 2016, https://www.salon.com/2016/11/03/the-dangerous-rise-of-alex-jones-how-austins-pet-conspiracy-kook-conquered-the-republican-party/.

10. Andy Borowitz, The Borowitz Report, New Yorker, https://www.newyorker.com/humor/borowitz-report#; Infowars, https://www.infowars.com/.

11. See Li Huang, Francesca Gino, and Adam D. Galinsky, "The Highest Form of Intelligence: Sarcasm Increases Creativity for Both Expressers and Recipients," Organizational Behavior and Human Decision Processes 131 (2015): 162–177.

12. Harper Neidig, "Fake News Giant: I Feel Bad about Putting Trump in the White House," The Hill (blog), November, 17, 2016, http://thehill.com/blogs/blog-briefing-room/news/306524-fake-news-writer-i-think-trump-is-in-the-white-house-because-of.

13. Becky Bratu, Erin Calabrese, Kurt Chirbas, Emmanuelle Saliba, Euronews, and Adam Howard, "Tall Tale or Satire? Authors of So-Called 'Fake News' Feel Misjudged," NBC News, December 15, 2016, https://www.nbcnews.com/news/us-news/tall-tale-or-satire-authors-so-called-fake-news-feel-n689421.

14. Steve Lambert, "The New York Times Special Edition," Steve Lambert (blog), November 2008, https://visitsteve.com/made/the-ny-times-special-edition/.

15. Will Oremus, "Stop Calling Everything 'Fake News,'" Slate, December 6, 2016, http://www.slate.com/articles/technology/technology/2016/12/stop_calling_everything_fake_news.html.

16. Pew Research Center, "Low Marks for Major Players in 2016 Election—Including the Winner," November 21, 2016, http://www.people-press.org/2016/11/21/low-marks-for-major-players-in-2016-election-including-the-winner/.

17. Thomas E. Patterson, "News Coverage of the 2016 General Election: How the Press Failed the Voters," Harvard Kennedy School, Shorenstein Center on Media, Politics and Public Policy, December 7, 2016, https://shorensteincenter.org/news-coverage-2016-general-election/.

18. Redacted Tonight, "Watch CNN Accidentally Explain How They're Fake News!," YouTube video, 9:35, November 4, 2016, https://www.youtube.com/watch?v=IOS2o1gTvHE.

19. Jack Coleman, "Quite Possibly the Funniest Thing That Brian Williams Has Ever Said," NewsBusters, December 7, 2016, https://www.newsbusters.org/blogs/nb/jack-coleman/2016/12/07/quite-possibly-funniest-thing-brian-williams-has-ever-said.

20. Pamela Engel and Natasha Bertrand, "3 events Brian Williams Is Suspected of Lying About," Business Insider, February 13, 2015, http://www.businessinsider.com/what-brian-williams-has-lied-about-2015-2.

21. Hadas Gold, "New Email Shows Brazile May Have Had Exact Wording of Proposed Town Hall Question before CNN," *Politico*, October 12, 2016, https://www .politico.com/blogs/on-media/2016/10/roland-martin-cnn-email-donna-brazile -wikileaks-229673.

22. Glenn Greenwald, "The 'Bernie Bros' Narrative: A Cheap Campaign Tactic Masquerading as Journalism and Social Activism," The Intercept, January 31, 2016, https://theintercept.com/2016/01/31/the-bernie-bros-narrative-a-cheap-false -campaign-tactic-masquerading-as-journalism-and-social-activism/; Ben Collins, "Hillary PAC Spends $1 Million to 'Correct' Commenters on Reddit and Facebook," Daily Beast, April 21, 2016, https://www.thedailybeast.com/hillary-pac-spends -dollar1-million-to-correct-commenters-on-reddit-and-facebook.

23. Ben Norton and Glenn Greenwald, "Washington Post Disgracefully Promotes a McCarthyite Blacklist from a New, Hidden, and Very Shady Group," The Intercept, November 26, 2016, https://theintercept.com/2016/11/26/washington-post -disgracefully-promotes-a-mccarthyite-blacklist-from-a-new-hidden-and-very-shady -group/.

24. Glenn Greenwald, "In the Democratic Echo Chamber, Inconvenient Truths Are Recast as Putin Plots," The Intercept, October 11, 2016, https://theintercept.com /2016/10/11/in-the-democratic-echo-chamber-inconvenient-truths-are-recast-as -putin-plots/.

VIII Solutions: Part Introduction

Although many of the authors in this book point toward solutions for fake news, this part most directly addresses attempts to mitigate its spread. The first two authors of this part discuss the role of platforms—the places where most misinformation circulates—in tackling the problem, the third discusses teaching fake news alongside the histories of other kinds of mass media to consider the similarities and differences of our contemporary moment to the past, and the fourth details a fake news "solution" that originated as an in-class activity, but turned into something much different after going viral. All of these authors point to larger issues that need to be considered as we address fake news, including the way platforms manage shared content, the need for broader civic engagement, and more support for education and academic freedom, all of which go well beyond calls for individuals to be careful more about what they share online.

More specifically, the first chapter in this part, "Platforms Throw Content Moderation at Every Problem" is by Tarleton Gillespie, who is a principal researcher in the Social Media Collective at Microsoft. His chapter explores how fake news evades detection by camouflaging itself as the kinds of content that platforms are designed to encourage. According to Gillespie, Facebook responded to fake news with four strategies, all of which are out of their existing content moderation playbook: kick fake news sources off their ad networks, partner with expert organizations, enlist users to flag dubious headlines, and promise to eventually solve it with artificial intelligence. Social media platforms have all constructed large-scale, moderation machines identifying, judging, and removing content: pornography, harassment, hate speech, obscenity, self-harm, and violence. But, as Gillespie argues, these current mechanisms of platform moderation are not perfectly tailored to each new problem, whether fake news, terrorist recruiting, revenge porn, or political bots. Discerning the fake from the genuine is not the same as identifying pornography or discouraging harassment, but because Facebook has responded with its existing moderation apparatus rather than developing new strategies for addressing fake news, future expectations, claims, tactics, and disputes will be shaped by it.

The second chapter in this part is "Normalizing Fake News in an Age of Platforms" by Paul Mihailidis, who researches media literacy, community activism, and civic life. This chapter discusses the ways that fake news has emerged in an age of platforms, online networks, and highly partisan political culture. Mihailidis argues that in order to reestablish credibility in news systems, we need to provide people the tools to identify false information, while also reestablishing the values that bring communities together to engage in meaningful dialogue and to understand news systems in the context of community. In other words, advocating for the development of media and news literacies will not fulfill their promise absent a larger civic mission. The chapter concludes with Mihailidis calling for value-driven approaches to engagement that move conversations of fake news from content to context, and educational responses to fake news from skills and critique to dialogue and meaning.

In the third chapter in this part, "Teaching 'Fake News' and Resisting the Privilege of Forgetting," film and media studies scholar Amanda Ann Klein discusses strategies for teaching fake news through her course "Reality TV, Fake News, and Media Literacy in the 21st Century." In this course, Klein works to give her students the critical tools necessary to find factually sound information while providing them with a historical overview of the technologies and formats used for communicating news and facts. Klein's class contextualizes fake news by first considering the development of radio and television for mass distribution, before exploring the emergence of computers, the internet, and algorithms in order to examine how our relationship with facts and truth shift when the amount of available data explodes and when that data can be conjured up instantly. Finally, Klein discusses whether and how educators can explain to students the differences between biased and fake news without appearing partisan, biased, or "fake" themselves in an era of threatened academic freedom.

The last chapter in this part is by media studies scholar and coeditor Melissa Zimdars, "Viral 'Fake News' Lists and the Limitations of Labeling and Fact-Checking." This chapter details Zimdars's entry into addressing the problem of fake news through a viral Google Doc, "False, Misleading, Clickbait-y, and/or Satirical 'News' Sources." Zimdars argues that her viral Google Doc, which was shared hundreds of thousands of times on social media and picked up by major news outlets around the world, reveals the limitations of individualized, reception-focused efforts to solving online misinformation. While media literacy and fact-checking efforts can play a role in making our media environment healthier, Zimdars instead calls for systemic changes to the way news is supported, greater regulatory control over social media platforms, and even the development of public social media alternatives.

Suggested Reading

danah boyd, "You Think You Want Media Literacy…Do You?," *Points* (blog), Data and Society, March 9, 2018, https://points.datasociety.net/you-think-you-want-media-literacy-do-you-7cad6af18ec2.

Dana Cloud, *Reality Bites: Rhetoric and the Circulation of Truth Claims in U.S. Political Culture* (Columbus: Ohio University Press, 2018).

Nicole A. Cooke, *Fake News and Alternative Facts: Information Literacy in a Post-Truth Era* (Chicago: American Library Association, 2018).

26 Platforms Throw Content Moderation at Every Problem

Tarleton Gillespie

In the wake of the 2016 U.S. presidential election, facing criticism over the prevalence of fake news, Facebook first proposed a trio of measures to address the problem: (a) clarifying part of the existing flagging system, marking "illegal, misleading, and deceptive content," to encourage users to flag news articles they felt were fraudulent; (b) enlisting fact-checking organizations like Snopes, FactCheck, and PolitiFact to assess some of these flagged news articles and mark them "disputed"; and (c) promising to pursue artificial intelligence (AI) techniques that might automatically discern the fraudulent from the genuine.[1]

Let's set aside not only the limitations of these responses, but also the profound problems of defining "fake news," of distinguishing hoaxes and falsehoods from propaganda and spin.[2] What I find revealing is that Facebook looked at the problem of fake news and saw it as a problem of content moderation, choosing as its first response to deploy its already-existing content moderation apparatus, or a souped-up version of it.

Every major social media company has built up a specific apparatus for content moderation.[3] Most take a customer service approach: users (and, increasingly, software) are tasked with identifying problematic content or behavior; platform moderators then engage in a procedural review, behind the scenes; they then decide to remove that content or not, based on their own guidelines and judgment. These procedures, built over more than a decade, have arguably been good enough for the needs of the platforms, in the sense that they have been able to scale to millions (or even billions) of users, to maintain enough promise of a healthy community that enough users regularly return, and to have kept up with new and more troubling phenomena as they emerged.

That, shall we say, is the best version of the story. Another is that a toxic culture of harassment, especially targeting women and minorities, appears to have rooted itself in social media, blithely tolerated by platform managers keen on encouraging their own ideas of free speech and profiting from the data they collect along the way; legislators in Europe and elsewhere are demanding more stringent interventions from social media platforms when it comes to hate speech and terrorist propaganda; and a flood of fraudulent news and conspiracy theories have eaten away at the public trust and influenced the way voters think, sufficiently perhaps to have had an effect on national elections. Even a high bar for success when moderating at this scale still allows hundreds of thousands of errors, and hundreds of thousands of oversights—each of which represents a user being wronged or left unprotected.

This system is starting to crack at the seams, and public disaffection for content moderation is joining other public concerns, about data privacy, targeted advertising, and the impact on journalism, in a fundamental reconsideration of the responsibility of platforms. Nevertheless, it is the system that's in place, firmly settled as *the way* platforms distinguish what they want to keep from what they want to remove.

Once a platform has a mechanism for moderation in place, it will tend to use it, regardless of whether or not it is suited to the new problem. This is deeper than just "when you have a hammer, every problem looks like a nail." Facebook has deeply invested in a complex, sociotechnical apparatus for moderating, with a complex division of a very large labor force, as its answer to an array of problems—one very particular kind of answer. It is compelled to deploy it whenever possible, for whatever problem; in fact, it comes to see the problem through its lens. But whatever your assessment of how effectively platforms moderate, fake news presents a new kind of challenge to platforms. There are some kinds of problems that simply cannot be cleaned up, because they are systemic, because the platform and the entire information ecosystem play into their circulation, because they reflect the very nature of the platform itself.

Moderation Wasn't Built to Handle Tactical Content

Early efforts at content moderation were designed with two kinds of problems in mind. The first were deliberate and obvious violations of the platform's guidelines, by those who rejected the rules or enjoyed mucking with the system: porn posted to platforms that clearly forbid it, trolls who invade communities to wreak havoc, Wikipedia vandals. These violations are obvious, in that the breach of the rules is clear, even if finding each and every violation isn't so simple. As the trolls got more sophisticated, the challenge of detection grew: 4chan-ers posting seemingly innocent videos with porn scenes embedded inside, or harassers engaged in organized efforts to swarm a victim without warning.

Platforms built their early moderation tools to keep the porn and trolls out. Obvious violations are politically easy, in part because they match and reassert the implied (or assumed) consensual norms of the community. But platforms quickly found that they faced a second kind of moderation challenge: instances in which the content or behavior in question was contested, in which there was no consensus about community norms. One user finds a photo offensive, another does not. One user feels harassed, the other believes it is all in good fun. One sees their speech as legitimately political, while their critics find it hateful. Sometimes these instances figured around a rule that was itself contested, or an exception that only some found reasonable: nudity policies that didn't suit women who felt that, if they could breastfeed in public, they should be able to do so on Facebook too; drag queens who felt they had the right to profiles using their stage names. Platforms reluctantly found themselves adjudicating their own policies around hotly contested cultural issues, weighing the opinions of users with different (even incompatible) beliefs, ethics, and cultures.

Platform moderation was designed to handle both kinds of moderation: to police the obvious violations and mediate the contested ones. But platforms increasingly face a third category: parasitic content.[4] Here I include misinformation, disinformation, propaganda—the kind of contributions that the unwieldy term *fake news* attempts to capture.[5] By "parasitic" I mean those contributions that are aware of the workings of the platform, and are designed with that awareness in mind—constructed to appear "genuine"[6]—but they take advantage of the circulation, legitimacy, and context the medium offers to do something beyond (or even counter to) its apparently genuine aims.

Like traditional forms of propaganda, fake news is designed to take advantage of the way the particular system works—procedurally, algorithmically, and financially. Fake news exploits platforms by simulating the very things platforms want to circulate, the very things platforms are opti-mized for.[7] If a fraudulent piece of propaganda can look just like news, then maybe some users will forward it like news. If it looks like news that aligns with the user's political beliefs, even better: maybe it will be shared as evidence of that political belief, as a performance of that political identity, as a badge of membership in that political tribe.[8] And if it looks like the kind of provocative, alluring, eminently clickable news that these platforms now thrive on, the kind that drives the "engagement" that is the economic imperative of commercial platforms, then platforms may be reluctant to remove it. Parasitic content that manages to circulate, or go viral, enjoys whatever patina of legitimacy that the platform offers other content that goes viral: appearing popular, hot, zeitgeist, or newsworthy.

Addressing parasitic content is fundamentally unlike the kinds of con-tent moderation that these platforms traditionally engage in. Fake news represents an "existential crisis" for social media platforms,[9] because it understands the platform and its incentives, and turns the platform against itself in ways that it will be reluctant to correct. Sometimes the develop-ers of fake news understand the mechanics and incentives of the system even better than the platform operators themselves. Like a virus, fake news thrives by understanding its host, using the system against itself. And, like a virus, rendering it inert may require altering the nature of the host itself—even the risk of killing it.

If that's not worrisome enough, let's acknowledge an ever more difficult truth that fake news makes plain. It's not just that someone with ill inten-tions can design a page to look like a news site or write a catchy headline. Parasitic content can emulate "genuine" content so well because *all* con-tent on social media platforms is, to some degree, tactical. In the broadest sense, all contributions to a platform attempt to take advantage of that plat-form, in that all contributions have aim and purpose. We flatter ourselves when we presume a simple distinction between (our) genuine contribu-tions and (their) devious ones: all users want their content to circulate—we are invited to communicate in this way—and all users seek to understand and exploit the system so that might happen, if only in little ways. *Parasitic* does not necessarily mean "nefarious," but it does reveal the opportunity that fake news exploits.

Much depends on who has access to different kinds of tools on the plat-form, and who enjoys a more or less sophisticated understanding of the system: I may know that including a hashtag in my post may help it circulate more widely or be found by more users; a newspaper partnered with a platform may be given more powerful tools and privileges that allow it to manage distribution in more sophisticated ways than I can; an advertiser or political campaign given access to personalized data has a still greater ability to utilize that system for its own ends. But in every case, the content has been outfitted to better exploit the system: make it as clickable as possible; work the system so it is more likely to be liked, retweeted, or forwarded; understand and optimize for the algorithms that pick and choose. Fake news not only emulates the look and feel of legitimate news; it emulates the tactics of legitimate news outlets, of all users, when we compete for attention in social media.

A Response That Better Acknowledges Platform Culpability

Facebook and Google did take other steps, besides content moderation, to combat fake news in ways that were more sober about the existential threat it posed, that acknowledged the way it took advantage of the platform's incentive structure. In November 2016, Facebook and Google removed what they deemed to be fraudulent providers from their advertising networks.[10] Their aim was to prevent them from making a quick profit from the advertising, thereby removing one of its most powerful incentives. Posts written by Macedonian teenagers, meant not to drive a political wedge into the U.S. electorate but to make a quick buck from an initial burst of "can you believe it?!" clicks and repostings, saw their ad revenue disappear.[11]

This was, of course, not a complete solution either. It only addressed those that were economically motivated; those motivated by politics would not likely be discouraged by this change. Still, it was a powerful step toward addressing the existential crisis of parasitic content. It recognized that the structural design of these ad networks offered a powerful incentive to the production of fake news, and more fake news was being produced to take advantage of that incentive.[12] Fake news has led platform managers to start acknowledging a harder truth: not just that there are harms on their platforms, or even that they might be held responsible for them in a legal sense, but that their platforms may in some way facilitate, encourage, entice, amplify, and profit from these harms. The platforms are not just available for misuse; they are structurally implicated in it.

Many commentators struggle to find the language for how platforms are implicated in their own misuse. We remain enamored with the idea that technologies are mere tools and that any detrimental consequences that follow do not fall at their feet. The simplest case to make is that social media platforms provide the tools to speak at zero cost, draw people into closer proximity, flatten the obstacles between them, deliver those contributions to others, allow them to persist, and organize them to be found. More perniciously, social media platforms curate users' contributions algorithmically, preferring some over others, according to specific logics of popularity and personalization. They reward popularity and virality and exaggerate its effects, and they reward homophily while offering the illusion of a gathered public.[13]

All this makes platforms ripe for fake news, conspiracies, and hoaxes. It's more than the mere fact that misinformation can circulate alongside true claims or that unvetted users can look like professional experts. Other tactics are available. Those looking to mislead can produce a whole lot of misleading content on the cheap, post it, and see what sticks. Popularity produces pathways of circulation that move their claims, and give them added social legitimacy.[14] Where disinformation used to require either highly constructed media campaigns or lateral networks of rumor, now individuals can try throwing a little grit into the system, to see what disrupts the most. Platforms amplify small interjections, when they seem like something worth sharing. And those deeply invested in such misinformation can produce not only the misleading claims, but whole networks of people and bots to circulate it and give the appearance of authentic popularity—an additional signal that platforms identify and use as justification to amplify further.

Spam, SEO, and Clickbait

Fake news is fundamentally unlike porn, harassment, and hate speech, in that it is designed to emulate exactly what the platform wants to distribute most. But there are other phenomena that we might call parasitic content, and platforms have already grappled with them in ways more suited to the challenges they pose: spam, search engine optimization (SEO) tactics, fake accounts, distributed denial of service (DDoS) attacks, clickbait, hoaxes, and bots. While these challenges have also, at times, been treated like content moderation problems, these "shady practices" pose much the same existential crisis that fake news does.[15]

Google and other search engines are in a constant battle against web designers trying to make their sites recognizable to the indexes, in the hopes that the site will be amplified as more relevant than it is otherwise. An entire industry, SEO, developed to pursue this end, promising to understand what Google's algorithms "want" in order to ensure that its clients' pages would be the lucky recipient of that desire.[16] In this battle, Google asserts the right to demote sites that don't play by its rules—a right that is sometimes disputed by those that are demoted, but rarely by search users. Like fake news, SEO attempts to understand the technical and incentive structure of search, and simulate features that will most likely lead search engines to deem it relevant. And like fake news, effective SEO threatens to undermine the very premise of search engines—if the top results on Google are there because those sites best approximated what the search engine looks for, of what value are those results?

Similarly, when Facebook began to struggle with clickbait, the question was whether Facebook's tendency to reward tantalizing headlines was having some aggregate damage on the quality of news, was incentivizing the wrong kind of information production. Like fake news, clickbait attempts to take advantage of the workings of the platform as a sociotechnical system. Because the mechanism for circulation is whether users click, packaging content in ways that maximized the appeal at that moment and in that form was strategically valuable for information providers who wanted readership, thrived on vitality, or simply had to make money in a moment when social media was becoming an increasingly dominant environment for news.[17]

Unlike Google's efforts to keep ahead of SEO, Facebook's efforts to address clickbait were at times controversial. News publishers complained that clickbait sites were getting an unfair advantage; when Facebook adjusted its newsfeed algorithm to privilege "authentic content," those sites complained that Facebook was picking winners and losers with an algorithm that should represent a level playing field.[18] The fortunes of specific outlets rose and fell as Facebook calibrated its algorithm to disincentivize the worst forms of clickbait, which it had itself called into existence.[19] (And, as with fake news, it is not as if "legitimate" journalism doesn't also engage in an effort to lure readers with an eye-catching headline or an exaggerated promise of what they might find in the article.[20] All news is parasitic in this way. These are all questions of degree and legitimacy.) Clickbait is, in many ways, a forbear of the fake news problem; it's not surprising that Facebook's response to fake news was continuous to its efforts to limit clickbait.

But more than anything, fake news may have more in common with spam. As spam is to e-mail, fake news is to social media: both are, as Finn Brunton put it, "the use of information technology infrastructure to exploit existing aggregations of human attention."[21] Spam wants to be circulated as a legitimate commercial appeal; fake news wants to be circulated as legitimate political fact. Spam often emulates (to varying degrees of sophistication) other familiar commercial, human, or institutional appeals: a bargain price for a desired product, a plea for assistance from a person in need, a customer service alert from a trusted bank. Some is amateur in its simulation and relatively easy to detect, while some is sophisticated enough to trick even a savvy user into clicking. And the economics are much the same: like fake news, spam doesn't have to trick everyone; it's a game of numbers, where even if a small percentage is fooled, the impact may be sufficient.

Conclusion

Traditional content moderation approaches, like tasking users with identification, making internal determinations of what should and should not circulate, and developing software to automate the detection of misinformation, are ill fitted to this existential threat. Fake news might not be something that can be policed away like porn. It not only simulates the news, and produces activity that simulates popularity; it makes plain that the system is already designed for tactical persuasion, already designed to reward the clickable over the true. Shutting off the flow of advertising revenue to fraudulent information providers was a powerful response; rather than policing away fake news, this changed the very terms on offer from the platform, undercutting the structural incentive that called it forth.

Perhaps it is possible to address fake news, not as bad content to be moderated away, but as a fundamental violation of the premise itself. Like spam, parasitic content must be treated as a conceptual violation of the premise of platforms themselves, rooted out for its own sake. It "provokes and demands the invention of governance and acts of self-definition on the part of those with whom it interferes."[22] Like SEO, it must be justified that this intervention is not editorial, but foundational. And as with clickbait, it must be disincentivized by changing the economic, political, and material structures and rewards that encourage it.

But, and this is the hardest part, it may require a sober rethinking of what Facebook really is, what Google really is; if these are in fact systems that value engagement over all other values, aspects of these underlying premises may need to change for the current flood of fake news to dwindle. "That is, the channel should be understood in terms of its capacity to fail, in the sense of being subject to a variety of parasites."[23] Social media platforms will have to decide whether fake news represents a violation of a core principle—perhaps one that was not well formed or articulated, like civic virtue or public collective obligation—or the unavoidable outcome of a principle too foundational to reconsider.

Notes

1. Casey Newton, "Facebook Partners with Fact-Checking Organizations to Begin Flagging Fake News" The Verge, December 15, 2016, http://www.theverge.com/2016/12/15/13960062/facebook-fact-check-partnerships-fake-news.

2. On the responses' limitations, see Robyn Caplan, Lauren Hanson, and Joan Donovan, *Dead Reckoning: Navigating Content Moderation after "Fake News"* (New York: Data and Society Research Institute, 2018). On defining "fake news," see Nicholas Jankowski, "Researching Fake News: A Selective Examination of Empirical Studies," *Javnost—The Public* 25, nos. 1–2 (2018): 248–255, https://doi.org/10.1080/13183222.2018.1418964; Johan Farkas and Jannick Schou, "Fake News as a Floating Signifier: Hegemony, Antagonism and the Politics of Falsehood," *Javnost—The Public* 25, no. 3 (2018): 298–314; On distinguishing hoaxes from propaganda, see Gilad Lotan, "Fake News Is Not the Problem," Data and Society, November 16, 2016, https://points.datasociety.net/fake-news-is-not-the-problem-f00ec8cdfcb.

3. Tarleton Gillespie, *Custodians of the Internet: Platforms, Content Moderation, and the Hidden Decisions That Shape Social Media* (New Haven, CT: Yale University Press, 2018).

4. Playing lightly off Michel Serres's idea of the "parasite." See Michel Serres, *The Parasite*, trans. Lawrence Schehr (Baltimore: Johns Hopkins University Press, 1982); also Paul Kockelman, "Enemies, Parasites, and Noise: How to Take Up Residence in a System without Becoming a Term in It," *Journal of Linguistic Anthropology* 20, no. 2 (2010): 406–421. Thanks to Dylan Mulvin for pointing me in this direction.

5. Caroline Jack, "Lexicon of Lies: Terms for Problematic Information," Data and Society, August 9, 2017, https://datasociety.net/output/lexicon-of-lies/.

6. Alexis Madrigal, "Why Facebook Wants to Give You the Benefit of the Doubt," *The Atlantic*, July 19, 2018, https://www.theatlantic.com/technology/archive/2018 /07/why-facebook-wants-to-give-you-the-benefit-of-the-doubt/565598/.

7. Tarleton Gillespie, "Algorithmically Recognizable: Santorum's Google Problem, and Google's Santorum Problem," *Information, Communication and Society* 20, no. 1 (2017): 63–80.

8. Francesca Polletta and Jessica Callahan, "Deep Stories, Nostalgia Narratives, and Fake News: Storytelling in the Trump Era," *American Journal of Cultural Sociology* 5, no. 3 (2017): 392–408.

9. Natasha Lomas, "Fake News Is an Existential Crisis for Social Media," Tech-Crunch, February 18, 2018, http://social.techcrunch.com/2018/02/18/fake-news-is -an-existential-crisis-for-social-media/.

10. Kaveh Waddell, "Facebook and Google Won't Let Fake News Sites Use Their Ad Networks," *The Atlantic*, November 15, 2016, http://www.theatlantic.com/technology /archive/2016/11/facebook-and-google-wont-let-fake-news-sites-use-their-ads -platforms/507737/.

11. Craig Silverman and Lawrence Alexander, "How Teens in the Balkans Are Duping Trump Supporters with Fake News," BuzzFeed News, November 3, 2016, https://www.buzzfeed.com/craigsilverman/how-macedonia-became-a-global-hub -for-pro-trump-misinfo.

12. Allegedly, Facebook had considered an upgrade to its newsfeed algorithm before the election that would have identified fake news / hoaxes, but because it appeared to disproportionately single out right-wing sites, it was shelved for fear of appearing politically biased; Michael Nunez, "Facebook's Fight against Fake News Was Undercut by Fear of Conservative Backlash," Gizmodo, November 14, 2016, http:// gizmodo.com/facebooks-fight-against-fake-news-was-undercut-by-fear-1788808204; Josh Constine, "Facebook Chose to Fight Fake News with AI, Not Just User Reports," TechCrunch, November 14, 2016, https://techcrunch.com/2016/11/14/facebook-fake -news/.

13. Ben Tarnoff and Moira Weigel, "Why Silicon Valley Can't Fix Itself," *The Guardian*, May 3, 2018, https://www.theguardian.com/news/2018/may/03/why-silicon-valley -cant-fix-itself-tech-humanism.

14. Karine Nahon, and Jeff Hemsley, *Going Viral* (Cambridge, UK: Polity Press, 2013).

15. Malte Ziewitz, "Shady Cultures," Theorizing the Contemporary, *Cultural Anthropology*, April 28, 2017, https://culanth.org/fieldsights/shady-cultures.

16. Dipayan Ghosh and Ben Scott. "Digital Deceit: The Technologies behind Precision Propaganda on the Internet," New America, January 2018, https://www.newamerica .org/public-interest-technology/policy-papers/digitaldeceit/.

17. Zizi Papacharissi, "The Importance of Being a Headline," in *Trump and the Media*, ed. Pablo Boczkowski and Zizi Papacharissi (Cambridge, MA: MIT Press, 2018), 71–77.

18. Will Oremus, "Facebook Is Cracking Down on Inauthentic Content," *Slate*, January 31, 2017, http://www.slate.com/blogs/future_tense/2017/01/31/facebook _is_cracking_down_on_inauthentic_content_in_the_news_feed.html.

19. Robyn Caplan and danah boyd, "Isomorphism through Algorithms: Institutional Dependencies in the Case of Facebook," *Big Data and Society* 5, no. 1. (2018), https://doi.org/10.1177/2053951718757253.

20. Kalev Laeetaru, "The Inverted Pyramid and How Fake News Weaponized Modern Journalistic Practice," *Forbes*, December 10, 2016, http://www.forbes.com/sites /kalevleetaru/2016/12/10/the-inverted-pyramid-and-how-fake-news-weaponized -modern-journalistic-practice/.

21. Finn Brunton, *Spam: A Shadow History of the Internet* (Cambridge MA: MIT Press, 2013), 199.

22. Ibid., 203.

23. Kockelman, "Enemies, Parasites, and Noise," 412.

27 Normalizing Fake News in an Age of Platforms

Paul Mihailidis

In 1957, the British Broadcasting Corporation's (BBC) *Panorama* news show produced a three-minute segment titled "Spaghetti-Harvest in Ticino," which told the story of a family in southern Switzerland harvesting spaghetti from a spaghetti tree.[1] The segment, produced for April Fools' Day, was the idea of *Panorama* cameraman Charles de Jaeger, who believed he could create a story that would trick many BBC viewers. With an approved budget of £100, De Jaeger used footage from a Pasta Foods factory near London, combined with a family vacationing in a hotel in Switzerland, to concoct a story about spaghetti breeding, cultivation, and harvesting. The show's voice-over was narrated by reputable broadcaster Richard Dimbleby, whose authority gave further credibility to the hoax.

The story aired on April 1 to an estimated 8 million viewers across Britain. At the time, pasta was not a regular household food in the country, and British families were unfamiliar with the origins of pasta. The day after the program aired, the BBC was inundated with hundreds of phone calls inquiring about the credibility of the story, but also to request more information about spaghetti cultivation and where they could purchase spaghetti trees. De Jaeger and Dimbleby created a compelling in-depth news feature, one that they found outlandish by premise. The BBC general director, Sir Ian Jacobs, could not verify the story and needed to conduct research to confirm the segment was indeed a joke.[2] The BBC released a comment on the segment and reaction that captured the moment: "Some viewers failed to see the funny side of the broadcast and criticized the BBC for airing the item on what is supposed to be a serious factual program. Others, however, were so intrigued they wanted to find out where they could purchase their very own spaghetti bush."[3] Decades later, CNN wrote that "Spaghetti-Harvest in Ticino" was "the biggest hoax that any reputable news establishment ever pulled."[4]

The relationship between news providers and audiences is complex. Stories like the BBC's "Spaghetti-Harvest in Ticino" provide a strong reminder about the negotiations of truth, narrative, and reception in news environments. And that the phenomenon of fake news is not new. Michael Schudson and Barbie Zelizer write, "To act as if today's fake news environment is fundamentally different from that of earlier times misreads how entrenched fake news and broader attitudes toward fakery have been."[5] A quick internet search of fake news history provides hundreds of examples of news organizations, journalists, and storytellers engaging in a range of approaches to their craft that can certainly be questioned. These examples indicate the complexity around what we understand as fake news, and show us why it is important to situate fake news in this present moment. John M. Hamilton and J. S. Tworek advocate for the need to explore news in the contexts of the institutions, technologies, and social norms that define it: "Thanks to new liberating technologies, anyone can be a reporter, their own editor, and their own newspaper delivery boy or girl. In this welter of half-baked rumor and deliberately planted misinformation, news has become a hazy fungible concept that alters civic discourse."[6]

This chapter discusses the ways fake news has emerged in an age of platforms, online networks, and a partisan political culture. It argues for a reading of the term *fake news* to be situated in the present and to be understood as weaponized for political impact. Based on this framing, this chapter comments on responses that involve educating people to better critique and deconstruct information in a digital culture. The chapter concludes with an argument in support of value-driven approaches to engagement that move conversations of fake news from content to context, and educational responses to fake news from skills and critique to dialogue and meaning.

Weaponizing Fake News in the Age of Platforms

In *Platform Capitalism*, Nick Srnicek explores the evolution of platforms as organizing principles for information and communication flows. Srnicek understands the evolution of platforms not as a particularly revolutionary phenomenon but rather as a continuum of technological evolutions that prioritize the capitalistic exploits of digital technologies.[7] Technologies have always worked to extract, Srnicek argues, and in this particular moment platforms embody four specific characteristics for capitalist gain.

First, as intermediary digital infrastructures, platforms enable the interaction of many different groups of interested parties, from advertisers and providers to consumers and users. Second, platforms embody network effects, where groups of people can help build ever-larger user and consumer bases, mapping new potential users along the way. Third, platforms employ cross-subsidization, which entails offering certain products and services for free to further extend the reach of the network. And fourth, platforms emphasize constant user engagement, through technologies of extraction, where they demand further attention in exchange for tidbits of compelling information that keep existing users engaged and that continually bring new users into an ecosystem.[8]

Understanding the impact of platforms on information flow and user engagement contextualizes the current moment of fake news. Platforms enable widespread collaboration and powerful dispersed networks to achieve collective outcomes when motivated toward an end goal.[9] However, as they have been further commodified and monopolized for capitalist gain, they have become subject to greater appropriation for economic gain and exploitation by those in power.[10] In her new book *Automating Inequality*, Virginia Eubanks articulates the role of platforms and their technologies in fracturing social infrastructure: "The skyrocketing economic insecurity of the last decade has been accompanied by an equally rapid rise of sophisticated data-based technologies in public services: predictive algorithms, risk models, and automated eligibility systems."[11]

As platforms have evolved to further exacerbate inequality, extract more resources from the poor, and exploit efficiencies, they have worked to dehumanize the core infrastructures in our daily communities. Douglas Rushkoff, in *Program or Be Programmed*, argues that platforms have dehumanized society by prioritizing isolation and commodifying the connections humans need to truly be together in the world.[12] James Cohen builds on this argument by critiquing algorithms, commonly seen as "ambivalent machines" that imbue neutrality. Cohen argues that algorithms are "pieces of code that are written by coders—human operators who imbue their intellect and talent into the program. Code is assumed to be structurally cold, but is actually imbued with the agenda, biases, and drawbacks of the coder."[13]

It is within this context that the term *fake news* becomes a tactic, or weapon, used by those working within platforms to achieve certain agendas or outcomes. In a recent piece for *The Guardian*, Evgeny Morozov writes that the problem is not so much fake news but rather "a digital capitalism that makes it profitable to produce false but click-worthy stories."[14] Morozov's critique positions fake news as but a small blip in the threat of platforms on democratic norms. Writes Morozov:

> The ease with which mainstream institutions, from ruling parties to think tanks to the media, have converged upon "fake news" as their preferred lens on the unfolding crisis says a lot about the impermeability of their world view. The big threat facing western societies today is not so much the emergence of illiberal democracy abroad as the persistence of immature democracy at home. This immaturity, exhibited almost daily by the elites, manifests itself in two types of denial: the denial of the economic origins of most of today's problems; and the denial of the profound corruption of professional expertise.[15]

We don't have to look far to see how political elites and those in power weaponize fake news for support, gain, and reach. What's interesting is not so much their co-option of platforms that support fake news, but rather the ways that such platforms have normalized a term like *fake news* for political gain.

A recently released study by researchers at the Massachusetts Institute of Technology (MIT) finds that fake news has significantly greater reach than other forms of information, and with significant extension across and within platforms.[16] In an *Atlantic* article that details the findings, Soroush Vosoughi, a coauthor of the study and a data scientist at MIT, explains: "It seems to be pretty clear [from our study] that false information outperforms true information ... and that is not just because of bots. It might have something to do with human nature."[17] The study focuses on true versus false stories shared on Twitter from 2016 to 2017, aggregating over 4.5 million impressions. Detailed in *The Atlantic* story:

> A false story reaches 1,500 people six times quicker, on average, than a true story does. And while false stories outperform the truth on every subject—including business, terrorism and war, science and technology, and entertainment—fake news about politics regularly does best. Twitter users seem almost to prefer sharing falsehoods. Even when the researchers controlled for every difference between the accounts originating rumors—like whether that person had more followers or was verified—falsehoods were still 70 percent more likely to get retweeted than accurate news. And blame for this problem cannot be laid with our robotic brethren. From 2006 to 2016, Twitter bots amplified true stories as much as they amplified false ones, the study found. Fake news prospers, the authors write, "because humans, not robots, are more likely to spread it."

The striking findings provide strong support for an ecosystem where politicians can leverage a term like *fake news* to advance an ideology, a political stance, or to galvanize support for or against political issues. A new study by Andrew S. Ross and Damian J. Rivers shows that the term *fake news* is used not only for political advocacy, but also to manipulate a politicians own spread of misinformation, and to justify unverified and false claims.[18] This is supported by a recent Tow Center study that highlighted how much mainstream news organizations spread, sustain, and exacerbate false stories through their coverage, and how this coverage surpassed that of factual stories.[19] These falsehoods spread in platforms that promote like-minded views, that circulate content far removed from sources, and that prioritize content that evokes *spectacle*, a term made popular by critical scholar Guy Debord, in discussing representation and media images in the 1960s.[20]

The weaponization of fake news in an ecosystem of connective platforms has led to a series of initiatives aimed to help citizens effectively respond to fake news. These initiatives often center on two priorities. Morozov and others call for a restructuring of our institutions so they are more accountable for their algorithms, and to assert regulatory norms of digital capitalism that work to disempower advertising and the need for online clicks.[21] Beyond increasing regulation, calls for media and news literacies are now common. There is general consensus that initiatives are needed to help audiences become more critical consumers of news and information, so that they may be able to identify false information and demand more credible sources. These media and news literacies, while well intentioned, often offer solutions to the wrong problems: namely, not only that fake news is a problem of a citizenry that lacks media savvy, but also that fake news is enabled by a citizenry no longer committed to the human interactions necessary for inclusive and vibrant civic engagement and participation.

Fighting "Fake News"

In the wake of its recent involvement in the spread of fake news in India that resulted in a deadly lynching, the social networking service WhatsApp announced that it was launching a digital literacy project to educate people about fake news and misinformation online.[22] The initiative, like many others, assumes the premise that if people are more educated, they will somehow be able to avoid such behaviors by identifying credible from false information. While this position is important, and WhatsApp is right to proactively take steps to reform and refute the spread of misinformation, many responses assume that a more skilled audience will help to constrain the spread of fake news, and reestablish credibility.

Initiatives that teach people how to identify fake information are needed. A recent study conducted at Stanford University found that children in U.S. middle schools had trouble differentiating credible from false information online.[23] Another recently published study finds that while fake news may be circulated and consumed by only a small percentage internet of users, that group is networked to spread information wide and to like-minded groups that are less apt to critique the information.[24] Efforts to build more critical information consumers can help to respond to this current moment, ensuring a public that is not complacent about the information they receive. But the weaponizing of a term like *fake news* demands more than an emphasis on skills.

Platforms that are designed to grab attention through continuous stimulation and the integration of personal expression with political information see human connection as a series of affirmations. People support each other with brief comments, likes, hearts, and stars, providing brief moments of connection that pass as quickly as they arise. The downside of this, of course, is that these fleeting moments take up more and more of our cognitive capacity, leaving little time and space for deep and meaningful connections to emerge, and time for judging the credibility and reliability of a message. Michael Bugeja writes that in this ubiquitous media environment we struggle with the "rigors of the human condition."[25] The need to constantly feel stimulated by and included in our online networks has taken over our capacity to engage in the types of dialogue and presence that create value and sense of belonging in the world.

The term *fake news* has settled nicely into the void between meaningful human connections and the priorities of the platform. In online spaces, where audiences find affirmation in peer support and credibility in information shared by those who share values and ideologies, deconstructing the credibility of information is less meaningful than finding information that supports particular worldviews. It is here where cries of "fake news" gain traction. And where the abilities of those online to share false information with like-minded communities finds legitimacy.

Reestablishing Human Connections in Platforms

At the outset of this chapter, I wrote of a particular information hoax that captured the attention of many. That hoax, while powerful, was fleeting. An experiment that created a flash of inquiry and then passed along. Today, false information is created not by news organizations but rather by individuals or small groups with particular aims and outcomes. They are seeded in spaces where communities can spread and sustain such ideas, and use mainstream media to legitimate and perpetuate them. In a recent report on the tactics used by internet subcultures to promote certain beliefs, Alice Marwick and Rebecca Lewis write: "Taking advantage of the opportunity the internet presents for collaboration, communication, and peer production, these groups target vulnerabilities in the news media ecosystem to increase the visibility of and audience for their messages."[26]

To reestablish credibility in news systems, it is necessary to provide people the tools needed to identify false information. Beyond this, however, efforts to combat the weaponization of fake news must focus on reestablishing the values that bring communities together to engage in meaningful dialogue, to support generative disagreement, and to understand news systems in the context of community. The work of media and news literacies will not fulfill their promise absent this larger mission. Approaches that prioritize such values focus on what Steven Sloman and Philip Fernbach write as "thinking with others."[27] Learning cultures that emphasize individual capacity often reduce the importance of community and human connection in how we understand and use information. Contextualizing platforms and social networks as "collaborative technologies" has further complicated this process.

Responses to fake news require a combination of further skills in media deconstruction along with values that support "being in the world with others toward common good."[28] The problem seems to come not from a lack of knowledge in the world, but rather from a lack of commitment to the rigors of democracy necessary to see across differences and support diverse ideas and ideologies. Like the "Spaghetti-Harvest in Ticino," false information will always have a place in our information ecosystem. The real question is whether it will be fleeting and playful, or whether it will continue to divide and perpetuate a culture of distrust.

Notes

1. To read more about the hoax, see "Spaghetti-Tree Hoax," Wikipedia, last modified May 23, 2019, https://en.wikipedia.org/wiki/Spaghetti-tree_hoax. To view the news clip, see MySwitzerland, "BBC: Spaghetti-Harvest in Ticino," YouTube video, 2:28, March 27, 2013, https://www.youtube.com/watch?v=tVo_wkxH9dU.

2. Leonard Miall, "Obituary: Lt-Gen Sir Ian Jacob," April 26, 1993, *The Independent*, https://www.independent.co.uk/news/people/obituary-lt-gen-sir-ian-jacob-1457544 .html.

3. BBC, "1957: BBC Fools the Nation," On This Day, http://news.bbc.co.uk/onthis day/hi/dates/stories/april/1/newsid_2819000/2819261.stm.

4. Saeed Ahmed, "A Nod and a Link: April Fools' Day Pranks Abound in the News," CNN, April 1, 2009, http://www.cnn.com/2009/US/04/01/april.fools.pranks/index.html.

5. Michael Schudson and Barbie Zelizer, "Fake News in Context" (paper presented at Disinformation Workshop, Annenberg School for Communication, University of Pennsylvania, Philadelphia, December 15–16, 2017), https://firstdraftnews.org/wp -content/uploads/2018/03/The-Disinformation-Ecosystem-20180207-v2.pdf.

6. John M. Hamilton and J. S. Tworek, "Fake News: A Modern History" (working paper presented at the Breaux Symposium: An Anatomy of Fake News, May 2–3, 2018, Washington, DC).

7. Nick Srnicek, *Platform Capitalism* (Cambridge, UK: Polity Press, 2017).

8. Ibid., 43.

9. See Clay Shirky, *Cognitive Surplus: Creativity and Generosity in a Connected Age* (New York: Penguin, 2010); James Surowiecki, *The Wisdom of Crowds* (New York: Anchor Books, 2005).

10. José van Dijck, *The Culture of Connectivity: A Critical History of Social Media* (New York: Oxford University Press, 2013).

11. Virginia Eubanks, *Automating Inequality: How High-Tech Tools Profile, Police, and Punish the Poor* (New York: St. Martin's Press, 2018), 9.

12. Douglas Rushkoff, *Program or Be Programmed: Ten Commands for a Digital Age* (New York: OR Books, 2010).

13. James Cohen, "Exploring Echo-Systems: How Algorithms Shape Immersive Media Environments," *Journal of Media Literacy Education* 10, no. 2 (2018): 145, https://digitalcommons.uri.edu/jmle/vol10/iss2/8/.

14. Evgeny Morozov, "Moral Panic over Fake News Hides the Real Enemy—the Digital Giant," *The Guardian*, January 8, 2017, https://www.theguardian.com/comment isfree/2017/jan/08/blaming-fake-news-not-the-answer-democracy-crisis.

15. Ibid.

16. Soroush Vosoughi, Deb Roy, and Sinan Aral, "The Spread of True and False News Online," *Science* 359, no. 6380 (2018): 1146–1151, http://science.sciencemag .org/content/359/6380/1146.

17. Robinson Meyer, "The Grim Conclusions of the Largest-Ever Study of Fake News," *The Atlantic*, March 8, 2018, https://www.theatlantic.com/technology/arc hive/2018/03/largest-study-ever-fake-news-mit-twitter/555104/.

18. Andrew S. Ross and Damian J. Rivers, "Discursive Deflection: Accusation of 'Fake News' and the Spread of Mis-and Disinformation in the Tweets of President Trump," *Social Media + Society* 4, no. 2 (2018), https://doi.org/10.1177/2056305118776010.

19. Craig Silverman, *Lies, Damn Lies, and Viral Content: How News Websites Spread (and Debunk) Online Rumors, Unverified Claims and Misinformation* (New York: Tow Center for Digital Journalism, 2015).

20. On circulation of content, see S. Shyam Sundar, "There's a Psychological Reason for the Appeal of Fake News," *New Republic*, December 8, 2016, https://newrepublic .com/article/139230/theres-psychological-reason-appeal-fake-news. See also Guy Debord, *Society of the Spectacle* (London: Bread and Circuses Publishing, 1967).

21. Morozov, "Moral Panic over Fake News."

22. "WhatsApp Working on Digital Literacy Programme to Curb Fake News," *Times of India*, July 20, 2018, https://timesofindia.indiatimes.com/companies/whatsapp -working-on-digital-literacy-programme-to-curb-fake-news/articleshow/65066869 .cms.

23. Sam Wineburg, Sarah McGrew, Joel Breakstone, and Teresa Ortega, *Evaluating Information: The Cornerstone of Civic Online Reasoning* (Stanford, CA: Stanford History Education Group, 2016), http://purl.stanford.edu/fv751yt5934.

24. Gordon Pennycook and David G. Rand, "Fighting Misinformation on Social Media Using Crowdsourced Judgments of News Source Quality," *Proceedings of the National Academy of Sciences* 116, no. 7 (2019): 2521–2526.

25. Michael Bugeja, *Interpersonal Divide in the Age of Machine* (Oxford: Oxford University Press, 2018), 10.

26. Alice Marwick and Rebecca Lewis, *Media Manipulation and Disinformation Online* (New York: Data and Society Research Institute, 2017), https://datasociety.net/pubs /oh/DataAndSociety_MediaManipulationAndDisinformationOnline.pdf.

27. Steven Sloman and Philip Fernbach, *The Knowledge Illusion: Why We Never Think Alone* (New York: Penguin, 2018).

28. Eric Gordon and Paul Mihailidis, eds., *Civic Media: Technology, Design, Practice* (MA, Cambridge: MIT Press, 2016), 3.

28 Teaching "Fake News" and Resisting the Privilege of Forgetting

Amanda Ann Klein

In a 1989 *New York* magazine article, journalist Eric Pooley lamented what he saw as a troubling trend in local news coverage: "The thoughtful report is buried because sensational stories must launch the broadcast: If it bleeds, it leads."[1] Scholars who study the media and the way its content is shaped and deployed have long known that much of the news on cable channels like CNN, Fox, and MSNBC, as well as network and local newscasts, tends to focus on content that generates ratings and viewership at the expense of content that is important, but which cannot be summarized in a sensational sound bite. These scholars have also long known that, in a bid for more eyeballs (and advertising dollars), news headlines, and even news content, can be purposely misleading, incorrect, or, yes, even "fake."

However, in the lead-up to, and following, the contentious 2016 U.S. presidential election, the term *fake news* was deployed more frequently, and in more contexts, than ever before, and not because Americans were suddenly becoming more media literate.[2] The prevalence of the term *fake news* coincided with a rise in conspiracy theories getting traction on social media and then finding their way into public discourse.[3] Take, for example, when White House advisor Kellyanne Conway cited something called the "Bowling Green Disaster," an event invented out of whole cloth, as a justification for the controversial travel ban by Donald Trump's administration in February 2017.[4] The concept of "fake news" has also been frequently deployed as a way to discredit a news story that was, in fact, accurate or true. For example, on May 31, 2018, President Trump tweeted: "Not that it matters but I never fired James Comey because of Russia! The Corrupt Mainstream Media loves to keep pushing that narrative, but they know it is not true!"[5] It is important to note here that Trump's Twitter-based pronouncements have become central to maintaining his base's support, riling up his opponents, chastising critics, and even testing out new policy ideas. This particular tweet was shared over sixty thousand times and favorited more than seventy-four thousand times, and bolsters Trump's frequent assertions that Robert Mueller's investigation, which the Federal Bureau of Investigation began in May 2017 to examine potential Russian interference in the 2016 U.S. presidential election, is founded on lies and is an unnecessary waste of taxpayer dollars. Indeed, just one year into his presidency, Trump was on record as making over 320 references to "fake news," almost always in response to negative coverage of his policies, comments, or administration.[6]

Teaching Fake News

With this broad co-optation of the term *fake news*, media studies scholars have found themselves in a difficult spot: How do we explain to our students when they can or cannot trust the news? How do we demonstrate that critical news is not necessarily biased or "fake" news? And how do we explain that difference without appearing partisan, biased, or "fake" ourselves? These questions led me to develop a new course at my university, a special topics seminar aimed at juniors and seniors in the spring of 2018 and titled "Reality TV, Fake News, and Media Literacy in the 21st Century." The goal of this course was to trace the various developments and changes in broadcast media that have led American consumers to a time and place where many of us (rightfully) do not trust the news media we read, see, and hear.

A central goal of the course was to arm students with the critical tools needed to find factually sound information about the world around us. Before the global spread of the printing press in the sixteenth century, it was difficult to find information about anything outside what you could personally verify. When we move forward in time to the circulation of newspapers in the seventeenth century, we are able to learn factually verifiable things about the world outside our immediate purview, and we are consuming the same facts as our neighbors reading the same newspaper. Again, there is an implicit trust that what we are reading is, in fact, from a reliable source and that this source would have no motivation for misleading us. Of course, even in the nineteenth century, there were incidents of the press lying or deceiving patrons in order to sell more newspapers, such as in 1835, when the *New York Sun* reported that some scientists had discovered life forms that resembled humans, only with hairy bodies and leathery wings, living on the surface of the moon. The story's publication, later dubbed the Great Moon Hoax, led the newspaper to sell out, which encouraged it to continue to publish more fake news stories about these apocryphal moon men.[7] Still, most nineteenth-century readers trusted their newspaper to deliver factual content.

The development and deployment of radio and television for the mass distribution of news in the twentieth century likewise carried an implicit trust, inherited from the media that preceded them (namely, print newspapers and newsreels that ran before cinemas screenings). I asked students to consider why this technology was developed, what it allowed consumers to do, how the creators and consumers of this technology identified problems or issues with these technologies, and then how creators, consumers, and legislators attempted to solve these problems (through regulation or deregulation). Students read about and discussed how the spread of commercial radio in the 1920s meant that Americans were able to access the same content at the same time, through a mass medium. Rather than buying a newspaper or venturing out to the movies to watch a newsreel, consumers could enjoy the radio, and the information it provided, without leaving the comfort or the intimacy of their home. Radio also acted as a democratizing technology: "Since it was, in principle, available to everyone, radio 'equalized' public life: it gave common access to events and entertainments that only a tiny minority had hitherto been privileged to enjoy."[8] We also discussed how, in the 1920s and 1930s, the medium of radio made the world feel like a smaller place when everyone with a radio could listen to the same content being broadcast at the same time. This instantaneity of shared content was a key development, and one piece of the puzzle we were putting together as a class. What does it mean when we can all learn the same information at the same time, while living in different spaces?

We also discussed the development of commercial television and some of TV's early attempts to capture authenticity and reality. We watched episodes of *Candid Camera* (1948–1991) and *Queen for a Day* (1945–1964) as a way to understand how and when TV first offered up the reactions and life stories of real people for entertainment. While *Candid Camera* promised to reveal humanity by filming people when they didn't realize it, *Queen for a Day* deployed human suffering as a real-life soap opera, making viewers feel good when, for example, widows with sick children were showered with gifts and prizes in exchange for telling their painful, personal stories on national TV. In either case, this kind of reality programming equated "reality" with entertainment, and the narratives and images of real people as inherently authentic records of the world. The class discussed how American media consumers' relationship with facts and authenticity has changed in relation to the technology we have developed for communicating authentic facts; technology is conditioning the way we understand the look and sound of reality and truth.

The next piece in our puzzle was the development of computers, the internet, and algorithms, and how our relationship with facts and truth shifts when the amount of available data explodes and when that data can be conjured up instantly. The class read and discussed Vannevar Bush's 1967 essay "Memex Revisited," in which Bush worried that the creation and publication of research and data was far outpacing the human mind's ability to organize, locate, and access that information in a timely manner.[9] He was particularly concerned about a problem that plagues us today: information overload. If attention is a finite commodity and information is increasingly boundless, how can we reconcile the two? Bush proposes a solution: a hypothetical microfilm viewing machine, a "memex," which mimics the way the human brain recalls information and makes connections between different concepts and ideas. While most file storage systems at that time were structured like indexes, with categories, subcategories, and hierarchies of information, Bush's hypothetical memex was structured by association, working much as the human brain does when searching for an answer. He describes a researcher who wants to know more about the distribution of hydrogen through steel: "All night memex plods on, at ten or more pages a second. Whenever it finds the words 'hydrogen' and 'diffusion' in the same item, it links that item into a new trail."[10] Here, Bush foretells the development of the modern search engine, which is able to process forty thousand queries per second, searching for the exact information a user seeks. What struck students the most about this particular essay is that Bush was describing the way the modern internet functions, decades before the launch of the first search engine, Archie, in 1990. We often think of the ways technology shapes how we think, but Bush's essay highlights how the ways we think can also shape the structure of technology.[11] Indeed, complex search algorithms, like Google's, make information retrieval and organization easier and faster, thereby giving human brains more free time to think and do and make. Bush described this as the "privilege of forgetting." But when this perspective bumps up against our current experience of the internet, a memex that exceeds Bush's wildest dreams, we can also see how the privilege of forgetting might also be one source of the current distrust of the news and the rejection of facts and science.

Fake news, as it is understood today, is successful primarily when its consumers do not attempt to remember previously established facts. For example, President Trump's aforementioned May 2018 tweet ("I never fired James Comey because of Russia!") directly contradicts a televised May 2017 interview in which Trump stated: "And, in fact, when I decided to just [fire James Comey], I said to myself, I said, 'You know, this Russia thing with Trump and Russia is a made-up story, it's an excuse by the Democrats for having lost an election that they should've won.'"[12] Of course, countless news outlets and social media users highlighted the contradiction in statements Trump made between May 2017 and May 2018, but for individuals who only read Trump's Twitter feed and who get their news from Fox News, Breitbart, or Infowars, three news sources that refrain from airing stories critical of the president, this statement can, in fact, be accepted as a truth. This is also Bush's privilege of forgetting. For those who do not wish to know more beyond what was said or declared today, it is very easy to believe the pastless present of Trump's Twitter account and search no further for proof or context.

In addition to giving my students a historical view of the technology and formats (radio, television, network news, reality television, cable news, social media) used for communicating news and facts, I wanted them to have the tools to verify on their own, without the aid of an "expert," whether or not a piece of news was truly "fake." To achieve this goal, I assigned a different print, television, radio, or online news source to each student, who was then required to consume that news source for ten weeks. With such a small seminar, I had only nine enrolled students, and so we were limited to tracking two print newspapers (the *New York Times* and *USA Today*); one online newspaper (the *Huffington Post*); three cable news channels (CNN, Fox, and MSNBC); one network news channel (NBC); one radio station (NPR); and one international news source (BBC).

Every week I assigned a single topic for my students to track, such as debates over the fate of children living in the United States under Deferred

Action for Childhood Arrivals (DACA) or the drought in Cape Town, South Africa,[13] and students were required to answer a series of questions about how their assigned news source addressed (or did not address) the week's topic. I asked students to list the major headlines related to the story, what they learned about this story from their assigned source, and if their source's coverage of this story changed or evolved over the course of the week. I also asked them how their assigned news source's coverage of this story differed or aligned with what they heard (or did not hear) about this story in their personal news consumption (through social media, peers, and other sources). For me, this was the key question of the semester: How do we reconcile the news we consume with our daily experience of the world?

For example, during the week of January 28–February 4, 2018, students were tasked with tracking stories related to a memo drafted by Republican congressman Devin Nunes (via #ReleasetheMemo), which accuses those participating in the Mueller investigation of bias against the president. The student tracking NBC explained, "Outside of the assignment, I have heard next to nothing about this story." The student tracking CNN wrote, "Throughout the week I maybe saw one video on YouTube or Facebook, but other than that there was little talk of this in my social media feed." The student tracking the *New York Times* had the most illuminating response:

> From my friends who are Republican, I've heard that the memo should be taken seriously and that the F.B.I. and Justice Department are guilty of abusing their power. From my friends who are Democrats, I've heard that the memo should not be taken seriously and that the F.B.I. and Justice Department were doing their job trying to find evidence to link Donald Trump's Campaign with some Russian Collusion.

Indeed, this question was always instructive because it gave me a window into how my students were learning about and understanding world events through their peers and personal news consumption. Every week students discussed their assigned topic and compared how their news source's coverage differed from or overlapped with their classmates' coverage. In general, students trust one another's perspective on current events and politics more than they trust mine, so it was especially effective for them to hear what their classmates' thought was biased and what was not. This work culminated in a twenty-minute class presentation and a 3,000-word final essay that offered a history of their assigned news source, identified its primary audiences, and explained whether or not ten weeks of reading that source led them to conclude that it was reliable and factually sound.

Teaching and Partisanship

The primary struggle of the course, however, was a personal one: How can I discuss current events and policies without appearing partisan or biased myself? This was more than an academic concern—as an employee of a state university, I am prohibited from using state resources (e.g., my classroom) to advocate for a particular political position. Additionally, in December 2017, the University of North Carolina (UNC) Board of Governors, the policy-making body supervising and managing the UNC system, approved a "free speech policy" for all seventeen of its campuses, including East Carolina University, where I work. The policy, modeled on a similar proposal drafted by the Goldwater Institute and distributed to conservative-leaning legislatures across the country, states that UNC schools now have the right to punish a student or faculty member who "substantially disrupts the functioning of the constituent institution or substantially interferes with the protected free expression rights of others."[14] Faculty, students, and staff who are found to violate this new policy are subject to suspension, expulsion, or termination of their employment. Because the UNC Board of Governors' policy does not define *disrupt* in any detail, the term remains broad, leading the American Civil Liberties Union of North Carolina, the American Association of University Professors, as well as faculty across the many UNC campuses to express their objections and concerns. Where is the line between "free speech" and "disruption," and who is the arbiter of this line? In this environment, teaching a class that asks students to determine whether certain news stories, many which have a political focus, are accurate or not, means I could risk appearing to advocate for a particular political position.

This is the environment in which all university instructors must now execute our craft. We must find a way to train our students to effectively seek out, and locate, what is true and what is false about their world, and, just as importantly, to understand why knowing the difference is more crucial than ever. This is not simply the task of the media studies professor or even the humanities professor; as a 2018 Gallup poll about climate change reveals, even the truth of science is up for debate.[15] While it can be chilling to be an instructor at a public university in this polarized political climate, I am also comforted to know that my profession gives me a tangible way to intervene and train the next generation to be better and smarter consumers. Ultimately, the main goal of teaching "Reality TV, Fake News, and Media Literacy in the 21st Century" was to equip my students with necessary information on the history, context, and function of broadcast journalism so that, when they left my class, they could feel confident in their ability to decide the value (or lack thereof) of the information they consume. Students learned that it is impossible to avoid all forms of bias in reporting, but that *most* news sources aim to be factually sound over and above political bias. However, this view of the news is only possible when eliminating content like op-eds, opinion news shows, and reporter (and presidential) tweets, etc. In other words, students also learned how to sort through the clutter of our boundless information age and home in on what is true, what is intended to inflame a portion of the electorate, and what is a little of both. My students learned that, like all privileges, the great privilege of forgetting enabled by the internet also comes with great responsibility.

Notes

1. Eric Pooley, "Grins, Gore, and Videotape—the Trouble with Local TV News," *New York*, October 9, 1989, 37.

2. Hunt Allcott and Matthew Gentzkow, "Social Media and Fake News in the 2016 Election," *Journal of Economic Perspectives*. 31, no. 2 (2017): 211–236.

3. Andrew Guess, Brendan Nyhan, and Jason Reifler, "Selective Exposure to Misinformation: Evidence from the Consumption of Fake News during the 2016 U.S. Presidential Campaign" (working paper, January 9, 2018), https://www.dartmouth.edu/~nyhan/fake-news-2016.pdf.

4. Samantha Schmidt and Lindsey Bever, "Kellyanne Conway Cites 'Bowling Green Massacre' That Never Happened to Defend Travel Ban," *Washington Post*, February 3, 2017.

5. Donald Trump (@realDonaldTrump), Twitter, May 31, 2018, https://twitter.com/realdonaldtrump/status/1002160516733853696.

6. Eugene Kiely, "Trump's Phony 'Fake News' Claims," FactCheck, January 16, 2018, https://www.factcheck.org/2018/01/trumps-phony-fake-news-claims/.

7. Matthew Goodman, *The Sun and the Moon: The Remarkable True Account of Hoaxers, Showmen, Dueling Journalists, and Lunar Man-Bats in Nineteenth-Century New York* (New York: Basic Books, 2008).

8. David Hendy, "Technologies," in *The Television History Book*, ed. Michele Hilmes (London: British Film Institute, 2003), 5.

9. Vannevar Bush, "Memex Revisited," in *Science Is Not Enough* (New York: William Morrow, 1967), 85–95.

10. Ibid., 93.

11. Hendy, "Technologies," 4.

12. Donald Trump, interview by Lester Holt, *NBC Nightly News with Lester Holt*, May 12, 2017.

13. In February 2018, news outlets reported that Cape Town, South Africa, was about to face "Day Zero," when the city would be forced to cut off taps to homes and businesses. Craig Welch, "Why Cape Town Is Running out of Water, and Who's Next," National Geographic, March 5, 2018, https://news.nationalgeographic.com/2018/02/cape-town-running-out-of-water-drought-taps-shutoff-other-cities/.

14. "Board of Governors Approves Free-Speech Policy for UNC Campuses," WRAL, December 15, 2017, https://www.wral.com/board-of-governors-approves-free-speech-policy-for-unc-campuses/17188508/.

15. Megan Brenan and Lydia Saad, "Global Warming Concern Steady despite Some Partisan Shifts," Gallup, March 28, 2018, https://news.gallup.com/poll/231530/global-warming-concern-steady-despite-partisan-shifts.aspx.

29 Viral "Fake News" Lists and the Limitations of Labeling and Fact-Checking

Melissa Zimdars

During the 2016 presidential primary season, I gleefully shared an article on Facebook alleging that Aaron Rodgers, who is the quarterback for the Green Bay Packers, attended a rally for presidential hopeful Bernie Sanders. The article spread like wildfire among my online friends group, many of whom are also overlapping fans of both the Packers and Bernie Sanders

Unfortunately, this article turned out to be from a fake news website, United Media Publishing. I was fooled by fake news. I implicitly trusted my many friends on social media sharing the story. The headline made me excited and hopeful about the primary election, and it did a good job of confirming what I wanted to believe as true about Rodgers: that he's a cool dude who shares my political views.

I share this anecdote to demonstrate just how easy it is to be "duped" by fake news. I have a Ph.D. in communication studies and I am a critical scholar, so you might think I would have been more careful. However, I do not (or at least did not) analyze each and every bit of information I come across online, especially on platforms I use for "fun," and I don't think I'm alone in this habit. Some evidence suggests many of us share or retweet without actually reading what we are sharing or retweeting,[1] which is definitely true in my instance of sharing fake news. The fact that I'm highly educated in the ways of critically analyzing media—and the fact that I see other highly educated people share similarly questionable sources—points to online misinformation as being more complicated than a lack of education, critical thinking skills, or digital media literacy.

Despite fake news being part of a complex problem involving the production, distribution, and reception of various kinds of information, the majority of current "solutions" to fake news deal primarily with reception and with individuals. Viral "fake news" lists, any one of the dozens of fake news library guides, browser plug-ins, debunking articles, pop-ups providing article information or context, and online media literacy quizzes, all attempt to get individuals to better understand online information. We tend to advance these kinds of "solutions" to problems partially because, as danah boyd argues, we exist in a neoliberal context that privileges and emphasizes individual agency.[2] It also *seems* easier to get individuals to change rather than, say, global media platforms. Just as environmental issues are too often addressed by encouraging consumers to buy energy efficient lightbulbs and reusable bags, while letting the largest polluters go unregulated, misinformation is too often addressed by encouraging individuals to analyze and fact-check sources, while letting a handful of companies continue to irresponsibly control global flows of information with little to no oversight.

Unless we remove more of the barriers for individuals to make sense of online information in this complex and cluttered media environment, these individualized solutions will, at best, prove ineffective and, at worst, exacerbate our misinformation problem.[3] I say this not to begrudge the goals behind these efforts—creators of these guides and consumer technologies looked for ways to help in the realms in which they operate, they looked for ways they could actually *do something*, just as I did—but rather to push us toward making more systemic changes with how and who produces and distributes our information.

This chapter thus details my entry into addressing the problem of fake news through a viral Google Doc, "False, Misleading, Clickbait-y, and/or Satirical 'News' Sources." I tell this story not because I believe this Google Doc has had a great impact on fighting online misinformation, but rather because its failures reveal the limitations of individualized, reception-focused efforts.

Viral "Fake News" Lists

While teaching Intro to Mass Communication in the fall of 2016, I became increasingly concerned by the types of sources my students were citing in their papers and in class discussions. Many of them were citing the same types of specious websites that I inadvertently shared the previous summer. When we entered into our journalism unit of the course, I decided to create a guide for helping them identify and analyze sources, titled "False, Misleading, Clickbait-y, and/or Satirical 'News' Sources." The guide contained everything from political yet generally reliable websites like Think-Progress to junk science websites like Natural News and fake news websites like United Media Publishing.

The morning before my lecture, I posted my in-progress guide to Facebook asking for input and suggestions for inclusion from my friends. When one friend asked to share the guide on a newsfeed to solicit further input, I switched the privacy setting from "friends" to "public." Within an hour it was shared almost two thousand times. Before I changed the original post's settings back to private a day later (after I started getting hateful comments on the post), it was already shared over twenty-five thousand times, although that number would grow to be significantly higher. In fact, it became one of the most shared "stories" about fake news in the fall of 2016 (and the basis for several other "most shared" stories about fake news during the same period by media outlets like NPR and *New York* magazine).[4]

I never intended my Google Document to be a stand-alone public resource, and I quickly worked to better organize and explicitly label the included websites upon receiving (rightfully) angry e-mails from Think-Progress, Upworthy, and Red State, among others, after they were inadvertently characterized as "fake news" in the press. You see, unbeknownst to me, I had inadvertently walked into a "maelstrom of controversy."[5] My Google Doc had been picked up by the *Los Angeles Times* and *New York* magazine, and as more news sources wrote about it, it became known as a list of fake news sites.[6] Indeed, it did contain quite a few fake news sites, but my resource was an attempt to capture a variety of online sources rather than just fake news. My Google Doc spread much as how fake news spreads: it tapped into an issue of growing concern, it "confirmed" either the reliability or unreliability of certain "news" sources (depending on one's personal beliefs), and it was reported on by some legitimate news organizations without vetting me or the Google Doc (and then other news organizations reported on it based on those reports). Somehow the resource went from an in-class activity to a "fake news list," and then from a "fake news list" to a research data set containing almost a thousand websites and part of digital media literacy resources created by libraries and schools around the country.[7]

The Limitations of Individualized "Solutions" to Fake News

Identifying and labeling websites as producers of fake news is complicated by the fact that there is not a clear way to address sources that we may not immediately categorize as fake news, but that also produce some of the most circulated false stories. For example, Sean Hannity's website, which I consider neither journalism nor a fake news site, published a story with the headline "Donald Trump Sent His Own Plane to Transport 200 Stranded Marines," and it generated over eight hundred thousand shares. The problem? This never happened,[8] yet the story was also picked up by a number of other websites, including Breitbart. Similarly, *The Independent* published a story about CNN accidentally airing hardcore pornography instead of an episode of *Anthony Bourdain: Parts Unknown*.[9] This story was then used as the source material for Fox 25 Boston and numerous other news and entertainment websites reporting the same thing (figure 29.1). The problem? This entire story was based on two hoax tweets. No one bothered to confirm the details in the story; instead, subsequent new stories were based on the original, which was based on false information.

As has become all too clear, even reputable news organizations and media entities regularly report on Google Docs, tweets, and blogs without

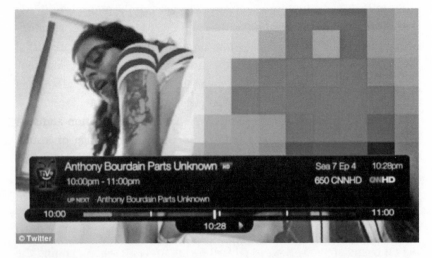

Figure 29.1
This manipulated image circulated on Twitter as "evidence" that CNN accidentally aired pornography.

necessarily digging into their credibility, and then other news organizations and media entities report on those stories that were based on Google Docs, tweets, and blogs (assuming the original stories to be accurate). This kind of information infidelity, and other practices plaguing contemporary news media, not only feeds public distrust of mainstream news organizations, and of information generally, but also gives support to accusations that the "real" news can be considered "fake news."[10] The media literacy strategy of checking additional news sources to confirm the details of a story is not a great option when so much of our mediasphere is polluted by fake news and faulty reporting. These confusing webs of misinformation entangling a variety of information sources also support an important point made by journalist Cory Doctorow: "We're not living through a crisis about what is true, we're living through a crisis about how we know whether something is true."[11]

Labeling fake news does not help us address *the problems of actual news*. In fact, labeling fake news may even de-emphasize the ways that different types of information sources interact and overlap, as demonstrated by these previous examples. Plus, attempting to label thousands of "news" websites is like playing a Sisyphean game of whack-a-mole: as soon as one source is analyzed, it may disappear and reappear as something else entirely. Labeling fake news and other types of online information is also unhelpful unless the person reading the labels views *the labeler* as credible or trustworthy. If readers disagree with the labeler or an applied label, it may just reinforce their existing beliefs about the source and the information circulated by it.[12] I received numerous e-mails to this effect; people said my resource supported their trust in websites like 100 Percent Fed Up and the *Washington Free Beacon* rather than challenged it.

Although I did receive thousands of messages of appreciation and suggestions for additions to my guide, I also received a barrage of insults and not-quite-threats to my safety (figure 29.2). Instead of contacting me directly to ask for removal from my resource, websites like Zero Hedge and Natural News attempted to discredit me as a "crybully professor" and "leftist totalitarian."[13] Other websites followed the same discrediting strategy, as exemplified by headlines like "Revealed: The Unhinged Feminist behind the Defamatory Hit List of Targeted Conservative Websites," "Bogus Hit List Is Removed after Radical Liberal Is Exposed, but Crying 'Fake News' Will Be New Weapon," and "Media Pushes Loony Leftist Professor's List of 'Fake

---

**LIST OF 'FAKE NEWS' BY PROFESSOR MELISSA
ZIMDARS INCLUDE DRUDGE, BREITBART,
ZEROHEDGE, INFOWARS AND THIS WEBSITE AS
GOOGLE, FACEBOOK CHANGE POLICY ON ADS...
DIDN'T THE MSM MEDIA RAN A LOT OF FAKE NEWS
ON TRUMP DURING ELECTION? FROM RIGGED
POLLS TO FAKE SCANDALS? REMEMBER :)**

POSTED ON NOVEMBER 16, 2016   UPDATED ON NOVEMBER 17, 2016

Figure 29.2
A headline from 70news.wordpress.com, which was one of the top Google news
results in November 2016 when searching for popular vote election results.

News' Conservative Sites."[14] These websites referred to me as a communist
infiltrator, super snowflake, fake professor, truth czar, and somehow both
an "elitist" (I have a Ph.D. and live on the East Coast) and a "nobody" (I
earned my Ph.D. from a state school in the Midwest and teach at a small
liberal arts college). Natural News and other websites also published my
contact information (and the contact information for my colleagues and
employer) and encouraged their readers to let me know what they thought
about being called a "moron" (despite the fact that I never referred to anyone as a moron).[15]

This backlash demonstrates, fundamentally, how communication
works. Individuals actively "decode" media texts and other forms of communication based on their own frameworks of knowledge, social contexts,
and relationships to production and technological infrastructures, among
other factors.[16] It is thus unsurprising that my guide helped some people,
while others did not care about it, did not find it useful, or fully rejected it
and me. My analysis and labeling, and later attempt to create a kind of taxonomy or continuum of online information, was appreciated by some and
viewed as "the biggest threat to freedom of speech" by others.[17]

Many of the problems with labeling fake news articles and websites parallel the problems and limitations with fact-checking. Just as many readers
of my list—or the websites that covered it—did not trust me, many do not
trust fact-checking organizations or news outlets debunking rumors and

conspiracies. For example, conservative "news" organizations frequently accuse Snopes not only of being liberally biased, but also of spreading outright lies. The Daily Caller, a conservative "news" website of questionable reliability, consistently publishes headlines like "Fact-Checking Snopes: Website's Political 'Fact-Checker' Is Just a Failed Liberal Blogger" and "Snopes Caught Lying about Lack of American Flags at Democratic Convention."[18] Fact-check organizations even feel compelled to evaluate other fact-checkers while fact-checking false claims about their own fact-checking, such as when FactCheck debunked a meme saying it had "exposed" Snopes.[19]

In the book *Reality Bites*, Dana Cloud argues that fact-checking "misses the forest in the trees." Its narrowness of focus on "just the facts" may debunk, for example, specific aspects of Hillary Clinton's e-mail scandal, but it does not necessarily help people make sense of or address concerns over whether Clinton is a trustworthy or ethical person. By focusing on specific, incorrect bits of information rather than engaging with the complexities of truth and falsehood, how "knowledge functions in service of power," and "who gets to shape facts for public sense making," fact-checkers miss the point.[20] Thus, instead of fact-checking, Cloud argues we should be engaged in frame-checking, where we try to understand how and why information is being framed in particular ways, how it's being used, or what emotions it inspires or values it references.

There are other problems with fact-checking, too, such as its potential to amplify misinformation.[21] Fact-checking also does not consider why people knowingly share information that is false.[22] Furthermore, fact-checking most often takes place after something has already been shared thousands of times,[23] and there is no guarantee that fact-checked information will reach the same audience as the original misinformation or that it will change anyone's mind. The fact-checking process and partnerships between organizations and tech companies may also lack transparency, be plagued by plagiarism, or exist solely to profit from search engine optimization, and "facts" themselves can be manipulated for a variety of reasons.[24] While fact-checking can serve an important function, particularly in terms of holding politicians accountable for what they say or acting as a resource for people trying to make sense of information, it is too often held up as the solution to fake news despite these kinds of issues and others.[25]

Moving beyond Individualized "Solutions" to Fake News

We have access to more sources of information than we ever have before, and we're having a hard time making sense of it all.[26] It can be difficult to identify fake news—just as it can be difficult to tell the difference between advertorials and editorials in magazines, between video press releases and nightly news segments on television. It's difficult to delineate between these forms of media precisely because they're designed to be that way. Making fake news a more challenging problem, perhaps, is the fact that in the digital era we now need to know the differences between native advertising, sponsored posts, contributor or community posts that neither undergo fact-checking nor are read by an editor, punditry-style "news," and poorly executed or obscure satire. And we need to do this while keeping track of a seemingly unlimited number of information sources that all look the same when presented to us in our social media feeds (each has a headline, accompanying image, and usually a story lede or description).

Thus, the problem of misinformation is not going to be overcome by social media platforms releasing public service announcements in newspapers about "spotting fake news" or promoting digital media literacy and fact-checking.[27] It's not going to be overcome by researchers promoting "critical thinking" as the most important solution in our current media context.[28] It's not going to be overcome by individuals and organizations taking it upon themselves to label, fact-check, or debunk misinformation. All of these solutions are far too focused on what individuals should read or do rather than on the underlying problems with contemporary journalism, the dominance of tech companies over our information systems and their general lack of public accountability, and governmental policies, in the United States at least, that are nonexistent, outdated, or exacerbating the problems of misinformation.

To address fake news and other forms of online information, we need reinvigorated local journalism, and more public funding for local media.[29] We need to assert more public control over communication systems and redistribute revenue from companies like Google and Facebook to public service news organizations.[30] We need publicly funded social media alternatives.[31] We need to push back against faulty claims of "free speech" that downplay the necessity of content moderation on social media platforms while allowing conspiracy sources to thrive.[32] We need to place less faith in "more speech" as a counter to false information in a "marketplace of ideas."[33] Ideally, we need to dismantle the capitalist systems underlying all of these issues and so many more. But, in the meantime, we need to understand that the proliferation of fake news and other kinds of misinformation is not caused by any one problem, and it will not be "solved" by any one "solution," especially ones that place the onus of responsibility on individuals.

Notes

1. Maksym Gabielkov, Arthi Ramachandran, Augustin Chaintreau, and Arnaud Legout, "Social Clicks: What and Who Gets Read on Twitter?" (paper presented at ACM SIGMETRICS / IFIP Performance, Antibes Juan-les-Pins, France, June 2016), https://hal.inria.fr/hal-01281190.

2. danah boyd, "You Think You Want Media Literacy...Do You?," *Points* (blog), Data and Society, March 9, 2018, https://points.datasociety.net/you-think-you-want -media-literacy-do-you-7cad6af18ec2.

3. Ibid.

4. NewsWhip, *The Rise of Hyper-Political Publishers* (NewsWhip Social Media Center, 2017), https://www.newswhip.com/wp-content/uploads/2017/05/The-Rise-Of-Hyper -Political-Publishers.pdf.

5. Ken Doctor, "The Fake News Wars Go Viral with Melissa's List," Nieman Lab, November 16, 2016, http://www.niemanlab.org/2016/11/the-fake-news-wars-go-viral -with-melissas-list/.

6. See Madison Malone Kircher, "An Extremely Helpful List of Fake and Misleading News Sites to Watch out For," *New York*, November 15, 2016, http://nymag.com /selectall/2016/11/fake-facebook-news-sites-to-avoid.html; Jessica Roy, "Want to Keep Fake News out of Your Newsfeed? College Professor Creates List of Sites to Avoid," *Los Angeles Times*, November 15, 2016, http://www.latimes.com/nation /politics/trailguide/la-na-trailguide-updates-want-to-keep-fake-news-out-of-your -1479260297-htmlstory.html. See also Will Oremus, "Stop Calling Everything 'Fake News,'" *Slate*, December 6, 2016, http://www.slate.com/articles/technology /technology/2016/12/stop_calling_everything_fake_news.html.

7. On the guide's use as a research data set, see Natasha Lomas, "Adblock Plus Wants to Use Blockchain to Call out Fake News," TechCrunch, June 13, 2018, https://techcrunch.com/2018/06/13/adblock-plus-wants-to-use-blockchain-to-call -out-fake-news/. On the guide's use as a media literacy resource, see, e.g., Harvard Library, "Fake News, Misinformation, and Propaganda," March 28, 2017, https:// guides.library.harvard.edu/fake.

8. David Emery and Brooke Binkowski, "Did Donald Trump Transport Stranded Troops on His Own Airplane?," Snopes, October 22, 2016, https://www.snopes.com /fact-check/donald-trumps-marine-airlift/.

9. Beatrice Verhoeven, "CNN Denies Report That Network Accidentally Aired 30 Minutes of Hardcore Porn," The Wrap, November 25, 2016, https://www.thewrap .com/cnn-denies-reports-that-network-accidentally-aired-30-minutes-of-hardcore -porn/.

10. Melissa Zimdars, "Information Infidelity: What Happens When the 'Real' News Is Considered 'Fake' News, Too?," Flow, December 16, 2016, http://www.flowjournal .org/2016/12/informational-infidelity/.

11. Cory Doctorow, "Three Kinds of Propaganda, and What to Do about Them," Boing Boing, February 25, 2017, https://boingboing.net/2017/02/25/counternarratives -not-fact-che.html.

12. For more information about information reception, please refer to the chapter by Danielle Polage and the chapter by Nicholas David Bowman and Elizabeth Cohen.

13. Tyler Durden, "Zero Hedge Targeted on Liberal Professor's List of 'Fake News' Sources," Zero Hedge, November 17, 2018, https://www.zerohedge.com/news/2016 -11-16/zero-hedge-targeted-list-fake-news-sources; Mike Adams, "Crybully Professor Names Natural News 'Fake News' Website along with Dozens of Others That Predicted the REAL Election Outcome," Natural News, November 16, 2016, https://www .naturalnews.com056040_Merrimack_College_fake_news_Melissa_Zimdars.html.

14. Jim Hoft, "Revealed: The Unhinged Feminist behind the Defamatory Hit List of Targeted Conservative Websites," Gateway Pundit, November 19, 2016, https://www.thegatewaypundit.com/2016/11/revealed-unhinged-feminist-behind -defamatory-hit-list-targeted-conservative-websites/; Samantha Chang, "Bogus Hit List Is Removed after Radical Liberal Is Exposed, but Crying 'Fake News' Will Be New Weapon," BizPac Review, November 19, 2016, https://www.bizpacreview.com /2016/11/19/bogus-hit-list-removed-radical-liberal-exposed-crying-fake-news-will -new-weapon-414026; "Media Pushes Loony Leftist Professor's List of 'Fake News' Conservative Sites," Titanic Brass, November 19, 2016, https://titanicbrass.com /2016/11/19/here-it-comes-media-pushes-loony-leftist-professors-list-of-fake-news -conservative-sites/.

15. Adams, "Crybully Professor."

16. Stuart Hall, "Encoding/Decoding," in The Cultural Studies Reader, ed. Simon During (New York: Routledge, 1993), 477–487.

17. On the guide viewed as a threat, see Claire Bernish, "Dear America, the 'Fake News' List Will Slaughter Freedom of the Press—and It's Everyone's Fault," Free

Thought Project, November 18, 2016, https://thefreethoughtproject.com/fake-news-slaughter-freedom-press-media/.

18. Peter Hasson, "Fact-Checking Snopes: Website's Political 'Fact-Checker' Is Just a Failed Liberal Blogger," Daily Caller, June 17, 2016, http://dailycaller.com/2016/06/17/fact-checking-snopes-websites-political-fact-checker-is-just-a-failed-liberal-blogger/; Peter Hasson, "Snopes Caught Lying about Lack of American Flags at Democratic Convention," Daily Caller, July 28, 2016, http://dailycaller.com/2016/07/28/snopes-caught-lying-about-lack-of-american-flags-at-democratic-convention/.

19. Viveca Novak, "Snopes.com," FactCheck, April 10, 2009, https://www.factcheck.org/2009/04/snopescom/; D'Angelo Gore, "Meme Falsely Claims We 'Exposed' Snopes.com," FactCheck, March 6, 2018, https://www.factcheck.org/2018/03/meme-falsely-claims-exposed-snopes-com/.

20. Dana Cloud, *Reality Bites: Rhetoric and the Circulation of Truth Claims in U.S. Political Culture* (Columbus: Ohio University Press, 2018), 52–74.

21. Whitney Phillips, "The Oxygen of Amplification: Better Practices for Reporting on Extremists, Antagonists, and Manipulators Online," Data and Society, May 22, 2018, https://datasociety.net/output/oxygen-of-amplification.

22. Whitney Phillips, *This Is Why We Can't Have Nice Things: Mapping the Relationship between Online Trolling and Mainstream Culture* (Cambridge, MA: MIT Press, 2015).

23. Sam Levin, "'Way Too Little, Way Too Late': Facebook's Factcheckers Say Effort Is Failing," *The Guardian,* November 13, 2017, https://www.theguardian.com/technology/2017/nov/13/way-too-little-way-too-late-facebooks-fact-checkers-say-effort-is-failing.

24. On partnering, see Mike Ananny, "Checking in with the Facebook Fact-Checking Partnership," *Columbia Journalism Review,* April 4, 2018, https://www.cjr.org/tow_center/facebook-fact-checking-partnerships.php. On plagiarism, see Craig Silverman, "A Marketing Site Deleted over 7,000 Articles after It Was Caught Stealing Fact-Checks and Plagiarizing," BuzzFeed, June 14, 2018, https://www.buzzfeed.com/craigsilverman/this-prolific-fact-checker-is-a-plagiarist?utm_term=.ycVqeL5YO#.jpPl4zYX. On manipulation of facts, see danah boyd, "What Hath We Wrought?" (keynote, SXSW EDU, March 7, 2018, Austin, TX), https://www.sxswedu.com/news/2018/watch-danah-boyd-keynote-what-hath-we-wrought-video/.

25. For more information about the limitations of fact-checking, see Alice Marwick, "Why Do People Share Fake News? A Sociotechnical Model of Media Effects," *Georgetown Law Technology Review* 2, no. 2 (2018): 474–512, https://www.georgetownlawtechreview.org/wp-content/uploads/2018/07/2.2-Marwick-pp-474-512.pdf.

26. See Luciano Floridi, *Information: A Very Short Introduction* (Oxford: Oxford University Press, 2010); Mark Andrejevic, *Infoglut: How Too Much Information Is Changing the Way We Think and Know* (New York: Routledge, 2013).

27. Rishi Iyengar, "WhatsApp Is Using Newspapers to Fight Fake News in India," CNN, July 10, 2018, https://money.cnn.com/2018/07/10/technology/whatsapp-india -newspaper-ads-fake-news/index.html.

28. The "Workshop on Digital Misinformation" preceding the 2017 International Conference on Web and Social Media, held in Montreal in May 2017, brought together computer scientists, social scientists, and even some journalists, fact-checkers, and representatives of Facebook and Google. After a day of presentations on misinformation networks, and fact-checking strategies, participants voted on what they believed to be the most important countermeasure to misinformation. The top choice? Critical thinking.

29. "Victory: New Jersey Dedicates Millions to Strengthen Local News Coverage," Free Press, July 2, 2018, https://www.freepress.net/news/press-releases/victory-new -jersey-dedicates-millions-strengthen-local-news-coverage.

30. Victor Pickard, "Break Facebook's Power and Renew Journalism," *The Nation* 306, no. 15 (2018): 22–24.

31. Diane Coyle, "We Need a Publicly Funded Rival to Facebook and Google," *Financial Times*, July 9, 2018, https://www.ft.com/content/d56744a0-835c-11e8-9199 -c2a4754b5a0e.

32. Sarah Emerson, "Facebook Is Using Bad Free Speech Arguments to Defend Infowars," Motherboard, July 13, 2018, https://motherboard.vice.com/en_us/article /bjbzdv/facebook-is-using-bad-free-speech-arguments-to-defend-infowars-conspiracy -theories.

33. Philip M. Napoli, "What If More Speech Is No Longer the Solution? First Amend-ment Theory Meets Fake News and the Filter Bubble," *Federal Communications Law Journal* 70, no. 1 (2018): 57–103, http://www.fclj.org/wp-content/uploads/2018/04 /70.1-Napoli.pdf.

Editors

Melissa Zimdars is an Assistant Professor in the Department of Communication and Media at Merrimack College. She earned her Ph.D. in Communication Studies from the University of Iowa and her M.A. in Media Studies and B.A. in Journalism and Political Science from the University of Wisconsin–Milwaukee. Zimdars is the author of *Watching Our Weights: The Contradictions of Televising Fatness in the "Obesity Epidemic"* (Rutgers University Press, 2019), and primarily researches global television programming, communication policies, and media industries. However, after a Google Doc she created went viral, Zimdars began working with a team of librarians and computer programmers to create tools for navigating fake news and other news websites through the OpenSources project. Zimdars's work has appeared in *Feminist Media Studies*, *Popular Communication*, *Television and New Media*, and *Flow*. She has also been interviewed about fake news by dozens of news outlets around the world, including the *Washington Post*, the *Boston Globe*, *The Guardian*, NPR, and BBC, and has presented on fake news at various libraries, museums, schools, private companies, and academic/trade conferences.

Kembrew McLeod is a Professor of Communication Studies at the University of Iowa and an independent documentary producer. A prolific author and filmmaker, he has written several books and produced documentaries that focus on popular music, independent media, copyright law, and pranksterism. His fifth book, *Pranksters: Making Mischief in the Modern World*, was published by New York University Press in 2014. McLeod also coproduced the documentary *Copyright Criminals*, which premiered at the 2009 Toronto International Film Festival and aired in 2010 on PBS's Emmy Award–winning documentary series *Independent Lens*. His first documentary, *Money for Nothing*, was programmed at the 2002 South by Southwest Film Festival and the 2002 New England Film and Video Festival, where it received the Rosa Luxemburg Award for Social Consciousness. McLeod's second documentary, *Freedom of Expression®: Resistance and Repression in the Age of Intellectual Property*, was distributed by the Media Education Foundation—where he also worked as an educational documentary producer. *Freedom of Expression®* serves as a companion to his book of the same title, which won the American Library Association's Oboler book award for "best scholarship in the area of intellectual freedom" in 2006. McLeod is also coauthor of the book *Creative License: The Law and Culture of Digital Sampling* and coeditor of the anthology *Cutting across Media: Appropriation Art, Interventionist Collage, and Copyright Law*, both published by Duke University Press in 2011. McLeod's music and cultural criticism have appeared in *Rolling Stone, Spin, Mojo*, the *New York Times*, the *Los Angeles Times*, the *Washington Post*, and the *Village Voice*.

Contributors

Mark Andrejevic is a Professor of Media Studies at Pomona College and a Visiting Research Professor at Monash University (Australia). He writes and teaches about surveillance, popular culture, and digital media. His current work focuses on the social implications of data mining, social sorting, and automated decision making. He is also the author of *Reality TV: The Work of Being Watched* (2004), *iSpy: Surveillance and Power in the Interactive Era* (2007), and *Infoglut: How Too Much Information Is Changing the Way We Think and Know* (2013).

Nicholas David Bowman is an Associate Professor of Journalism and Creative Media Industries in the College of Media and Communication, Texas Tech University. Bowman earned his Ph.D. from Michigan State University. His research looks at the cognitive, emotional, behavioral, and social demands of interactive media. He is a former newspaper and radio journalist.

Mark Brewin earned his Ph.D. from the University of Pennsylvania and is currently an Associate Professor of Communication at the University of Tulsa in Oklahoma. A former newspaper reporter, his primary interests are in the history of journalism and the history of political communication, dating from the early modern period to the present.

Benjamin Burroughs is an Assistant Professor of Emerging Media in the Hank Greenspun School of Journalism and Media Studies at the University of Las Vegas, Nevada. His research focuses on streaming media and technology, media industries, and social media. His work has been published in *New Media and Society*, *Journal of Broadcasting and Electronic Media*, *Social Media + Society*, and *Continuum*. He earned two Masters degrees in Global Media and Communication from the University of Southern California and the London School of Economics and Political Science and his Ph.D. in Communication Studies from the University of Iowa.

Elizabeth Cohen is an Assistant Professor of Communication Studies at West Virginia University. She earned her Ph.D. at Georgia State University, and her research specializes in the psychological motivations and effects of social media use.

Colin Doty received his Ph.D. in Information Studies from the University of California, Los Angeles, in 2015. He teaches at several universities in the Southern California area. His research focuses on misinformation, the information society, and new media. His chapter in this volume is based on his work as a research consultant with the Advancing New Standards in Reproductive Health (ANSIRH) program at the University of California, San Francisco.

Dan Faltesek is an Assistant Professor of Social Media at Oregon State University. His research explores the relationships between institutions and infrastructures of social media and the interfaces and texts we know as social media. This approach crosses communication, political economy, computer science, graphic design, and other fields as a translational approach to social media research.

Johan Farkas is a Ph.D. fellow at Malmö University, Sweden. His research interests include political communication and participation and online propaganda. Farkas has published on "cloaked Facebook pages" in *New Media and Society* and *Critical Discourse Studies*, and his work on fake news as a floating signifier is published in *Javnost—The Public*.

Cherian George is an Associate Professor in the Journalism Department of Hong Kong Baptist University, where he also serves as director of the Centre for Media and Communication Research. His latest book is *Hate Spin: The Manufacture of Religious Offense and Its Threat to Democracy* (MIT Press, 2016), and he is the author of three other books: *Singapore: The Air-Conditioned Nation* (Landmark, 2000); *Contentious Journalism and the Internet: Towards Democratic Discourse in Malaysia and Singapore* (National University of Singapore Press and University of Washington Press, 2006); and *Freedom from the Press: Journalism and State Power in Singapore* (National University of Singapore Press, 2012). Since 2013, he has been the editor of the journal *Media Asia*.

Tarleton Gillespie is a Principal Researcher in the Social Media Collective at Microsoft Research in New England. He is also an adjunct Associate Professor at Cornell University and the author of *Wired Shut: Copyright and the Shape of Digital Culture* (MIT Press, 2009) and coeditor of *Media Technologies: Essays on Communication, Materiality, and Society* (MIT Press, 2014). A forthcoming book examines the relationship between content guidelines on social media platforms and "appropriate" user contributions.

Dawn R. Gilpin is an Associate Professor at the Walter Cronkite School of Journalism and Mass Communication at Arizona State University. She earned her Ph.D. in Mass Media and Communication at Temple University and has published research in numerous journals and edited volumes, including *Communication Theory, Journal of Public Relations Research*, and *A Networked Self* (Routledge, 2011), among others. Her research broadly addresses organizational and collective identity construction, with a specific focus in recent years on online gun culture.

Gina Giotta is an Assistant Professor of Communication Studies at California State University, Northridge. In addition to her work on nineteenth- and twentieth-century visual culture, she studies the political economy of network culture and changing forms of production as they relate to unwaged communicative work and the sexual division of labor online.

Theodore L. Glasser is a Professor of Communication, Emeritus, at Stanford University. Glasser's teaching and research focus on media practices and performance, with emphasis on questions of press responsibility and accountability. His books include *Normative Theories of the Media: Journalism in Democratic Societies* (with Clifford Christians, Denis McQuail, Kaarle Nordenstreng, and Robert White), winner in 2010 of the Frank Luther Mott–Kappa Tau Alpha award for best research-based book on journalism / mass communication and a finalist for the Association for Education in Journalism and Mass Communication's Tankard Book Award; *The Idea of Public Journalism*, an edited collection of essays, recently translated into Chinese; *Custodians of Conscience: Investigative Journalism and Public Virtue* (with James S. Ettema), which won the Society of Professional Journalists' award for best research on journalism, the Bart Richards Award for Media Criticism, and the Frank Luther Mott–Kappa Tau Alpha award for the best research-based book on journalism / mass communication; *Public Opinion and the Communication of Consent* (edited with Charles T. Salmon); and *Media Freedom and Accountability* (edited with Everette E. Dennis and Donald M. Gillmor). His research, commentaries, and book reviews have appeared in a variety of publications, including *Journal of Communication*, *Journalism and Mass Communication Quarterly*, *Critical Studies in Mass Communication*, *Journalism Studies*, *Policy Sciences*, *Journal of American History*, *Quill*, *Nieman Reports*, and the *New York Times Book Review*.

Amanda Ann Klein is an Associate Professor of Media Studies at East Carolina University. Klein teaches courses in film history, theory, and aesthetics. Her primary research and teaching interests include film history and historiography, film genres and genre theory, African American cinema, exploitation films, television studies, and subcultural studies. She is the author of *American Film Cycles: Reframing Genres, Screening Social Problems, and Defining Subcultures* (University of Texas Press, 2011) and coeditor of *Cycles, Sequels, Spin-offs, Remakes and Reboots: Multiplicities in Film and Television* (University of Texas Press, 2016).

Paul Levinson is a Professor of Communication and Media Studies at Fordham University in New York City. His nonfiction books, including *The Soft Edge* (1997), *Digital McLuhan* (1999), *Realspace* (2003), *Cellphone* (2004), *New New Media* (2009; 2nd ed., 2012), *McLuhan in an Age of Social Media* (2015), and *Fake News in Real Context* (2016), have been translated into twelve languages. He coedited *Touching the Face of the Cosmos: On the Intersection of Space Travel and Religion* in 2016. His science fiction novels include *The Silk Code* (winner of the Locus Award for Best First Science Fiction Novel of 1999), *Borrowed Tides* (2001), *The Consciousness Plague* (2002), *The Pixel*

Eye (2003), *The Plot To Save Socrates* (2006), *Unburning Alexandria* (2013), and *Science Fiction and Fantasy Writers of America* (1998–2001). His stories and novels have been nominated for Hugo, Nebula, Sturgeon, Edgar, Prometheus, and Audie awards. He appears on CNN, MSNBC, Fox News, the Discovery Channel, National Geographic, the History Channel, NPR, and numerous TV and radio programs and was listed in the *Chronicle of Higher Education*'s "Top 10 Academic Twitterers" in 2009.

Adrienne Massanari is an Assistant Professor in the Department of Communication at the University of Illinois at Chicago. Massanari's research centers on the social and cultural impacts of new media, gaming, information architecture and user-centered design, crowdsourcing, youth culture, and digital ethics. Her work has appeared in *New Media and Society, First Monday, Journal of Computer-Mediated Communication*, and *Journal of Information Technology and Politics*. In her book *Participatory Culture, Community, and Play: Learning from Reddit* (Peter Lang, 2015), she analyzed the culture of the social news and community site Reddit. She also has more than ten years of experience as a user researcher, information architect, usability specialist, and consultant in both corporate and educational settings.

Sophia A. McClennen is a Professor of International Affairs and Comparative Literature at Pennsylvania State University, founding Director of the Center for Global Studies, and Associate Director of the School of International Affairs. She studies human rights, satire, and politics, and her recent work includes *Is Satire Saving Our Nation?* (2014), coauthored with Remy Maisel, and *The Routledge Companion to Literature and Human Rights* (2015), coedited with Alexandra Schultheis Moore.

Panagiotis Takis Metaxas is a Professor of Computer Science at Wellesley College studying the propagation of (mis)information on the Web and online social media, the power of crowdsourcing, and developing tools that support the privacy of the user while estimating the trustworthiness of the information the user receives. Metaxas is also Faculty Director for the Albright Institute of Global Affairs and an affiliate at Harvard's Center for Research on Computation and Society.

Paul Mihailidis is an Associate Professor in the School of Communication at Emerson College in Boston, where he teaches media literacy and civic media. He is also Principal Investigator and Faculty Director of the Engagement Lab at Emerson College, where he is Director of the M.A. in Civic Media: Art and Practice. Mihailidis also directs the Salzburg Academy on Media and Global Change, a project that gathers young media makers and activists from around the world to build media responses to the globe's pressing problems. His research focuses on the nexus of media, education, and civic voices. His books *Civic Media: Technology, Design, Practice* (MIT Press, 2016; with Eric Gordon) and *Media Literacy and the Emerging Citizen* (Peter Lang, 2014) outline effective practices for participatory citizenship and engagement in digital culture. He earned his Ph.D. from the Philip Merrill College of Journalism at the University of Maryland, College Park.

Benjamin Peters is an Assistant Professor of Communication at the University of Tulsa in Oklahoma. His work examines how media—and information technologies in particular—take shape differently across different regimes of space, time, and power. He received his Ph.D. and M.Phil. from Columbia University.

Whitney Phillips is an Assistant Professor of Communication, Culture, and Digital Technologies at Syracuse University. She is the author of *This Is Why We Can't Have Nice Things* (MIT Press, 2015) and coauthor of *The Ambivalent Internet* (Polity Press, 2017).

Victor Pickard is an Associate Professor at the University of Pennsylvania's Annenberg School for Communication. He has published numerous scholarly articles and book chapters, and his popular writing has appeared in outlets such as *The Guardian*, the *Huffington Post*, *The Nation, Jacobin,* and *The Atlantic*. He is the author of *America's Battle for Media Democracy* and coeditor of *Media Activism in the Digital Age* (with Guobin Yang), *The Future of Internet Policy* (with Peter Decherney), and *Will the Last Reporter Please Turn out the Lights* (with Robert McChesney). Currently, he is working on a book about the future of digital journalism.

Danielle Polage is an Associate Professor of Psychology at Central Washington University. She received her Ph.D. in Cognitive Psychology from the University of Washington in 1999 and her B.A. in Mathematics from Emory University in 1993. She specializes in memory research, particularly false memories, lying, and other psychology and law issues. Her main focus of research is the effects of lying on the liar's memory for the truth and the memory effects of exposure to false information. She is the author of nine published articles and has presented her research at conferences all over the world.

Stephanie Ricker Schulte is Associate Chair and Associate Professor of Communication at the University of Arkansas. She holds a Ph.D. in American Studies from George Washington University in Washington, D.C., and researches communication technologies, popular culture, and transnational media policy. Her first book, *Cached: Decoding the Internet in Global Popular Culture* (New York University Press, 2013; Critical Cultural Communication series), is a transnational political and cultural history of the internet that examines the multidirectional relationships between technological design, American culture, and policy making. Her work has appeared in shorter form in *Television and New Media, Journal of Transnational American Studies, Mass Communication and Society, Feminist Studies, American Behavioral Scientist, Journal of Communication, American Studies,* and *Journal of New Media and Culture.*

Leslie-Jean Thornton is an Associate Professor in the Walter Cronkite School of Journalism and Mass Communication at Arizona State University. She was the top editor at six newspapers in the New York–Connecticut metro area and earned her Ph.D. from the University of North Carolina at Chapel Hill.

Anita Varma is the Program Manager for the Trust Project (Journalism Ethics). Varma works across many Trust Project areas, including newsroom partner relations, research, bookkeeping, and scheduling. She also coordinates public engagement activities related to developing strategies for improving trust in news. Varma earned a Ph.D. in Communication from Stanford University.

Claire Wardle is a leading expert on social media, user-generated content, and verification. Her research sits at the increasingly visible and critical intersection of technology, communications theory, and mass and social media. She is cofounder and leader of First Draft News, the world's foremost nonprofit focused on research and practice to address mis- and disinformation. First Draft is housed at the Shorenstein Center on Media, Politics and Public Policy at the John F. Kennedy School of Government at Harvard University, where Wardle is a Research Fellow. Previously, she was the Research Director at the Tow Center for Digital Journalism at the Columbia Journalism School. Wardle has worked with newsrooms and humanitarian organizations around the world, providing training and consultancy on digital transformation. She earned a Ph.D. in Communications and an M.A. in Political Science from the University of Pennsylvania.

Sheng Zou is a doctoral student at Stanford University. Zou is interested in critical theory and cultural studies, particularly issues related to the politics of representation, the workings of ideology, and the affective dimension of digital media production and user participation. Zou earned an M.A. in International Journalism and Communication from Tsinghua University and a B.A. in International Relations and English from Beijing Foreign Studies University.

Index

Note: page numbers followed by "f" refer to figures.